Frederick H. Cryer is Project Director
of the Dead Sea Scrolls Initiative,
Institute for Biblical Exegesis,
University of Copenhagen.
Thomas L. Thompson is Professor of
Old Testament, Institute for Biblical
Exegesis, University of Copenhagen.

JOURNAL FOR THE STUDY OF THE OLD TESTAMENT SUPPLEMENT SERIES

290

Editors
David J.A. Clines
Philip R. Davies

Executive Editor
John Jarick

COPENHAGEN INTERNATIONAL SEMINAR

6

General Editors
Thomas L. Thompson
Niels Peter Lemche

Associate Editors
Frederick H. Cryer
Mogens Müller
Hakan Ulfgard

Sheffield Academic Press

Qumran between the Old and New Testaments

Frederick H. Cryer and
Thomas L. Thompson

Journal for the Study of the Old Testament
Supplement Series 290

Copenhagen International Seminar 6

Copyright © 1998 Sheffield Academic Press

Published by
Sheffield Academic Press Ltd
Mansion House
19 Kingfield Road
Sheffield S11 9AS
England

Typeset by Sheffield Academic Press
and
Printed on acid-free paper in Great Britain
by Bookcraft Ltd
Midsomer Norton, Bath

British Library Cataloguing in Publication Data

A catalogue record for this book is available
from the British Library

ISBN 1-85075-905-7

CONTENTS

In 1997 it is now fifty years since the first of the Dead Sea Scrolls became known. The discovery of these texts have been dramatic in many ways. First, the story of the discovery itself is dramatic. But, also dramatic have been the series of hypotheses which have followed. We need not discuss the drama around the 'unofficial' publication, which was provoked by the apparently delayed official publication.

A couple of years ago, a few books and a couple of television programs renewed public interest in the Dead Sea Scrolls. It was once again claimed that these texts in reality are sources for earliest Christianity, which, accordingly, must have appeared radically different than the New Testament writings would have us believe.

This renewed interest offered the occasion for the Institute for Biblical Exegesis at the University of Copenhagen to intensify its study of the Essenes and of the texts from the Dead Sea. This was done not least through plans to host a Scandinavian conference on the topic, 'Qumran between the Old and the New Testaments', from 19 to the 22 June, 1995, at Schaeffergården, just north of Copenhagen. The purpose was to bring together the latest understanding of the Dead Sea texts and their significance. To achieve this, we invited four international scholars at the centre of Qumran studies. These were Professor Florentino García Martínez from Groningen, Professor Hartmut Stegemann from Göttingen, Professor Emanuel Tov from Jerusalem and Professor Ben Zion Wacholder from Cincinnati. Around these four main lectures, the rest of the program developed in the form of lectures and seminars directed by local Scandinavian scholars.

It should be mentioned that the study of the Dead Sea texts builds on a tradition at our institute. Two of the former professors of the Old Testament have been influential in this field. Professor Eduard Nielsen had introduced the Dead Sea Scrolls to a more popular audience.[1] In 1959,

---

1. *Håndskriftfundene i Juda Ørken: Dødehavsteksterne* (Copenhagen: Gad Forlag, 1956).

together with Benedikt Otzen, the later professor of Old Testament in Århus, he published a distinguished, text-critically based translation of the most important of the Dead Sea texts, along with a brief commentary.[2] Professor Svend Holm-Nielsen published his doctoral disputation, *Hodayot: Psalms from Qumran,* in 1960.[3] This study has since been continued in a number of articles by others.

It is at the same time interesting that this research has a prehistory at the University of Copenhagen. For instance, the professor of Old Testament, Flemming Friis Hvidberg (1897–1959) had written his doctoral disputation on the *Damascus Document* which had been found in Cairo in 1896.[4] Hvidberg determined the date of this text between 63 BCE and 70 CE. He believed that the text was more pharisaical than Sadducean in tone. That it might have something to do with the Essenes did not then occur to him. Similarly, the professor of New Testament, Holger Mosbech (1886–1953) had published his disputation on the Essenes in 1916,[5] in which the possibility that there should be a connection with the *Damascus Document* was not even discussed. The ancient sources, Philo, Josephus and Pliny the Elder, render such an idealistic picture of the Essenes that it was first with the discovery of the texts at Qumran that we can confidently connect them with those who are revealed precisely as sectarians, whose voice we hear in the *Damascus Document.*

The study of the Dead Sea Scrolls has demonstrated in a steadily increasing manner their relevance for the study of both the Old and the New Testaments. While there had begun to be a tendency to marginalize the Qumran community and its texts, it is clear today that this textual discovery has given us a unique insight into a part of the Judaism from which Christianity arose. Whereas earlier one had to refer to later texts for everything essential, here we have textual material in hand in which not only the content, but the physical documents themselves are older than our other sources for Jesus' contemporary Judaism.

---

2.   *Dødehavsteksterne: I oversættelse og med noter* (Copenhagen: Gad Forlag, 3rd edn, 1960).

3.   (Acta Theologica Danica, 2; Aarhus: Århus Universitet, 1960).

4.   *Menigheden af den nye Pagt i Damascus: Nogle Studier over de af Salomo Schechter fundne og under Titelen 'Fragments of a Zadokite Work' udgivne Genizafragmenter ('Damascusskriftet')* (Copenhagen: Gad Forlag, 1928).

5.   *Essæismen: Et Bidrag til Senjødedommens Religionshistorie* (Copenhagen: Schultz, 1916).

At least as significant is the new knowledge that the extensive discovery of biblical manuscripts and especially manuscript fragments has given us about the development of Judaism's Bible. The joy of some over having confirmation for the antiquity of the later Masoretic text type could hardly be dampened by the discovery that this so-called proto-Masoretic text was not the only one that has been found. Other text forms have come to light that inform us that a single uniform biblical text is the result of a lengthy process of transmission and that there can no longer be any sense in speaking about an 'original' or 'base' text. Among other things, this has brought the Septuagint out of the cold regarding the question about how Judaism's Bible looked around the beginning of this era.

Finally, it is significant that the climate of biblical research during the past decade has been able to show a growing desire to understand Jesus and earliest Christianity within the context of, or at least in close connection with, contemporary Judaism. Here, the Dead Sea Scrolls give us first-hand knowledge of another Jewish sect, which shows evidence of 'structural similarities' (Niels Hyldahl) with what we also find in New Testament Christianity, not least in regard to both the interpretation of Scripture and self-understanding. It is to be hoped that the time is past when someone like Herbert Braun, with reference to the Judaizing tendency in the Gospels, can formulate it as an acknowledgment that one must deal with the acceptance of a certain amount of Judaism even in regard to Jesus.[6] Jesus was a Jew and must be understood within the context of the Judaism of his time.

Schaeffergården created a fine framework around four productive and delightful days. The climate of the conference was developed by a pronounced wish to receive and share knowledge. Our four international guests: Florentino García Martínez, Hartmut Stegemann, Emmanuel Tov and Ben Zion Wacholder made outstanding contributions here, not merely through their own lectures, but also to a great degree through their great readiness to participate in the discussions of the conference's other contributions. In my role as director of the hosting institute, I would like to extend to them and to the other lecturers and seminar leaders many thanks for their efforts.

---

6. See *Spätjüdisch-häretischer und frühchristlicher Radikalismus: Jesus von Nazareth und die essenische Qumransekte* (BHT, 24; 2 vols.; Tübingen: J.C.B. Mohr, 2nd edn, 1969), II, p. 1.

At the same time, I would also like to express warm thanks for the support of the University of Copenhagen's theological faculty, of which our institute is a part. Not least do I wish to thank our dean, Professor Jens Glebe-Møller, as well as the various foundations, who generously made it possible for the Scandinavian members of the conference to take part without other expenses than that of their travel. These thanks are extended to the following foundations:

Queen Margrethe's and Prince Henrik's Foundation
The Palestine Foundation
G.E.C. Gads Foundation
Højgaard's Foundation
The State Research Counsel for the Humanities
The Initiative on Hellenism
Norfa
Consul George Jorck and his wife Emma Jorck's Foundation
The General Fund of the University of Copenhagen

Mogens Müller
Director
Institute for Biblical Exegesis, University of Copenhagen

ABBREVIATIONS

ABD	David Noel Freedman (ed.), *The Anchor Bible Dictionary* (New York: Doubleday, 1992)
ALUOS	Annual of Leeds University Oriental Society
AnBib	Analecta biblica
ANET	James B. Pritchard (ed.), *Ancient Near Eastern Texts Relating to the Old Testament* (Princeton: Princeton University Press, 1950)
ANRW	Hildegard Temporini and Wolfgang Haase (eds.), *Aufstieg und Niedergang der römischen Welt: Geschichte und Kultur Roms im Spiegel der neueren Forschung* (Berlin: W. de Gruyter, 1972–)
ANTJ	Arbeiten zum Neuen Testament und Judentum
ATANT	Abhandlungen zur Theologie des Alten und Neuen Testaments
BA	*Biblical Archaeologist*
BASOR	*Bulletin of the American Schools of Oriental Research*
BBB	Bonner biblische Beiträge
BEATAJ	Beiträge zur Erforschung des Alten Testaments und des antiken Judentums
BETL	Bibliotheca ephemeridum theologicarum lovaniensium
BH	Biblia Hebraica
BHK	R. Kittel (ed.), *Biblia hebraica* (Stuttgart: Württembergische Bibelanstalt, 1937)
BHS	*Biblia hebraica stuttgartensia*
BHT	Beiträge zur historischen Theologie
Bib	*Biblica*
BibRes	*Biblical Research*
BiOr	*Bibliotheca orientalis*
BZ	*Biblische Zeitschrift*
BZAW	Beihefte zur *ZAW*
CB	*Cultura bíblica*
CBQ	*Catholic Biblical Quarterly*
ConBNT	Coniectanea biblica, New Testament
ConBOT	Coniectanea biblica, Old Testament
CRINT	Compendia rerum iudaicarum ad Novum Testamentum
DBSup	*Dictionnaire de la Bible, Supplément*
DJD	Discoveries in the Judaean Desert
DSD	*Dead Sea Discoveries*

EI	Eretz Israel
ETL	*Ephemerides theologicae lovanienses*
GTA	Göttingen Theologische Arbeiter
HKAT	Handkommentar zum Alten Testament
HSM	Harvard Semitic Monographs
HSS	Harvard Semitic Studies
HTR	*Harvard Theological Review*
HUCA	*Hebrew Union College Annual*
IDB	George Arthur Buttrick (ed.), *The Interpreter's Dictionary of the Bible* (4 vols.; Nashville: Abingdon Press, 1962)
IEJ	*Israel Exploration Journal*
IES	Israel Exploration Society
IOS	*Israel Oriental Society*
JANES	*Journal of the Ancient Near Eastern Society*
JANESCU	*Journal of the Ancient Near Eastern Society of Columbia University*
JBL	*Journal of Biblical Literature*
JJS	*Journal of Jewish Studies*
JNES	*Journal of Near Eastern Studies*
JNSL	*Journal of Northwest Semitic Languages*
JQR	*Jewish Quarterly Review*
JSOT	*Journal for the Study of the Old Testament*
JSOTSup	*Journal for the Study of the Old Testament*, Supplement Series
JSPSup	*Journal for the Study of the Pseudepigrapha*, Supplement Series
JSS	*Journal of Semitic Studies*
LCL	Loeb Classical Library
LXX	Septuagint
MSU	Mitteilungen des Septuaginta-Unternehmans
MT	Masoretic Text
NRSV	New Revised Standard Version
NTL	New Testament Library
NTOA	Novum Testamentum et orbis antiquus
NTS	*New Testament Studies*
NTT	*Norsk teologisk tidskrift*
OBO	Orbis biblicus et orientalis
OCT	Oxford Cuneiform Texts
OTS	*Oudtestamentische Studiën*
PAM	Palestine Archaeological Museum
RB	*Revue biblique*
REB	Revised English Bible
REJ	*Revue des études juives*
RevQ	*Revue de Qumran*
RSV	Revised Standard Version
RTP	*Revue de théologie et de philosophie*
SBLDS	SBL Dissertation Series
SBLSP	SBL Seminar Papers

SEÅ	*Svensk exegetisk årsbok*
SHANE	Studies in the History of the Ancient Near East
SJOT	*Scandinavian Journal of the Old Testament*
SNTSMS	Society for New Testament Studies Monograph Series
SR	*Studies in Religion/Sciences religieuses*
ST	*Studia theologica*
STDJ	Studies on the Texts of the Desert of Judah
SUNT	Studien zur Umwelt des Neuen Testaments
SWBAS	Social world of Biblical Antiquity Series
TAPA	*Transactions of the American Philological Association*
TDOT	G.J. Botterweck and H. Ringgren (eds.), *Theological Dictionary of the Old Testament*
TLZ	*Theologische Literaturzeitung*
TRE	*Theologische Realenzyklopädie*
TRu	*Theologische Rundschau*
TZ	*Theologische Zeitschrift*
VT	*Vetus Testamentum*
VTSup	*Vetus Testamentum*, Supplements
WMANT	Wissenschaftliche Monographien zum Alten und Neuen Testament
WUNT	Wissenschaftliche Untersuchungen zum Neuen Testament
ZAW	*Zeitschrift für die alttestamentliche Wissenschaft*

LIST OF CONTRIBUTORS

Anders Aschim, The Norwegian Lutheran School of Theology, Oslo

Per Bilde, University of Århus, Århus, Denmark

Ellen Juhl Christiansen is an independent scholar living in Risskov, Denmark

Frederick H. Cryer, University of Copenhagen, Denmark

Torleif Elgvin, Luthersk Bibel-og Menighetsseminar, Oslo, Norway

Jesper Høgenhaven, University of Copenhagen, Denmark

Robert W. Kvalvaag, Høgskolen i Oslo, Norway

Neils Peter Lemche, University of Copenhagen, Denmark

Florentino García Martínez, Qumrân Instituut—RUG

Sarianna Metso, Trinity Western University, Canada

Staffan Olofsson, Teologiska Institutionen, Uppsala, Sweden

Allan Rosengren Petersen, University of Copenhagen, Denmark

Thomas L. Thompson, University of Copenhagen, Denmark

Emanuel Tov, Hebrew University of Jerusalem, Israel

Håkan Ulfgard, Lund University, Sweden

Ben Zion Wacholder, Hebrew Union College, Jewish Institute of Religion

THE GENRE OF 11QMELCHIZEDEK

Anders Aschim

1. *The Melchizedek Document from Qumran Cave 11*

Those in charge of this conference have chosen as its subject: *Qumran between the Old and New Testaments.* This paper will deal with one of the smaller documents from Qumran, at least in terms of the amount of inscribed fragments preserved. Nevertheless, it offers an excellent illustration of the challenges which the Qumran material represents for biblical scholars from both disciplines, of the possibilities as well as the limitations.

From this point of view, three features of the document are noteworthy:

1. It makes heavy use of texts from the Hebrew Bible, mainly by way of explicit quotations (see below, §2).
2. The text has a number of interesting points of contact with the New Testament.[1]
3. The condition of the document, however, is so fragmentary that it is very difficult to determine precisely both the meaning of the text itself and its significance for biblical studies.

This last feature is, of course, *the* fundamental problem of Qumran research, and various approaches have been developed in order to solve it. Concerning our document, J. Carmignac states: 'To arrive at a fair

---

1. For example, it uses Isa. 61 in a way that reminds a New Testament reader of Jesus' synagogue sermon in Nazareth, Lk. 4.16-30. It introduces the figure of Melchizedek in a way reminiscent of the Letter to the Hebrews. And it utilizes the expression 'the anointed one', so important for New Testament Christology. See further M. de Jonge and A.S. van der Woude, '11Q Melchizedek and theNew Testament', *NTS* 12 (1966), pp. 301-26; P.J. Kobelski, *Melchizedek and Melchireša'* (CBQMS, 10; Washington: Catholic Biblical Association, 1981), pp. 99-137.

interpretation of this document, the first question to resolve is that of its literary genre'.[2] Accordingly, the purpose of this paper is to try, once more, to determine the literary character of 11QMelch as precisely as possible.

Thirteen fragments of this manuscript are preserved.[3] They have been given the siglum 11Q13 or 11QMelch. Nine of the fragments were successfully located by the original editor, A.S. van der Woude, who was able to show that they contain the remains of three consecutive columns of text. However, only 25 lines from the middle column (col. 2) can be reconstructed into a readable, running text with any degree of probability. An important recent contribution has been given by E. Puech,[4] who has suggested locations for the remaining fragments. Especially interesting is his attempt to reconstruct col. 3. Still, there is not much left of this column, and scholars have mainly been working with col. 2.

2. *11QMelch and the Pesharim*

The most important structural feature in column 2 of 11QMelch is the alternation between explicit biblical quotations and interpretations. Both are introduced in a technical way, by the use of certain formulas.[5] This is clearly an *exegetical* work. The structure of the text reminds one

2.   J. Carmignac, 'Le document de Qumran sur Melkisédeq' (*RevQ* 7 [1970], pp. 343-78), p. 360, quoted with approval in J.T. Milik, 'Milkî-ṣedeq et Milkî-reša' dans les anciens écrits juifs et chrétiens' (*JJS* 23 [1972], pp. 95-144), p. 109.

3.   A.S. van der Woude, 'Melchisedek als himmlische Erlösergestalt in den neugefundenen eschatologischen Midraschim aus Qumran Höhle XI', *OTS* 14 (1965), pp. 354-73 (355). A fourteenth, very small fragment that appears on the photograph PAM 43.979 is noted in Milik, 'Milkî-ṣedeq', p. 96 n. 4, in Kobelski, *Melchizedek*, p. 3 n. 2, and in E. Puech, 'Notes sur le manuscrit de XIQ-Melchîsédeq', *RevQ* 12 (1987), pp. 483-513 (485 n. 6). In addition, F. García Martínez, 'Texts from Qumran Cave 11', in D. Dimant and U. Rappaport (eds.), *The Dead Sea Scrolls: Forty Years of Research* ([STDJ, 10; Leiden: E.J. Brill; Jerusalem: Magnes Press Yad Izhak Ben-Zvi, 1992], pp. 18-26), pp. 23-24, reports that E. Puech 'has found a small fragment of this ms that does not appear in the photographs'. English translation of the text in F. García Martínez, *The Dead Sea Scrolls Translated: The Qumran Texts in English* (trans. W.G.E. Watson; Leiden: E.J. Brill, 1994), pp. 139-40.

4.   Puech, 'Notes'.

5.   'As it is written...' (2.9, 23), 'As he says...' (2.2, 10, 11, 15, 18, 25), 'Its interpretation' (2.12, 17), 'That is...' (passim), etc.

strongly of the so-called 'pesharim', like the famous Habakkuk commentary from Qumran Cave 1 (1QpHab). Even the word 'pesher' itself turns up in 11QMelch (2.4, 12, 17). There are also significant differences, however, between 1QpHab and 11QMelch. The former quotes the complete text of Habakkuk, chs. 1–2—and that text only—section by section. Each section is followed by a pesher, an interpretation. In 11QMelch, the structure is more complex. Quotations come from different parts of the Bible. Some serve as base texts for elaborate interpretation (Lev. 25.13 in 2.2-9; Ps. 82.1-2 in 2.9-14; Isa. 52.7 in 2.15-24), while other texts are cited or alluded to as part of supplementary arguments.[6] Two biblical texts stand out, in that quotations or allusions are found spread throughout the column: Lev. 25.9-13 (2.2, 6, 7, 25) and Isa. 61.1-2 (2.4, 6, 9, 13).

In his 1970 journal article on 11QMelch, J. Carmignac made a distinction between two categories of pesher. The first one he called '*péshèr* "continu"'. In these works a biblical text is systematically and sequentially interpreted. The other type he named '*péshèr* "discontinu" ou "thématique"'. Such works interpret different biblical texts that have been grouped together by the way of a central idea.[7]

The classification of works according to the categories of 'continuous' and 'thematic' pesharim has become commonplace in Qumran research. In general, scholars have accepted Carmignac's attribution of 11QMelch to the genre 'thematic pesher'. If we ask what is actually the unifying theme behind the various biblical texts interpreted in 11QMelch, however, scholarly opinions differ.[8]

---

6. Deut. 15.2 in 2.2-3; Ps. 7.8-9 in 2.10-11; Dan. 9.25 or 26 in 2.18; Isa. 8.11 in 2.24. Cf. G.J. Brooke, 'Melchizedek (11QMelch)', in *ABD* IV, pp. 687-88.

7. Carmignac, 'Le document', pp. 360-61. A corresponding distinction was introduced by H. Stegemann, in connection with the document 4Q252, then called 'Patriarchal Blessings'. Stegemann prefers the word 'midrash' for the thematic type ('Weitere Stücke von 4QpPsalm 37, von 4QPatriarchal Blessings und Hinweis auf eine unedierte Handschrift aus Höhle 4Q mit Exzerpten aus dem Deuteronomium', *RevQ* 6 [1967], pp. 193-227, esp. pp. 213-17). The editor of 11QMelch, van der Woude, used 'midrash' in a similar way to characterize 11QMelch, 'Melchisedek', p. 357.

8. Some find it in the figure of Melchizedek, here clearly an angelic figure, e.g., J.A. Sanders, 'The Old Testament in 11QMelchizedek' (*JANESCU* 5 [1973], pp. 373-82), p. 379 n. 5, and A. Steudel, *Der Midrasch zur Eschatologie aus der Qumrangemeinde (4QMidrEschat$^{a.b}$): Materielle Rekonstruktion, Textbestand,*

This paper will question the validity of the category 'thematic pesher', and consequently also the designation of 11QMelch as a specimen of this literary type. To this end, a short survey of some aspects of the pesher genre is necessary.

3. *Aspects of the Pesher Genre*[9]

a. *Pesher Work and Pesher Unit*
The word *pesher* is used in multiple ways in Qumran research and it may describe phenomena on different levels. It may be helpful to introduce an elementary distinction between two hierarchical levels of textual phenomena, one more, the other less comprehensive.

In this paper, I shall use the expression 'pesher unit' to signify the lower level, the small textual unit. A pesher unit in its most simple form consists of a quotation and an interpretation. It uses a distinctive technical terminology: interpretations are always and quotations sometimes introduced by certain formulas; the most characteristic of the interpretation-formulas include the word *pesher*.[10] There is, of course, much more to say about the distinct traits of pesher. For the present purpose, however, these formal observations will be sufficient.[11]

Gattung und traditionsgeschichtliche Einordnung des durch 4Q174 ('Florilegium') und 4Q177 ('Catena A') repräsentierten Werkes aus den Qumranfunden (STDJ, 13; Leiden: E.J. Brill, 1994), p. 184. Carmignac prefers 'la délivrance des justes, comparée à l'année jubilaire' ('Le document', p. 362). Milik, on the other hand, determines the theme as the periods of history, with special regard to the activity of angels in each of them. This is dependent on his hypothesis that 4Q180, 4Q181 and 11QMelch are three copies of a work called 'Pesher on the Periods', ('Milkî-ṣedeq', p. 110).

9. For an overview of the extensive literature on the *pesharim*, see M.P. Horgan, *Pesharim: Qumran Interpretations of Biblical Books* (CBQMS, 8; Washington: Catholic Biblical Association, 1979); D. Dimant, 'Pesharim, Qumran', *ABD* V, pp. 244-51.

10. Horgan, *Pesharim*, pp. 239-44.

11. A more complete description would include a certain hermeneutical perspective, through which the scriptural text is applied to the interpreter's own time. A discussion of the relationship between *pesher* and *midrash* would be included. Cf. in addition to the works mentioned in the previous notes, G.J. Brooke, 'Qumran Pesher: Towards the Redefinition of a Genre', *RevQ* 10 (1981), pp. 483-503. I agree with Brooke in that the pesharim may adequately be described as 'Qumran midrashim'. The similarities with techniques for the interpretation of dreams, visions

For pesher in its more comprehensive meaning I shall use the expression 'pesher work'. A pesher work may be defined as a literary work consisting of a series of pesher units.[12]

b. *Different Types of Pesher*
According to recent scholarship, pesher units occur in three types of larger literary contexts: in 'continuous' pesharim, in 'thematic' pesharim, and as 'isolated' pesharim within non-pesher works.[13]

1. *'Continuous' Pesharim.* At least 15 manuscripts from Cave 1 and 4 are placed in this category.[14] Characteristic of the 'continuous pesher' is its close dependence on the sequence of the biblical text. In a paradigmatic work of this type, the quotations are supposed to cover the complete text of a biblical book, and that text only.

In fact, no extant copy of the pesharim covers a *complete* biblical text. This is partly due to their fragmentary state. 4Q169 = 4QpNah probably *did* contain the whole biblical text. But from the material remains we know with certainty that 1QpHab did *not* contain ch. 3 of the prophetic book—whatever the reason for that may be.

There are, furthermore, some other important deviations from this ideal pattern. In several cases, continuous pesharim turn out to be less continuous than often supposed, in that they omit parts of the biblical text (4Q162 = 4QpIsa^b, 4Q163 = 4QpIsa^c, and 4Q171 = 4QpPs^a). 4Q163 = 4QpIsa^c also cites scriptural texts other than the base text.[15]

and omens would also be underlined, with special emphasis on the similarities with the book of Daniel. Cf. the works of M. Fishbane, 'The Qumran Pesher and Traits of Ancient Hermeneutics', in *Proceedings of the Sixth World Congress of Jewish Studies*, I (Jerusalem: World Union of Jewish Studies, 1977), pp. 97-114; *idem*, *Biblical Interpretation in Ancient Israel* (Oxford: Clarendon Press, rev. edn, 1988), pp. 443-524.

12. Cf. K. Koch, *Was ist Formgeschichte? Methoden der Bibelexegese* (Neukirchen-Vluyn: Neukirchener Verlag, 5th edn, 1989), pp. 29-31, who distinguishes between 'Gliedgattung' and 'Rahmengattung'.

13. Dimant, 'Pesharim', p. 245; L.H. Schiffman, *Reclaiming the Dead Sea Scrolls: The History of Judaism, the Background of Christianity, the Lost Library of Qumran* (Philadelphia: Jewish Publication Society of America, 1994), p. 224.

14. Dimant, 'Pesharim', pp. 245-47. In addition, three very fragmentary texts have been identified as pesharim by some scholars. See Horgan, *Pesharim*, p. 1.

15. Horgan, *Pesharim*, pp. 86-87, 95; H. Stegemann, *Die Essener, Qumran, Johannes der Täufer und Jesus: Ein Sachbuch* (Herder Spektrum, 4128; Freiburg:

2. *'Thematic' Pesharim.* This is the (sub-)genre to which 11QMelch is generally ascribed. A 'thematic pesher' also consists of pesher units, but, unlike the 'continuous pesher', it cites and comments on scriptural texts from different parts of the Bible. These, it is assumed, have been chosen to illustrate a certain central idea. A brief analysis of the most important documents that are supposed to belong to this genre is given to test this assumption.

a. *4Q252.*[16] Formerly called 'Patriarchal Blessings', now 'Pesher on Genesis[a]', 4Q252 is a much debated and very interesting document. This is true also in terms of its literary character. One of its commentators says that the text consists of 'a series of exegetical remarks, some with lemmas, and some without, situated sequentially and covering Genesis 6–49, but with no overt principle governing its choice of passages on which to comment'.[17] Actually, most of the exegetical remarks preserved do not conform to the pesher pattern; 'rewritten Bible' or 'paraphrase' may be more adequate labels. However, distinct pesher units do also occur, at least in the part of the document which comments on the blessings of Genesis 49 (col. 4-5).

It may not be appropriate to characterise this text as a pesher work. The official editor of the text, G.J. Brooke, uses the more neutral term 'commentary on Genesis'. Nevertheless, the work has certain features that may be of some importance for the study of the pesher genre, in particular, the so-called thematic pesharim. In the words of Brooke, 'It is selective, both in that it does not aim to provide commentary on the whole of Genesis, and in that, at least for some of its pericopae, it seems to be citing material from other scriptural and non-scriptural sources. Nevertheless, it does not seem to deviate from the sequence of the text of Genesis in its ordering of its units of commentary. Genesis thus acts as a controlling influence on the structure of the commentary.'[18]

Herder, 1994), pp. 176, 179; Schiffman, *Reclaiming the Dead Sea Scrolls*, pp. 228-30.

16. For the state of publication, cf. G.J. Brooke, 'The Genre of 4Q252: From Poetry to Pesher', *Dead Sea Discoveries* 1 (1994), pp. 160-79 (160 n. 1). Translation in García Martínez, *Dead Sea Scrolls Translated*, pp. 213-15.

17. M.J. Bernstein, '4Q252: From Re-Written Bible to Biblical Commentary', *JJS* 45 (1994), pp. 1-27 (5).

18. Brooke, 'The Genre of 4Q252', pp. 178-79.

b. *4Q174 and 4Q177*. In the *editio princeps,* these manuscripts are entitled 'Florilegium' (4Q174) and 'Catena A' (4Q177) respectively.[19] The 'Florilegium' in particular has been invoked as a textbook example of a thematic pesher. In this scroll, verses from different parts of the Bible are cited and commented on. Primary emphasis is on citations from 2 Samuel 7, Psalms 1–2 and Deuteronomy 33.

Two major studies of these documents may allow for a somewhat different understanding of their literary character. G.J. Brooke has given a very careful study of 4Q174, not least from a form-critical point of view.[20] And recently A. Steudel has offered a new reconstruction of the manuscripts 4Q174 and 4Q177. She understands them as two manuscripts of the same work, a work which she has entitled 'Midrash on Eschatology'.[21]

Both studies emphasise the structural significance of the Psalms citations for the work. If Steudel's reconstruction is correct—and, indeed, I think there are good reasons to accept it—by far the longest part of the work consists of pesher units commenting on selected verses from the book of Psalms (mainly *incipit* verses, but sometimes others as well), most often in the canonical sequence. Several of these pesher units have a complex structure, in that they also use secondary citations from other parts of the Bible. This Psalm-commenting part of the work is introduced by the formula: *midrash min…* (4Q174 1-2.1.14), the opening words of Psalm 1 immediately following. Actually, this would be a fitting superscription to a 'Midrash Tehillim'. Why not read this work as another 'Pesher on Psalms'?

19. J.M. Allegro, *Qumran Cave 4/I* (DJD, 5; Oxford: Clarendon Press, 1968); 4Q174: pp. 53-57 + Pl. XIX-XX; 4Q177: pp. 67-74 + Pl. XXIV-XXVa. Cf. J. Strugnell, 'Notes en marge du volume V des "Discoveries in the Judaean Desert of Jordan"', *RevQ* 7 (1970), pp. 163-276 (220-25, 236-48). Translation in García Martínez, *Dead Sea Scrolls Translated,* pp. 136-37, 209-11.

20. G.J. Brooke, *Exegesis at Qumran: 4QFlorilegium in its Jewish Context* (JSOTSup, 29; Sheffield: JSOT Press, 1985).

21. Steudel, *Midrasch.* An English summary of her work is available in A. Steudel, '4QMidrEschat: "A Midrash on Eschatology" (4Q174 + 4Q177)', in J. Trebolle Barrera and L. Vegas Montaner (eds.), *The Madrid Qumran Congress: Proceedings of the International Congress on the Dead Sea Scrolls, Madrid 18–21 March, 1991* (STDJ, 11.2; Leiden: E.J. Brill; Madrid: Editorial Complutense, 1992), pp. 531-41.

The first part of 4Q174 departs from this pattern. It consists of two shorter sections. The first quotes the blessing of Moses, Deuteronomy 33, with short comments. This section is, unfortunately, rather poorly preserved. The second, and the most well-known, passage of the work cites and comments on the oracle of Nathan, 2 Samuel 7. If the work is a pesher on Psalms, the presence of these passages requires an explanation. It is possible that different works were written on the same scroll, or that the scroll represents some sort of anthology. More likely, however, these sections were thought of as an 'exordium', introducing the running commentary.

c. *4Q180 and 4Q181*.[22] These manuscripts play a special role in the study of 11QMelch because of the influential hypothesis of J.T. Milik. Based on their similarities in outlook, vocabulary and interest, he concluded that the three manuscripts were actually copies of the same work, a work to which he gave the title 'Pesher sur les Periodes'.[23] These are, in fact, the opening words of 4Q180, where the beginning of the manuscript is preserved. Milik further conjectured the existence of a 'Book of Periods', now lost, on which the work was a commentary.

Several scholars have accepted this hypothesis;[24] others have been more reserved. For a number of reasons, I do not believe that these manuscripts belong together.[25]

22. *Editio princeps:* Allegro, DJD, 5, pp. 77-80; pl. XXVII and XVIII. Cf. Strugnell, 'Notes', pp. 252-55. Translation in García Martínez, *Dead Sea Scrolls Translated*, pp. 211-13.

23. Milik, 'Milkî-ṣedeq', pp. 109-12, 122-24.

24. Kobelski, *Melchizedek*, pp. 50-51; Brooke, 'Melchizedek'.

25. D. Dimant, 'The "Pesher on the Periods" (4Q180) and 4Q181', *IOS* 9 (1979), pp. 77-102, rejects the unity of 4Q180 and 4Q181 and questions several of Milik's reconstructions. A. Steudel points to differences in form as well as content between 4Q180/181 and 11Q13, *Midrasch*, p. 184, and especially 'אחרית הימים in the Texts from Qumran', *RevQ* 16 (1993), pp. 225-46 (234 n. 48). More closely related to 4Q180 from a formal point of view—perhaps even another copy of the work??—is the recently published document 4Q464; M.E. Stone and E. Eshel, 'An Exposition on the Patriarchs (4Q464) and Two Other Documents (4Q464ᵃ and 4Q464ᵇ)', *Le Muséon* 105 (1992), pp. 243-64. On the question of the existence of a 'Book of Periods', see R.V. Huggins, 'A Canonical "Book of Periods" at Qumran?', *RevQ* 15 (1992), pp. 421-36.

The manuscript 4Q180 has some peculiarities compared to other documents using the word pesher. Mostly, the word is used to connect a biblical text to its interpretation. In this document, however, there is no antecedent—no biblical text being explicitly referred to. The unusual formula *pesher 'al* is also striking.[26] It seems to function as a sort of superscription. The expression 'Pesher on the Periods' is probably not a superscription to the whole work, however.[27] In 1.7 there is a similar formula introducing the next section of the text: 'Pesher on "Azazel and the angels…"' To judge from the extant fragments, the work is related to a biblical story, if not to a biblical text. Says D. Dimant: 'After a general introduction, the Pesher presents a detailed treatment of the Period of the Ten Generations — from Shem to Abraham'.

There is more work to be done on this text. The issue here is limited: to underline the ties to the Genesis story—if not to the Genesis text. It probably does not belong to the genre 'pesher work' in a strict sense. 4Q252 may be the closest relative.

3. *'Isolated' Pesharim.* In some instances in the Qumran library, pesher units occur as parts of a non-pesher work. This very interesting phenomenon is probably of some significance for the understanding of the history of the genre, a subject too extensive to be treated in the present context. Most of the instances are found in the Admonitions of the *Damascus Document* (CD), but 1QS 8.14-16 also contains a pesher on Isa. 40.3.[28] 4Q252 may perhaps be considered another case of this category.

c. *Conclusions regarding the Pesher Genre*
From these observations, the following tentative conclusions may be drawn:

1. *Pesher units* may occur in different contexts: In pesher works, that is, collections of pesher units, but also as parts of non-pesher works.
2. A primary connection to one biblical text seems to be a fundamental feature of *pesher works*. Also in the so-called 'thematic pesharim' such connections are discernible.

---

26. Although not unique, as often stated. It also appears in 4Q464 3 2 7.
27. Cf. Strugnell, 'Notes', p. 252.
28. Dimant, 'Pesharim', p. 248.

3.   Pesher works may be described as more or less *continuous* with regard to their treatment of the primary biblical text. Some cite the whole sequence of the biblical text, verse by verse, line by line, while others are selective in their choice of verses to comment upon. As a rule, the sequence of the biblical text is respected.

4.   Pesher works may be described as more or less *complex* with regard to their use or non-use of supportive biblical texts. Some works quote the primary text only, while others cite secondary texts as well.

5.   The category 'thematic pesher', however, does not seem useful for the classification of pesher works. It turns out to be difficult to formulate the central ideas around which the so-called 'thematic pesharim' are supposed to be organized, except in very general terms (e.g. 'eschatology'). Furthermore, if the previous points are valid, the category seems unnecessary.

The implications of these observations may be summarized in the words of M.J. Bernstein: 'There is either one sort of pesher or many, but not exactly two'.[29] Bernstein, who has studied in detail the use of formulas to introduce biblical citations within different pesher works, concludes that in this respect 'the extant pesharim occupy points along a continuum'.[30] This seems to be the case also as concerns the two parameters briefly studied here, the degree of continuous citation of the primary text and the use of secondary citations.[31]

4. *The Genre of 11QMelch*

It is time to apply the results of the above survey to the main question: that of the genre of 11QMelch.

---

29. M.J. Bernstein, 'Introductory Formulas for Citation and Re-Citation of Biblical Verses in the Qumran Pesharim: Observations on a Pesher Technique', *Dead Sea Discoveries* 1 (1994), pp. 30-70 (34). Bernstein's statement borrows an expression used by J. Kugel to characterize biblical parallelism.

30. Bernstein, 'Introductory Formulas', p. 69.

31. The use of secondary texts in pesher works calls for further study. It seems that the more continuous pesharim make less use of this device, whereas the less continuous make more extensive use of it (compare 4Q174 + 4Q177, 4Q163, and 1QpHab). The picture is, however, more complicated. It has been pointed out that

a. *Pesher Units as Part of a Non-Pesher Work?*

To my knowledge, no-one has yet examined the possibility that 11QMelch might actually be a non-pesher work.[32] In that case, the chain of pesher units in 11QMelch 2 would be regarded as 'isolated' pesharim, belonging to a work of unknown literary type. The context is too fragmentary to determine its overall genre, and form criticism will not help us much further.

One argument may speak in favour of such a solution: if 11QMelch were a pesher work, one also would expect to find scriptural citations and/or the typical formulaic language of the genre *outside* of col. 2. In fact, such traits are very difficult to identify. The reconstruction of the word *pishrô* in frag. 5, line 4 is possible, but far from certain.[33]

The validity of this argument is, however, limited. The remains are minute and do not allow safe conclusions. On the other side, the chain of pesher units present in col. 2 would be unusually long and complex if they were part of a non-pesher work. This speaks against the solution.

b. *Pesher on a Biblical Text?*

Hence, I will try to read 11QMelch as a pesher work based on one biblical text. It is clearly complex; the work utilizes secondary citations from a variety of biblical writings. And it is possibly non-continuous, commenting only on selected passages from the primary text.

The last remark is of some importance. Instead of a somewhat myopic search for references to scriptural verses immediately preceding or following those preserved in the work,[34] we may profitably search in the wider literary context of the primary biblical text. But which is this text? There are, in fact, two candidates.

---

sections of the pesharim have been influenced by passages from biblical books other than the primary texts, but without explicitly quoting the passages. Cf. B. Nitzan, *Pesher Habakkuk: A Scroll from the Wilderness of Judah* [Hebrew] (Jerusalem: Mosad Bialik, 1986); M. Kister, 'Biblical Phrases and Hidden Biblical Interpretations and Pesharim', in D. Dimant and U. Rappaport (eds.), *The Dead Sea Scrolls: Forty Years of Research* (STDJ, 10; Leiden: E.J. Brill; Jerusalem: Magnes Press/Yad Izhak Ben-Zvi, 1992), pp. 27-39.

32. A hint of this possibility is given in Steudel, *Midrasch*, p. 196 n. 1.

33. Milik, 'Milkî-ṣedeq', p. 100; Kobelski, *Melchizedek*, p. 23; Puech, 'Notes', p. 503.

34. Cf. Milik, 'Milkî-ṣedeq', pp. 100-101, on Lev. 25.8.

1. *Pesher on Isaiah?* 'Isa 61 1-2 is the unifying scriptural base of the 11QMelch pesher', according to J.A. Sanders.[35] References to this text are scattered throughout the whole of col. 2.

I have earlier been inclined to describe 11QMelch as a pesher on Isaiah.[36] An additional argument for this *may* be found in frag. 11, line 3 (part of col. 3 in Puech's reconstruction). The text of 11QMelch is here reconstructed as *ḥômat* (or: *ḥômôt*) *Yerûshalayim*—'the wall(s) of Jerusalem'. A similar expression is found in the wider literary context of Isa. 61.1-2–62.6.

Some formal arguments, however, speak against this solution. Most important is the fact that in the preserved part of the text, Isa. 61.1-2 is not explicitly quoted and commented upon;[37] rather, the references occur in pesher comments on other texts.[38]

2. *Pesher on Leviticus?* We are left with the other option, here in the words of J.A. Fitzmyer: 'The thread which apparently runs through the whole text and ties together its various elements is Lv. 25'.[39] Indeed, several explicit references to this chapter are spread throughout 11QMelch 2. Formally, they are treated in a standard pesher manner. I propose to describe 11QMelch as *a pesher on (a part of) Leviticus*.

---

35. J.A. Sanders, 'Dissenting Deities and Philippians 2.1-11', *JBL* 88 (1969), pp. 279-90 (286 n. 29). Cf. M.P. Miller, 'The Function of Isa. 61.1-2 in 11Q Melchizedek', *JBL* 88 (1969), pp. 467-69; Sanders, 'Old Testament', esp. pp. 374 and 379 n. 5.

36. A. Aschim, 'Verdens eldste bibelkommentar? Melkisedek-teksten fra Qumran', *Tidsskrift for Teologi og Kirke* 66 (1995), pp. 85-103 (98).

37. See, however, Puech's reconstruction of 2.4.

38. Miller, 'Function', p. 469. In addition, the citation of Isa. 52.7 is introduced with a long and complex formula including a reference to 'the words of the prophet Isaiah'. This may seem somewhat awkward if the primary text is taken from the same book.

39. J.A. Fitzmyer, 'Further Light on Melchizedek from Qumran Cave 11', in *idem, Essays on the Semitic Background of the New Testament* (Sources for Biblical Study, 5; London: Chapman, 1971), pp. 245-67 (251) (originally in *JBL* 86 [1967], pp. 25-41). The same opinion is stated, e.g. by Bernstein, 'Formulas', p. 60 n. 94 (though somewhat hesitantly), and D. Dimant, 'Qumran Sectarian Literature', in M.E. Stone (ed.), *Jewish Writings of the Second Temple Period* (CRINT, 2.2; Assen: Van Gorcum; Philadelphia: Fortress Press, 1984), pp. 483-550 (521 n. 187).

A word of caution is appropriate. It is difficult to detect references to Leviticus in the remaining parts of the work (i.e. outside col. 2). There is also a formal problem in that the citations do not always occur in the sequence of the biblical text. Thus, 25.13 is quoted early in col. 2, 25.9 later.[40] However, I would like to point out that within col. 2 there are a couple of possible intertextual links to other parts of Leviticus, which, in my opinion, deserve further investigation.

The significance of the *Day of Atonement* in 11QMelch 2.7-8 goes far beyond Lev. 25.9, where it occurs merely as a means of dating the proclamation of the Year of Jubilee. In 11QMelch, it is obviously a matter of great importance to the author that the proclamation of the eschatological liberation—and judgment—takes place on this very day. One may consider the possibility of an implicit reference to such passages as Leviticus 16 or 23.26-32, which may have been interpreted earlier in the work. This is, however, impossible to verify from the material remains and belongs to the field of speculation.

Another intertextual link seems more probable. In 11QMelch 2, 'exile and return' is a dominant theme. This is combined with an eschatological expectation based on a sabbatical chronology. In Lev. 26.33-45 exile is interpreted as punishment for—among other things—failure to keep the commandment concerning the sabbatical year: 'Then the land shall rest, and enjoy its sabbath years. As long as it lies desolate, it shall have the rest it did not have on your sabbaths when you were living on it' (Lev. 26.34-35 NRSV). This text is clearly a part of the background for 'chronomessianic' speculations (a term coined by B.Z. Wacholder), a widespread phenomenon in Judaism in antiquity, at least since Dan. 9.24-27 and the Apocalypse of Weeks in *1 Enoch*, 11QMelch being itself a typical example.[41] To my knowledge, it is to the credit of P. Garnet to have demonstrated the importance of this same text also

---

40. Further, it is often claimed that the pesharim treat prophetic texts only. This picture is, however, too simplistic. It is true that pesharim treat Scripture *as oracles*, and in so far as prophecy. But there are pesher works on Psalms, and several works, both of pesher and non-pesher kind, which contain pesher units based on parts of the Pentateuch (4Q252, 11QMelch, CD).

41. B.Z. Wacholder, 'Chronomessianism: The Timing of Messianic Movements and the Calendar of Sabbatical Cycles', *HUCA* 46 (1975), pp. 201-218 (202) on Lev. 26 (210-11) on 11QMelch. See also Steudel, 'אחרית הימים', pp. 233-36.

for Qumran ideas of salvation and atonement.[42] He does not, however, explore its eventual significance for 11QMelch. In view of its thematic proximity to 11QMelch 2, as well as its literary proximity to Leviticus 25, a connection is not improbable.

5. *Concluding Remarks*

The approach taken in this paper has been rather limited. It has been strictly synchronic, and strictly formal—even limited to a very small selection of formal traits. It is appropriate to relate this approach briefly to some other questions that should be addressed to the text, the full treatment of which, however, go beyond the scope of this paper.

1.	The approach is not inconsistent with the more diachronic approach taken by traditional form criticism. To write the *Gattungsgeschichte* of the pesher literature is a fully legitimate project, and several promising attempts have been made.[43] This involves, however, evidence of diverse kinds, too extensive to be included here: discussion of the development of form, content and vocabulary, the palaeography of individual manuscripts, references to historical events, and so on.

2.	The focus on the smaller literary unit, the pesher unit, also allows for classical form criticism in another respect: The individual unit may have a *prehistory* prior to its inclusion in the pesher work of which it is presently a part. This may well be the case with 4Q252, a very complex document from a formal point of view. It may also explain some traits of 4Q174 + 4Q177,[44] and it cannot be excluded in the case of 11QMelch.

42. P. Garnet, *Salvation and Atonement in the Qumran Scrolls* (WUNT, 2.3; Tübingen: J.C.B. Mohr, 1977), esp. pp. 113, 118-19.

43. Stegemann, *Die Essener*, pp. 167-87; Steudel, *Midrasch*, pp. 193-201. On 11QMelch in particular, see Puech, 'Notes', pp. 507-10. These scholars are in agreement concerning the dating of 11QMelch: it is written towards the end of the second century BCE, and it is probably the oldest extant work of a pesher type.

44. Schiffman, *Reclaiming the Dead Sea Scrolls*, pp. 230-31; R. Bergmeier, 'A. Steudel: Der Midrasch zur Eschatologie aus der Qumrangemeinde (rec.)', *TLZ* 120 (1995), pp. 138-39.

3.   Still unsolved are the questions about the *function* and *setting* of this type of literature.[45] These are questions that need to be readdressed on a broad basis.[46]

45. Various attempts have been made: T.H. Gaster (*The Dead Sea Scriptures* [Garden City, NY: Anchor Press/Doubleday, 3rd edn, 1976]), paraphrases the text as 'a series of notes for a sermon' (p. 389); for Stegemann, it belongs to the group of 'Schriftgelehrte Abhandlungen' (*Essener*, p. 167). Brooke has proposed a connection to a liturgical setting, perhaps the Day of Atonement (*Exegesis*, pp. 322-23).

46. Since the completion of the manuscript, the official edition of 11QMelch (by F. García Martínez, E.J.C. Tigchelaar and A.S. van der Woude) has appeared, *Qumran Cave 11/II* (DJD, 23; Oxford: Clarendon Press, 1998), pp. 221-41, pl. XXVII.

Among recent contributions to the study of 11QMelch, two stand out as particularly valuable. In *La croyance des Esséniens en la vie future: Immortalité, résurrection, vie éternelle? Histoire d'une croyance dans le Judaïsme ancien* (2 vols.; EBib, 21-22; Paris: Gabalda, 1993), II, pp. 513-62, E. Puech has revised his edition and commented upon many aspects of the text. F. Manzi, *Melchisedek e l'angelologia nell'Epistola agli Ebrei e a Qumran* (AnBib, 136; Rome: Pontificio Istituto Biblico, 1997), treats 11QMelch in detail on pp. 51-96. His volume includes a comprehensive bibliography.

Editions of two additional texts treated in the paper have also appeared in the DJD series: 4Q464 (Exposition on the Patriarchs) by E. Eshel and M.E. Stone in *Qumran Cave 4/XIV: Parabiblical Texts, Part 2* (DJD, 19; Oxford: Clarendon Press, 1995), pp. 215-30, pl. XXVIII, and 4Q252 (Commentary on Genesis A) by G.J. Brooke in *Qumran Cave 4/XVII: Parabiblical Texts, Part 3* (DJD, 22; Oxford: Clarendon Press, 1996), pp. 185-207, pls. XII-XIII.

THE ESSENES IN PHILO AND JOSEPHUS

Per Bilde

1. *Introduction*

Before the emergence of Qumran and its literature, the accounts of Philo and Josephus on the Essenes were studied regularly, generally in the context of Ancient Judaism or Early Christianity.[1] After the discovery of the Dead Sea Scrolls, interest in classical Jewish sources on the Essenes increased because of the importance of these documents in attempts to identify the community behind the Scrolls.[2] Rather quickly the general consensus developed that the community behind the scrolls should be identified with the Essenes or a group close to the Essenes.[3] As a result, the interest in Philo's and Josephus's accounts of the Essenes decreased partly because research now concentrated on the

1. Cf. the history of earlier research in S. Wagner, *Die Essener in der wissenschaftlichen Diskussion vom Ausgang des 18. bis zum Beginn des 20. Jahrhunderts: Eine Wissenschaftsgeschichtliche Studie* (BZAW, 79; Berlin: Alfred Töpelmann, 1960).

2. Cf., e.g., R. Marcus, 'The Qumrân Scrolls and Early Judaism', *BibRes* 1 (1956), pp. 9-47; *idem*, 'Philo, Josephus, and the Dead Sea Yahad', *JBL* 71 (1952), pp. 207-209; A. Dupont-Sommer, *Les écrits esséniens découvets près de la Mer Morte* (BH; Paris: Payot, 1959), esp. pp. 31-81, 100-18; G. Vermes, 'Essenes and Therapeutai', *RevQ* 3 (1962), pp. 495-504.

3. Today, the hypothesis that the Qumranites were Essenes is accepted by most scholars. Cf., e.g., G. Vermes, *The Dead Sea Scrolls: Qumran in Perspective* (London: SCM Press, 3rd edn, 1994 [1977]), pp. 100-18; E. Schürer, *The History of the Jewish People in the Age of Jesus Christ (175 B.C.–A.D. 135): A New English Version* (rev. G. Vermes, F. Millar and M. Black; Edinburgh: T. & T. Clark, 1979), II, pp. 583-85; T. Rajak, 'Ciò che Flavio Guiseppe vide: Josephus and the Essenes', in F. Parente and J. Sievers (eds.), *Josephus and the History of the Greco-Roman World: Essays in Memory of Morton Smith* (Leiden: E.J. Brill, 1994), pp. 141-60 (142-43); J.C. VanderKam, *The Dead Sea Scrolls Today* (Grand Rapids: Eerdmans; London: SPCK, 1994), pp. 71-98.

scrolls themselves and partly, naturally enough, because the classical Jewish descriptions were generally interpreted as second-hand sources wrapped in Hellenistic redactions, or even that the descriptions in Philo and Josephus were regarded as Hellenized distortions of the actual Essenes, whom we can find only in the writings from Qumran.[4] In contrast to their opinions on Philo and Josephus, the same scholars tend to regard the Dead Sea Scrolls as rather untouched by Hellenistic culture and representing genuine and pure Palestinian Jewish religion.[5]

However, during the last decades, the discussion of the identity of the Qumran community has been revived by Schiffman's hypothesis that the Qumranites were 'Zadokites' close to the Sadducees, by the 'Groningen Hypothesis,' according to which they were a splinter group which had broken out of a broader Essene movement, and with Stegemann's and other hypotheses which are all variants of the same paradigm.[6] These theories have created a new situation, also with respect to Philo's and Josephus's accounts of the Essenes, because these two accounts seem to indicate a similar situation with several—partly different and partly related—Essene communities.

In the present paper I aim at a renewed presentation and discussion of the accounts of Philo and Josephus on the Essenes in the light of the new discussion of the Qumran community's identity and early history: what is the character of each of these two (sets of) accounts? How are they related to each other? What were the interests and intentions of their authors? And how reliable are these accounts?

I propose to proceed as follows. I begin by examining the descriptions of the Essenes (and Therapeutes) by Philo and Josephus and aim at bringing out explicitly the contents and character of each account. I

4. Thus, e.g., Marcus, 'The Qumrân Scrolls', pp. 28-29; B.J. Roberts, 'The Qumran Scrolls and the Essenes', *NTS* 3 (1956–57), pp. 58-65; R. Bergmeier, *Die Essenerberichte des Flavius Josephus: Quellenstudien zu den Essenertexten im Werk des jüdischen Historiographen* (Kampen: Kok Pharos, 1993), pp. 10-11; H.-Aa. Mink, 'Qumran: Aspekter af brydningen mellem jødedom og hellenisme', *Hellenismestudier* 9 (1995), pp. 52-64.

5. Thus, e.g., Bergmeier, *Die Essenerberichte*, p. 10.

6. Cf. L.H. Schiffman, 'Origin and Early History of the Qumran Sect' *BA* 58 (1995), pp. 37-48; F. García Martínez, *The Dead Sea Scrolls Translated: The Qumran Texts in English* (Leiden: E.J. Brill, 1994), pp. lii-liv; H. Stegemann, *Die Essener, Qumran, Johannes der Täufer und Jesus: Ein Sachbuch* (Freiburg: Herder, 1993), pp. 194-226; and the surveys in Vermes, *The Dead Sea Scrolls*, pp. 100-18; VanderKam, *The Dead Sea Scrolls Today*, pp. 71-98.

intend to do this by coining a number of headings that are meant to summarize a certain subject in each text and setting them up in lists. Later I compare the various lists of headings with the intention of discovering connections between the texts and producing statistical material which can be used in the interpretation. I continue with an analysis of the evidence, with the aim of systematically determining the profile of Philo's and Josephus's accounts and their possible mutual interrelations.

I emphasize the uncertainty of this attempt: already the selection and naming of headings are defective, and so is the evaluation of similarities and differences. Therefore, I have to stress that it is only the tendencies of my results that really count as significant, not the specific numbers, percentages and other details.

2. *Philo*

a. *Every Good Man is Free (Philo-a)*

In his stoicizing treatise, *Quod omnis probus liber sit* ('Every Good Man is Free', here Philo-a), presumably written in the beginning of the first century CE, the young Philo (ca 20 BCE–45 CE) presents various groups of 'wise' people as exemplifying his main thesis, according to which only the truly wise man is genuinely free. Having presented examples of wise Greeks, Persians and Indians, Philo turns to 'Palestinian Syria', and he underlines that this region 'too, has not failed to produce high moral excellence'.[7] This is the case especially among the Jews 'including as it is said,[8] certain persons...called Essenes' (75a). Paragraphs 75-91 are devoted to the description of this group, and the Essenes are presented as follows:

1. Number: they are 'more than four thousand . . . ' (75a).
2. Name: their name, the 'Essenes', is interpreted by Philo 'as a variation... of *hosiotēs* (holiness)', and he assumes that this

---

7. I have borrowed the English translation of the ancient authors from the Loeb Classical Library, here F.H. Colson (trans.), *Philo* (LCL, IX; Cambridge, MA: Harvard University Press; London: Heinemann, 1967). The relevant paragraphs (75-91) are quoted in full in Eusebius from Caesarea (c. 260–340 CE), *Praep. Evang.* 8.12.

8. This wording (*legontai*) can be interpreted as indicating Philo's use of a (written?) source. See section 5.b.

name has been given to them 'because they have shown themselves especially devout in the service of God' (75b).

3. Sacrifice: they do not offer animal sacrifices, but instead present their own minds as a spiritual sacrifice (75c).

4. Locality: they 'live in villages and avoid the cities because of the iniquities which have become inveterate among city dwellers' (76a).

5. Work: they work with their hands either on the land or in other peaceful and beneficial crafts (76b).

6. Agriculture: (76b).

7. Craft: (76b).

8. Wealth: they do not accumulate property, neither gold nor land, but are content with providing their daily necessities (76c).

9. Frugality: instead, they regard frugality as the true kind of richness, for, as the only people in the world who have voluntarily assumed poverty, 'they are esteemed exeedingly rich, because they judge frugality with contentment to be, as indeed it is, an abundance of wealth' (77, cf. 84b).

10. Weapons: they do not produce any kind of weapon (78a).

11. Commerce: they have no idea of commerce and look with contempt on all kinds of greed (78b).

12. Slaves: they do not own slaves, and in their community 'all are free, exchanging services with each other' (79a).

13. Equality: they reject the owning of slaves especially because, in agreement with 'the statute of Nature, who mother-like has born and reared all men alike', they regard all men to be equal (79b, cf. 84e).

14. Philosophy: in 'philosophy' they only cultivate the disciplines of theology and ethics (80a, cf. 88).

15. Holy Scriptures: they study ethics eagerly, taking 'for their trainers the laws of their fathers', laws which they regard as being of divine origin (80b, cf. 81-82).

16. Sabbath: they study these laws 'at all times, but particularly on the seventh days' (81a); on that day 'they abstain from all other work', and assemble in their synagogues . . . (81b).

17. Synagogue: (81b).

18. Hierarchy: here, 'arranged in rows according to their ages . . . ' (81c).

19. Allegory: thus, they listen to the reading of the words of their books, and to the 'allegorical' interpretation presented by a person 'of especial proficiency' (82).

20. Piety: in this way 'they are trained in piety, holiness, justice . . . love of God, love of virtue, love of men' (83).

21. Purity: in their 'love of God' they attach particular importance to 'religious purity'(84a).

22. Oaths: likewise, they demonstrate this attitude 'by abstinence from oaths' and by 'veracity' (84b).

23. Theology: further, by their belief that God 'is the cause of all good things and nothing bad' (84c).

24. Simplicity: they show their 'love of virtue, by their freedom from the love of either money or reputation or pleasure, by self-mastery and endurance, again by frugality, simple living . . . ' (84d).

25. Ethics: they demonstrate their 'love of men' by benevolence, equality 'and their spirit of fellowship' (84e, cf. 79b).

26. Hospitality: this fellowship may be seen in the fact that their houses are open and shared by all (85a); especially, they practise hospitality towards members of their own order (85b).

27. Common property: they are the only community in the world with common property, including even clothes and food (86a-b); they put all earned wages 'into the common stock and allow the benefits thus accruing to be shared by those who wish to use it' (86c).

28. Common clothes: (86a).

29. Common meals: (86b, cf. 91).

30. Sick and elderly: they take care of the sick and elderly as if they were their real relatives (87).

31. Truly free: accordingly, in contrast to Greek philosophers, Philo stresses that the Essene 'philosophers' (cf. 88a) are men of ethical practice whom he describes as 'athletes of virtue' (*athlētas aretēs*). By such deeds they establish 'the liberty which can never be enslaved' (*ex hōn hē adoulōtos eleutheria*) (88b, cf. 84d).

32. Admired by rulers: Philo concludes that even unsympathetic and cruel rulers have admired the Essenes: 'they all treated them as self-governing (*autonomois*) and freemen by nature and extolled their communal meals and that ineffable sense of

fellowship, which is the clearest evidence of a perfect and supremely happy life' (89-91).[9]

In this account Philo describes the Essenes as a numerous group of Jewish 'philosophers', genuinely free men, holy ascetics, living in villages where they have established well-organized 'communistic' communities with common ownership of property, clothes and meals, without slaves, a strange mixture of equality and hierarchy, common care for the sick and the elderly, with hard labour, no commerce and no production of weapons. Religiously, the Essenes are characterized by a spiritualized reinterpretation of the traditional animal sacrifices, by their absorption in the Holy Scriptures which they interpret allegorically, with a strict interpretation and practice of Jewish law and ethics, especially of the Sabbath, with rejection of oaths, and with strong emphasis on religious purity—a community which has been admired by all, even cruel rulers.

b. *Hypothetica (Philo-b)*
In his work, *Praeparatio Evangelica* (8.6.1–11.18), Eusebius brings two extracts from a work by Philo. Eusebius informs us that the first comes from the second book of a (lost) work by Philo, *Hypothetica*, and that the second extract which describes the Essenes comes from another (lost) work by Philo entitled 'Apology for the Jews'.[10] In the second extract (*Praep. Evang./Hyp.* 11.1-18, here Philo-b) Philo describes the Essenes as follows:

1. Identity: the 'Lawgiver'[11] has trained multitudes of his kinsmen 'for the life of fellowship' (*epi koinônian*), and these men are called Essenes (11.1a).

---

9. A similar situation is described in Philo, *Hyp.* 11.18 and in Josephus, *Ant.* 15.371-79. Cf. M. Petit, 'Les Esséens de Philon d'Alexandrie et les Esséniens', in D. Dimant and U. Rappaport (eds.), *The Dead Sea Scrolls: Forty Years of Research* (Leiden: E.J. Brill; Jerusalem: Magness Press/Yad Izhak Ben Zvi, 1992), pp. 139-55 (154-55, and section 3.a.1).

10. Colson remarks: 'The general asumption is that these <three> are one and the same' (*Philo*, p. 407; cf. P. Borgen, 'Philo of Alexandria', in M.E. Stone (ed.), *Jewish Writings of the Second Temple Period: Apocrypha, Pseudepigrapha, Qumran Sectarian Writings, Philo, Josephus* (CRINT 2.2; Assen: Van Gorcum, 1984), pp. 233-82 (247). Therefore, I follow Colson in calling this work *Hypothetica* as well.

11. Presumably Moses, cf. Philo, *Vit. Cont.* 63, and Josephus, *War* 2.145, 152.

2. Name: this name is given to them because of their holiness (11.1b, cf. number 2 in the above list).
3. Locality: they are said to live in many cities and villages in Judaea (11.1c).
4. Associations: here, they are 'grouped in great societies of many members' (11.1d); below (11.5) it is stated that they live together in free associations (*kata thiasous, hetairias kai susitia*) where they practice fellowship and common meals.
5. Admission: new members are recruited, not by birth, but by personal choice, based 'on their zeal for virtue and desire to promote brotherly love (*dia de zēlon aretēs kai philanthrōpias...*)' (11.2).
6. Mature men: thus, new members of the Essene associations are not children or youths, but elderly, mature men—'no longer carried under by the tide of the body nor led by the passions, but enjoying the veritable, the only real freedom' (11.3).
7. Common property: their freedom 'is attested by their life': they have no private property, no slaves and no riches, but they hand over their belongings to a 'public stock and enjoy the benefit of them all in common' (11.4).
8. Slaves: they have no slaves (11.4).
9. Common meals: they have common meals (11.5, cf. 11.1).
10. Work: they spend their time working from sunrise to sunset, with great energy and regardless of bad weather and with the same zeal as gymnastic competitors (11.6).
11. Asceticism: they regard their 'exercises' as being of a more durable value for man than the practices of the athletes (11.7).
12. Agricultural work: some of them till the land, others take care of cattle-breeding and bee-keeping (11.8).
13. Craft: still others work in handicrafts in order to gain their livelihood (11.9).
14. Common treasury: the money they earn is brought to a designated treasurer who takes care of buying what the community needs (11.10).

Cf. A. Paul, 'Flavius Josèphe et les Esséniens', in D. Dimant and U. Rappaport (eds.), *The Dead Sea Scrolls: Forty Years of Research* (Leiden: E.J. Brill; Jerusalem: Magnes Press/Yad Izhak Ben-Zvi, 1992), pp. 125-38, (131-32), who emphasizes Josephus's predilection for the word 'Lawgiver'(*nomothetēs*).

15. Frugality: thus having a common life and a common table, they are content because they are 'lovers of frugality who shun expensive luxury as a disease of both body and soul' (11.11).

16. Common clothes: even their clothes they have in common, one set in winter and one in summer (11.12).

17. Sick and elderly: they willingly take care of the sick and the old men, who are 'treated as parents' (11.13).

18. Marriage and continence: they avoid marriage, regarding it an obstacle for their common life as well as for their practice of continence (11.14a).

19. Low opinion of women: another reason is their view of women as selfish, jealous and disturbing the religious life of their husbands (11.14b-15). Especially if they get children, women become even more 'hostile to the life of fellowship' (11.16-17). They think that a man bound to wife and children 'has become a different man and has passed from freedom into slavery' (11.17).

20. Admired by rulers: the description concludes by referring to the fact that not only common people, but even mighty kings admire this way of living of the Essenes (11.18, cf. n. 9 above).

In this piece Philo describes the Essenes as a popular voluntary association of pious, mature Jews, living in cities and villages in Judaea, organized in 'communistic' societies with common property, meals and clothes, with no slaves, taking care of the sick and elderly, busily working from morning to evening in agriculture and crafts, living a simple life in modesty and frugality, abstaining from sexual love and marriage because of a negative view of women, being admired by rulers in power.

Accordingly, this account is closely related to Philo-a, though with stronger emphasis on the character of the Essene community as a voluntary association with individual admission, and on their inclination to celibacy.[12]

---

12. Petit characterizes *Hyp.* 11.1-18 as 'beaucoup plus réaliste que celle de *Prob.*' ('Les Esséens de Philon', p. 155), an evaluation which I find difficult to accept. Generally, Petit describes both accounts as 'apologetic' representations 'd'une communauté de "parfaits" juifs sur le modèle des thiases philosophiques hellénistiques' ('Les Esséens de Philon', p. 155).

c. *The Contemplative Life (Philo-c)*

In the treatise *De vita contemplativa* ('The Contemplative Life', here Philo-c) Philo describes the so-called *Therapeutae*, a strange Jewish group living near Alexandria which Philo himself explicitly brings in connection with the Essenes (§1). As not only Philo, but also (other) scholars of name regard the Therapeutes as related to the Essenes,[13] it is necessary to include this description in an examination of the Essenes in classical Jewish sources.

In contrast to the two former accounts, the whole content of Philo-c is devoted to the same subject (of the Therapeutes) and, accordingly, the description is much more diffuse. In the introduction Philo refers to his earlier discussion(s) of the Essenes, and categorizes them as a group 'who persistently pursued the active life'. By contrast, the Therapeutes are described as a community 'who embraced the life of contemplation' (*peri tōn theōrian aspasamenōn*) (§1). Philo continues by assuring us: 'In doing so I will not add anything of my own procuring to improve upon the facts…, but shall adhere absolutely to the actual truth' (*all' atechnōs autēs periechomenos tēs alētheias*)[14]—and describes the Therapeutes as follows:

1. Philosophy: the Therapeutes are presented as 'philosophers' (2a, cf. 16, 26, 28, 34, 67, 69).
2. Name: Philo derives their name from *therapeuō*, 'either in the sense of "cure" because they' cure not only man's body, but, in particular, his soul when it is oppressed by diseases inflicted by city-life, 'or else in the sense of "worship", because nature' itself has taught them to worship the Supreme God (*to on*) (2b).
3. Piety: their piety is compared with that of the worshippers of the 'elements' (3-5), of the 'demi-gods' (6), of different kinds of images (7) and of the Egyptian holy animals (8-10).
4. Spiritual vision: in contrast, the Therapeutes are able to 'see' (*blepein*) in a spiritual way, and they worship the invisible deity in a mystical or ecstatic way (11-12, cf. 28a).

---

13. Cf. Vermes, 'Essenes and Therapeutai'; Schürer, *The History of the Jewish People*, II, pp. 554-97, esp. pp. 595-97; G. Vermes and M.D. Goodman (eds.), *The Essenes according to the Classical Sources* (OCT, 1; Sheffield: Sheffield Academic Press, 1989), pp. 15-17; Bergmeier, *Die Essenerberichte*, pp. 41-48.

14. Does this expression indicate the use of a (written?) source? See n. 8 and section 5.b.

5. Abandoning private possessions: they are so absorbed by this 'blessed life' and divine wealth that 'they abandon their property' to their relatives or friends (13). Philo compares this act with similar ones of famous Greeks—and finds that of the Therapeutes to be superior (14-17).

6. Leaving the family: the next step of the Therapeutes is to give up their family, friends and fatherland (18).

7. Migration: they move, not to another city, because city-life 'is full of turmoils and disturbances', but 'outside the walls pursuing solitude in gardens or lonely bits of country' (19-20).

8. Locality: this type of life can be found in several places in the world, but in particular in Egypt, 'and especially round Alexandria' (21). The best of these people 'journey from every side to settle in a certain very suitable place which they regard as their fatherland'; it is situated 'above the Mareotic Lake' (22); it is rich and has a pleasant climate (23).

9. Housing: here, the Therapeutes live in simple houses, situated at a suitable distance from each other (24).

10. Private sanctuary: 'in each house there is a consecrated room', a 'sanctuary' (*semneion*), where they 'are initiated into the mysteries of the sanctified life' (*ta tou semnou biou mystēria telountai*) (25a).

11. Holy Scriptures: here, they enjoy no drink and food, but only 'laws and oracles delivered through the mouth of prophets, and psalms and anything else which fosters and perfects knowledge and piety' (25b). By studying these books they 'keep the memory of God alive...' (25-26, cf. 28b).

12. Prayer: every day they pray at dawn and at sunset (27a); at sunrise 'they pray for a fine bright day,' fine and bright in the true sense of the heavenly daylight which they pray may fill their minds' (27a, cf. 66 and 89b).

13. Allegory: they spend the day 'entirely in spiritual exercise' (28a). They study their Holy Scriptures 'and seek wisdom from their ancestral philosophy by taking it as an allegory, since they think that the words of the literal text are symbols of something whose hidden nature is revealed by studying the underlying meaning' (28b, cf. 75-78).[15]

---

15. Compare 1QpHab 2.7-10; 7.1-5 on the Teacher of Righteousness whom God has given insight to interpret all the 'secrets' in the books of the prophets. In

14.   Other books: in addition to the 'Biblical' books they have writ-
      ings from the founders of the group who have formulated the
      principles for their allegorical interpretation (29a). They con-
      tinue this tradition by composing hymns to God (29b, cf.
      80).[16]

15.   Sabbath: six days a week they study at home (cf. 25-26, 28,
      34), but 'every seventh day they meet together as for a general
      assembly...' (30a, cf. 36). Here, the oldest among them comes
      forward and gives a 'well-reasoned and wise discourse' (31).

16.   Sanctuary/synagogue: accordingly, the Therapeutes have a
      'common sanctuary' (32a).

17.   Order and hierarchy: in the assembly they 'sit in order accord-
      ing to their age in the proper attitude...' (30b, cf. 66-67).

18.   Separation of men and women: their sanctuary is divided by a
      wall in two parts, one for men and one for women (32-33, cf.
      69).

19.   Asceticism/self-control: they regard self-control (*engkrateian*)
      the foundation for all other virtues (34a). Therefore, they limit
      their consumption of food and drink (34b-35 and 37b, cf. 69).

20.   Common meals: but on the seventh day they have a proper,
      but simple meal of bread, salt, hyssop and water (36-37a, cf.
      40-82).

21.   Modesty in clothing: as their houses and meals their clothes
      are simple, in winter a skin coat and in summer a light shirt
      (38).

22.   Simplicity: thus, they generally stick to simplicity which they
      regard as the source of truth (39).

this paper it is impossible systematically to compare and to analyse the connections
between the accounts of Philo and Josephus on the Essenes, on the one hand, and
the Dead Sea Scrolls, on the other. I can only mention a few cases in order to
illustrate this aspect of the subject. For a systematical comparison, see T.S. Beall,
Josephus' Description of the Essenes Illustrated by the Dead Sea Scrolls (SNTSMS,
58; Cambridge: Cambridge University Press, 1988) on Josephus only; Vermes and
Goodman (eds.), *The Essenes*; Bergmeier, *Die Essenerberichte*; Rajak, 'Ciò che
Flavio Guiseppe vide', pp. 156-58 (only on *War* 2).

16.   This piece of information is unique to the accounts under examination and it
immediately brings to mind the 'sectarian' literature in the Dead Sea Scrolls.
Bergmeier, who is detecting the sources behind Philo's and Josephus's descriptions
of the Essenes (Therapeutes), does not comment on this text in Philo (Bergmeier,
Die Essenerberichte, pp. 41-48).

In paragraphs 40-63a Philo makes a long excursus on the contrast between the gatherings and common meals of the Therapeutes, on the one hand, and the immoderate parties of 'other people', not least the Greeks, on the other. Philo remarks that 'the disciples of Moses' (cf. n. 11) regard the Greek excesses 'with supreme contempt' (63b).

23. Pentecost: in contrast to these parties of the gentiles, Philo describes how the Therapeutes celebrates the festival of seven weeks, probably Pentecost (65):[17] they gather, stand in an orderly way, lift their eyes and hands to heaven and pray (66, cf. 27). Then they sit down to eat (67). Philo emphasizes the simplicity of the couches and the meal (69b).

24. White robes: at the festival of Pentecost the Therapeutes are dressed in white robes (66a).

25. Hierarchy: at the common meal 'the seniors recline according to the order of their admission' (67a).[18]

26. Women: women, 'most of them aged virgins', take part as well (68a). During the meal, the men sit by themselves to the right and the women to the left (69a).[19]

27. Slaves: they have no slaves 'as they consider that the ownership of servants is entirely against nature' (70). At the festival of Pentecost the serving is provided by young free men (71-72).

28. Simple meal: no wine is served, only water. Likewise, no animal flesh is put on the table. As on the seventh days (cf. 36-37a), the food consists of bread with salt and, sometimes, hyssop (73, cf. 81).

29. Wine: they abstain permanently from wine (73-74).

30. Vegetarianism: they do not serve flesh (73).

31. Silence: during the dinner—and at most other occasions—there is silence (75a).

---

17. Thus Colson, *Philo*, pp. 152-53.

18. Here, Philo might suggest an admission procedure like the one we know from Qumran (1QS 5-6), Josephus, *War* 2.137-42 and Philo-b (no. 5, *Hyp.* 11.2). In his discussion of *War* 2.137-42 compared to 1QS 6.13-23, Bergmeier does not include these texts of Philo (*Die Essenerberichte*, pp. 97-102).

19. This wording, as well as the whole context, suggests that no ordinary marriage was practised among the Therapeutes; cf. Vermes and Goodman (eds.), *The Essenes*, p. 15.

32.   Allegory: the silence is only broken by the president who 'discusses some question arising in the Holy Scriptures...' (75b-76). The audience listens as on the meetings on the sabbaths (77, cf. 30-31). 'The exposition of the sacred scriptures treats the inner meaning conveyed in allegory' (*hai de exēgēseis tōn hierōn grammatōn ginontai di' hyponoiōn en allēgoriais*, cf. n. 15). In this way, the soul is able to reach 'the inward and hidden through the outward and visible' (78, cf. 29).

33.   Hymns: after the discourse, the president sings a hymn, 'either a new one of his own composition or an old one by poets of an earlier day...' (80, cf. 29b). After him 'all the others take their turn'. Then follows the meal already described (81-82, cf. 64-75).

34.   Choirs: after the meal follows another service: all stand up, 'form themselves' into two choirs (of men and women) and sing hymns to God (83-84, cf. 80 and 29b). Later, the two choirs unite and sing together in imitation of the choir of the Israelites after having been saved through the Red Sea (85-88). 'Thus they continue till dawn, drunk with this drunkenness in which there is no shame...' (89a).

35.   Morning prayer: in the early morning they stand 'turned to the east and when they see the sun rising they stretch their hands up to heaven and pray for bright days and knowledge of the truth...' After the prayers they return to their houses to continue 'their wonted philosophy'[20] (89b, cf. 27 and Josephus-c no. 18).

In §90 Philo concludes his description by a eulogy of the pious Therapeutes.

In this long text Philo describes the Therapeutes as a voluntary association of pious Jewish 'philosophers' in Egypt, including women, having abandoned their possessions, family and fatherland, and migrated to a place on the countryside outside Alexandria, organized in a 'communistic' society with common property, common sacred meals, equality

---

20. Cf. §§80 and 29b; Josephus-c no. 18. Petit 'Les Esséens de Philon', pp. 144-46, refers to the related texts in 1QH 12.6-7; 1QS 10.2-3, and several rabbinical texts.

(including women) combined with hierarchy, without slaves (but members serving), living an ascetic, vegetarian and wine-less life in simplicity, silence, frugality and continence, spending all their time, not on working, but on prayer, worship, meditation, mysticism, contemplation and study of the holy writings, either in their own simple houses, or in their common sanctuary. Great emphasis is put on the study and allegorical interpretation of the Holy Scriptures and of their own books, and on their religious service which they perform in white robes and with choirs and hymns, both on the Sabbaths and at the festival of Pentecost.

d. *Similarities and Differences*
Philo's three accounts are related in varying degrees.

Philo-a, Philo-b and Philo-c: we have the following cases of correspondence: 1. frugality: a-9, b-15 and c-21 (22, 28, 29, 30); 2. common meals: a-29, b-9 and c-20; that is, two cases out of 32, 20 and 35, or about 6%, 10% and 7%, which is not significant.[21]

Philo-a and Philo-b: here, we have the folowing cases of correspondence: 1. name: a-2 and b-2;[22] 2. work: a-5 and b-10; 3. agricultural work: a-6 and b-12; 4. craft: a-7 and b-13; 5. common property: a-27 and b-7; 6. sick and elderly: a-30 and b-17; 7. admired by rulers: a-32 and b-20; that is 7 cases out of 32 and 20, or about 28% and 35% respectively.

Philo-a and Philo-c: here we have the following cases of correspondence: 1. locality: a-4 and c-8; 2. slaves: a-12 and c-27; 3. philosophy: a-14 and c-1; 4. Holy Scriptures: a-15 and c-11 (13, 32); 5. synagogue: a-17 and c-16; 6. hierarchy: a-18 and c-17 (25); 7. allegory: a-19 and c-13 (32); 8. piety: a-20 and c-3 (4, 10. 11, etc.); 9. simplicity: a-24 and c-22; that is 9 cases out of 32 and 35, or about 22% and 25% respectively.

Philo-b and Philo-c: here, we have the following cases of correspondence: 1. aceticism: b-11 (15) and c-19 (5, 20-22, etc.); 2. marriage and continence: b-19 and (c-26 [18]); 3. common clothes: b-16 and c-21; that is three cases out of 20 and 35, or about 15% and 9% respectively.

---

21. Here, we are dealing with such small numbers that, with the uncertainty factors taken into account, no reliable statistical conclusions can be drawn.

22. If the second interpretation of *therapeuō* in Philo-c (*Vit. Cont.* § 2b) is preferred, we have a case of triply common material.

In Philo-a we have the following cases of special material: 1. number: a-1; 2. sacrifice: a-3; 3. weapons: a-10; 4. commerce: a-11; 5. equality: a-13; 6. purity: a-21; 7. oaths: a-22; 8. theology: a-23; 9. ethics: a-25; 10. hospitality: a-26; and 11. truly free: a-31; that is 11 cases out of 32, or about 30%.

In Philo-b we have the following cases of special material: 1. identity: b-1; (2. locality: b-3); 3. associations: b-4; 4. admission: b-5; 5. mature men: b-6; 6. common treasury: b-14; (7. marriage and continence: b-18); and 8. low opinion of women: b-19; that is six (eight) out of 20, or about 30%.

In Philo-c we have the following special material: (1. name: c-2); 2. spiritual vision: c-4; 3. abadoning private possessions: c-5; 4. leaving the family: c-6; 5. migration: c-7; (6. locality: c-8); 7. housing: c-9; 8. private sanctuary: c-10; 9. prayer: c-12; 10. other books: c-14; 11. separation of men and women: c-18; 12. pentecost: c-23; 13. white robes: c-24; (14. women: c-26); 15. wine: c-29; 16. vegetarianism: c-30; 17. silence: c-31; 18. hymns: c-33; 19. choirs: c-34; and 20. morning prayer: c-35; that is 17 (20) out of 35, or about 55%.

The survey appears to confirm what one expects, that Philo-c stands somewhat apart. On the other hand, solid interrelations between Philo-c and the other two accounts, especially between Philo-a and Philo-c, have been discovered.

3. *Josephus*

Josephus (37–c. 100 CE) brings a great deal of material on the Essenes, first and foremost in the long section in *War* 2.119-61 (here Josephus-c), but also in the *Antiquities of the Jews* (*Ant.*) 18.18-22 (here Josephus-b), and in a number of minor accounts (here Josephus-a).[23] Generally, Josephus's descriptions of the Essenes are ones of admiration, precisely like those of Philo. In Josephus's case, this attitude may not be unconnected with his claim that, as a youth, he had personally been

23. *War* 1.78-79; 2.113, 567; 3.11; 5.145; *Ant.* 13.171-73, 298, 311-13; 15.371-73, 374-79; 17.346-48; 18.11, 18-22; *Life* 10-11. Beall, *Josephus' Description*, presents a detailed examination of all texts in Josephus on the Essenes in their relation to the writings from Qumran. Bergmeier, *Die Essenerberichte*, analyses the most important of these texts regarding the possibility of one or more sources behind Josephus (and Philo).

in close contact with the Essenes (*Life* 10-11).[24] In the survey of Josephus's information of the Essenes I will proceed as follows: first, I will examine Josephus-a, then turn to the more extensive report in Josephus-b, and conclude with the lengthy piece in Josephus-c.

a. *The Minor Accounts (Josephus-a)*

1. Prophecy: *War* 1.78 (= *Ant.* 13.311-13) tells a short story about a certain Judas who was a trustworthy prophet 'of Essene extraction' (*Essaios ên genos*). In *War* 2.113 (= *Ant.* 17.346-48) we hear of another Essene prophet, Simon, who was able correctly to interpret a dream by king Archelaos. In *Ant.* 15.373-79 there is a longer story about a third Essene prophet, Menachem, predicting the future kingship of Herod the Great who, by the way, is said to have treated Menachem (and the Essenes generally) well.[25] In the long section on the Essenes in Josephus-c the writer notes that there were prophets among the Essenes, men 'who profess to foretell the future, being versed from their early years in holy books...' (*War* 2.159, cf. *Ant.* 13.311).

2. Pacifism?: in *War* 2.567 (and 3.11) Josephus states that among the Jewish military leaders who were appointed at the beginning of the revolt against Rome in 66 CE there was a certain *Joannês ho Essaios* ('John the Essene'). In this context it may not be inappropriate to call to mind that the military leader in Galilee, Josephus, who himself claimed to have been a prophet,[26] maintains that, as a youth, he had been in touch with the Essenes (*Life* 10-11). This information agrees with the fact that in *War* 2.119-61 Josephus does not state that the

24. Similarly Petit, 'Les Esséens de Philon', pp. 153, 155, and, especially, Rajak, 'Ciò che Flavio Guiseppe vide', pp. 144-45, 155, 159. Bergmeier, *Die Essenerberichte*, pp. 20-21, dismisses this text as unreliable.

25. Cf. the remarks in Philo-a (*Omn. Prob. Lib.* 89-91) and Philo-b (*Hyp.* 11.18) on the admiration of the Essenes by cruel (Jewish?) rulers, cf. Petit, 'Les Esséens de Philon', p. 154. Bergmeier assumes the existence of a specific written source, 'Die Essäer-Anekdoten', behind these stories of Essene prophets (*Die Essenerberichte*, pp. 13-18).

26. Cf. *War* 3.399-408, esp. 3.400. See the interpretation in P. Bilde, *Flavius Josephus between Jerusalem and Rome: His Life, his Works, and their Importance* (JSPSup, 2; Sheffield; Sheffield Academic Press, 1988), pp. 47-52, 189-91.

Essenes rejected the use of arms. On the contrary, in §125 we learn that, on their journeys, the Essenes carried 'arms as a protection against brigands'. Further, in §§152-53 we are informed about the tortures that the Essenes suffered during the war against Rome (66–70/74 CE), although this does not imply that the Essenes themselves used arms. Finally, a hint in the same direction may be seen in the fact that on Masada the excavators found texts closely related to those found near Khirbet Qumran.[27] Accordingly, it may be concluded that Josephus does not explicitly describe the Essenes as pacifists.[28]

3.   Theology: in *Ant.* 13.171-73 (a short parallel to *War* 2.119-61 and *Ant.* 18.11-25) Josephus presents briefly the three most important 'parties' or 'schools' in Judaism: the Pharisees, the Sadducees and the Essenes.[29] In §172 the idea of 'Fate' (*heimarmenê*) is singled out as the main criterion, and the Essenes are said to believe 'that Fate is mistress of all things, and that nothing befalls men unless it be in accordance with her decree'. In *Ant.* 18.18 we find a sort of key to interpret this strange language: 'The doctrine of the Essenes is wont to leave everything in the hands of God'.[30] Thus, Josephus may have chosen the expression 'Fate' for pedagogical reasons, in an attempt to make easier the understanding of his Hellenistic-Roman readers.[31]

27. Cf. Y. Yadin, *The Ben Sira Scroll from Masada: With Introduction, Emendations and Commentary* (Jerusalem: The Israel Exploration Society, 1965); *idem, Masada: King Herod's Fortress and the Zealot's Last Stand* (London, 1966), chapters 13–14.

28. As we have seen, it is also not stated in Philo that the Essenes did not use weapons, only that they did not produce them; cf. Philo-a (*Omn. Prob. Lib.* 75).

29. Bergmeier, *Die Essenerberichte*, pp. 56-66, argues that these texts presuppose a specific source on the three Jewish 'philosophical' schools: 'Die Drei-Schulen-Quelle'. However, the 'philosophy' terminology emerges in *Life* 12, too, and this fact suggests that this terminology can also be interpreted as Josephus's own.

30. Beall, *Josephus' Description*, pp. 113-14; Bergmeier, *Die Essenerberichte*, pp. 65-66 and VanderKam, *The Dead Sea Scrolls Today*, pp. 76-78, demonstrate the similarity between Josephus on this point and the writings of Qumran, mainly 1QS 3 and 11.10-11.

31. Cf. section 5.a and d. On this issue generally, see Bilde, *Flavius Josephus between Jerusalem and Rome*, pp. 165-67.

4.   Philosophy: in *Ant.* 15.371 we are told that the Essenes follow 'a way of life taught to Greeks by Pythagoras', although Josephus does not specify this information. He might think of the esoteric, closed circles of the Pythagoreans, of their asceticism or of their mysticism.[32] Apart from this case, Josephus uses the 'philosophical' terminology in *Ant.* 18.11 and *Life* 12 as well when writing on the Jewish religious groups.

5.   Locality: in *War* 5.142-45 Josephus describes the so-called First Wall, and in this context he refers to the 'gate of the Essenes' (*tên Essênôn pylên*). In our context the geographical location of this gate is not decisive.[33] But the very name reflects an interesting possibility: the existence of an Essene community in Jerusalem.[34]

None of these minor accounts is meant as a general report on the Essenes. They are all short reports of isolated events, episodes, either anecdotes on named Essenes[35] or small pieces of information. All belong in other contexts with different plots and points, and in these contexts the minor accounts on the Essenes are presented *en passant* with the aim to illustrate the context in question.[36]

b. *Antiquities of the Jews 18 (Josephus-b)*
In *Ant.* 18.11 Josephus returns to the terminology, mentioned above (in section 3.a.3 and 4), writing that the Jews 'from the most ancient times, had three philosophies pertaining to their traditions...', and in *Ant.* 18.18-22 Josephus describes the Essenes as follows:

1.   Theology: they tend to 'leave everything in the hands of God' (18a).

32.   Cf. note d in the Loeb edition of the *Antiquities*, VIII, p. 179. Bergmeier (*Die Essenerberichte*, p. 80) argues that *Ant.* 15.371 reveals Josephus's use of a Pythagorean source: 'Die pythagoraisierende Essener-Quelle'. This source is assumed to be rather extensive and to lie behind most of *War* 2.119-61 and *Ant.* 18.18-22 (pp. 79-107).

33.   On this problem, see Y. Yadin, 'The Gate of the Essenes and the Temple Scroll', in *Jerusalem Revealed: Archaeology in the Holy City 1968–1974* (Jerusalem: The Israel Exploration Society, 1975).

34.   Cf. Philo-b (*Hyp* 11.1) and Josephus-c no. 12 (*War* 2.124).

35.   Cf. Bergmeier, *Die Essenerberichte*, pp. 13-18 and 114.

36.   However, precisely for that reason the information they contain deserves serious consideration regarding its historical reliability.

2. Anthropology: they 'regard the soul as immortal' (18b).
3. Ethics: they strive towards 'righteousness' (18c, cf. 20a on the general 'virtues' of the Essenes).
4. Relations to the Temple: they 'send votive offerings to the temple, but perform their sacrifices employing a different ritual of purification'. Therefore, they 'are barred from those precincts of the temple that are frequented by all people and perform their rites by themselves' (19a).
5. Work/agriculture: they work exclusively in agriculture (19b).
6. Common property: they 'hold their possessions in common' and all have an equal share (20b).
7. Number: they are 'more than four thousand' men (20c).
8. Women and marriage: no women are allowed among the Essenes because women may cause division in their community (21a).
9. Slavery: they do not own slaves because they regard slavery as unjust (21b).
10. Equality: instead, they work for one another (21c).
11. Officials: they elect administrators to take care of the economic problems of the community (22a).
12. Priests: likewise they elect 'priests to prepare bread and other food' (22b).

Finally, Josephus states that the Essenes' manner of life is very similar to 'that of the so-called Ctistae among the Dacians' (22c) whom, unfortunately, we do not know.[37]

In contrast to Josephus-a the description in Josephus-b is a general report, although it is much shorter than that in Josephus-c. Josephus-b is a presentation of high admiration of the Essenes as a numerous religious community with its own characteristic theology, anthropology and ethics, with (negative) relations to women and family life, having problematic relations to the Temple in Jerusalem, although priests play an important role in the community. The Essenes are organized as a

37. Bergmeier (*Die Essenerberichte*, pp. 81-83) discusses this text and—on the basis of Pliny, *Hist. Nat.* 4.80: *Getae, Daci Romanis dicti* ('the Getes, by the Romans called the Dacians')—he identifies the Ctistae with the Getes. The Getes are known as Thracians from Herodotus (4.93-94), Strabo, Poseidonius and Hermippos who connects the Thracians with the Jews and with Pythagoras. In this way the Essenes in *Ant.* 18.22, too, are related to Pythagoras.

'communistic' society living by agriculture, having common property, no slaves, equality and elected administrators.

c. *War 2 (Josephus-c)*

In Josephus-c we have the writer's longest and most famous account of the Essenes, from which we get the following information:

1. Aim: they cultivate 'sanctity' (119b).
2. Solidarity: they are more closely-knit together than the other Jewish groups (119c).
3. Asceticism: they 'shun pleasures as a vice and regard temperance (*engkrateian*) and the control of the passions as a special virtue (*aretên*)' (120a).
4. Marriage and women: they hold marriage in contempt because of their low esteem for women; however, they do not completely reject family life and propagation (120b and d, cf. 160-61).
5. Adoption: instead of natural propagation they 'adopt other men's children' (120c).
6. Low opinion of women: they have no confidence in the faithfulness of women (120-21).
7. Common property: they despise wealth and practise a 'community of goods' which Josephus holds 'truly admirable' (122a); new members of the society are supposed to leave their property to the community (122c).
8. Equality: thus they practise complete economic equality (122b and d).
9. Oil: they refuse the use of oil considering it to be impure (123a).[38]
10. White robes: they are always dressed in white (123b, cf. 137).
11. Officials: they elect leaders to administrate the activities of the community (123c).
12. Locality: they do not live concentrated in one city, but rather in large groups in 'every town' (124a).
13. Hospitality: thus they can travel all over the country without expenses, for everywhere they are well received by their fellow-Essenes (124). In every city there is an official with the

---

38. Here, even Bergmeier (*Die Essenerberichte*, p. 95) admits the surprising agreement with the Dead Sea Scrolls (CD 12.16; 4Q513 13.4).

specific duty to receive and take care of travelling Essenes (125b).

14. Weapons: therefore, on their journeys, they do not need to carry anything with them 'except arms as a protection against brigands' (125a).

15. Discipline: they are very disciplined and remind us of a group of children under strict command (126a, cf. 132-33).

16. Modesty in dress: they keep their dress and shoes until they are worn out (126b).

17. Commerce: there is no market economy in their community, but they exchange objects among themselves (127, cf. 122).

18. Morning prayer: at sunrise they practice a peculiar, old morning prayer towards the sun 'as though entreating him to rise' (128, cf. 148 and Philo-c no. 12 and 35).

19. Work: after the morning prayer they are sent to work hard until the fifth hour (129a); after an interruption of a purifying bath and a meal they return to their work until evening (131 c).

20. Bath and purity: at the fifth hour they assemble, change their clothes and clean themselves in cold water (129b, cf. 123a).

21. Common meals: after the purification and under the exclusion of the novices they walk silently to the eating room 'as to some sacred shrine' (129c); then they sit down in silence and have their simple meal (130); after sunset the same procedure is repeated, and guests may take part in their meal (132a).[39]

22. Priests: before and after the common meal a priest 'says a grace' (131).

23. Silence: no noise is heard, and 'they speak in turn, each making way for his neighbour' (132b, cf. 126a); to outsiders 'the silence of those within appears like some awful mystery' (§133a, cf. 129c); however, it is due only to the sobriety and modesty of the Essenes (133b).

24. Obedience and 'free enterprise': they are obedient to their superiors in all matters except two—'the rendering of assistance and compassion' (134a); the only limit for charity is a prohibition against helping relatives (134b).

---

39. In P. Bilde, 'The Common Meal in the Qumran-Essene Communities' (forthcoming), I have examined all the texts on common meals in Philo and Josephus as well as in the Dead Sea Scrolls.

25. Self-control: they master their anger and temper; they are loyal and peaceful (135a).
26. Oaths: therefore, their words are reliable, and they avoid swearing as unnecessary (135b).[40]
27. Holy Scriptures: they 'display an extraordinary interest in the writings of the ancients' (136a).
28. Healing: they are interested in healing, and, with this aim, they investigate the Scriptures as well as 'medicinal roots and the properties of stones' (136b).[41]
29. Admission procedure: they have strict rules for the admission of new members who are supposed to pass through three years of gradual preparation and testing (137-42); during the first year the candidate stays outside the community where he is being instructed in its teaching and rules, and provided with a hachet (137a, cf. 148), a loin-cloth and a white dress (137b, cf. 123b); later, he is admitted to parts of the community life (138a), and only after two more years of testing is the candidate completely admitted into the society (138b).
30. The oath of admission: the preparatory period is concluded by a series of oaths promising piety towards God and justice towards men: that he will abstain from harming others; that he will 'for ever hate the unjust and fight the battle of the just' (139);[42] that he will remain loyal to men and rulers; that he will never abuse his power, should he himself get an office; that he will always stick to the truth and expose liars; that he will abstain from stealing and unjust gain; that he will hide nothing from his fellow Essenes, and reveal 'none of their secrets to others' (141); that he will transmit the rules of the community exactly as he received them; that he will abstain from robbery; that he will 'preserve the books of the sect and the names of the angels' (142).

---

40. Cf. *Ant.* 15.371 on King Herod the Great's exemption of the Essenes from the demand of an oath of loyalty.

41. Beall, *Josephus' Description*, pp. 72-73, draws attention to the striking parallel in 1QS 4.6-7. In contrast, Bergmeier, *Die Essenerberichte*, p. 87, refers to Pythagorean parallels.

42. Here again, we have a case being remarkably close to the Qumran writings, esp. 1QS 1.9, cf. the discussion in Beall, *Josephus' Description*, p. 79. In this case,

31. Expulsion: those who seriously transgress these laws are expelled from the community (143a); as such, a former member of the sect often continues to feel bound by the eating laws of the order, he cannot 'partake of other men's food, and so falls to eating grass and wastes away and dies of starvation' (143b); therefore, they often 'in compassion…receive many back in the last stage of exhaustion' (144).

32. Lawsuits: they are 'careful in their trial of cases', their courts have at least 100 members, and their decisions are 'irrevocable' (145a).

33. The Lawgiver: they have great respect for the name of the 'Lawgiver' (presumably Moses, cf. note 11), and blasphemy is punished with death (145b).

34. The elders and the majority: they respect their 'elders' and the majority (146).

35. Spitting: they are 'careful not to spit into the midst of the company or to the right' (147a).[43]

36. Sabbath: they are 'stricter than all Jews in abstaining from work on the seventh day' (147b); they prepare the food on the day before, and they 'do not venture to remove any vessel or even go to stool' (147c).

37. Latrines: in this context Josephus informs us about the habits of the Essenes regarding defecation: they select distant places where they dig a hole, 'and wrapping their mantle about them, that they may not offend the rays of the deity, (cf. 128) sit above it'; having discharged themselves they cover the hole (148-49).

38. Hierarchy: they are divided by seniority into four grades (cf. 137-42), and the juniors are regarded as impure by the seniors (150).

39. Lifetime: because of the simplicity of their life their lifetime is remarkably long (151a).

40. Perseverance: they endure danger, pain and death (151b); during the war with the Romans, they went through severe

too, Bergmeier, *Die Essenerberichte*, p. 91, prefers to refer to a Pythagorean parallel.

43. Once again, we are confronted with a famous amazing case of correspondence between Josephus and the Writings from Qumran (1QS 7.13), cf. Beall, *Josephus' Description*, pp. 96, 125; Bergmeier, *Die Essenerberichte*, p. 103.

persecution and torture determined to obtain immortality (152-53).[44]

41.   Anthropology: they believe that the body is corruptible, but 'that the soul is immortal and imperishable' (154a); being of another origin the souls are caught, 'as it were, in the prison-house of the body' (154b); but when they are liberated from the body, 'then, as though liberated from a long servitude, they rejoice and are borne aloft' (155a); thus they share 'the belief of the sons of Greece... that for virtuous souls there is reserved an abode beyond the ocean... while they relegate base souls to a murky and tempestuous dungeon...' (155b[-58]).[45]

42.   Prophecy: by virtue of their familiarity with the holy Scriptures some of them have the gift of prophecy (159).

43.   Another group: finally, Josephus informs his readers that he is aware of a separate group of Essenes differing from the main group only by its positive view on marriage (160); however, these Essenes take care to show that their interest in marriage does not stem from carnal lust, but only from their wish to beget children.[46]

The description in Josephus-c is the most comrehensive of the classical Jewish accounts.[47] It is a report of high admiration for the Essenes as a well-organized religious community characterized by its low esteem for women and marriage, although they do not agree completely on this point. They live in cities that are well organized as 'communistic' associations, with common property and meals, no commerce, equality, and elected leaders and administrators. They work hard the whole day. Their way of life is characterized by self-control, frugality and asceticism. Their discipline and order is impressive. Their religious life comprises morning prayer towards the sun, baths of purification, common

44.   Cf. 2 Macc. 6-7; 1QS 1.17-18.

45.   According to Paul ('Flavius Josèphe', pp. 132-37), *War* 2.151-58 is created by Josephus and presented here as a proper Jewish 'answer' to the epistle of Paul (1 Cor. 15) and Christianity propagating the idea of the resurrection of the body.

46.   161, cf. 120b. Rajak ('Ciò che Flavio Guiseppe vide', p. 157) evaluates this information as historically important.

47.   According to Rajak ('Ciò che Flavio Guiseppe vide', pp. 149-151), in *War* 2.119-61, Josephus followed a Greek philosophical and ethnographical model for describing the ideal society.

sacred meals, intensive study of the holy Scriptures, healing, great care with respect to lawsuits, strict interpretation of the Law of Moses bearing on the Sabbath, purity and oaths; they practise silence and wear white robes. Further, they have peculiar practises in relation to the use of oil, healing, respect for the name of Moses and prophecy. Their admission procedure is long and complicated in contrast to the rules for expulsion. The endurance of the Essenes during persecution and torture has been remarkable, but has to be understood in connection with their belief in the immortality of the human soul.

d. *Similarities and Differences*
Josephus's accounts of the Essenes are related and different at the same time.

Josephus-a, Josephus-b and Josephus-c: there are no obvious cases of correspondence.

Josephus-a and Josephus-b: there is one case of correspondence: theology: a-3 and b-1; that is one out of five and twelve cases, or 20% and 9%; because of the element of uncertainty this number cannot be regarded as significant.

Josephus-a and Josephus-c: we have the following cases of correspondence: 1. prophecy: a-2 and c-42; (2. locality: a-5 and c-12); that is one (two) out of five and 43 cases, or about 30% and 3%; not significant.

Josephus-b and Josephus-c: we have the following cases of correspondence: 1. anthropology: b-2 and c-41; 2. ethics: b-3 and c-24; 3. work: b-5 and c-19; 4. common property: b-6 and c-7; (5. women and marriage: b-8 and c-4/43); 6. equality: b-10 and c-8; 7. officials: b-11 and c-11; 8. priests: b-12 and c-22; that is seven (eight) cases out of 12 and 43, or about 60% and 8%.

In Josephus-a we have the following cases of special material: 1. pacifism?: a-2; 2. philosophy: a-4; and (3. locality: a-5); that is two (three) cases out of five, or about 50%.

In Josephus-b we have the following cases of special material: 1. relations to the Temple: b-4; 2. number: b-7; (3. women and marriage: b-8); 4. slavery: b-9; that is three (four) cases out of 12, or about 30%.

In Josephus-c we have the following cases of special material: 1. aim: c-1; 2. solidarity: c-2; 3. asceticism: c-3; (4. marriage and women: c-4); 5. adoption: c-5; 6. low opinion of women: c-6; 7. oil: c-9; 8. white robes: c-10; (9. locality: c-12); 10. hospitality: c-13; 11. weapons: c-14;

12. discipline: c-15; 13. modesty in dressing: c-16; 14. commerce: c-17; 15. morning prayer: c-18; 16. bath and purity: c-20; 17. common meals: c-21; 18. silence: c-23; 19. obedience and 'free enterprise': c-24; 20. self-control: c-25; 21. oaths: c-26; 22. Holy Scriptures: c-27; 23. healing: c-28; 24. admission procedure: c-29; 25. the oath of admission: c-30; 26. expulsion: c-31; 27. lawsuits: c-32; 28. the Lawgiver: c-33; 29. the elders and the majority: c-34; 30. spitting: c-35; 31. Sabbath: c-36; 32. latrines: c-37; 33. hierarchy: c-38; 34. lifetime: c- 39; 35. perseverance: c-40; 36. another group: c-43; that is 34 (36) cases out of 43, or about 70%.

The survey confirms what is expected, namely the fact that Josephus-c stands apart with a remarkably high percentage of special material. On the other hand, there are solid relations between Josephus-c and the other two accounts, especially Josephus-b.

4. *Philo and Josephus*

a. *Philo-a*
Turning to Philo-a and comparing its contents with the material in the three accounts in Josephus, one can see the following results:

Philo-a corresponds with Josephus-a in the following cases: (1. locality: P-a-4 and J-a-5); 2. philosophy: P-a-14 and J-a-4; 3. admired by rulers: P-a-32 and J-a-1; that is two (three) out of 32 cases, or about 7 (10)%; hardly significant.

Philo-a corresponds with Josephus-b in the following cases: 1. number: P-a-1 and J-b-7; 2. sacrifices: P-a-3 and J-b-4; 3. agricultural work: P-a-5/6 and J-b-5; 4. slaves: P-a-12 and J-b-9; 5. equality: P-a-13 and J-b-10; 6. theology: P-a-23 and J-b-1; 7. ethics: P-a-25 and J-b-3; 8. common property: P-a-27 and J-b-6; that is 7 out of 32 cases, or about 20%.

Philo-a corresponds with Josephus-c in the following cases: 1. name/holiness: P-a-2 and J-c-1; 2. work: P-a-5 and J-c-19; 3. frugality/asceticism: P-a-9 and J-c-3/9/16; 4. commerce: P-a-11 and J-a-17; 5. equality: P-a-13 and J-c-8; 6. Holy Scriptures: P-a-15 and J-c-27; 7. Sabbath: P-a-17 and J-c-36; 8. hierarchi: P-a-18 and J-c-15/23/24/34; 9. purity: P-a-21 and J-c-20; 10. oaths: P-a-22 and J-c-26; 11. ethics: P-a-25 and J-c-24; 12. hospitality: P-a-26 and J-c-13; 13. common property: P-a-27 and J-c-7; 14. common meals: P-a-29 and J-c-21; that is 14 out of 32 cases, or about 40 %.

Finally, in Philo-a, as compared with the three accounts in Josephus, we have the following special material: (1. locality: a-4); 2. crafts: a-7; 3. wealth: a-8; 4. weapons: a-10; 5. allegory: a-19; 6. simplicity: a-24; 7. sick and elderly: a-30; 8. truly free: a-31; that is seven (eight) out of 32 cases, or about 22%.

However, we have already seen that from this material numbers (1), 5, 6 and 7 reappear in Philo's two other works (cf. section 2.d). Number 8 and, to some extent, number 6 are clearly marked by the overall theme of the treatise as a whole: *freedom*, and can therefore be regarded as 'redactional'. Accordingly, we have only genuinely special material in numbers 2, 3 and 4.

My analysis points to the conclusion that almost all the material in Philo's first tractate is 'traditional'. This conclusion indicates that Philo used sources, probably one or more (written?) source(s) to which Josephus, too, had access.[48]

b. *Philo-b*
Comparing Philo-b with Josephus's three accounts on the Essenes turns out as follows:

Philo-b corresponds with Josephus-a in the following cases: (1. admired by rulers/prophecy: P-b-20 and J-a-1); and (2. locality: P-b-3 and J-a-5); that is none, one or two cases out of 20, which is 10%, at most; hardly significant.

Philo-b and Josephus-b correspond in the following cases: 1. common property: P-b-7 and J-b-6; 2. slaves: P-b-8 and J-b-9; 3. agricultural work: P-b-12 and J-b-5; (4. common treasury: P-b-14 and J-b-11); 5. marriage and continence: P-b-18 and J-b-8; (6. low opinion of women: P-b-19 and J-b-8); that is four (six) out of 20 cases, or about 25%.

Philo-b and Josephus-c correspond in the following cases: 1. name/ aim: P-b-2 and J-c-1; (2. locality: P-b-3 and J-c-12); 3. admission: P-b-5

48. Against Petit who concludes that Philo did not use written sources when he wrote the two accounts on the Essenes ('Les Esséens de Philon', pp. 153-55). From his analysis of the accounts of the Essenes (Therapeutes) in Philo and Josephus, Bergmeier (*Die Essenerberichte*, pp. 23-48) draws the conclusion that Philo and Josephus had two common sources: the 'hellenistisch-jüdische Essäer-Quelle' and the 'pythagoraisierende Essener-Quelle' (pp. 48 and 114). Rajak claims that in *Ant.* 18.18-22 Josephus is dependent on Philo-a ('Ciò che Flavio Guiseppe vide', pp. 147-48).

and J-c-29; 4. common property: P-b-7 and J-c-7; 5. common meals: P-b-9 and J-c-21; 6. work: P-b-10 and J-c-19; 7. asceticism: P-b-11 and J-c-3/16; (7) common treasury: P-b-14 and J-c-11); (8. common clothes: P-b-16 and J-c-10/16); 9. marriage and continence: P-b-18 and J-c-4; 10. low opinion of women P-b-19 and J-c-4; that is seven (ten) out of 20 cases, or about 40%.

Thus, in Philo-b, as compared with the three accounts in Josephus, we have the following special material: 1. identity: b-1; 2. associations: b-4; 3. mature men: b-6; 4. crafts: b-13; 5. sick and elderly: b-17; that is five out of twenty cases, or 20%.

We have already seen that from this material, numbers 2, 4 and 5 reappear in one or both of the other two accounts by Philo (cf. section 2.d). As number 1 is obviously a 'redactional' introduction we have only number 3 left as special material, and even this item might be interpreted as 'redactional'.

Accordingly, in Philo-b as well we find that almost all the material seems to be 'traditional', a fact indicating the use of one or more (written?) source(s) which seem to have been used by Josephus, too (cf. n. 48).

c. *Philo-c*

When we compare Philo-c with Josephus's three accounts we get the following results:

Philo-c corresponds with Josephus-a in one case: philosophy: P-c-1 and J-a-4; that is about 3%; not significant.

Philo-c and Josephus-b correspond in the following cases: (1. abandoning private possessions: P-c-5 and J-b-6); (2. women/marriage: P-c-26 and J-b-8); 3. slaves: P-c-27 and J-b-9; that is two (three) out of 35 cases, or about 7%; not significant.

Philo-c and Josephus-c correspond in the following cases: (1. name/ healing: P-c-2 and J-c-28); 2. Holy Scriptures: P-c-11 and J-c-27; 3. prayer/morning prayer: P-c-12/35 and J-c-18/37; 4. Sabbath: P-c-15 and J-c-36; 5. order and hierarchy: P-c-17/25 and J-c-15 (23, 24, 34); 6. asceticism: P-c-19 and J-c-3; 7. common meals: P-c-20 and J-c-21; 8. modesty in clothing: P-c-21 and J-c-16; 8. white robes: P-c-24 and J-c-10; 9. simple meal: P-c-28 and J-c-21; 10. silence: P-c-31 and J-c-23; that is nine (ten) out of 35 cases, or about 27%.

Accordingly, in Philo-c, as compared with the three accounts in Josephus, we have the following special material: 1. name: c-2; 2. piety:

c-3; 3. spiritual vision: c-4; 4. leaving the family: c-6; 5. migration: c-7; 6. locality: c-8; 7. housing: c-9; 8. private sanctuary: c-10; 9. allegorical interpretation: c-13 (cf. 32); 10. other books: c-14; 11. separation of men and women: c-18 (cf. 26); 12. simplicity: c-22; 13. Pentecost: c-23; 14. Wine: c-29; 15. flesh: c-30; 16. hymns: c-33; 17. choirs: c-34; that is 17 out of 34 cases, or 50%.

It has already been shown that some of this material reappears in Philo's two other accounts (cf. section 2.d): Philo-c (as defined above) corresponds with Philo-a in the following cases: 1. piety: c-3; 2. locality: c-6; 3. allegorical interpretation: c-9; 4. simplicity: c-22. There is no overlapping between Philo-c (as defined above) and Philo-b.

The results of this survey indicate that in Philo-c the writer had at his disposal a solid block of special material illustrating the life, cult and teaching of the Therapeutes which differs from the Essenes on some important points. On the other hand, however, in a great number of cases the Therapeutes appear to be closely related to the Essenes as described in Philo and Josephus (cf. n. 48).

d. *Josephus-a*

Above (in sections 4.a.b and c), it has been shown that (parts of) the material in Josephus-a reappears in Philo's accounts:

Josephus-a corresponds with Philo-a in two (three) cases; out of a total of five, that is about 50%. However, the small numbers here represent an important element of uncertainty.

Josephus-a corresponds with Philo-b in two uncertain cases; not significant.

Josephus-a corresponds with Philo-c in one case; out of a total of five cases that is 20%; not significant.

Accordingly, the result is that, compared with Philo's three accounts, the following special material occurs in Josephus-a: number 2: pacifism?

Taken together with the findings of the survey in section 3.d these results indicate that almost all the material in Josephus-a is 'traditional'.

e. *Josephus-b*

Above (in sections 4.a.b and c) it has been shown that (parts of) the material in Josephus-b reappears in Philo's accounts:

Josephus-b corresponds with Philo-a in seven cases; out of a total of 12 that is about 60%.

Josephus-b corresponds with Philo-b in four (six) cases; out of a total of 12 that is about 42%.

Josephus-b corresponds with Philo-c in two (three) cases; out of a total of 12 cases that is about 18%.

Accordingly, the result is that there is no special material at all in Josephus-b.

Taken together with the findings of the survey in section 3.d these results indicate that all material in Josephus-b is 'traditional' (cf. n. 48).

f. *Josephus-c*

Above (in sections 4.a.b and c) it has been shown that (parts of) the material in Josephus-c reappears in Philo's accounts:

Josephus-c corresponds with Philo-a in 14 cases; out of a total of 43 that is about 34%.

Josephus-c coresponds with Philo-b in seven (ten) cases; out of a total of 43 that is about 18%.

Josephus-c corresponds with Philo-c in nine (ten) cases; out of a total of 43 that is about 22%.

These results imply that in Josephus-c, as compared with all the other accounts (both in Philo and in Josephus), there exists the following special material: 1. solidarity: c-2; 2. adoption: c-5; 3. oil: c-9; 4. weapons: c-14; (5. bath and purity: c-20); (6. self-control: c-25); (7. healing: c-28); 8. admission procedure: c-29; 9. admission oath: c-30; 10. expulsion: c-31; 11. lawsuits: c-32; 12. the Lawgiver: c-33; 13. spitting: c-36; 14. latrines: c-37; 15. lifetime: c-39; 16. perseverance: c-40; 17. another group: c-43; that is 14 (17) out of 43 cases, or about 40%.

Taken together with the findings of the survey in section 3.d these results indicate that the material in Josephus-c seems to consist of two parts, one 'traditional' in the sense that it reappears in the other accounts of Philo and Josephus, and one of special material suggesting either 'redactional' creativity or a special source. However, as several of these 'special material' items in Josephus-c overlap with features in the Dead Sea Scrolls (esp. numbers 3, [5], 8, 9 and 13), the first alternative should be excluded. Accordingly, I conclude that the special material, or, at least substantial parts of it, stems from a special source.[49]

49. Bergmeier does not consider the possibility that in *War* 2.119-61 in addition to the two sources used by both Philo and Josephus (cf. n. 48), Josephus had access to a third source. Rajak concludes her analysis of *War* 2.119-61 with the assumption that, on the one hand, Josephus was dependent on a Greek model (cf. n. 47); on

5. *Interpretation*

a. *Philo's and Josephus's Presentation of the Essenes (Therapeutes)*
The accounts of Philo and Josephus present the same general picture of
the Essenes (Therapeutes): they are described as an admirable voluntary association of pious and extremely virtuous men, living a simple,
disciplined and healthy common life. Apart from the Therapeutes, the
Essenes are pictured as a peculiar social group, clearly separated from
the society as a whole, distinguished by a high degree of fellowship and
common economy, working hard with their hands in agriculture and
crafts. Their piety is characterized by intensive study of the Holy Scriptures, by spiritualization of such traditional religious values as Scripture
and Temple, by prayer, by severe ethical demands, by frugality and by
a certain degree of asceticism.

It is obvious that Philo and Josephus have the same attitude of admiration for the Essenes (Therapeutes), whom they describe in positive
and praising terms.[50]

Basically, however, they present the Essenes (Therapeutes) in the
same way as they generally present Judaism and the Jewish people.
Both writers describe Judaism as a sort of ideal 'philosophy', able to
compete with Greek philosophical schools and with Hellenistic-Roman
religions.[51] In this general context they present the Essenes as the Jewish elite.[52] They describe the Essenes as representing the highest quality
of Judaism and Jewish values and, therefore, as the best bid of the
Jewish people in the international, Hellenistic-Roman, religio-philo-
sophical debate on social ethics, legislation and the ideal and utopian
society.

the other hand, all the information in *War* 2 came from his own experiences with
the Essenes (cf. n. 24), Rajak, 'Ciò che Flavio Guiseppe vide', pp. 151-58.

50. Cf. Paul, 'Flavius Josèphe'; Rajak, 'Ciò che Flavio Guiseppe vide', pp. 145
and 147. This 'redaction critical' element in Philo and Josephus is gravely
underestimated in Bergmeier.

51. Cf. Philo-a §88; Philo-c §63b; Josephus-a number 4; Josephus-b 18.20, and
Apion 1.1-56 and so on. On Philo generally, see Borgen, 'Philo of Alexandria',
pp. 252-59, and on Josephus, see Bilde, *Flavius Josephus between Jerusalem and
Rome*, pp. 173-206.

52. Similarly Borgen, 'Philo of Alexandria', pp. 248 and 249; Paul, 'Flavius
Josèphe', pp. 130-32, 138; Petit, 'Les Esséens de Philon', p. 155; Rajak, 'Ciò che
Flavio Guiseppe vide', p. 146.

In this debate ideas about social justice, equality, common property, frugality, (partly sexual continence) and a simple life in the country, outside the 'destructive' cities, were essential. These ideas were cultivated by nearly all philosophical schools, especially the Stoics, but also the Pythagoreans, the Platonists and the Cynics.[53] In the Hellenistic period these schools had developed new ideas of the ideal life, both for the individual and for society. These ideas were characterized by a general tendency of critical reaction against the 'modern' luxurious life-style of the wealthy city-dweller of the Hellenistic-Roman civilization. Instead, both philosophers and religious prophets taught the 'salvation' and bliss of a return to the simple, moderate and frugal life on the country-side. These ideas could develop into outright ideals of undisguised asceticism (*engkrateia*), best known from the Pythagoreans, the Cynics, the early Christians and the Gnostics.

The short description of the Essenes in Pliny (23–79 CE) (*Nat. Hist.* 5.17.4) reflects the same ideas. Here, Pliny presents this sect as:

> the solitary tribe of the Essenes, which is remarkable beyond all other tribes in the whole World, as it has no women and has renounced all sexual desire, has no money, and has only palm trees for company. Day by day the throng of refugees is recruited to an equal number by numerous accessions of persons tired of life and driven thither by the waves of fortune to adopt their manners.[54]

Accordingly, Pliny, too, describes the Essenes as an ideal community, living in the wilderness where they had rid themselves of money, sexuality and other 'modern' detrimental phenomena. And to this community came great numbers of individual applicants who were tired of the urban life of Hellenistic-Roman civilization.

It was precisely on these points that Philo and Josephus were able to play their Jewish trumpcard of the Essenes. For the Essenes were no airy idea of the sort that were found in the Greco-Roman moral and utopian writings. The Essenes were a piece of historical reality. And precisely by having been practised in an actual community, the example of the Essenes was superior to all (other) Hellenistic-Roman

---

53. On this debate, see D. Mendels, 'Hellenistic Utopia and the Essenes', *HTR* 72 (1979), pp. 207-22 (with references to relevant literature); Rajak, 'Ciò che Flavio Guiseppe vide', pp. 149-51 (on *War* 2).

54. The translation is borrowed from the Loeb edition: H. Rackham, *Pliny: Natural History* (LCL; Cambridge, MA: Harvard University Press; London: Heinemann, 1942), p. 277.

theoretical ideas. In my opinion, this view of the Essenes was the main reason why this community came to play a significant role in the apologetic projects of our two Jewish authors.

Against this background it is not surprising that Philo and Josephus present the Essenes in a 'Hellenistic' way (cf. sections 1 and 5.d). They wrote in Greek and adressed themselves to a Hellenistic-Roman audience with the message that the Essenes had in an optimal way realized precisely some of the ideals and utopias of the same Hellenistic-Roman world. Of course, this had to be done in a way which could be understood (cf. note 51).

Although Philo and Josephus agree to a great extent in their accounts of the Essenes (and Therapeutes)—both in their 'redactional' aims and in the contents—they also have their own peculiar interests. Unfortunately, in this context I cannot go deeper into this problem, but shall have to restrict myself to the following few remarks: Philo puts a particular emphasis on such aspects of the life of the Essenes (Therapeutes) as allegory, frugality, asceticism and 'freedom'. And Josephus seems to cultivate a particular interest in prophecy, theology, anthropology, eschatology, priests, admission procedure and, generally, in details and modifications such as Josephus-c numbers 9, 28, 35, 37 and 43. Theoretically, such differences can be interpreted either as 'redactional' additions, or as 'redactional' selections from one or more other, more comprehensive, source(s) (cf. sections 4.f and 5.b). However, in both cases one may be allowed to trace the editorial hand of the writer in question.

b. *One or More Common Source(s) behind Philo and Josephus?*
In this analysis I found connections between all the examined accounts. This interesting situation demands closer scrutiny of the issue of 'redaction' and 'tradition': how can one best explain all the results of this examination?

The analysis revealed an impressive amount of material that was common to Philo and Josephus. Almost all the elements in Philo-a and Philo-b reappear either in Josephus or in Philo-c. The same is the case in Josephus-a and Josephus-b. Only in the more extensive accounts, Philo-c and Josephus-c, did I find a considerable amount of special material. At the same time, however, I found particularly solid connections precisely between these two texts.[55]

55. Bergmeier, too, has noticed these connections, and he explains them as due

Further, it is important to notice the strong 'redactional' interests in Philo and Josephus at the same time as there are astonishingly few specific 'redactional' traces in their texts. This fact, as I believe it to be, excludes the interpretation of the special material in Philo and Josephus as being due primarily to 'redactional' creativity in the sense of invention. In that case I believe that the additions would have had a more easily recognizable 'redactional' character. Consequently, not only the common material but also much of the special material may be interpreted as 'traditional'.

Accordingy, I suggest that the results of this analysis should be interpreted as indications of the use by Philo and Josephus of traditional material; in other words, of one or more, possibly written, sources.[56]

This hypothesis receives additional support from the expression *legontai* in Philo-a §75, and, perhaps, also from Philo-c 1 (cf. nn. 8 and 14).

c. *The Therapeutes*

Geza Vermes has argued in detail for the idea that the Therapeutes should be regarded as 'an Egyptian off-shoot of the Palestinian ascetic movement of the Essenes'.[57] My analysis (cf. section 2.d and 4.c) has confirmed the existence of so many connections between Philo-c and all the other accounts—especially, however, to Josephus-c—that I must join Vermes in his conclusion.[58] Philo-c seems to describe a Jewish

---

to the use of the common 'Pythagoraising' source (cf. nn. 32 and 48), which he thinks was used also by Pliny (*Die Essenerberichte*, p. 107).

56. In earlier research this hypothesis was often assumed; cf. Wagner, *Die Essener in der wissenschaftlichen Diskussion*, pp. 193-209, 234-36. In more recent literature, it has often been generally suggested (cf. M. Hengel, 'Qumran und der Hellenismus', in M. Delcor and H. Baillet *et al.* [eds.], *Qumrân: Sa piété, sa théologie et son milieu* [BETL, 46; Paris-Gembloux: Editions Duculet, 1978], pp. 333-72 [340]; Mendels 'Hellenistic Utopia', pp. 213-14, 218), but rarely argued in detail. An exception is Bergmeier who argues at length for the assumption that, in his various accounts on the Essenes, Josephus must have used four different written sources (*Die Essenerberichte*, esp. pp. 114-117). As mentioned earlier, Petit rejects the idea that Philo used written sources, e.g. Nikolaos from Damascus or such sources that can be traced in Rabbinic literature.

57. Vermes and Goodman (eds.), *The Essenes*, p. 17.

58. Similarly Bergmeier who, however, argues that Philo's (Pythagoraising) source originally defined the Therapeutes as Essenes and placed them near the Dead Sea (*Die Essenerberichte*, pp. 41-48, esp. p. 43) (cf. Pliny, *Nat. Hist.* 5.73).

diaspora group both closely related to the Essenes and different from them on a few important points. In fact, this conclusion is close to what Philo himself suggests in his description of the Therapeutes (*Hyp.* §1).

d. *Philo, Josephus, Hellenism and the Dead Sea Scrolls*
Another good reason to reopen the discussion of classical Jewish sources on the Essenes in relation to the Dead Sea Scrolls is the discussion about Judaism and Hellenism. In his principal work on this subject, Martin Hengel has generally questioned the construction in earlier research of an antithesis between these two worlds. And in a related article, Hengel has demonstrated that, to a large extent, also the Qumran community, as we know it from the Dead Sea Scrolls, appears to have been greatly influenced by Hellenistic ideas, structures and institutions.[59]

I believe that Hengel is right. What we find—both in the accounts of Philo and Josephus on the Essenes (Therapeutes) and in the writings from Qumran—is not far from being a Jewish adaptation of one version of the well-known voluntary Hellenistic association.[60] Generally, we know this phenomenon as the Hellenistic *koina*: circles of individuals with a common interest in philosophy, religion or some other subject. I do not refer to commercial or burial clubs in this connection, but to the philosophical schools and the mystery religions.[61] Individuals were admitted into such associations only after a personal 'conversion' and a formal application. Generally, the full members of this type of association shared a number of doctrines, and in the mystery religions these had to be kept secret from the outside world. In such Hellenistic associations the members had access to a particular 'knowledge', or to some kind of 'mysteries'. Often, these doctrines were rediscovered in 'old'

59. Cf. M. Hengel, *Judentum und Hellenismus: Studien zu ihrer Begegnung unter besonderer Berücksichtigung Palästinas bis zur Mitte des 2.Jh.s v.Chr.* (WUNT, 10; Tübingen: Mohr Siebeck, 2nd edn, 1973), pp. 394-453; also, *idem,* 'Qumran und der Hellenismus'.

60. Cf. Hengel, 'Qumran und der Hellenismus, pp. 347-52; M. Weinfeld, *The Organizational Pattern and the Penal Code of the Qumran Sect: A Comparison with Guilds and Religious Associations of the Hellenistic-Roman Period* (NTOA, 2; (Fribourg: Editions Universitaires; Göttingen: Vandenhoeck & Ruprecht, 1986); Paul, 'Flavius Josèphe', p. 155.

61. Cf. A.D. Nock, *Conversion: The Old and the New in Religion from Alexander the Great to Augustine of Hippo* (Oxford: Oxford University Press, 1935; repr. Lanham, MD: University Press of America, 1988), pp. 1-16, 138-86.

(Holy) Scriptures such as the works of Homer, Plato, Egyptian or Persian traditions which were then interpreted allegorically. Finally, members of such associations were subject to a more or less strict discipline.

Philo and Josephus describe the Essene (Therapeutic) associations in these Hellenistic terms. However, these terms not only fit the descriptions of Philo and Josephus, but the Dead Sea Scrolls as well.[62] Also in the Qumran community, as known from the primary sources, we are confronted with the characteristic voluntary Hellenistic association. Moreover, in their teaching as well, we find recognizable Hellenistic ideas such as individualism, personal choice, spiritualization, dualism, asceticism, frugality and so on.[63]

Accordingly, I think we have to confirm and support Hengel's hypothesis, that not only are the descriptions in Philo and Josephus Hellenistic, but, to a large extent, the writings from Qumran as well. This hypothesis opens for a rearrangement of the whole scene of discussing the Dead Sea Scrolls, the accounts of Philo and Josephus on the Essenes (Therapeutes), Judaism and Hellenism.

First, I think we have to forget about the idea that the accounts in Philo and Josephus are 'Hellenized distortions' of the historical reality which we find in the Dead Sea Scrolls (cf. notes 4 and 5). In fact, the accounts of Philo and, especially, of Josephus correspond with the Dead Sea Scrolls to a very large extent, as has often been demonstrated (cf. notes 2-3, 15-16, 18, 30, 38-39 and 41-43).

Secondly, it should be noticed that these two groups of writings represent two different types of Hellenization. In the Dead Sea Scrolls, the Hellenistic 'spirit' is mainly implicit, unconscious and unwitting, and in Philo and Josephus it is mainly conscious and explicit. But none of the two groups of writing could escape their Hellenistic-Roman context.

Thirdly, it has to be taken into consideration that the Dead Sea Scrolls, on the one hand, and the accounts of Philo and Josephus, on the other, represent two different literary genres. The texts from Qumran are the community's own writings aiming at internal religious consumption. In contrast, the two Greek-writing authors are outsiders who give a summarized presentation aiming at a non-Jewish world.

---

62. Cf. Hengel, 'Qumran und der Hellenismus', pp. 347-52; Weinfeld, *Organizational Pattern*.

63. Cf. Hengel, 'Qumran und der Hellenismus', pp. 352-72.

Fourthly, the two groups of writings may describe several, partly different, groups.

Finally, therefore, I suggest that the accounts in Philo and Josephus should be regarded as relevant sources to the Essenes/the Qumran community, also in cases where they do not *verbatim* correspond with the Dead Sea Scrolls.[64]

64. Similarly, Rajak, 'Ciò che Flavio Guiseppe vide', pp. 156-57.

THE CONSCIOUSNESS OF BELONGING TO GOD'S COVENANT AND WHAT IT ENTAILS ACCORDING TO THE DAMASCUS DOCUMENT AND THE COMMUNITY RULE

Ellen Juhl Christiansen

One of the pertinent questions about Jewish identity is whether Israel has a special status apart from or among other peoples. In this context I shall explore the consciousness of belonging to a covenant, examining the use of the covenant in the *Damascus Document* (CD) and the *Community Rule* (1QS) and considering how the idea might have functioned as an identity term within these two documents. My concern is that while ברית (covenant) in the biblical background stands for a divinely-established covenant relationship with Israel as a nation, the interpretation hereof in these two texts limits covenant relationship to a voluntarist group within Israel.

Whereas most scholars look upon the two Dead Sea texts as representatives of one and the same community and assume that these reflect one Essene community, I shall treat these texts in their own context, and consider them as belonging to different strands of the Essene movement.[1] In line with this, I shall focus on how these texts reflect a change from an ethnic to a particularistic definition of what covenant-belonging means. For an ethnic interpretation, the *Book of Jubilees* is a good example. Even a cursory reading of it will show that the concern here is to maintain Jewish *ethnic* distinctiveness. The attitude here is that Jewish practices, such as circumcision, honouring the Sabbath and dietary observances, were to be maintained and, as a consequence, Gentile practices were to be avoided. For this the author makes use of the

---

1. I shall treat the documents in their present, redacted form, disregarding the literary critical analyses, since this makes good sense from the point of view of group identity.

covenant as a designation for Jewish national identity, basically oper-
ating with *one* covenant, eternally established and valid, with boundaries defined by birth, and envisaging it as a covenant with ethnic
Israel. For a narrower interpretation, CD and 1QS provide several characteristic features of a changed covenant identity.[2]

It is well known that covenant does not always function in the same
way, nor is it used in the same sense, in Jewish literature. When I
choose covenant I do so because it is the most important metaphor for
social identity, describing both a wide ethnic and a narrowly-defined
group identity in the First Testament.[3]

The Hebrew ברית designates a *relationship* among humans who are
not related by kin, and between God and God's people. Essentially,
ברית stands for a *formal agreement* that is made between two or more
parties, either between equals or imposed by a superior on an inferior
party. Such an agreement has both secular and religious overtones, as is
also the case with English 'covenant'.[4] The covenant concept in its
social and political sense was familiar to the cultures surrounding ancient Israel, although in the First Testament ברית has primarily
religious connotations. When humans relate to God this is seen as both
a vertical and a horizontal relationship, as the biblical covenant narratives show, arising, on the one hand, from a consciousness of belonging
to a covenant established in past events, and based, on the other hand,
on common rituals and a common law. When ברית, always in the
singular, stands for group identity in its horizontal aspect it is actu-
alized in blessings and obligations for Israel; in its vertical aspect it
is experienced as divine presence within Israel. Thus covenant entails
human response as the presupposition for blessings fulfilled.

For *group identity* two basic distinctions need to be made. First, identity is national or *ethnic identity* when based on a common heritage, on
shared norms, rites and beliefs. For this I shall adopt Meredith B.

---

2.   The rationale for this change has been dealt with in details in my *Covenant
in Judaism and Paul: A Study of Ritual Boundaries as Identity Markers* (Leiden:
E.J. Brill, 1995).

3.   Particularly illuminating is E.W. Nicholson, *God and his People: Covenant
and Theology in The Old Testament* (Oxford: Clarendon Press, 1986).

4.   The English 'covenant' draws on both the Hebrew ברית and the Greek
διαθήκη. The expression 'secular covenants' is used by G.E. Mendenhall,
Covenant, IDB, I, pp. 716-17. Secular covenants are of four types related to
(a) suzerainty, (b) parity, (c) a superior patron and (d) promissory oaths.

McGuire's 'civil religion'.[5] Although McGuire applies the term to
modern American society with its diverse ethnic and religious groups
in particular, it may also be used to describe group identity in an ancient society to which a common space, common beliefs, common ethical norms and a shared lifestyle are pertinent. Secondly, identity may
be based, not on ethnic criteria, but on conversion; that is, on the indi-
vidually-made commitment to a group's life-style and values.[6] When
identity thus builds on *a personal choice* of group membership this may
be termed 'religious particularism' because group solidarity is created
by the beliefs and norms as defined by the group.[7] This is the case when
a religious group sees itself as the only legitimate religion, claiming
that other groups with different beliefs and norms are illegitimate
religions or have false beliefs. 'Particularism' has the advantage over
other terms, such as 'sectarianism', in that it is less anachronistic, thus
more suitable as a term for group belonging in societies in antiquity.[8] A
particularistic understanding of, for instance, belonging to the covenant
tends to transcend national and ethnic belonging, or even to spiritualize
social identity. But in its extreme form, particularism is, as an expression of individualism, a threat to the sociality of a group, since it is
conflict orientated.

1. *Covenant Conditions in the Damascus Document*

The tendency to narrow down covenantal belonging from national to
ethical criteria was noted already by Ernst Lohmeyer.[9] His paradigm,
whereby 'covenant' has a past, present and future meaning, is still

5. M.B. McGuire, *Religion: The Social Context* (Belmont: Wadsworth, 3rd
edn, 1991), pp. 179-81. 'Civil religion' was used before McGuire by, e.g. R.N.
Bellah, *Beyond Belief: Essays on Religion in a Post-Traditional World* (New York:
Basic Books, 1970); originally it was coined by Jean Jacques Rousseau.
6. With McGuire, *Religion*, p. 71, I define conversion as transformation
inasmuch as 'it changes the sense of who one is and how one belongs in the social
situation'.
7. See McGuire, *Religion*, pp. 190-91.
8. 'Sect' and 'sectarian' is neither very accurate, nor appropriate, for a first-
century group which is not opposed to a church. 'Particularism', on the other hand,
is useful for describing a group that looks on itself as the only true heir to tradition,
the rightful recipient of God's revelation, of the real manifestation of truth.
9. E. Lohmeyer, *Diatheke: Ein Beitrag zur Erklärung des neutestamentlichen
Begriffs* (Leipzig: I.C. Hinrich, 1913), p. 119.

useful for CD.[10] Thus, from the point of view of both an ethnic and a particularistic identity ברית stands for a past, present and future relationship. Moreover, it epitomizes validity and obedience to the law.[11] As we shall see, in CD there is a tension between ethnic identity with a strong awareness of the past and a particularistic self-understanding which limits membership to those who belong by choice and subscribe to voluntarist group conditions. The fact that the author of 11QTemple makes very little use of the term ברית and, when used, applies it in its biblical context of divine law given to all Israel is worth noting.[12] This may be due to its being composed outside Qumran hence of a different origin, as many scholars now assume.[13] Be that as it may, CD needs to be analyzed from the viewpoint of its bearing witness to a community with restricted membership.

a. *Covenant Validity*

1. According to CD, the covenant has its origin in God, in whose nature and will it is grounded, and on whose promise covenant-validity rests.[14] This basic belief is seen particularly in the uses of qualifying adjuncts to ברית as in ברית אל 'covenant of God' (CD 3.11; 5.12; 7.5; 13.14; 14.2; 20.17) and בריתו 'his covenant' (CD 1.17; 3.13; 8.1; 19.3) indicating that the covenant is valid due to its divine origin. Here CD presupposes the First Testament idea of *one covenant* of divine establishment. While different covenantal manifestations may be hinted at, they are never referred to as plural covenants. Clearly God's promise of

10. Lohmeyer, *Diatheke*, p. 115.

11. For CD K.G. Kuhn, *Konkordanz zu den Qumranschriften* (Göttingen: Vandenhoek & Ruprecht, 1960), p. 37, enumerates 42 occurrences: CD 1.4, 17, 18, 20; 2.2; 3.4, 10, 11, 13; 4.9; 5.12; 6.2, 11, 19; 7.5; 8.1, 18, 21; 9.3; 10.6; 12.11; 13.14; 14.2; 15.2, 3, 5, 6, 8, 9; 16.1, 12; 19.1, 13, 14, 16, 31, 33; 20.12 (twice), 17, 25, 29.

12. According to Y. Yadin, *The Temple Scroll* (Jerusalem: Israel Exploration Society, 1983), II, p. 437, there are 5 occurrences: 2.4 (citing Exod. 34.12); 20.14 (covenant of salt); 29.10 the covenant made with Jacob (on festival laws on sacrifices); 55.17 on laws against idolatry; and 59.8 as part of the laws concerning the royal authority.

13. See, for instance, the articles by H. Stegemann and G.J. Brooke in D. Dimant and U. Rappaport (eds.), *The Dead Sea Scrolls: Forty Years of Research* (Leiden: E.J. Brill, 1992).

14. The faithfulness of God is further found in the expression that God keeps the covenant oath, e.g. CD 8.15 and 19.28.

blessing, life and peace to Israel is inherent in the covenant, but its validity is by implication also conditional on Israel keeping the law, as the allusions to the Sinai covenant in 3.13, 15.5 and 16.1 show.[15]

2. Another fundamental idea is the belief that ברית concerns God's relationship with a people, as obvious in ברית לישראל (CD 3.13; cf. 15.8-9), in ברית לכל ישראל (CD 15.5) and ברית ועם כל ישראל (CD 16.1). These phrases for 'covenant with all Israel' express an awareness of continuity, particularly with Sinai. Essentially, they contain the idea that God's covenant is for the whole people of Israel, but from the contexts in which they are used, a change can be observed. By explicating that covenant is 'to return to the Law of Moses' (15.9), CD shows a tendency to narrow covenant down, to exclude some from God's covenant with Israel.

3. The *validity* of the covenant builds on the belief that the covenant relationship was *established by God* in the past for the future, as is evident from the expression in 3.4 'covenant for eternity' ברית לעולם.[16] A variant is found in CD 3.12-16:

> But with them that held fast to the commandments of God who were left over of them, God established His covenant with Israel even until eternity, by revealing to them hidden things concerning which all Israel had gone astray. 'His holy sabbaths' and His glorious appointed times, His righteous testimonies and His true ways and the requirements of His desire, 'which man shall do and live thereby', *these* he laid open before them' (trans. C. Rabin).

Two things are expressed here: first, the covenant is established by God. Therefore, it has eternal validity. Secondly, God's covenant is with those who have kept the commandments. This, then, means that the covenant concerns only a part of Israel, and hence has a limited validity. While CD presupposes the covenant stories about Noah (Gen. 9) and Abraham (Gen. 17), as is evident from the choice of vocabulary in the whole passage, it also narrows covenant down by letting legal observance be a condition for the validity of the relationship.

15. See, e.g. R.F. Collins, 'The Berith-Notion of the Cairo Damascus Covenant and its Comparison with the New Testament' *ETL* 39 (1963), pp. 555-94, esp. p. 561.

16. Cf. 15.5: והבא בברית לבל ירשראל לחוק עולם. Note that for law/ordinances CD use קדש (20.30) or עדק (20.11; 20.31; 20.33), not עולם.

4. Validity is based on the belief that God is known as one who 'remembers' the covenant, or even 'the covenant of ancestors'.[17] By using זכר CD clearly draws on a First Testament covenant vocabulary and theology and thus shows an awareness of a historical dimension.[18] What does it mean that God remembers the covenant? Does it imply blessing or curse? Or both?

In CD 1.4-5 we find the statement, 'But when He remembered the covenant of the ancestors, He caused a remnant to remain of Israel and gave them not up to be consumed' (trans. C. Rabin).[19] This idea that God preserved a remnant that has roots in the past is an important factor determining the identity of the community, linked as it is to a belief in the validity of covenantal blessings. However, God's remembering means not only mercy, but also wrath. Thus, the phrase ברית האבות 'covenant of the ancestors' (CD 8.18 and 19.31) appears in a context of both love and hate, meaning that those who belong to 'the covenant of the ancestors' are loved by God because they are obedient to its laws, while all who do not obey the law will become the object of the wrath of God. The rationale for this is taken from history. Since Israel did not in the past walk according to the law, it was given over to its enemies and punished, hence 'the land was made desolate' (CD 3.10, cf. 5.20–6.2). Similarly, we find the expression, 'vengeance of the covenant' נקם ברית (CD 1.17-18, cf. 19.13) containing the idea that God punishes the unfaithful. Thus a pattern of faithfulness is evoked by a reference to history. Ultimately, the validity of the ethnic covenant is at issue.

5. Ethnic validity is once more at stake when covenant is used with a reference to *individuals* of the past. Although these references are few, the author seems to suggest that human *faithfulness* is a *condition* for belonging to God's covenant. When Abraham is mentioned in CD 3.2-4 together with Isaac and Jacob, they serve as examples of obedience

17. CD 1.4: ובזכרו ברית ראשנים. This is a quotation from Lev. 26.45, in the context of which God remembered the previous covenant relationship as a favour to Israel, hence a reference to validity; cf. also CD 6.2. Parallel is ברית האבות, CD 8.18 and 19.31, cf. Jer. 34.13; 31.32 and Deut. 9.5 and 7.8.

18. Cf. Gen. 9.15-16; Isa. 64.8; Jer. 31.34. See H. Eising, 'זבר', *TDOT*, IV, pp. 70-71.

19. I have replaced Rabin's 'forefathers' with 'ancestors'. When using the term שארית CD 1.4-5 qualifies it as the remnant of Israel alluding to Ezra 9.8, 13-15, or to the First Testament prophets' hope for a remnant that will restore Israel, its land and people. See, for instance, Isa. 8.16-18; 11.16; 28.5; 37.31-32; 44.17; Mic. 2.12; 4.6-7; 5.7-8; Jer. 25.20; 39.3; 40.15; 41.10; Ezek. 9.8; 25.16.

and are accepted by God as a result of this.[20] Once, in CD 12.11, we find the 'covenant of Abraham' ברית אברהם. The wider context is the section on halakhic laws in CD 9–16, the narrower context mentions slaves who belong to the covenant of Abraham.[21] Since this refers to the fact that all males who are part of a Jewish household are required to keep the law of circumcision (cf. Gen. 17.23), the covenant of Abraham is here synonymous with circumcision.[22] From these two contexts it follows that those who did *not* keep the commandments were punished as unacceptable partners, while those who did were within the covenant.

There is possibly an allusion in CD 4.1-10 to another individually-based covenant. Here *Levi* is mentioned in connection with covenant, representing a covenant with the priesthood, related to atonement.[23] Malachi 2.8-9 is possibly in the background, with its twofold understanding of priestly service: to guard knowledge and to give instruction (torah).[24] If this is the case, CD acknowledges that it is a priestly task and responsibility to mediate knowledge and to give instruction, and as a result, it sees priestly service extended into a non-cultic sphere. Consequently a narrower *priestly covenant* emerges at the expense of a broader ethnic covenant. This will be more obvious when we turn to 1QS.

In sum, while CD bases its covenant on the divine will and order in the past, it also stresses that that covenant has an eternal validity, hence making it into a relationship with God in its present and future aspect. When covenant is related to a remnant's faithfulness it has keeping the law as content. When covenant validity is no longer grounded in God's

---

20. CD 3.2: אוהבים לאל ובעלי ברית לעולם, 'friends of God and partners of the covenant', cf. *Jub.* 6.19 and 19.9.

21. The context in 12.6-11 concerns laws on the relation to Gentiles.

22. Thus, F.F. Hvidberg, *Menigheden af den nye Pagt i Damascus: Nogle Studier over de af Salomo Schecter fundne og under Titlen 'Fragments of a Zadokite Work' udgivne Genizafragmenter ('Damaskusskriftet')* (Copenhagen: Gads, 1928), p. 165; E. Lohse, *Die Texte aus Qumran: Hebräisch und Deutsch* (Munich: Kösel, 1971), p. 290; and C. Rabin, *The Zadokite Documents* (Oxford: Clarendon Press, 1954), p. 61.

23. Of note is CD 4.9 where 'covenant with the ancestors' is related to atonement. The verbal expression is כפר, which in Num. 25.13 is used in connection with the act of revenge and atonement of Phinehas, cf. Sir. 45.23.

24. Cf. Collins, 'The Berith-Notion', p. 559.

promises to be faithful, the covenant idea has changed, human obedience being equally stressed. Thus, identity of a particularistic type has begun to emerge.

b. *Covenant Obedience*

The emphasis on covenant conditions leads to a reinterpretation of the First Testament double promise of *land and offspring* by focusing on the land as a place of holiness and on the requirements for remaining within the people. This is particularly the case with the phrase 'new covenant in the land of Damascus', unique for CD. Moreover, the relationship between covenant obedience and the *status* of the people is also at stake. The key question is, what is the locality of this land? Following from this, who qualify as members of Israel?

It is one of the characteristic features of CD that it takes the exile as a point of departure, and with this, the *loss of the land* is interpreted as a result of sin. This is obvious from CD 1.4-12 and 6.2-11. Moreover, in CD 2.14-16 the present disobedience of Israel is described as parallel to the exilic situation.[25] In line with this, disobedience is condemned as in CD 2.7-9:

> For God has not chosen them from of old, <from the days of> eternity, and before they were established He knew their works and abhorred the generations when they arose, and He hid His face from the land from their arising until their being consumed (trans. C. Rabin).

The same idea is expressed in CD 5.20-21 and 3.10. Because the covenant was violated through sins in the past, 'the land became desolate'.

This leads to the belief that the anger of God is caused by *not* doing, which again is equal to a breach of the covenant (CD 3.1-12).[26] Hence, the motivation for keeping the law is found in God's punishment of

---

25. In CD, disobedience to the God-given law, as acts of transgression, is the main substance in sin, cf. E.P. Sanders, *Paul and Palestinian Judaism* (London: SCM Press, 1977), p. 273.

26. Thus the history of Israel's past, from the sons of Noah, is a history of *not doing* the will of the creator. All Israel had gone astray by not observing the Sabbath, the Festivals, the way and will of God (CD 3.14-15) and for this disobedience destruction is the responsive act of God (CD 3.10-11). Conversely, obedience gives a guarantee of salvation (CD 3.15-16). Likewise, those who 'walk in perfection of holiness' according to instructions are promised life for a thousand generations (CD 7.5-7). Cf. Lohmeyer, *Diatheke*, p. 118: 'Hier werden Gnade und Gesetz unmittelbar in eins geschaut, und das Gesetz damit selbst Bürgschaft des Heils'.

those who disregard the divine will. Moreover, CD ties the motivation for law obedience to the command to separate clean and unclean, holy and profane, by means of which covenant is interpreted narrowly as a *priestly* covenant (CD 6.17; 7.3). This is explicitly referred to in the phrase 'the men of perfect holiness' (20.2, 5, 7), designating the priestly community, or perhaps members of the community who have a special, perhaps a higher, status within it.[27] Whether this is a status of order within the community, or of authority over it, is difficult to say from the material at hand. What is significant is the connection between covenant and obedience.

It is characteristic that nowhere in CD is the possession of the land said to be a present or future blessing of the covenant for the people.[28] Rather, when employing 'land of Damascus', CD refers to it in either a literal-geographical or a metaphorical-symbolic sense.[29] The problem emerges most clearly in the expression from CD 6.5, a midrash of Num. 21.18:

> The Well is the Law. And those that dug it are 'they that turned from (from impiety) of Israel' who went out from the land of Judah and sojourned in the land of Damascus (trans. C. Rabin).[30]

Scholars disagree on the meaning of this passage, some taking it literally either to mean a departure from Judah to Damascus, implying an exile in Damascus,[31] or, still literally, as a 'Qumran community' outside

---

27. Thus, G. Forkman, *The Limits of the Religious Community: Expulsion from the Religious Community within the Qumran Sect, within Rabbinic Judaism, and within Primitive Christianity* (CB, 5; Lund: C.W.K. Gleerup, 1972), p. 66, interprets 'the men of perfect holiness' as an inner group, 'in contrast to the outer circle of members on the novice level', parallel to 1QS 8.20. However, there is no clear evidence for such a distinction here.

28. Cf. H. Lichtenberger, 'Alter Bund und neuer Bund', *NTS* 41 (1995), pp. 400-14, esp. p. 404.

29. Thus 'Damascus' means either a geographical locality (literally, Damascus, or transferred, of Qumran) or it is a symbol for a place of refuge. For a survey of this problem, see P.R. Callaway, *History of the Qumran Community: An Investigation* (JSPSup, 3; Sheffield: Sheffield Academic Press, 1988), pp. 121-27.

30. P.R. Davies, *The Damascus Covenant: An Interpretation of the 'Damascus Document'* (JSOTSup, 25; Sheffield: Sheffield Academic Press, 1983), p. 93, in accordance with his whole approach, maintains that the phrase means 'captivity of Israel', designating those who literally went out of Israel to live in captivity.

31. This is the classical approach for which Hvidberg, *Menigheden*, e.g. p. 113, is a typical representative.

the Qumran site—perhaps a reference to Damascus as a place of refuge for the 'Qumran community'.[32] In both cases a change of *place* is implied, by some sort of relocation to a new district (cf. CD 2.5; 6.1). Most scholars, however, would prefer a metaphorical interpretation, so that Damascus means a symbolic place, in terms of it being a symbol of refuge. From the point of view of covenant theology, Damascus is perhaps best understood as a place defined by its holiness. That holiness requires a place, or even a land, seems to be implied in CD 1.7-8:

> He visited them; and He caused to grow forth from Israel and Aaron 'a root of cultivation, to possess His land'[33] and to wax fat in the goodness of His soil (trans. C. Rabin).

In this passage 'land' occurs as elaboration to what is said in CD 1.4: 'When He remembered the covenant of the ancestors'. However, if we keep in mind that not all Israel shall 'possess the land', but only a faithful 'remnant', an obvious change of covenant identity has taken place. Because the emphasis is on the few who are conscious that covenant relationship entails obedience, in reality the remnant community replaces 'Israel'. And by focusing on obedience as a human quality, the idea of a place as sacred land has given way to the demand for holiness of those who inhabit it.[34] What is most significant about 'land' is that it is, if not spiritualized, at least transformed *from locality to lifestyle*.

Thus, CD acknowledges a continuation of God's revelation by referring to the covenant. Although covenant stands for both law and blessings in principle, in reality covenantal blessings are never accentuated. CD is concerned with covenant in its continuation hoping the remnant will inherit past promises through obedience. This means obedience becomes a means of covenant identification. When this is the case, covenant is *conditional on obedience*. Moreover, from the converse idea of disobedience as breach of the covenant, a hope for renewal of a broken covenant, for a restoration of people and land, emerges and becomes a demand for purity, as we shall see below.

---

32. For references, see Davies, *The Damascus Covenant*, p. 17.

33. An echo of Isa. 60.21, but not a quotation.

34. Thus Hartmut Stegemann, '"Das Land" in der Tempelrolle und in anderen Texten aus den Qumranfunden', in Georg Strecker (ed.), *Das Land Israel in biblischer Zeit: Jerusalem-Symposium 1981 der Hebräischen Universität der Georg-August-Universität* (GTA, 25; Göttingen: Vandenhoek & Ruprecht, 1983), p. 165.

c. A 'Broken Covenant' and the 'New Covenant'

If the covenant is identified as law, it follows that disobedience is a *breach of the covenant*. But if breach of covenant brings God's anger and subsequent punishment, how is the covenant relationship to be restored?

With respect to vocabulary for covenant breach, CD uses a variety of terms: (a) עבר, to transgress the covenant/the ordinances (CD 1.20; 16.12), (b) עזב, to forsake the covenant/the commandments (CD 3.11; cf. 8.19; 19.33) and (c) מאס to despise the covenant/the ordinances (CD 20.11; cf. 8.19; 19.32). This variety is, as we shall see, more a matter of style than of content, thus confirming that law and covenant are two sides of one coin.[35] With regard to the 'new covenant', the fact remains that it was neither given nor established by God, but was rather based on what humans had entered into in the past.

1. When CD deals with the broken covenant and atonement, God is always the subject of the atoning act (CD 2.4-5; 3.18; 4.6-10; 20.34) except in the ambiguous passage, CD 14.19, in which the Messiah of Aaron and Israel will make atonement for transgressions. Apart from this, we find the idea that humans may turn from sin by choosing to enter the covenant, which in CD 4.9-10 is defined as a covenant God established 'to make conciliation for their trespasses'. Atoning sacrifices are probably presupposed in CD 9.14; 11.17-23; 16.13, and the view that the atoning function is enacted by the community seems to be indicated in 4.6-9 and 7.5, where perfect behaviour may be a substitute for sacrifices.[36] When one looks at the instances where the notion of the broken covenant occurs they fall roughly into two categories: Israel of the past, and enemies and/or apostates of the present community.

CD deals with breach of the covenant by using Scripture to identify who are 'in' and who are 'out'.[37] Thus CD draws on the First Testament idea that God punishes those who break the covenant, interpreting

35. The same tendency to identify covenant as obedience to the law of Moses can be found in CD 15.9-10, ' the oath of the covenant which Moses concluded with Israel'. Cf. 16.2, 5: 'law of Moses'; CD 5.8; 8.14; 19.26: 'Moses said' and CD 5.21: 'the commandments of God given by the hand of Moses'.

36. See Sanders, *Paul*, p. 299.

37. For the view that CD's use of Scripture is 'a success pattern', see W.O. McCready, 'Pattern for Identity in the Damascus Covenant', in *Proceedings of the Eighth World Congress of Jewish Studies, Jerusalem August 16-21 1981* (Division A; World Union of Jewish Studies:Perry Foundation for Biblical Research, 1981),

Scripture in a positive and a negative way. In a way, this runs through as a theme in CD 1.2–8.21, where the author moves backwards and forwards between past and present, between cause and effect.

On the one hand, Scripture is quoted, or echoed, to prove both the negative and the positive effects of what covenant relationship meant in *past* history, and on the other, Scripture is used as a foundation for creating an awareness of what covenant relationship means in the *present* situation. In this way, an identification of the present members of the community is given. They are those who have entered into the covenant, 'people of understanding' or 'people of wisdom', for whose sake God will remember the covenant, that is, *restore the relationship*. The purpose of these scriptural interpretations seems to be to create an awareness of present identity that can be recognized from the past, reflected as it is in the First Testament characters and events.

CD 3.21–4.2 quotes and interprets Ezek. 44.15 by adding a significant future dimension that is not found in the First Testament. By considering this passage in the context of identity, I shall suggest that the reuse of Ezekiel may throw light particularly on the goal of the group. I shall quote the full passage from 3.18–4.4:

> But God in His wonderful mysteries made conciliation for their trespass and pardoned their impiety, 'and He built them a sure house' in Israel, the like of which has not stood from ancient times even until now. They that hold fast to it are destined for eternal life and all glory of man (אדם) is theirs; as God swore to them by the hand of the prophet Ezekiel, saying: 'The priests and the Levites and the sons of Zadok, who kept charge of My sanctuary when the children of Israel strayed from Me, they shall approach <Me to minister unto Me, and they shall stand before Me to offer> Me fat and blood'.[38] The Priests are 'they that turned (from impiety) of Israel' who went out from the land of Judah; and <the Levites are> they that joined themselves with them; and the sons of Zadok are the elect of Israel, the ' men called by name' who shall arise in the end of days (trans. C. Rabin).

pp. 85-90. By this he means that CD presents Israel's history in a pattern that in the context of the present community serves to identify faithfulness, both in its continuation to the past and in its sameness at present.

38. In Ezek. 44.15 there is only one group, the priests who qualify as descendants of Zadok: 'But the levitical priests, the descendants of Zadok, who kept the charge of my sanctuary'. Its function is to be in charge of the sacrificial system. In CD there are three groups, an interpretation made possible by the twice added 'and'. Cf. Hvidberg, *Menigheden*, p. 84.

The train of thought runs from God's initial forgiveness to God's establishment of a 'sure house' and into a promise of eternal life for those who remain faithful. The passage refers to Ezekiel, builds on it and explains the phrase 'sure house'.

The main problem is that 'house' is ambivalent, because either temple or dynasty could be implied. There are several passsages in the First Testament that speak of a promise of house. (1) If 'sure house' alludes to the promise in 1 Sam. 2.35 of a house for the sons of Zadok, it could be a term for a priestly family. (2) If there is an allusion to 2 Samuel 7, the promise of house may refer to a Davidic dynasty as well as a temple.[39] In view of this, 'house' in CD 3.18–4.4 could contain the same ambivalence of dynasty and temple. Perhaps 'house' is best taken as a synthesis of a continuation of the Davidic dynasty and of the community of priests serving at the temple (either the real or the spiritualized temple).[40] (3) If forgiveness and eternal life are the central issues, Ezekiel 44 is applied in a community context, interpreting it to refer to the exilic origin of the community and the eschatological restoration. In that case the reference to the 'sons of Zadok' could refer to a group that will join in the eschatological age.[41] (4) If CD 3.18–4.4 is parallel to the other scriptural references that have faithfulness as their theme, then this passage refers to a community's understanding of its origin, its present interest in cultic holiness perhaps reinterpreted in ethical terms by adding that God's act of forgiveness is valid for the contemporary faithful and adding also the future dimension, the common goal, and eternal life. By means of such a *pattern of faithfulness,* everyone in the community is defined in relation to everyone else. Thus, those who went out are identified as those who in the past turned from Israel. The 'going out' is then not literally but metaphorically a turning away from (Israel's) sin. And those who 'joined' them should be identified as a

39. Dynasty: 7.11, 16-17, 25, 27, 29; temple: 7.5, 6-7, 13. Cf. 1 Sam. 25.28; 1 Kgs 11.38; 1 Chron. 22.6.

40. For this view, see G. Klinzing, *Die Umdeutung des Kultus in der Qumrangemeinde und im Neuen Testament* (SUNT, 7; Göttingen: Vandenhoeck & Ruprecht, 1971), pp. 75-80. He states: 'Die am *Haus festhalten* (3.20) entsprechen denen, die den Dienst am *Heiligtum bewahrt* haben (4.1f.)', p. 78 (author's italics), in which case the temple is not spiritualized. For Klinzing 'house' is equivalent to temple, a self-designation for the community.

41. Noted by Hvidberg, *Menigheden*, p. 86, and J. Liver, 'The "Sons of Zadok" in the Dead Sea Sect', *RevQ* 6 (1967–69), pp. 3-30.

past and present group who made a conscious choice of covenant commitment. Finally those who 'shall arise in the end of the days' refers to a present and/or future addition to the community.

If this is correct, the passage shows that various groups are identified in relation to each other, history being the foundation, but origin is not an issue, because essentially they all belong to 'the elect of Israel', and all are identified in their status as faithful to God's covenant law. The self-understanding that is involved is particularistic, because *covenant* stands for an *exclusive relationship* between Israel, or part of Israel, and its God.

This means that the present awareness of belonging to God's covenant, is both an awareness of belonging to a history of faithfulness and a consciousness that obedience is necessary in order *to restore the broken covenant,* that is to reclaim its validity in its original aspect of promise.[42] When the emphasis is on faithfulness, human commitment is a necessary condition for covenant relationship.

2. CD uses the phrase ברית החדשה בארע דמשק 'the new covenant of the land of Damascus' in four places, CD 6.19; 8.21; 19.33-34 and 20.12. The expression 'new covenant' is notably ambiguous. The question is *not* whether 'new covenant' is an allusion to Jeremiah 31 or not.[43] Even if there is an allusion to Jeremiah, it is of note that the context there is covenant as 'new law' with a different quality to the covenant relationship.[44] With respect to 'new', the problem is whether

42. A.S. Kapelrud, 'Der Bund in den Qumranschriften', in S. Wagner (ed.), *Bibel und Qumran: Beiträge zur Erforschung der Beziehungen zwischen Bibel- und Qumranwissenschaft* (Festschrift Hans Bardtke; Berlin: Evangelische Haupt-Bibelgesellschalt 3[u], 1968), pp. 137-49, esp. p. 147; Sanders, *Paul,* p. 242, cf. p. 295; Collins, 'The Berith-Notion', p. 566.

43. Scholars disagree whether CD is drawing on Jeremiah or not in its use of the term 'new covenant'. For a balanced view, see Callaway, *History,* p. 126, who states that there is a *possible dependence* on Jer. 31 or traditions arising from it. To be fair, some find a *clear allusion* to Jer. 31.31. Thus, e.g. M. Black, *The Scrolls and Christian Origins: Studies in the Jewish Background of the New Testament* (London: Thomas Nelson and Sons Ltd, 1961), p. 91; Young Ki Yu, 'The New Covenant: The Promise and its Fulfilment: An Inquiry into the Influence of the Covenant Concept of Jer. 31.31-34 on Later Religious Thought with Particular Reference to the Dead Sea Scrolls and the New Testament' (PhD thesis, Durham, 1989), chapter 3. Others *deny any direct allusion* on the basis that the differences are too great, e.g. Collins, 'The Berith-Notion', pp. 571-79.

44. See my *Covenant,* pp. 54-59.

the newness in CD lies in *God's* restoring the already existing relationship to its eternal validity, by recollecting promises, not in adding or changing prescriptions; or in *humanity's* attempt to restore a relationship by reinforcing the already-given obligations.

Most significant perhaps is the fact that the term 'new covenant' is *never* opposed to an 'old covenant'.[45] Consequently, 'new covenant' cannot be understood simply as replacement of an old covenant.[46] Rather, 'new covenant' is used as distinct from a *broken* covenant; hence the problem is related to covenant validity. Does 'new covenant' presuppose a new content? Is it a term related to identity? If it is, does it emphasize a different type of relationship to God?

If newness refers to the *content* of a covenant, newness must be seen in relation to the two aspects, conditions and promises. Perhaps the real issue in CD 6.18-20 is a controversy over the calendar, in which case the 'new covenant' community is opposed to the establishment; hence 'new covenant' stands for a particular content of calendric laws and their interpretation.[47] It could be argued, as does E.P. Sanders, that the new covenant was established because new revelations were discovered.[48] Against Sanders, I propose that 'hidden things' (3.14) means not 'new' revelations but radicalized demands, new ways of interpreting the already-existing covenant laws on keeping the Sabbath and other festivals. By means of a strict observance of the law, a new and different quality of covenant relationship is made possible.[49] This reflects covenant in its aspect of eternal law. If this is correct, then 'new covenant' may be a polemical phrase, coined by one group in opposition to

45. Thus stressed by A. Jaubert, *La notion d'alliance dans le judaïsme abord de l'ère chrétienne* (PatSor, 6; Paris: Cerf, 1963), p. 210, following Lohmeyer, *Diatheke*, pp. 119-20. Also Lichtenberger, 'Alter Bund', pp. 404-405.

46. It seems to be a necessary condition in CD for a 'new covenant' that the prescriptions of the ('old') law are constantly taught, and that the law has to be kept according to its correct interpretation. Cf. Lohmeyer, *Diatheke*, p. 119. I fail to see how Kapelrud, in *Bibel und Qumran*, p. 14, can justify the view that CD operates with an old covenant.

47. See H. Lichtenberger and E. Stegemann, 'Zur Theologie des Bundes in Qumran und im Neuen Testament' *Kirche und Israel* 6 (1991), pp. 134-46, esp. p. 135.

48. Sanders, *Paul*, p. 242.

49. This would be in line with the the *book of Jubilees* and its emphasis on keeping Sabbath and Festivals, both for the sake of uniting the people, and because of the validity of the covenant obligations.

another. Be this as it may, my concern here is that the interpretation of
'new covenant' is within the context of identity. This raises the question: is the term 'new covenant' seen in continuity with or in contrast to
a past covenantal identity?

If 'new covenant' is an identity term, newness could be understood to
mean a restored covenant of promise and law by adding an eschatological dimension.[50] If the hope that God will remember initial
promises and renew them is inherent in 'new covenant,' then 'new'
refers to restoration of the law, to what was fulfilled in the past in the
coming of the 'teacher of righteousness'. Another possible explanation
is that CD applies the aspect of promise, and then 'new' could refer to
the First Testament message of forgiveness, which in CD's interpretation becomes a realized-eschatological promise. It is noteworthy
that where Jeremiah understands 'new covenant' as future, CD takes
'new covenant' as a past and present reality.[51] All this, therefore, points
to 'new covenant' as an expression of a self-understanding within the
community, although not necessarily a self-designation. Moreover, it
points to covenant as a *presently-realized different relationship with
God* which builds on a prophetic foundation of forgiveness based also
on a priestly interpretation of the law. The wider perspective of this is
that obedience restores and maintains a relationship with God, out of
which hope for all Israel or part of it grows. Of note is the fact that
there is a tension between the theology that emphasizes human
commitment as a means of restoration and the idea that change is exclusively the result of God's creative act.[52]

If this is correct, 'new covenant' refers to the same covenant, meaning that God has reestablished the broken relationship, and by implication 'new covenant' equates new conditions for one and the same
covenant.

In order to restore the broken covenant, a conscious choice needs to
be made. This choice is referred to in the language designating
movement, such as CD's phrase כל באי ברית 'all who enter (or have

50. See Lohmeyer, *Diatheke*, p. 120: 'Um der Berith mit den Vorfahren willen
sendet Gott den Messias und mit ihm die "neue Ordnung"; diese neue ist eine
Repristination der alten'.

51. Or as Collins, 'The Berith Notion', p. 582, formulates it: 'the eschatological
new covenant has become *concrete* in a *historical* realization' (author's italics).

52. This tension resolved is in the context of Paul, Gal. 4.6, who claims that the
status of being 'children of God' is a divine decision, not a human choice.

entered) the covenant', used as an address or in explanations.[53] In the First Testament it may be used literally or figuratively, the latter sense most likely being the one used in CD to express entering into either a community or a certain belief-system. Transformation takes place when submission to the will of God is expressed ritually as 'to cross' or 'enter' into a covenant. This response is the actual establishment of the covenant, when entry is tied to commitment, to legal observance, and covenant identity is based on legal principles and boundaries are drawn accordingly. From this perspective, covenant entry finds its immediate goal and purpose in a group relationship, although the ultimate goal may be to escape from God's judgment.[54]

Thus while CD is conscious of past tradition, values and beliefs, it is also aware of a broken covenant. When the concern is with renewal, this is related to covenant in its obligatory aspect, the reinforcement of the law. CD expects humans to enter the covenant, restoring its validity; the demand is to reach perfection through obedience to the law as interpreted by a priestly group. In this way identity has been narrowed down from an ethnic to a priestly covenant, which is clear, particularly where the awareness of being part of the priestly 'new covenant' creates a consciousness of a narrow covenant which ultimately creates a boundary within Israel.

2. *Covenant Awareness in the Community Rule*

Unlike CD, a continuity with the past is *not* expressed in covenantal terms in 1QS. The term 'Israel' seems to be used in a much narrower sense than in CD. The possibility that 1QS applies 'covenant' in a different way, stressing similar or different values, exists. Thus it is conspicuous that the term 'new covenant' is not found, and that other identity terms, such as *yahad*, seem to be preferred. Despite this, 'covenant' remains an important category for identity featuring eschatological hope and ecclesiological awareness.

a. *A Priestly Eschatological Covenant*
In 1QS there are various contexts in which a covenant terminology occurs.[55] As in CD, the phrase 'covenant of God' is used, thus 1QS

---

53. CD 2.2; 3.10; 6.9, 11, 19; 8.1, 21; 9.3; 12.11; 13.14; 19.13-14, 33-34.
54. Cf. CD 3.20 and 7.4-6.
55. See Kuhn, *Konkordanz*, p.36, who lists 32 occurrences of ברית in 1QS.

10.10 ברית אל and 1QS 5.18, 19, 22 בריתו. As in CD, we also find the epithet 'eternal,' thus ברית עולם (1QS 3.11; 4.22-23; 5.5; 8.9) and 'covenant of grace' ברית חסד in 1QS 1.8. Frequently we see that the covenant is a relationship into which humans enter, expressed as באי ברית or עבר ברית.[56] Of particular note is the lack of continuity with the past, that there seems to be no interest in maintaining that the covenant was established with Israel at Sinai, or that the present community is in continuity with historical Israel. Instead of drawing on covenant history, 1QS focuses on covenantal theology. The historical rationale for being in or belonging to the covenant is lacking, which is highly significant. This indicates that a change from ethnic to a particularistic identity has been made, that self-understanding in the community behind 1QS is more exclusive than in CD. I shall now substantiate this statement.

1. When 1QS uses the characteristic expression, 'the covenant of God', it may at best be presupposed that a covenant was established in the past; nowhere is there a clear reference to such an event. Rather the context sets 'the covenant of God' in a dualistic scheme, good–evil, or light–darkness, suggesting that 'covenant of God' stands for a *timeless principle*. If this is the case, then the attitude to covenantal belonging has changed, in comparison to, for instance, the *Book of Jubilees*, inasmuch as some belong to the covenant because they are loved by God or are within the realm of light. Others, by being created evil, are hated by God, and since they belong to the realm of darkness, they are therefore outside God's covenant.

2. The idea that the covenant is 'remembered', by God or by humanity, is absent. Not only is the phrase (familiar from CD), 'covenant with the ancestors' absent, but rather surprisingly, so is the idea of a covenant being established with First Testament figures such as Noah, Abraham, Isaac, and Jacob, who do not even appear as examples of behaviour, as models of obedience, or in interpretations in which the covenant idea features. The one exception to this is Moses, who is explicitly given the role of mediator of the law (1QS 1.3 and 8.15). But

Thus 1.8,16, 18, 20, 24; 2.10, 12, 13, 16, 18; 3.11; 4.22; 5.2, 3, 5, 8, 9 (twice), 10, 11, 12, 18, 19, 20, 22 (twice); 6.15, 19; 8.9, 10, 16; 10.10. Note that of these, 10 are in the section concerning entry to the community (1.16–3.18) and 16 are in the section on community structure (5.1–7.25).

56. For באי ברית see 1QS 1.7-8; 2.12, 18; 3.11-12; 5.8, 20; 6.14-15; 10.10. For עבר ברית see 1.16, 18, 20, 24; 2.10, 11.

even when the name of Moses is used, this is not in a reference to the historical establishment of the covenant, but rather to the legal principle of the covenant relationship, stressing the obligatory aspect of the covenant. Thus the phrase in 1QS 5.8 לשוב אל תורת מושה, 'to return to the law of Moses', clearly addresses the present community by qualifying the law further as that which 'has been revealed to the Sons of Zadok, the keepers of the covenant'. This type of argument attests to the identification of covenant with law.

3. There is *no* consciousness of belonging to a people whose existence has its origin in the divine establishment of the covenant. No reference to the experiences of the exile, as in the opening of CD, is found. The history of Israel is referred to only in passing in 1QS 1.21-25, a confessional formula which has little or no historical perspective. Thus the liturgical framework and confessional content of both the positive phrases, 'the favours of God manifested in his mighty deeds' and 'merciful grace to Israel' (1.21-22), and of the negative phrase, 'the iniquities of the children of Israel, all their guilty rebellions and sins' (1.23), do not refer to history. At most there is an allusion to something that belongs to the history of salvation which may mean no more than that the covenant ritual provides an occasion for the community to express a shared destiny.[57] A clear awareness, as in CD, of a common past uniting present Israel with the Israel of past and future, be it in faithfulness or unfaithfulness, is not articulated.

4. Where CD is conscious of a faithful remnant, seen as heir to the covenant by being faithful, but also in historical continuity, 1QS seems not to be conscious of a remnant within or from Israel. However, there is a certain consciousness of continuity in the phrase 'Sons of Zadok', albeit primarily as an awareness of belonging to a *priestly line*, thereby claiming a priestly covenantal inheritance from the past going back perhaps to the covenant promised to Phinehas.[58] If this is the case, two things are notable. On the one hand, the 'Sons of Zadok' may be the *leadership* of the community, although not meant in a cultic context (1QS 5.2, 9).[59] However, there seems to be no difference in rank or authority between priests in general and the sons of Zadok, when 1QS

57. As Sanders, *Paul*, pp. 243-47, has noted, there is in both CD and 1QS a particularistic tendency, inasmuch as 'the sectarians' refrained from calling themselves 'Israel', and their being conscious of being chosen out of Israel.

58. Cf. Num. 25.12-13.

59. Cf. Liver, 'The "Sons of Zadok"', p. 28.

5.2 is compared to 6.19. On the other hand, if, as in CD, it is a priestly function to *interpret the law* within and for the community, this is not limited to leaders. To study the law is a duty in which all members of the community need to be engaged. According to 1QS 5.9, the priests' function is to 'keep the covenant' and 'seek His will'. This means the covenant is based on the principle of law, rather than on history.

When the priestly function is to interpret the law, this may throw light on the meaning of the unique expression, בריתם 'their covenant' in 1QS 6.18-20:

> Then when he has completed one year within the Community, the Congregation shall deliberate his case with regard to his understanding and observance of the Law. And if it be his destiny, according to the judgement of the Priests and the multitude of the men of their Covenant, to enter the company of the Community, his property…shall be handed over to the Bursar of the Congregation (trans. G.Vermes).

The best way to interpret 'their covenant' is to take the suffix as referring *not* to the divine origin, but to priestly establishment, or commitment. Consequently when לרוב אנשי 'the multitude of the men' is qualified with 'their covenant' it means not a covenant consisting *of* priests, rather a covenant based on priestly commitment; priests and lay members together have a commitment to study and teach the law and to live accordingly. New members joining the community enter it in order to participate in a priestly covenantal commitment, a continuous study of the law. The purpose of this is to begin a *restoration* of the covenantal relationship, covenant being understood primarily in its obligatory aspect, its validity based on a legal principle.

5. With a lack of consciousness of past history, it cannot occasion surprise that the First Testament covenantal blessing, of becoming a people and possessing a land, is not the focal point of 1QS. This leads to the question of eschatology. Thus, 1QS 4.6-8:

> And as for the visitation of all who walk in this spirit, it shall be healing, great peace in a long life, and fruitfulness together with every everlasting blessing and eternal joy in life without end, a crown of glory and a garment of majesty in unending light (trans. G. Vermes).

It is clear that the emphasis has *shifted* from concrete blessings of place and collective existence, to an individualized reward, which is expressed in future categories, as eschatological hope. The concern is with covenantal blessings of peace and long life, building on the dualistic principle of goodness and truth and applying the divine promise individually, not collectively. In the perspective of future judgment, reward includes the hope of vindication, which is expected when the Messiahs of Israel and of Aaron overthrow all evil (1QS 9.11; cf. 1QSa 2.12-22).

Rather than giving a rationale for the covenant validity from past events, 1QS finds validity in a reference to the two spirits of light and darkness. Although applying covenantal terms, the document concentrates its interest on how the covenant is valid for the present community. And from this change one may conclude that the force and dynamic of the covenant concept lie in the ecclesiological usage of the covenant and in the application of this to the present life of the community.

6. With regard to eschatology, of particular interest is the expression, 'eternal covenant', explicitly mentioned in four passages, in 1QS 3.11; 4.22-23; 5.5; 8.9. Of these, three are in a context where life in obedience brings *atonement,* by means of which the eternal covenant is established; 1QS 4.22 is in the context of God's final judgment. This could indicate that the community has a function that is equivalent to priestly service, and that God's presence is to be found within the community behind 1QS, rather than in the Jerusalem temple. If this is the case, then the community sees itself as a group to which the promise of the eternal, priestly covenant has been given. This points to a theology of election for which CD shows surprisingly little concern for.

First, there is in 1QS 11.7-9 clear evidence that *God is the subject* of election, and that *the community* has been set apart as the 'eternal possession' of God, hence the community, not all Israel, is *the object* of election:

> God has given them to His chosen ones as an everlasting possession, and has caused them to inherit the lot of the Holy Ones. He has joined their assembly to the Sons of Heaven to be a Council of the Community, a foundation of the building of Holiness, an eternal Plantation throughout all ages to come (trans. G. Vermes).

This is part of the concluding section of 1QS, 9.26b–11.22. Election is here set both in an ecclesiological and an eschatological setting. On the one hand, we find that 'the chosen' are united with angels to be part of heaven; on the other hand, being chosen means being set apart for God, to form a 'council of the community', סודם לעצת יחד, to be God's eternal possession.[60] Whereas the idea that the community is an 'eternal

60. In some cases (e.g. 1QS 2.25; 8.5 or CD 19.35) the whole community is in

plantation' brings associations with the covenant of priests,[61] the 'eternal assembly' סוד עולמים[62] associates the present covenant relationship with future fulfilment. As for covenant-belonging, this is now confined to those who choose to accept it, or to live in accordance with its law and who will accordingly escape judgment. What thus characterizes the community of 1QS is both a future and a realized eschatology.[63] Moreover, a tension between the present existence of the community and its future existence is seen when the expression, 'those whom God has chosen', is qualified as being 'an eternal possession', belonging to the sphere of heaven. The same tension between present and future is found in the idea of election of the 'upright'. Thus, 1QS 4.22-23:

> (After being purified) the upright may have understanding in the knowledge of the Most High and the perfect way of insight into the wisdom of the sons of heaven. For it is they whom God has chosen for the eternal covenant, and to them shall all the glory of Adam belong (trans. Michael A. Knibb).

The exclusiveness inherent in the idea of a divine election (in both 1QS 11 and 4) is now transferred to the eternal covenant.[64] Even if exclusiveness of election is in line with what we find in some parts of the First Testament, the exclusiveness in 1QS is stronger than there, being referred to in covenant terms. In 1QS there is no indication that God's election for an eternal covenant is an election of Israel to become a superior people, as in the *Book of Jubilees*.[65] Rather more significant is the idea that God's election is thought of as *coinciding* with the community as 'the elect'. Thus, election designates that some are chosen *out of Israel*, to live a life in obedience.[66] There is, however, no reason

mind, so that סוד seems to be almost identical to ברית, as suggested by E. Kutsch, 'Bund', *TRE* 7, p. 404.

61. Cf. CD 1.7-8. Here מטעת is used of the faithful remnant, that is, to 'inherit the land', to receive the blessings of the covenant.

62. See also 1QS 2.25, 1QH 3.21, cf. 1QH 4.25, סוד קדושים.

63. Cf. B. Otzen, 'Sekthåndbogen', in E. Nielsen and B. Otzen, *Dødehavsteksterne: I oversættelse ogh med noter* (Copenhagen: Gads, 1959), p.95; A.R.C. Leaney, *The Rule of Qumran and its Meaning: Introduction, Translation and Commentary* (London: SCM Press, 1966), p. 253.

64. Expressed elsewhere in the phrase, 'the congregation of the elect', עדת בחירו, cf. 4QpPs 37 2.5; 3.5.

65. No interest in God's election of a location, such as Zion in *Jub.* 1.17, or a place for God's special presence, is found.

66. For an election of the people, see 1QM 10.9; 4QpPs 37.4. Cf. also 4QFlor

to believe that election for the eternal covenant is limited to priests. Further, when 1QS identifies 'the elect' with the 'upright' by proclaiming that they are the heirs of the covenant (promises and obligations), 1QS claims the covenant in its eternal validity for its community. It follows from this that ethnic Israel may by divine decision be excluded from a covenantal relationship, because neither is an entirely ethnic Israel chosen, nor does it live a life in obedience.[67]

Secondly, it is important to acknowledge that, as in the First Testament, *election is for a purpose*, a task.[68] Since election, understood individually as well as collectively, is closely associated with obedience in 1QS, this answers the question of the purpose or goal of the eternal covenant. This is clear from the opening paragraph of 1QS 1.1-8, in which the tasks are to seek God, to do what is right, to 'love what God has chosen and hate all that He has rejected' (1QS 1.3-4; cf. 1.9) also qualified as 'the covenant of loyalty or fidelity' (1QS 1.8).[69] In line with this, the command to the community is: to hate falsehood and to love truth (1QS 2.24; 4.2-4; 9.17); to engage especially in 'eternal hatred' for the 'people of perdition' (1QS 9.22; cf. 1.10). In addition, it is to engage in love towards 'the children of light', or the members of the community (1QS 1.9).[70] Thus, the interpretation of love turns into a double command, to hate and to love, attributing a dualistic principle that is *not* found in the First Testament in this form, nor in CD. This shows that in 1QS the concern is with the idea that those elected should be true to the obligatory covenant.

When election is thus understood in terms of covenant obligations, then *collective* belonging implies that the goal of present life is obedience, and from the perspective of future judgment, the hope is

---

1.18-19 which refers to the nations over against Israel. It does not follow from this identification that the community called itself 'true Israel', as Sanders, *Paul*, p. 245, rightly stresses.

67. This is implied also in 1QH 14.15; 15.23; 16.13; 17.21, but note the fragmentary character of these texts.

68. Cf. T.C. Vriezen, *Die Erwählung Israels nach dem A.T.* (ATANT; Zürich: Zwingli Verlag, 1953), p. 46.

69. Against G. Vermes, I take חסד ברית in 1QS 1.8 to be more than 'covenant of grace', because it contains both promise and obligations, hence 'covenant of loyalty or fidelity'. Cf. 'troskabspagten' as in Otzen, *Dødehavsteksterne*, pp. 46-47. See further, G. Vermes, *The Dead Sea Scrolls: Qumran in Perspective* (London: SCM Press, 1982 [1977]), p. 167.

70. Also expressed as 'lovingkindness' in 1QS 2.24; 5.4, 25; 8.2; 10.26.

eschatological reward for the community. This I see reflected in 1QS
8.5-10:

> When these are in Israel, the Council of the Community shall be estab-
> lished in truth. It shall be an Everlasting Plantation, a House of Holiness
> for Israel, an Assembly of Supreme Holiness for Aaron. They shall be
> witnesses to the truth at the Judgement, and shall be the elect of Good-
> will who shall atone for the Land and pay to the wicked their reward. It
> shall be that tried wall, that precious corner-stone, whose foundation
> shall neither rock nor sway in their place (Isa xxviii,16). It shall be a
> Most holy Dwelling for Aaron, with everlasting knowledge of the Cove-
> nant of justice, and shall offer up sweet fragrance. It shall be a House of
> Perfection and Truth in Israel that they may establish a Covenant accord-
> ing to the everlasting precepts. And they shall be an agreeable offering,
> atoning for the Land and determining the judgement of wickedness, and
> there shall be no more iniquity (trans. G. Vermes).

This passage contains a number of ideas, from the point of view of both
the community's present self-understanding, especially its purpose, and
its awareness of its future existence. Two ideas in particular are of concern here. One matter of interest is election being related to *atonement*.
Thus, the most important function of the temple, to bring sacrifices and
to atone for sins and transgressions, is now a function of the community
of the elect. From this it follows that the community sees itself as
belonging to a covenant that is based on priestly principles of purity,
and established by humanity (1QS 8.10), by those who chose to join it
and therefore covenantal identity is particularistic.

The other issue here is the change in the role which the human partner plays in the covenant establishment. This is clear from the metaphorical language, 'Everlasting Plantation', 'House of Holiness for
Israel', 'Assembly of Supreme Holiness for Aaron', 'tried wall', 'precious corner-stone', and 'a Most holy Dwelling for Aaron', 'House of
Perfection', and 'Truth in Israel', all of which refer to the community,
and in a particular way call to mind the *priestly* covenant *commitment.*
What seems most significant is that these metaphorical expressions
refer to what is expected of the human partner with respect to covenant
membership. By using terms for priestly purity and holiness, 1QS has
changed the emphasis, stressing both covenantal obedience and a status
of perfection, rather than belonging by birth. We note again a *change*
from an ethnic to a particularistic covenant relationship.

In short, the consciousness of the *past* is almost eliminated in 1QS,
and when present, it is at best ambivalent. From the perspective of

identity, 1QS has the *present* covenant as its central focus, and the most important covenant aspect is that of covenant *obedience*. The group's self-understanding builds on the conviction that election means being obliged to live according to the law and being devoted to the study of Torah. Because the eternal covenant in 1QS is interpreted in these categories, with atonement as its primary characteristic, adding also an eschatological dimension, the covenant idea has *to a large degree been transformed*. Since the group behind 1QS focuses its attention on covenant restoration, covenant membership entails a radically changed life-style based on priestly perfection, that is, on purity boundaries.

b. *Ecclesiological Consciousness and Covenantal Awareness*
In 1QS identity can also be expressed in other ways. Although it would be useful to examine all, or several other, identity terms, this is beyond what is feasible. Particularly one term יחד calls for attention. It is significant that this term is used more often than ברית in 1QS.[71] A brief look at *yahad* will clarify whether the prominence given to this term implies a particularistic self-understanding.

1. An ecclesiological consciousness is found in the expression in 1QS 5.5-6, 'a foundation of truth for Israel, for the community of the everlasting covenant', the latter a translation of ליחד ברית עולם. Whereas several commentators have emphasized that the phrase should be understood as a reference to the true Israel, so that Israel is synonymous with the community, this is not the issue here.[72] What is characteristic in relation to identity is that יחד is used of and by a group that sees itself united for a purpose. Both noun and adverb are frequent in 1QS, the verb less so. As a noun it means 'union', as an adverb 'together'.[73] While *yahad* is not used as a term for any community outside

71. Conversely in CD, where only CD 20.1, 14, 32 attests to the usage.
72. Thus P. Wernberg-Møller, *The Manual of Discipline: Translated and Annotated with an Introduction* (Leiden: E.J. Brill, 1957); Otzen, *Dødehavsteksterne*, p. 67; Knibb, *The Qumran Community*, 1987, p. 107. Differently, Sanders, *Paul*, p. 245, who points to the consciousness of the community as being forerunner of the true Israel.
73. First Testament usage is rare, and not in a context of identity; see, e.g. Deut. 33.2 using the noun, or Ps. 86.11, using the verb, in piel, 'unite'. For full studies of the concept and its use in the Dead Sea Scrolls, see particularly, J. Maier, 'Zum Begriff יחד in den Texten von Qumran' *ZAW* 72 (1960), pp. 148-66, and P. Wernberg-Møller, 'The Nature of YAHAD according to the Manual of Discipline and Related Documents', *ALUOS* 6 (1966–68), pp. 56-81.

the Dead Sea Scrolls, it may have been adapted here under the influence of the Greek κοινωνία.[74] Its frequent use in 1QS and variety of meanings point to the importance of the term, stressing union, unity or togetherness.[75] Nevertheless, there is no evidence that it is employed as a proper name. Rather, there seems to be a deliberate use of יחד in the context of a community, stressing that the community is united in ideology as well as practice, in a common cause and with a common goal.[76] Given the fact that יחד is a parallel term to ברית, both terms are ecclesiological concepts used to designate group identity, although not necessarily used of one group only, or even of a group united in all matters concerning organization, theology and practice.

2. When *yahad* is qualified as יחד אל (1QS 1.16; 2.22), as יחד קודש (1QS 9.2, 7-8; cf. 1QSa 1.9), as ברית יחד (1QS 3.12), or as יחד אמת (1QS 2.24), this is a language similar to the covenantal language, with the same consciousness of belonging to God's covenant, hence sharing ecclesiological self-understanding. Moreover, when the community members are called 'people of the community', אנשי יחד (1QS 5.1; 6.21; 7.20; 8.11, 16; 9.5, 7, 10, 19) or 'multitude of the men of the community', רוב אנשי היחד (1QS 5.2-3; 6.19), this implies that *yahad* is to be distinguished from הרבום 'the many'.[77] It is of note that particularly in relation to acceptance of new members, to expulsion or

---

74. Thus suggested by M. Weinfeld, *The Organizational Pattern and the Penal Code of the Qumran Sect: A Comparison with Guilds and Religious Association of the Hellenistic Roman Period* (NTOA, 2; Göttingen: Vandenhoek & Ruprecht, 1986), pp. 13-14, based on Josephus, *War* 2.122, 123 as evidence. Cf. also M. Hengel, 'Qumran und der Hellenismus', in M. Delcor (ed.), *Qumran: Sa piété, sa théologie et son milieu* (BETL, 46; Paris: Duculot, 1978), pp. 333-72. There may be a parallel to the use in Acts 2.42, but a comparative study of יחד and κοινωνία, in both Second Testament and classical texts, is needed to substantiate whether there is a (mutual?) influence.

75. Thus Wernberg-Møller, 'The Nature of YAHAD', esp. p. 70.

76. Wernberg-Møller, 'The Nature of YAHAD', pp. 70-71, maintains that יחד is not a term for 'a clearly defined religious sectarian body'. Rather it seems to refer to a 'reform movement' within Judaism with an emphasis on law observance. Further, p. 61, he argues for membership not of one community but of a *local branch* on the basis of 1QS 6.13-16 (italics mine). Maier, 'Zum Begriff', p. 150 points to the theological understanding of יחד and denies that there is a reference to organization, cf. 1QS 2.26; 3.7 and 9.2.

77. רבים refers to priests and laity, thus 1QS 6.1 and frequently also CD 13.7; 14.7,12; 15.8. The Greek translation of this is either πλῆθος, or οἵ πολλοί, according to Weinfeld, *Organizational Pattern*, pp. 14-16; cf. Josephus, *War* 2.146.

punishment of present members, the *yahad* has a status of authority, which is clear from the expression, עצת היחד, the 'council of the community'.[78] This group is either its governing body,[79] or it is the whole community gathered for decisions.[80] However, the language is far from transparent and it is impossible to make a decision for one against the other interpretation. Be that as it may, the preference in 1QS for יחד to designate union and unity, points to another way of expressing the awareness of being a community created from, but also *within,* the wider ethnic Israel. By being a parallel term to 'covenant' it reflects a self-understanding that makes a point of using a different terminology than the one used in the First Testament and CD. It testifies to a narrower type of ecclesiology than one defined by ethnic principles.

3. As in CD the most frequent use of covenantal language is found in relation to entry into the community.[81] 'Entry into the covenant' appears in the liturgical part in 1.16–2.18. This may be interpreted either as a rite of initiation or as a ritual of covenant renewal. The latter is most likely, because the choice is between 'the reign of God' and 'the reign of Belial', indicating that the rite is repeated and the choice is not once only. It is of note that separation from outsiders is inherent in the ritual marking entry; hence from the fact that the community demands separation from others, despite their being born inside Israel, we may conclude that a particularistic ecclesiology is present.

To sum up, the covenant concept of 1QS builds on the idea of a priestly structure, of priestly qualities related to purity. Especially when the use of *yahad* is taken into consideration, a *change of identity* becomes clear. Out of a national identity a particular religious group is conceptualized. No longer are the people, or the land, the objects of interest, or the focus of covenantal blessing. This change of focus is particularly obvious when the group adopted *yahad* as identity term. By

---

78. עצה, council (counsel), seems in some instances a parallel term for community; see Otzen, *Dødehavsteksterne*, p. 47.

79. 1QS 8.1, 'judges of the congregation', and 1QSa 1.29, 'tribal chiefs judges and officers' both seem to indicate a leadership with a different authority to that of the community. Possibly the same is found in 4QFlor 1.17.

80. Cf. 1QS 3.2; 5.7; 6.3, 10; 7.2, 22, 24 and 11.8.

81. Either באי ברית as in 1QS 1.7-8; 2.12, 18; 3.11-12; 5.8, 20; 6.14-15; 10.10; or באי יחד as in 1QS 1.16; 2.26; 3.2; 5.7. Elsewhere I have dealt with covenant entry in more detail; see *Covenant*, pp. 162-83.

means of this change of terminology, 1QS signals a different ecclesiological awareness. No longer is the important factor ethnic belonging; rather, it is the shared religious belief and practice that create unity. Whether this reflects a movement for reform of the wider society, or an internal renewal with no impact on national and religious identity, is difficult to assess from the material at hand.

3. *Conclusion*

While from the point of view of identity, a covenantal relationship is not necessarily exclusive by nature, it nevertheless becomes exclusive when ethnic identity is no longer inherent in covenantal theology. CD, on the one hand, refers to the idea of the 'covenant with the ancestors', in principle given to all Israel, but in practice to a narrow group, one which is *entered by human choice* rather than one affirmed by undergoing the rite of circumcision. On the other hand, since the covenant is a relationship based on faithfulness and obedience, covenantal identity builds on obedience. Due to the nature of CD, the real concern is for those who are inside the community, with a view to keeping those who are in the covenant inside by emphasizing the importance of being faithful. Potentially, Israel is the object of a call to return to the covenant; in practice, however, only the few who respond are counted as within the covenantal boundaries. In this way, exclusive boundaries reflect a particularistic identity. What emerges is a relatively *closed community* whose self-image is that of a remnant, called to preserve priestly purity by demanding ritual and ethical obedience and faithfulness. Because of this, there is a *change of identity*, from an ethnic covenant to a particularistic covenant. Eventually there is a change in the relationship between God and Israel, or God and humanity.

For 1QS, the covenant of the past is no longer important. The emphasis on 'eternal covenant' points to a *change of covenant theology* with a view to the future realization of a covenant defined in elitist terms. Belonging to a 'new covenant' is not expressed. Rather, what is significant is the idea that the covenant relationship with God is *established*, not by God, but by humans who enter in order to fulfil the covenant obligations. Members are requested to practise a strict observance of the law as interpreted in and by the community behind 1QS. This then reflects that *human acceptance* of God's covenant is the factor that establishes a covenant relationship.

The establishment of one or more communities that embody the true relationship with God is a clear example of a movement away from a 'civil religious society' to a 'particular religious society'. Conditional covenant membership in both CD and 1QS is another example of this change, although the community behind 1QS is more exclusive than the one behind CD. Both *exclude* all born Jews who have not made a conscious choice to enter the covenant, abandoning ethnic identity and clinging to a particularistic identity that has priestly purity and internally-created community rules as a characteristic feature.

When identity changes, the understanding of the relationship with God changes. The change is *from* CD's view that the entrance to the (new) covenant is the beginning of a future restoration of Israel's relationship with God, *to* 1QS's idea of a pure community preserving a place for the presence of God with itself and awaiting the eschatological judgment and restoration of the covenant of God with the elect. This community is identified by its hope of receiving 'everlasting blessing and eternal joy in life without end, a crown of glory and a garment of majesty in unending light' (1QS 4.7-8). And thus a *radical breach with the First Testament and its covenant identity* has taken place.

GENESIS IN QUMRAN

Frederick H. Cryer

In terms of the praxis of theory formation, it has long been acknowledged that people persistently attempt to accommodate new information to pre-existent theoretical bases. There is nothing wrong with this;
knowledge is, after all, relational by nature. Moreover, it is only by
comparison with the known that the new and unknown can be made
intelligible. If such new information should prove consonant with the
extant theory, it then merely serves as trivially supporting evidence, and
I *do* mean to say 'trivially', because one would never have devised a
theory in the first place without *some* supporting evidence, and a theory
does not become more solid merely by increasing the instantiation of its
examples. It is where new evidence either *clashes* with existing theory
or cannot comfortably be made to fit into it that scholars and natural scientists find their mettle tested, and where a theory may be seen to need
either adaptation or replacement. The danger, of course, is that scholars
may not for psychological reasons be prepared to acknowledge a conflict, so that he or she continues to attempt to fit inconvenient information into a theoretical framework that is no longer appropriate.

Now in connection with the understanding of the development of the
Pentateuch modern study has taken place within a framework of assumptions—I decline now and forever to use that much-abused word,
'paradigm'—that are *traditional* in nature. This is merely to say that,
until 1947, we were not in possession of truly ancient Hebrew-language
editions of the Pentateuch and had to make do with the evidence of the
Septuagint, which was itself only attested in manuscript evidence
dating from well into the Common Era; and, naturally, of the Samaritan
Pentateuch, the manuscript tradition which is much younger still, no
matter how far back we may suppose it to have begun. The Renaissance
and Reformation insistence on the accurate reconstruction of the original text of ancient documents meant that a great deal of emphasis has

traditionally been placed on the use of the early translations and paraphrases of the Old Testament text to aid us in our reconstructions.
Again, there is nothing wrong in all this; knowledge is, as I have said,
relational in nature, so we were compelled to use these documents *faute
de mieux*. And, lest I be misunderstood, let me hasten to add that it was
in many respects entirely proper to do as I have sketched out here.

The tradition as to the origin of the text of the Old Testament, as is
well known, traces it back in *4 Ezra* 14.18-48 to Ezra's writing down of
the canon in the thirtieth year after the fall of Jerusalem, which is to
say, in 557 BCE. Of course, it has long been obvious that this date is
much too early, at least as far as the whole of the Old Testament is
concerned, as such works as Chronicles, Daniel and Esther, to mention
but a few, were clearly written long after this date. But there have been
numerous scholars who have been prepared to argue for an early canon-
ization of the *Pentateuch alone*, followed by the accretionary growth of
the rest of the Old Testament. The reason for this is the evident fact of
the great importance assigned in early Judaism to the Pentateuch vis à
vis the other biblical books, which would seem to reflect an earlier crys-
tallization of the Pentateuchal materials. Also, tradition insists that the
schism between the Samaritans and the Jews of the Jerusalemite temple
took place over the issue of the expansion of the canon beyond the
books of the Pentateuch. Parenthetically, it should be remarked that this
schism has proved singularly difficult to put a date to, with assumptions
ranging from the fifth century in earlier times, down to the second in
recent proposals.

Thus whether it was formalized or merely implicit, the develop-
mental hypothesis has asserted that an *ancient Pentateuch* was the nucleus around which the other Old Testament documents collected, and
the assumption of an ancient Pentateuch has justified the use of many
different types of textual evidence, including, primarily, the Septuagint
and the Samaritan Pentateuch, to reconstruct it.

The discovery and evaluation of the documents from Khirbet Qumran, as well as new insights into the formation of the canon of the Old
Testament, have provided reasons for questioning the adequacy of this
model. To take the last-mentioned of these quantities first, there is
today a spectrum of arguments as to the origin of the canon. One pole
of this spectrum is demarcated by the insistence of the conservative
scholar, R.T. Beckwith, that the canon came into being virtually as
early as is affirmed by the tradition itself. Beckwith is inclined to take

almost every reference in mishnaic and early rabbinical tradition to the word 'Torah' to be a reference to the same text corpus with which we are familiar today as the Pentateuch, and he is undismayed by the quite various enumerations of the books of the Bible mentioned in rabbinical and Early Christian tradition and in Josephus and Ben Sira. At the other end of the spectrum is my colleague Niels Peter Lemche, who simply points out that, in the form that has come down to us, the Old Testament cannot be shown to pre-date the Hellenistic period.

I shall not enter into this discussion here at this time, although for the record I should like to register my agreement with Lemche. As far as the above-mentioned spectrum of views is concerned, however, one thing should be obvious, which is that the mere fact that it is possible to debate the matter extensively and plausibly from two quite opposite points of view means that we are short on hard facts. It cannot be *demonstrated* that the Torah of the second century BCE was identical with the Torah of Rabbi. This observation alone is sufficient to show that it is not possible to utilize the above-mentioned model as to the history of the canon as a historical interpretative framework for the development of the Pentateuch.

Hence it will be necessary for scholars to seek to employ some more stringent empirical criteria in order to characterize the development of the text of the Pentateuch and other Old Testament documents than has up to the present been the case. Of course, it will always be possible for scholars to claim that, even once we have arrived at a well-supported conjectural ur-text of the entire Old Testament, or even of the Pentateuch alone, it itself would be merely a faithful rendition of a pristine and much earlier original text. The existence of such an original text, however, would by its nature be an object of faith and not on the order of the conjectural knowledge that is available to the scholar.

When I speak of using more objective criteria, I should like to stress at the outset that the hypothesis of the *sectarian nature* of the society or societies underlying the documents from Khirbet Qumran has, in my opinion, served as a prodigious red herring which, or so I contend, has distracted scholars from approaching the texts objectively. Every characteristic in these texts that does not agree with what scholars take to have been the character of 'mainstream' or 'proto-Pharisaic' Judaism has immediately been filed under the rubric of 'sectarian' or 'Essene' theology, or else it has on occasion been labelled 'Saduccaean', 'Hasidic', or the like, with or without the adjective 'proto-' attached. One should instead stop to consider that the earliest access we have to the textual basis of Pharisaic Judaism is the references in the Mishna, and that the Mishna was (a) first completed around 200 CE, and (b) is only available to us in mediaeval copies. Likewise, whatever the truth or falsehood of the references in Philo, Josephus and Pliny the Elder to an alleged 'Essene' community living in the Judaean wilderness at the northern end of the Dead Sea, these references derive from the close of the first century of the Common Era or the beginning of the second. Finally, a point that is becoming increasingly delicate, the connection between the so-called 'villa' and the depositions of documents in the caves has always been tenuous, today more so than ever.

When we consider that two recent separately conducted series of Carbon 14 datings of the documents in question, one undertaken in Zurich and the other in Arizona, have arrived at a spectrum of dates for these documents ranging from the end of the fourth or beginning of the third century BCE to the end of the first or the beginning of the second century of the Common Era, it becomes difficult to characterize as 'sectarian' a social group that is virtually *coterminous* with early Judaism itself. A 'sect' is by definition a breakaway movement from a well-established orthodoxy, and we have at present no reason to imagine that such an orthodoxy existed prior to the existence of the documentary tradition from Khirbet Qumran. Furthermore, the chronological horizon provided by the Carbon 14 studies bridges over periods when, to the best of our knowledge, the so-called 'villa' was not even inhabited. This has prompted scholars such as Niels Peter Lemche and Philip Davies to speculate that the contents of the caves are actually depositions of the temple community in Jerusalem, made to safeguard them from destruction at the hands of the Hasmonaeans or, if later, the Romans, a conclusion to which Norman Golb would, of course, subscribe, if in modified form, though for his own reasons. Naturally, this hypothesis would make intelligible the long chronological horizon of the documents that have come down to us, at the cost of dispelling some of our conceptions as to the integration of Jewish theology in the period in question.

Whatever the truth of the matter may ultimately prove to be, I suggest, then, that we will be better served in our attempts to understand the documents from Khirbet Qumran on their own merits, rather than with reference to the 'sectarian hypothesis' that has guided their interpretation up to the present.

To take but a single example of what I am speaking of, scholars have long been aware that the Qumran documents included a sizable number of texts that have been form-critically defined as *halakhot*, which is to say, interpretative rulings based on pre-existent legal material. Indeed, Professor Lawrence H. Schiffman of New York University has written two entire monographs and numerous articles on the so-called Qumran *halakhot*. In his most recent contribution, a brief article in *The Biblical Archaeologist*, Schiffman refers to the fascinating document 4QMMT, called after a phrase in its epilogue *Miqsat ma'ase hatora*, 'some precepts on the Law', as the *Halakhic Letter*. This is not entirely Schiffman's idea, as the term was used already by Elisha Qimron eleven years previously to designate this document, which, incidentally, is not a 'letter': there were at least six copies of it in the caves, and I know no one so fond of his own words that he keeps so many copies, not even in the age of the information revolution. Although it may reproduce epistolary form reasonably faithfully, this text clearly served an *exemplum*-function in its ancient context. I could accept this usage and the notion of *halakha* in Qumran better if the term were actually in use in Qumran's own documentation. As it is, it looks to me as if Mishnaic terminology, whose actual date we can only guess at, has been reapplied anachronistically to the Qumran materials. The language and script of 4QMMT have been, in my opinion correctly, assigned by their publishers, Elisha Qimron and John Strugnell, to 'the last four centuries BCE' without possibility of narrowing the date by other than conjectural means. This dating can only gain support from the recent conclusion of the Arizona laboratory that the Habakkuk Pesher must date from the third to the first century BCE, as this text refers to the Teacher of Righteousness, who is assumed to be the speaker or author of 4QMMT. But since the Tannaitic period which gave rise to the *halakha* ended with Rabbi around 200 CE, the extent of the anachronism in question could conceivably be more than half a millennium. I need hardly stress the absurdity of reading ancient texts through a five-hundred year younger system of categories which has itself been subjected to one and a half millennia of exegesis.

It is notoriously difficult for Christian—and in particular Protestant—scholars to read, for example, the Pauline epistles, without somehow smuggling either Augustine or Martin Luther into their readings; it is apparently equally difficult for Jewish scholars to avoid reading their own literary and religious history into the texts from Khirbet Qumran. I think that it is entirely intelligible that this should be so; it has never-theless had profound, not always helpful, consequences for our under-standing of the Qumran documents.

What has prompted my thinking along these lines has been a growing awareness on the part of those engaged in the publication of the Qum-ran biblical texts that the tradition of these texts cannot be characterized as attempts to faithfully pass on an authoritative, finally-shaped text. As far back as 25 years ago, James A. Sanders, who published the Qumran Psalter, concluded that there was so much variation both in the text, arrangement, and superscriptions of the Psalms in Qumran that, in his words,

> ...if there had already been a closed canon of Psalms since the fourth century, or since late Persian times..., even a 'liturgical collection' of canonical and non-canonical psalms would surely reflect the accepted canon where it existed.

Of course, the seriousness of Sanders's observation depends on one's view of the role played by the Psaltar in the formation of the biblical canon, and he was much and vociferously criticized for his brave forthrightness at the time. Moreover, this sort of observation has per-sisted up to the present day. As is well known, Emmanuel Tov has been proclaiming the simultaneous co-existence of a wide variety of dis-parate texts in Qumran from at least as far back as the end of the 1970s; his detailed portraiture of this argumentation has increased from work to work, culminating recently with his fine introduction to the textual tradition of the Hebrew Bible.

In a closely-argued study which appeared in 1988, Eugene Ulrich has studied what he has termed 'intentionally variant editions of the biblical text', taking his examples in 4QpalaeoExod[m], as well as the Qumran editions of the books of Samuel, Jeremiah, and the Aramaic-language part of Daniel.

In an interim report on the publication of 4QJudg[a] published in 1989, J. Trebolle Barrera recorded a singular observation. This is that the text itself covers the material presented in MT of Judg. 6.2-13, with the reservation that the Qumran edition of this text lacks vv. 8-10, that is, fully a fourth of this short text. But Trebolle Barrera further noted that scholars as far back as George Foot Moore, writing around the turn of the century, had recognized vv. 8-10 on source-critical grounds as a redactional expansion of the text. In 4QJudg[a], then, we have objec-tive evidence as to the correctness of Moore's assertion. It is to Trebolle

Barrera's credit that he acknowledged that, and I quote,

> the contribution of 4Q goes far beyond the domain of the history of
> textual transmission reaching the fields of literary criticism and editorial
> history of the entire book.

It occurred to me that if literary or source criticism and textual criticism could police each other reciprocally *en miniature*, in conjunction with the fine detail of the textual traditions of various Biblical works, would the same not also be possible *en large*, that is, at the macrotextual level of the transmission of chapters and verses? Now as a test of this hypothesis in conjunction with Pentateuchal documents what I propose to do is, as a thought experiment, to ignore the tradition as to the preexistence of a long-established Pentateuchal text. We shall then proceed to examine the Qumran manuscript tradition of the book of Genesis to see what forms that tradition takes; this is to be compared with traditional literary-critical theories as to the growth and structure of the book, as an independent control instance. It is proper to use literary criticism for this purpose, as the structural and compositional insights of source criticism have been arrived at on *formal* grounds that are basically irrelevant to considerations of the age of the Pentateuchal literature. Finally, I shall offer a brief glance at other Qumran Pentateuchal literary traditions as a further control.

Proleptically, I should like to state that the extremely lacunary nature of the Pentateuchal documents in Qumran will prevent our drawing any very astonishing conclusions. However, I think we should bear in mind the following recommendation by Eugene Ulrich, which he presented at the Madrid Dead Sea Scrolls conference in March of 1991:

> We should not begin our thinking with a vision of a unified *Biblia Hebraica* or modern Bible, but rather with an image of a flexible number of sacred scrolls with varying degrees of closeness or distance from a center called 'Torah', whose periphery was vague.

Although, as should be apparent by now, I am not entirely convinced of the centrality of 'Torah' to the stream of textual tradition, this picture of an indeterminate number of alternative texts which are so distinct from one another that my colleague, Thomas Thompson, calls them *compositional variants*, can serve as the contrasting hypothesis to the traditional theory of a single, ancient textual tradition.

Preliminary to studying the attestation of Genesis in the caves it should be noted that I am concerned solely with documents that are clearly attempts to preserve *text* as such. I am excluding consciously both the Pesharim and the parabiblical texts, the former because we do not actually know whether the Pesharim gloss text of the biblical or some other tradition, the latter because the relationship between the 'biblical' and the 'paraphrastic biblical' has yet to be firmly established. There are places where, for example, the book of *Jubilees* and Genesis run fully parallel for anything from a half verse up to several whole ones; but *Jubilees* only becomes a witness to the biblical text if one assumes without proving that the biblical text was already extant prior to the composition of *Jubilees*. Similar considerations will naturally apply also to the Pesharim.

A survey of the Qumran Genesis fragments reveals that the caves will originally have contained at least 16 separate copies of the text (or 19, if we accept Davila's distinction of 4QGen[h] as in reality representing four different MSS), although the extent of completeness of these copies we shall naturally never know. Eleven of these texts have been studied in great detail by James R. Davila and others in *Discoveries in the Judaean Desert*, vol. XII, which appeared in 1994. The others have been presented in various publications. For a convenient survey of the rest, I shall here rely on Uwe Glessmer's 'Liste der biblischen Texte', which appeared in *Revue de Qumran* in 1994. Since the textual tradition is extremely fragmentary, I shall for the sake of argument simply assume that if a known chapter of the MT is in Qumran represented by so little as a single verse it will originally have existed there in full. Thus I shall be concerned solely with lacunae of chapter length. I hope in this fashion also to avoid overstating my argument, which is, after all, ultimately a grandiose argument from silence.

The first thing that strikes the eye in conjunction with the textual basis of Genesis in Qumran is that chs. 7–16 are absent from the manuscript tradition. There is a citation from Gen. 12.4-5 in 4QGen[hpara], but for the very reason that this is not a precise citation of the text known to us from the LXX, MT and SP I shall ignore it here. Chapters 20 and 21 are also absent, as are chs. 25 and 28–33 (although there is a bit of chs. 33–34 on some fragments which seem to have come from Wadi Muraba'at), 38, 44, 46 and 50. Of course, the lacunae in question are advanced here with every conceivable reservation owing to the flukes of preservation. Nevertheless, it should be remarked that the Genesis manuscripts were deposited in caves 1, 2, 4, 6 and 8, a dispersion which should have, or so one might think, ensured reasonable chances for survival. This is to be compared with the fact that the considerably shorter book of Exodus was in Qumran preserved in 16 manuscripts (plus 14 brief references in phylacteries and mezuzoth), distributed over caves 1, 2, 4 and 7, and yet is lacunary only with respect to a single chapter (ch. 38)!

There is accordingly a strong possibility that the missing segments of text in the Genesis collection are not owing to the accidents of time. Let us consider: as attested, Qumran's Genesis possessed the two creation narratives plus the account of the fall, Cain and Abel, and, apparently, a list of pre-flood patriarchs, plus a brief instruction to Noah to build an ark and prepare it, because God purposes to destroy mankind. There was no table of nations, nor any story of a tower of Babel, with mankind's attendant dispersion over the face of the earth. There must naturally have been some kind of Abraham narrative prior to the P-covenant and circumcision of Abraham and Ishmael in ch. 17, but there is no hint of the Abraham and Lot theme, nor of the battle with the Mesopotamian interlopers and the Melchizedek interlude, nor of the JE covenant with Abraham in Genesis 15. The absence of Genesis 14 is, naturally, intelligible in light of the fact that in other Qumranic fragments Melchizedek is a quasi-messianic figure, associated with the end-time. Moreover, literary criticism since at least August Dilmann in the nineteenth century has been aware of the awkward fit of Genesis 14, with its portrayal of a warlike Abraham, with the rest of the Abraham narratives, which without exception depict him as a man of peace. Then, too, if the Qumran tradents had known of it, Genesis 15 would no doubt have been problematical from a number of viewpoints. It contains the reference to the four hundred years the Israelites will have to serve in Egypt, waiting for the Amorites' sin-account to be fulfilled; this is a redactional bridge that enables Genesis to bridge over Exodus and to point forward to the conquest of the land as well. Finally, the chapter contains the strange depiction of Yahweh entering into a covenant in the form of a smoking oven, or at least some kind of physical manifestation, which may have been theologically objectionable to some. In other words, one can advance good reasons for the non-inclusion of the chapter, while only the dogmatism of the four-source theory insists that a Yahwistic or Yahwistic-Elohistic covenant narrative would *have* to be included in Genesis.

To pick up the thread again: without ch. 16, Ishmael is not born of an Egyptian mother, although the promised Isaac is assured of Yahweh's blessing instead of him. The Lot who is saved in chs. 18–19 is then not necessarily kin to Abraham; in fact, the only kin relation stated in connection with him in these chapters is his apical paternity of the Moabites and Ammonites, via incest.

Now Genesis 20, the story of Abraham and Sarah's sojourn in the court of Abimelek of Gerar, has long been recognized as a straightforward doublet of 12.10-20, one which recurs in yet another incarnation in Genesis 26. It is therefore intelligible that ch. 20 is absent from the Qumran tradition. On the other hand, as Isaac's birth is promised in the surviving ch. 17 and the lad is endangered in ch. 22, it is likely that his birth narrative in ch. 21 was part of the Qumran collection which time has not spared.

Sarah's death and the purchase of the cave of Machpelah formed part of the Qumran tradition, as did the bride-purchase of a wife for Isaac in ch. 24; however, the extensive list of Abraham's Arab wives and offspring as well as Ishmael's non-Israelite descendants failed to be stated. Isaac's sojourn in Gerar is reported (ch. 26), as is Jacob's stealing of the blessing in ch. 27, but Isaac's death, Jacob's flight to Paddan-Aram, and the entire cycle of his thriving and wiving there, as Shakespeare has it, goes unreported. This makes sense in view of the fact that Jacob's entire sojourn in Paddan-Aram has been regarded since the nineteenth century as a mere entertaining and occasionally semi-comical expansion of a straightforward picaresque narrative; but it is one that overdimensions Jacob at the expense of both Abraham and Isaac.

We might find that it strains the bounds of credibility that Jacob thus should proceed to Shechem with a full complement of unaccounted-for offspring. However, one should consider what has been won by the non-mention of these chapters, for we are spared the story of Jacob obtaining wives from the non-Israelite Aramaeans, just as the silence as to ch. 25 spares us Abraham's and Ishmael's non-Israelite progeny. We are also spared the narrative in 31.43-54 of the making of a covenant with the non-Israelite Laban; and the narrative in ch. 32 of Jacob's self-abasement before Esau, the eponymous ancestor of the non-Israelite Edomites. Contrariwise, ch. 34, with its tale of rapine and revenge, and of the eradication of the threat of miscegenation with the non-Israelite Shechemites, *is* preserved: a fiercely particularistic conclusion. This xenophobic thrust is, however, not developed in all respects, as ch. 36 is preserved and describes in detail the children of Esau, although, admittedly, Israelite tradition does not apostasize the Edomites as it does other peoples.

The Joseph narrative is related more or less as we are familiar with it, with one signal exception. It has always been evident to source critics that ch. 38, with its remarkable story of Tamar's righteous harlotry and Judah's inadequacy and mendacity, is a completely irrelevant digression from the Joseph narrative. The tradents of the tradition of Genesis in Qumran apparently thought so, too, as the chapter is nowhere in evidence. Chapter 44, in which Joseph plays cat-and-mouse with his brothers and Judah is rehabilitated with a noble speech, simply develops and enriches both characters without materially advancing the plot: the mere announcment of Joseph's survival would surely suffice as a dramatic device to get Jacob down to Egypt. Moreover, as Judah has not been humiliated by a ch. 38, he is not in need of extensive rehabilitation in ch. 44; nor does the Qumran Genesis collection conclude that he is, as the contents of this chapter are unattested in their collection. The narrative material preserved in ch. 45 of our book of Genesis, in which Joseph reveals himself to his brothers and Pharaoh commands them to settle in Egypt, *is* material to the story, and hence is preserved, whereas P's lengthy list of those Jacob brought with him, in ch. 46, is not, and does not figure in the tradition. Finally, there is no trace of ch. 50, the narratives of the death and embalming of Jacob and Joseph; conceivably, the references to foreign burial practices dictated the omission of this chapter or else prevented its composition, although, as with Genesis 15, it serves as a bridge to much wider perspectives in the Pentateuch and hence is clearly redactional, so it may not even have been *known* to the Qumran tradents, whoever they were.

In sum, although we must be extremely hesitant because of the lack of concrete evidence, the Genesis manuscripts in Qumran seem to have the character of a very 'Israelite' collection, as most reference to foreign peoples or practices is lacking. In modern times, scholars from Gerhard von Rad to H.H. Schmid have marvelled at and been impressed by the *universalism* of the hypothetical Yahwist, which they see attested already in the narrative of the calling of Abraham in Genesis 12. This motif is, however, nowhere near as evident in Qumran's Genesis as it is in the Genesis traditions of the MT, the LXX or the SP.

In short, the Qumran Genesis just barely makes sense as an independent composition, although there are many narrative elements not present in it which do make good reading in the Genesis of the MT, the LXX and the SP. However, its *Tendenz* is quite clear, and thus does give the collection coherence as a redactional phase in the development of the Pentateuch. What it lacks is mostly reference to the peoples surrounding Israel, which would integrate it into the world at large; and passages which would serve to integrate it into the larger narrative of the Pentateuch.

As a control, we might just glance at the lacunae in the other Pentateuchal manuscript traditions. As mentioned previously, the only lacuna in Qumran Exodus is ch. 38, which includes the description of the altar of burnt offering, but also the mirrors for the ministering women, and all the interior hangings for the court of the Tabernacle, plus the reckoning of the cost of it all. It is not inconceivable that some details such as the mirrors of the ministering women led to the omission of this chapter or to the failure to compose it, but it contains so much else that is integral to the account of the Tabernacle that the non-existence was possibly owing to the vagaries of time and the worms that devour ancient manuscripts.

Leviticus is attested by at least 11 manuscripts, ranging from masoretic to proto-Septuagintal text to targumic text; only ch. 12, dealing with a woman's uncleanness following birth, is not represented. As this is an autonomous block of legislation, it is difficult to say whether its omission could be consciously motivated or is accidental.

Numbers is in Qumran's collection represented by at least seven distinct manuscripts, and hence is the most poorly-attested of the Pentateuchal manuscripts; its lacunae are, however, interestingly reminiscent of those in Genesis, though again, without a parallel to the extended narrative structure of Genesis it is difficult to be certain of some matters. Chapter 6, containing the instructions concerning the Nazirite vow, but also the Aaronide blessing, is wholly absent. Of course, there is now objective evidence to the effect that the Aaronide blessing was traditional material; its absence here is therefore possibly not accidental. The next sizable lacuna is ch. 10, comprising the instructions for the making of the silver trumpets and the account of the breaking up of the camp and their 'setting out by stages from the wilderness of Sinai' plus the march order of the tribes and the words of signal: 'Arise O Lord, and let thy enemies be scattered'; and, at close of day, 'Return, O Lord, to the ten thousand thousands of Israel'. Scholars have identified the latter on form-critical grounds as an ancient prayer of assembly, once thought to have been used in Israel's nomadic past, back when there were still scholars who believed that Israel *had* a nomadic past; or in conjunction with military activity in settled times. I can think of no plausible reason for their omission, if they were pre-existent in a Pentateuchal Numbers tradition, and the cause may be chance. Chapter 15 is also without witness; it contains detailed instructions pertaining to the burnt offering, the firstfruits of the grain, the high-priestly atonement sacrifice on behalf of the people, and the narrative of the execution of the man gathering firewood on the Sabbath. Clearly, the absence of the chapter on the altar of burnt offering in Exodus 38 could be related to this omission here, which is in any case compensated for by legislation elsewhere. In consideration of the apparent ambiguity in the texts found in Qumran towards the high-priestly office, the absence of the reference to priestly atonement is wholly intelligible on theological grounds.

The next major 'omission' is Numbers 17, which includes the second part of the account of 'strange fire', in which Eliezer the priest uses the censers of the burned ones to plate the altar, while Aaron is directed to offer atoning incense for the people's mutiny, as well as the anecdotal wonder-narrative of Aaron's staff, which is used to enhance his authority. Given the non-attestation of the Aaronide blessing from Numbers 10, as mentioned above, this lack, too, is wholly intelligible on theological grounds.

Chapter 28, with extensive recommendations pertaining to both the burnt offering and the Passover, is also absent. In view of the other passages on the altar of burnt offering and the offering itself which are missing from this manuscript tradition, this is hardly surprising, although the lack of reference to the Passover is. Otto Eissfeldt regarded both chs. 28 and 29 as expansions of P's original cultic calendar; he would no doubt have found it gratifying to discover their absence here.

Chapter 30, which contains the regulations limiting a woman's right to swear cultically-binding oaths, is absent, which agrees completely with the absence of ch. 6, dealing with the Nazirite oath. There is an evident theological tendency at work here, and we should perhaps recall that the early Christians, too, objected to oath-taking.

Chapter 31, dealing in Pentateuchal Numbers tradition with Israel's revenge on the Midianites, is likewise 'absent' and, given the previously-mentioned 'omission' of the Sihon and Og narratives, as well as the lack of the narratives dealing with the king of Arad and of Balak, the son of Zippor, this is of a piece. Moreover, the failure to mention such foreign peoples rhymes with the similar failure observed above in the case of the Qumran Genesis collection.

Finally, ch. 34, which details the boundaries of Israel-to-be, is unattested in the Qumran collection, which knows instead only ch. 35, with its list of Levitical cities of refuge. Moreover, ch. 34 specifies that the division is to be performed by Joshua ben Nun and Eleazar the priest, an apportionment that first takes place in Joshua 14–19. The instructions in Numbers 34 are hence, again, redactional bridging statements that link, in this case, the Pentateuch or Tetrateuch to the book of Joshua, forming, if you will, a Hexateuch. We have seen previously that also the Genesis collection apparently fails to include many such redactional linkages.

The book of Deuteronomy is attested in Qumran by fragments of at least 27 different manuscripts, plus a handful of references in phylacteries and mezuzoth. German scholarship was preoccupied back in the 1970s and the beginning of the 1980s with a search for what scholars termed 'die Mitte des Alten Testaments', which is to say, the 'centre' of the Old Testament as a corpus of texts. My own *Lehrmeister* in the university of Bochum, Professor Dr Siegfried Herrmann, suggested that that 'centre' was to be found in the book of Deuteronomy, a decision with which the tradents behind the Qumran collection apparently agreed, as every chapter of that book is attested in the manuscript fragments that have come down to us.

In short, the deficits of the Qumran Pentateuchal collection vis à vis the masoretic Pentateuchal tradition include a good deal of expansional narrative material, such as the account of Jacob's sojourn in Paddan-Aram. But they also include material with a specific theological *Tendenz*: there is an absence of text which might serve to enhance the authority of the Aaronide line—and, in retrospect, it is not inconceivable that the lack of a Melchizedek text in Qumran's Genesis could harmonize with this tendency. There is a lack of reference to the peoples around Israel, to Israel's territorial borders, to legislation regulating the taking of oaths, to references to burnt offerings and the cultic calendar, to texts describing events reported elsewhere in the Pentateuch or Hexateuch, and finally, and interestingly, to magic, as neither Aaron's staff nor the apotropaic image of Nehushtan was apparently included.

Of course, all of the above observations are offered, as stated previously, with only the greatest hesitation, as the manuscript tradition is notoriously lacunary by its very nature. But it seems to me that there is nevertheless a commonalty of features in the differences between Qumran's collection and the traditional collection of material (MT, LXX, SP) that it would not be too daring to suspect some underlying intentionality behind these differences. Moreover, the apparently systematic nature of the minuses of Qumran's Genesis versus the traditional collection prompt one to ask whether the worms that decimated so many manuscripts so thoroughly in the caves of Qumran had acquired theological and national-particularistic tastes. But only closer analysis could answer the question as to whether the Qumran tradition is in reaction to a pre-existent Pentateuchal tradition, or whether it is merely yet another manuscript tradition that existed alongside of that one. One thing, however, is certain: whichever answer should prove to be the correct one, we are in any case forced to conclude that it was possible for the tradents in Qumran to exercise vast independence with respect to the manuscript traditions that underlie the modern MT, LXX and SP. And that conclusion is itself sufficient to place yet another questionmark next to the notion of an ancient and authoritative Pentateuchal text.

THE MYSTERY TO COME:
EARLY ESSENE THEOLOGY OF REVELATION

Torleif Elgvin

4QInstruction (previously designated *Sapiential Work A* or *4QMusar Lemevin*) presents us with previously unknown material that enriches our knowledge of the sapiential and apocalyptic traditions of the second century BCE.[1] This paper concentrates on two interrelated aspects of the theology of this book: revelation and the elect community.

4QInstruction is preserved in seven fragmentary copies, one from Cave 1 (1Q26) and six from Cave 4 (4Q415, 416, 417, 418a, 418b, 423).[2] Six copies display early Herodian script (30–1 BCE), while one (4Q423) represents a late Herodian hand (1–50 CE). The large number of copies and the fact that this book was being copied even until a late stage in the history of the Qumran settlement show that it was highly

---

1. For an introduction to *4QInstruction*, see my papers, 'Wisdom, Revelation, and Eschatology in an Early Essene Writing', *SBLSP 34* (Atlanta: Scholars Press, 1995), pp. 440-63; 'Early Essene Eschatology: Judgement and Salvation According to Sapiential Work A', in D.W. Parry and S.Y. Ricks (eds.), *Current Research and Technological Developments on the Dead Sea Scrolls* (Leiden: E.J. Brill, 1996), pp. 126-65. 'Admonition Texts from Qumran Cave 4', in M.O. Wise, N. Golb, J.J. Collins and D.G. Pardee (eds.), *Methods of Investigation of the Dead Sea Scrolls and the Khirbet Qumran Site: Present Realities and Future Prospects* (New York: New York Academy of Sciences, 1994), pp. 179-94; and further, D. Harrington, 'Wisdom at Qumran', in E. Ulrich and J. VanderKam (eds.), *The Community of the Renewed Covenant: The Notre Dame Symposium on the Dead Sea Scrolls* (Notre Dame: University of Notre Dame Press, 1994), pp. 137-52.

2. The Hebrew text of the various fragments is available in B.Z. Wacholder and M.G. Abegg, *A Preliminary Edition of the Unpublished Dead Sea Scrolls: The Hebrew and Aramaic Texts from Cave Four: Fascicle Two* (Washington: Biblical Archaeology Society, 1992). The DJD edition of *4QInstruction* (by J. Strugnell and D. Harrington, I am responsible for one of the copies) is in preparation.

regarded within the Essene Community.[3] Two of the copies (4Q415 and 4Q416) were rolled in the less common way with the beginning on the inside of the scroll when they were deposited the last time, a fact that probably indicates that these scrolls were still in active reading use by 68 CE.[4] I have elsewhere calculated the length of the book to be between 26,000 and 31,000 letter spaces, and located most of the major fragments within the original scrolls.[5]

4QInstruction is a didactic book that provides instruction for man's relation to his fellowman and to God. Most of the book is an address to the wise and understanding individual in the second person singular. Large parts of the book consist of wisdom sayings, often in proverbial form, that provide practical admonitions for life in family and society in the areas of relations with parents, wife, and children; financial matters (loans and surety); working ethics (relations to superiors and subordinates); agricultural matters (seasons and festivals, sanctification of the first-born of the livestock), and so on. A lengthy section with such material, comprising approximately four consecutive columns, is preserved by the overlapping fragments 4Q417 1/4Q416 2 (this section probably covered cols. 3–6 in both scrolls).

Further, the book contains discourses which deal with eschatology and the revelation of God's mysteries to the elect. These discourses abound with apocalyptic material. An eschatological discourse on the coming judgment and the lots of the elect and the ungodly occupies two full columns of the book (4Q416 6.17–8.15, 4Q416 frgs. 4, 1, 3). Another discourse which elaborates on the future judgment of the wicked and salvation of the righteous occupies almost a full column (4Q418 frag. 69).[6] A lengthy discourse on the revelation of God's mysteries and the heavenly *Book of Hagi* is followed by a fragmentarily-preserved exhortation to praise the God who provides knowledge (4Q417 frag. 2,

---

3. Further, probably only copies of the most important books were hidden in Cave 1; see H. Stegemann, *Die Essener, Qumran, Johannes der Täufer und Jesus* (Freiburg: Herder, 4th edn, 1994), pp. 89-90.

4. T. Elgvin, 'The Reconstruction of Sapiential Work A', *RevQ* 16 (1995), pp. 559-80.

5. Elgvin, 'Reconstruction'. The original 4Q417 scroll contained between 17 and 20 columns, each of approximately 28 lines of 50-60 letter spaces. The length of this scroll was approximately 260 cm (+/– 30 cm).

6. On the eschatological discourses, see T. Elgvin, 'Early Essene Eschatology'. 4Q418 161 could derive from a third discourse on the last days.

probably cols. 9 and 10 out of approximately 18 columns, see discussion of the main section below). 4Q418 frag. 81 (approximately col. 17 out of around 25 columns) preserves almost a full column of text which deals with the spiritual inheritance of the elect and his eschatological community. Exhortations which deal with the hope of the righteous are also interspersed with wisdom sayings.

1. *Milieu of Origin*

A number of phrases and motifs from the Hebrew sections of Daniel recur in *4QInstruction*, especially those related to wisdom, revelation, and the elect.[7] As there is no clear literal dependence between Daniel and *4QInstruction*, it seems probable that both are dependent on a common tradition. The circles behind *4QInstruction* might be related to the *maskilim* of the book of Daniel,[8] although our book must be dated well after the persecution of Antiochus, as there are no references to any persecution of righteous Jews. Both books reflect scribal activity and a quest for divine communication; neither is concerned with the sacrificial cult of the temple.[9] Only two small passages deal with purity matters or priestly traditions. In its eschatology, *4QInstruction* is apocalyptic, not restorative, which indicates a distance from the Maccabean/Hasmonean establishment.

The terminology of *4QInstruction* is closely related to *The Rule of Discipline*, the *Damascus Document* and the *Hodayot*.[10] *4QInstruction*

---

7. The most important are גלה, רז, יודע/דעת, להבין/מבין, השכיל/משכיל/שכל, חיי עולם, חרפה, קודשים/קדוש/קודש. It should be noted, however, that *4QInstruction* understands קץ as 'period' like the sectarians, not as 'end' like Dan. 8–12.

8. Cf. J.J. Collins, 'Was the Dead Sea Sect an Apocalyptic Movement?', in L.H. Schiffman (ed.), *Archaeology and History in the Dead Sea Scrolls: The New York University Conference in Memory of Yigael Yadin* (Sheffield: Sheffield Academic Press, 1990), pp. 25-51.

9. Cf. P.R. Davies, 'Reading Daniel Sociologically', in A.S. van der Woude (ed.), *The Book of Daniel in the Light of New Findings* (Leuven: Peeters, 1993), pp. 345-61.

10. The discourses have more 'sectarian terminology' than the sections with wisdom sayings. The wisdom sayings might reflect an older tradition, to which a writer close to the early Essene community added discourses of his own. On sectarian terminology in *4QInstruction*, see T. Elgvin, 'Admonition Texts', pp. 184-86.

seems to have been influential in the framing of sectarian thinking and parlance. One phrase known from 1QH[a] 10.27-28 also occurs in *4QInstruction*: לפי דעתם יכבדו איש מרעהו 'according to their knowledge they shall be honoured, each one by his neighbour', 4Q418 55.10. It is likely that this hodayah quotes from *4QInstruction*, the examples of influence from *4QInstruction* upon the *Hodayot* are legion. Terminological similarities can be observed also with *The Book of Mysteries* (1Q27, 4Q299/300/301).

Apart from early sectarian writings, the books of *Enoch* seem to be the closest relative of *4QInstruction*. Most parallels are found in the *Book of Watchers* and the *Epistle of Enoch*. Our wisdom composition shares with *1 Enoch* the themes of the final judgment of the wicked and the glorious hope of the righteous. In both books divine wisdom is given the elect of the remnant community only through revelation. Terminological similarities indicate some kind of dependence between these writings. Both works foresee that the elect shall 'inherit the earth' (*1 En.* 5.7; 4Q418 81.14; cf. Mt. 5.4) and use the phrase 'eternal planting' for the elect community (*1 En.* 10.16; 84.6; 93.5, 10; 4Q418 81.13; 4Q423 1–2.7). These phrases recur in sectarian writings (CD 1.7-8; 8.14-15; 1QS 8.5-6; 11.8; 1QH[a] 6.15; 8.6, 10, 20; 4QpPs[a] 2.2-11). The phrase 'they shall walk in eternal light' occurs in both compositions.[11] Some important Enochic themes are not mentioned in *4QInstruction*: the interest in cosmology, the spatial dualism between heaven and earth, the ontological dualism between humans and the world of the spirits and the fall of the angels.

In its terminology, *4QInstruction* is closer to the writings of the *yaḥad* than to the *Enoch* literature. It is thus more probable that *4QInstruction* draws upon the books of *Enoch* than the other way around. The presupposition of the remnant community could point to a situation between MMT (160–52 BCE) and 1QS/CD (last decades of second century BCE), before sectarian theology had crystallized, for the origin of *4QInstruction*. In this case, *4QInstruction* should be seen as a representative of the wider Essene movement, not of the *yaḥad*. The lack of

---

11. *1 En.* 92.4, 4Q418 69 14. In the same line of this passage on the eschatological lot of the elect we find the triad אור עולם...כ]בוד...רוב הדר. The same triad is found in the description of the bliss of the righteous in 1QS 4.7-8 וכליל כבוד עם מדת הדר באור עולמים 'a crown of glory and a garment of honour in eternal light', and in 1QH[a] 12.15 about the lot of the elect הדר כבודכה לאור ע]ולם 'the honour of Your glory in eternal light'.

polemics against the Jerusalem establishment makes another option more likely: to ascribe *4QInstruction* to the pre-teacher community mentioned in CD 1. If so, *4QInstruction* would have its origins in one of the groups that provided the background for the Essene movement, and which used the *Enoch* literature and possibly authored parts of it. Tentatively, I would date the composition of *4QInstruction* to somewhere between 160 and 130 BCE. The discourse in 4Q418 frag. 69 draws upon the *Epistle of Enoch*. This fact supports a date for the origin of the *Epistle* in the first half of the second century BCE rather than in the second half.[12]

The admonitions presuppose life in a regular society where they also deal with outsiders, although the addressee is related to some kind of community. He has knowledge of the community's interpretation of the Scriptures and God's mysteries, and is exhorted to continue his meditation and study. The work does not reflect a hierarchically structured community like the *yaḥad*.

The author/redactor seems to be a lay teacher who addresses 'the enlightened', the members of his community. His advices are related to the everyday life-situations of his readers, to the challenges posed by family life, business matters, finances and job relations. At the same time, he is preoccupied with eschatological issues: the hope of the righteous and his knowledge of the secrets of God are to provide perspective for his everyday situation, and he needs to be reminded of this. Although *4QInstruction* is a literary product, the book reflects the experience of a teacher relating to a specific audience. The active use of a

12. Cf. G.W.E. Nickelsburg, 'Enoch, First Book of', *ABD* II, pp. 508-16. The Epistle was probably composed in pre-Essene circles slightly before the middle of the century: G.W.E. Nickelsburg, 'The Epistle of Enoch and the Qumran Literature', *JJS* 33 (1982), pp. 333-48; *idem*, '*1 Enoch* and Qumran Origins: The State of the Question and some Prospects for Answers', *SBLSP* (1986), pp. 34-60; J.C. VanderKam, *Enoch and the Growth of an Apocalyptical Tradition* (Washington: Catholic Biblical Association, 1984), pp. 142-49; J.J. Collins, *The Apocalyptic Imagination: An Introduction to the Jewish Matrix of Christianity* (New York: Crossroad, 1984), pp. 52-53; *idem*, 'Wisdom, Apocalypticism, and Generic Compatibility', in L. Perdue, B.B. Scott and W.J. Wiseman (eds.), *In Search of Wisdom* (Louisville: John Knox Press, 1993), pp. 65-85. A later dating of the *Epistle of Enoch* is still held by Koch (the time of Hyrcanus): K. Koch, 'Sabbatstruktur der Geschichte: Die sogenannte Zehn-Wochen-Apokalypse (I Hen 93.1-10 91.11-17) und das Ringen um die alttestamentlichen Chronologien im späten Israelitentum', *ZAW* 95 (1983), pp. 403-30.

wide range of literary traditions points to scribal circles as the milieu of origin.

2. *The Lot of the Elect and the Remnant Community*

In *4QInstruction*, revelation is connected to the elect community, 'the spiritual people' (4Q417 2.1.18, see below). The individual member is partaker of the eschatological gifts of God and has been revealed His mysteries. An investigation of the theology of the community and the state of the elect reveal further 'sectarian' characteristics of this book.

The idea of the community as the true remnant of Israel is especially prominent in 4Q418 frag. 81. I will discuss this passage, which was located somewhat after the middle of the 4Q418a scroll, in more detail. Parallels with sectarian literature will be noted.

Fragment 81 preserves almost a full column of text. Its 20 lines preserve the full height of the column; lines 1-14 are discussed below. This text stands out among the preserved parts of *4QInstruction* with its lofty, poetic language. The main themes, the remnant community and the spiritual inheritance of the elect, are described in different ways. Phrases and sub-themes are frequently repeated.[13] The passage represents a radical reinterpretation of the Solomon tradition. Close parallels to Solomon's prayer and God's promise to him in 1 Kgs 3.6-14 can be observed,[14] which indicates that the wisdom that God gave Solomon

---

13. The root קדש is represented in lines 1, 4 (3x), 11, 12 (2x); המשילכה 'He gave you authority' in lines 3, 9, 15; separation (נזר, בדל) from flesh (רוח בשר, תעבות נפש) in lines 1, 2 (2x); inheritance (נחלה, ירש) in lines 3 (4x), 11, 14; wisdom phrases (שכל, לקח, חכמי לב, חכמה, בין) in lines 9, 15 (2x), 17 (2x), 18, 19, 20 (2x); the elect community (מטעת עולם, אנשי רצון) in lines 10, 13; the fountain image (מקור) in lines 1 (2x), 12; God's creation and preordination in lines 2, 20. The inheritance of the elect is described with the words כבוד (l. 5); בכור (l. 5); טוב (l. 6 [twice], l. 19).

14. Cf. the following phrases which recur in 4Q418 81: 1 Kgs 3.6 חסד גדול (2x)—line 8 ובחסד וברחמים; 1 Kgs 3.9 להבין בין־טוב לרע—a theme recurring in *4QInstruction*, 4Q417 2.1.10, 4Q418 2.7, 4Q423 1-2.7; 1 Kgs 3.9, 11, 12 להבין, משפט, לב שמע לשפט—line 15 ואתה מבין; line 18 ואז תבין; 1 Kgs 3.9, 11 נבון, הבין; 1 Kgs 3.12 לב חכם ונבון—line 20 וכול—line 7 דרוש משפטיו הבין לשמע; 1 Kgs 3.13 וכבודכה הרבה מאדה—line 5 נתתי לך גם־עשר גם־כבוד; חכמי לב השכלו; 1 Kgs 3.13 תמלא ושבעתה ברוב טוב—line 19 וטובתי לכה אתן ואתה {ל}הלוא לכה טובו line 6; כול שומרי דברו וקו]מי חוקיו—line 8 ואם תלך בדרכי לשמר חקי ומצותי 1 Kgs 3.14; ובאמונתו הלך תמוד line 6; line 14 יתהלכו כול נוחלי ארץ. In this context one should

(cf. 1 Kgs 3.28; 4.29; 14.17; cf. 2 Sam. 14.17, 20) now is bequeathed to the elect in the community of the eternal planting.

שפתיכה פתח מקור לברך קודשים ואתה במקור עולם הלל [ ]שׁ הבדילכה מכול   1

רוח בשר ואתה הבדל מכול אשר שנא והנזר מכול תעבות נפׁשׁ [כי]א הוא עשה כול   2

ויורישם איש נחלתו והוא חלקכה ונחלתכה בתוך בני אדם ובנחלתו המשילכה ואתה   3

בזה כבדהו בהתקדשכה לו כאשר שמכה לקדוש קודשים לכול [ ] ‏ ̊בל ובכֿוֿ‏לֿ[]לֿ[ ]   4

הפיל גורלכה וכבודכה הרבה מאדה וישימכה לו בכור ב[עצתו ה]לֿ[וא אמר לכה?]   5

מטובתי לכה אתן ואתה {ל} הלוא לכה טוֿבו ובאמונתו הלך תמיד]   6

מעשיכה ואתה דרוש משפטיו מיד כול יריבכה כול מיל̇ן והוא על כול[‏]15   7

אהבהו ובחסד {עולם} וברחֿמֿים על כול שומרי דברו וקנאת̇ [על כול שונאיהו?]   8

ואתה שכ[ל] פתח לכה ובאוצרו המשילכה ואיפת אמת פ̇[קד] לכה   9

אתכה המה ובידכה להשיב אף מאנשי רצון ולפקוד ע̇ל̇ [אנשי בליעל   10

עמכה בֿטֿרם תקח נחלתכה מידו כבד קדושיו ובט̇ [רם   11

פתח̇[מ]קֿ̇ור כול קֿדֿשים וכול הנקרא לשמו קודשי̇[ם   12

עם כול קֿ̇צים הדרי פארתו למטעת עוֿ[לם   13

[]י̇ה תבֿלֿ בֿוֿ יתהלכו כול נוחלי ארץ כי בשמ̇[ו נקראו?   14

[יהיו]

He [1]opened your lips as a fountain to bless the holy ones. And you, as an eternal fountain praise [ ].. He separated you from all [2]the spirit of flesh. <Hence> you shall separate from everyone He hates and keep apart from all abominations of the spirit. [Fo]r He made everyone [3]and bequeathed them, each man his inheritance, and He is your portion and your inheritance among the sons of men. [In] His [inhe]ritance He gave you authority. And you, [4]honour Him for that when you sanctify your-self to Him. As He set you to sanctify the holy ones for all].. and among all[ ] [5]He cast your lot and greatly increased your glory, and set you as His firstborn in[His council (?). Did He]n[ot say to you(?)] [6]'My favour I will give you'? Is not His goodness yours? <So> walk always in His faithfulness[...] [7]your deeds. And you, seek His judg-ments from the hands of all your opponents all ..[...He acts in...toward all who] [8]love Him and in mercy and kindness toward all who keep His word, but His zeal [is against all who hate Him(?)] [9]He opened for you insig[ht], gave you authority over His storehouse and determined the accurate ephah [for you ...] [10]they are with you. It is in your hands to turn aside wrath from the men of <His> favour and punish[the men of Belial(?)...] [11]with you. Before you take your portion from His hand,

note the historic allegory in *1 En.* 89.45-50 which describes Solomon as more glorious than David. This *Tendenz* points to wisdom circles as the milieu of origin.

15. The early photo PAM 40.618 shows some additional letters on the left edge of lines 7, 8 and 10.

honour His holy ones, and be[fore you...] [12]He opened[a foun]tain
<for> all the ho[ly] ones, all who by His name are called holy o[nes, ...
they will be] [13]for all the eras the splendours of His sprout, as an
[ete]rnal planting [ ] [14]...the earth, in it will walk all those who inherit
the land, for by [His] name[are they called' (4Q418 81.1-14).

Line 1: The column starts with an exhortation to praise the angels:
use your lips as a fountain of praise. The praise of the elect is described
as מקור עולם 'an everflowing fountain'. The fountain image is frequent
in the *Hodayot*: God is likened to a fountain (cf. Jer. 2.13; 17.13; Ps.
36.10), for example, 1QH[a] 1.4 כיא] אתה אלי מקור ד[עת.[16] The phrase
פתח מקור, here a perfect, is used of God opening a fountain in the
believer in 1QH[a] 2.18; 10.30; 18.10 (מק]ור פתחתה בפי עבדכה 'You
have opened a [foun]tain in the mouth of Your servant'), 12, 13. The
phrase מקור עולם is found in 1QH[a] 6.17-18; 8.8; 10. 31; 1QSb 1.3, 6.
The phrase לברך קודשים 'bless the holy ones' has the same meaning as
לקדוש קודשים in line 4 and possibly כבד קודשיו in line 11.[17]

Lines 1-2: As God separated you from the ungodly, so shall you keep
apart from them and from every abomination; הבדל מכול אשר שנא
והנזר מכול תעבות נפֹש. To separate from the ungodly is a well-known
theme in QL; cf. 1QS 1.3-4; 5.1, 10, 18; 1QH[a] 14.10-11; CD 6.14-15.
For a similar use of the root שנא, cf. 1QS 1.4, 10; 9.16. The root נזר is
frequently used in sectarian writings about separation from outsiders,
CD 6.15; 7.1; 8.8; 1QH[a] 4.19. For the phrase תעבות נפֹש, cf. 1QH[a]

---

16. Stegemann's reconstruction, quoted from S. Tanzer, 'The Sages at Qumran:
Wisdom in the Hodayot' (PhD dissertation, Harvard University, 1987), p. 28.

17. The word קדושים/קודשים is regularly used on the angels in the sectarian
writings: 1QS 11.8; 1QH[a] 3.22, 11.12; 1QM 1.16, 10.12, 12.1, 7, 15.14. Exceptions
to this rule are found in 1QM 9.8 which designates the priests as קודשים, 1QH[a]
frag. 15.7 עם רוב טוב קדושים 'with an abundance of good things the holy ones',
4QMidrEschat (4Q177) 10.2 לקד[ו]שים אשר [בא]רץ 'for the hol[y ones who are]on
e[arth'. Cf. Prov. 30.3 דעת קדשים אדע where קדשים is used on the wise ones. This
is the only place in the Bible where קודשים is used about men in a non-priestly
context. Within *4QInstruction* קדושים is used on the elect in line 12 of this text and
4Q417 2.1.19. Cf. also 1QS 5.18 which uses the term איש הקודש on the elect, and
4QMidrEschat 3.4 which designates those who can enter the eschatological temple
קדושי שם. *1 En.* 1.9; 14.23, 25 uses 'holy ones'of the angels, while 97.5 uses it on
the elect. I interpret 'bless/sanctify/honour the holy ones' in lines 1, 4 and possibly
11 as blessing the angels, not the brethren of the community. In contrast, when
קודשים appears twice in line 12 it is a designation for the members of the community, as it is in 4Q417 2.1.19 (see below).

להתקדש לכה מכול תועבות נדה 11.10-11 'that he may be holy for You with no abominable uncleanness'; 1QS 4.21 מכול תועבות שקר 'from all abomination and falsehood'; CD 7.1, 3 להזיר מן נזונות כמשפט...ולהבדל מכל הטמאות כמשפטם 'keep from fornication according to the statute... and keep apart from every uncleanness according to the statutes relating to each one'.

Lines 2-7: The Creator is the source of each man's inheritance. He has given you, one of the elect, a glorious lot and made you His first-born son. Therefore praise Him and the holy angels, walk in faithfulness toward Him and ask for His judgments.

In lines 3-5 the lot of the elect is described with the words נחלה ,ירש (3x), חלק and גורל. These words denote the spiritual-eschatological inheritance of the elect community both in QL and synagogue liturgy:[18] For ובדדכיהן יתהלכו...לפי וייורישם איש נחלתו (line 3) cf. 1QS 4.15-16 נחלת איש 'in their paths they walk...according to each man's portion'; יתהלכו...וכפי נחלת איש באמת וצדק 4.24 'they walk...according to each man's portion of truth and righteousness'.

The promise to Aaron/Levi (Num. 18.20 אני חלקך ונחלתך בתוך בני ישראל, Deut. 10.9 יהוה הוא נחלתו—their inheritance will be priestly dues instead of a piece of land), is in *4QInstruction* reinterpreted as a promise to the elect individual: 'He <=God> is your portion...'; cf. 1Q26 1.7 (=4Q423 4.3a-4) ואמר לו אני חל]קכה ונחלתכה בתוך בני אדם? 'He said to him: I will be [your po]rtion [and your inheritance among the sons of men(?)'. The circles behind *4QInstruction* interpreted Ps. 16.5-11 (v. 5 יהוה מנת־חלקי וכוסי) and 73.23-28 (v. 26 וחלקי אלהים לעולם) as promises about eternal life for the righteous.[19] In a contrasting interpretation Qoh. 5.17 and 9.9 use the same phrases to justify

---

18. M. Weinfeld, 'The Heavenly Praise in Unison', in I. Seybold (ed.), מקור חיים: *Festschrift für Georg Molin an seinem 75. Geburtstag* (Graz: Akademische Drucku. Verlaganstalt, 1983), pp. 427-37. Cf. Zech. 3.7; Mal. 2.7; Dan. 7.18. For further references in *4QInstruction*, see 4Q418 69 12-14 ובֹ]ני שמים אשר חיים עולם נחלתם...תנחלו כֹ]בֹוד ורוב הדר אתם 'the sons of heaven, whose inheritance is eternal life...also you [will inherit g]lory and abundant honour'; 4Q416 6.20 (= 4Q416 4.3) ואתה מבין שמחה בנחלת אמת 'man of understanding, rejoice in the inheritance of truth'.

19. G. von Rad has demonstrated that the late postexilic psalms 16 and 73 spiritualize the prerogative of the Levites, '"Gerechtigkeit" und "Leben" in der Kultsprache der Psalmen', *Festschrift für A. Bertholet* (Tübingen: J.C.B. Mohr, 1950), pp. 225-48.

the earthly pleasures as man's inheritance, כי הוא חלקך בחיים כי הוא חלקו.

משל in *Hip'il* is frequently used in *4QInstruction* on being in a position of authority.[20] Both in 4Q416 2.3.11-12 ובנחלת כבוד המשילכה 'He gave you authority over a glorious inheritance' and lines 3, 9, 15 of our text, the meaning of המשילכה is God setting the elect into a glorious inheritance. The word גורל is often used in sectarian writings on the lot of the elect: 1QS 2.2 אנשי גורל אל 'the men of God's lot', 11.7-8 וינחילם בגורל קדושים 'He gave them inheritance in the lot of the holy ones', 1QH[a] 11.11-12 ובגורל עם קדושיכה 'have a portion with Your holy ones'.

The state of the elect is described in the category of divine sonship: וישימכה לו בכור ב[עצתו?] (line 5) 'He set you as His firstborn in[His council(?)]'. In three cases, *4QInstruction* calls the addressee a firstborn son of God;[21] cf. 1Q26 3.2 where Milik's reading should be corrected from כי אתה לו לבן ב[כור ל]חיד to כי אתה לי לבן ב[כור, 4Q418 69.15 ואתה בן[ ]בכור.[22] The theme of divine fatherhood in the Bible and early Jewish tradition is comprehensive. *4QInstruction* is one of many compositions that draws upon the traditions about the people of Israel[23] and the anointed king/messianic figure[24] as God's son, and conveys divine sonship to the individual elect.[25] *4QInstruction* seems to be the first

20. Elgvin, 'Admonition Texts', p. 187.

21. In contrast, 4Q416 2.2.13 והיו[ת לו לבן בכור probably describes the relation to a superior.

22. The word [בכור appears on a small fragment which should be located at the lower left corner of 4Q418 frag. 69; cf. Elgvin, 'Early Essene Eschatology?

23. Exod. 4.22; Deut. 32.6; Hos. 11.1; Jer. 3.19; 31.20; Isa. 43.6-7; 64.7; Mal. 2.10; Sir. 36.14; *Jub.* 1.24; 2.20; 4Q504 (4QDibHam[a]) 1-2 recto 3.4-7; 4Q474 1-3 בן אהוב 'a beloved son', יו[כ]ח בבן יד[י?]ך 'he will adm]onish a dea[r] son'.

24. 2 Sam. 7.14; Pss. 2.7; 89.27-28; 4QFlor 1.11; 4Q246 (4QApoc ar) 2.1; *1 En.* 105.2; 4Q369 (4QPrayer of Enosh) 1.2.6; *T. Levi* 4.2.

25. Sir. 4.10, 'Be like a father to orphans, and as a husband to widows, then God will call you a son (ואל יקראך בן), show mercy and rescue you from the pit'; 23.1, 'Lord, father and master of my life'; 51.10 (Geniza version), וארומם יי אבי אתה כי אתה גבור ישעי 'I will praise the Lord "You are my Father, for You are the Mighty One of my salvation"'; 4Q372 (4QapocrJoseph[b]) 1.16, ויקרא אל אל גבור להושיעו מידם ואמר אבי ואלהי אל תעזבני ביד הגוים 'he called to God the Mighty to save him from their hands and he said, "My Father, my God, do not abondon me into the hands of the nations"'; 4Q460 5.6 (possibly a prayer of Judah or Levi), לוא אתה עזבתה לעבדכה [אבי ואדוני 'You did not abandon Your servant...My Father and my Lord'; 1QH[a] 9.35-36, כי אתה אב לכול [בני] אמתכה 'You are a

(and possibly only) source to call the elect individual a firstborn son of God. The designation בכור 'firstborn' is taken from Exod. 4.22, cf. *Jub.* 2.20.[26]

Lines 5-6: ה[ל]וא אמר לכה[?] וטובתי לכה אתן ואתה הלוא לכה טובו 'Did He]n[ot say to you (?)] 'My favour I will give you'? Is not His goodness yours?' The last (missing) part of line 5 introduced this divine promise which opens line 6. These words cannot be identified with any biblical verse; cf., however, the promise to Solomon, 1 Kgs 3.11-14.

Father for all [the sons] of Your truth', cf. 1QS 4.5, 6; 1QH[a] 4.32-33; 7.29-30; 9.35; 11.9, 11).

26. The theme of divine sonship has a continued history of reception and reinterpretation in Jewish tradition, both on Egyptian and Palestinian soil. The Egyptian sources are: Sap. Sol. 2.16-18, 'If the righteous is God's son (εἰ γάρ ἐστιν ὁ δίκαιος υἱὸς θεοῦ), he will help him and rescue him from the hand of his enemies', 5.5; *Joseph and Aseneth* has Gentiles calling Joseph 'God's son' (6.2-6) and the proselyte Aseneth becoming a 'daughter' of God (ch. 12). *T. Abr.* 12 portrays Abel 'like a son of God' (ὅμοιος υἱῷ θεοῦ) in heaven. According to Philo, God begets Isaac who consequently is a divine son of God (*On the Cherubim* 45; *On the Change of Names* 131; *On Flight and Finding* 168). Abraham is blessed by God and adopted as his only son, God is inscribed as his Father, *On Sobriety* 56-57. *Logos* is an archangel and God's firstborn, *On the Confusion of Tongues* 146. Based on Exod. 4.22, *The Prayer of Joseph* 3-8 describes Jakob-Israel as a preexistent archangel, 'commander among the sons of God', 'the firstborn of all living'.

If we turn to Palestinian sources, *T. Levi* 4.2 promises Levi 'to be a son, helper and servant before God'. *Ps.-Philo* 16.5 has the righteous sons of Korah expressing that God is their true father: 'Our father has not begotten us, but the Most Powerful has formed us. And now if we walk in his ways, we will be his sons.' Late rabbinical sources preserve a 'charismatic-mystical' tradition where individual pious miracle workers (e.g. Honi the Circledrawer, early first century BCE, Chanina ben Dosa, late first century CE) have a son-Father relation to God or are called by him, 'my son'. Ancient prayers of the Siddur address God as a merciful father (אבינו מלכנו אב הרחמן). Tannaitic sources indicate that the Pharisees adressed God as 'Father in Heaven'. In the Gospels, Jesus is portrayed as having a unique relation with his heavenly father, and he calls his disciples 'sons of your heavenly father'. *Test. Jud.* 24.1-3 speaks about the sons of Juda, the people of the Messiah 'that you might become His true sons'. *4 Ezra* 6.58 calls the people of Israel God's firstborn, 7.28-29 mentions 'my son Messiah'.

It is noteworthy that of these sources only a few use the word בכור/πρωτότοκος, 'firstborn': Exod. 4.22; *Jub.* 2.20; *The Prayer of Joseph*; 4QDibHam; *4 Ezra* (all about the people of Israel); Philo on *logos*; Ps. 89.28; 4Q369 (on the Davidic king/a messianic figure); and the New Testament (on Jesus, Lk. 2.7; Rom. 8.29; Col. 1.15, 18; Heb. 1.6; on the congregation, Heb. 12.23).

The 'favour' (טובתי) and 'goodness' (טובו) which God conveys upon the elect probably include both spiritual and material gifts.

The statement of lines 7-8, על כול] אהבהו ובחסד וברחֿמֿים על כול שומרי דברו וקנאתוֿ] על כול שונאיהוֿ? 'He acts in…toward all who] love Him and in mercy and kindness toward all who keep His word, but His zeal [is against all who hate Him(?)', is a free rendering of Exod. 20.5-6 יהוה אלהיך אל קנא פקד עון…לשנאי ועשה חסד לאלפים לאהבי ולשמרי מצותי. Although the literal meaning of the words from Exod. 20.6 is that God's mercy is over all who keep his word, our text has only the elect of the remnant community in mind.

Lines 9-11: God gave you insight, His resources are at your disposal, you can guard the community against His wrath, and protect it against the men of evil. Receive your portion and praise His angels. אנשי רצון, 'the men of <His> favour' (line 10), is a designation for the community which is under God's mercy. In sectarian writings this phrase is a technical term for the members of the community, cf. 1QH[a] 4.32-33; 11.9 בני רצונכה/רצונו, 1QS 8.6 בחירי רצון.[27] The same phrase is found in 4Q298 (4Qcr Words of a Sage to Sons of Dawn) 1.3-4 וי[ד]עים דר[ש]ו] א[לה והשיב[ו] א[נשי רצו]נו [לדרך] חיים 'And those who know have pursued these things, men of His favour have turned to the way of life'; and Lk. 2.14 ἐν ἀνθρώποις εὐδοκίας. Our text provides the first occurrence of this New Testament phrase in Hebrew.

The individual has power to protect the community against (God's) wrath, וביידכה להשיב אף מאנשי רצון ולפקוד עֿל] אנשי בליעל?. The same thought is found in 4QShir where the songs of the sage have apotropaic power: he shall make known God's splendour, 'in order to frighten and ter[rify] all the spirits of the angels of destruction and bastard spirits, demons…', 4Q510 1.4-5.[28] For the phrase להשיב אף 'turn aside wrath' cf. 1QM 3.9 לוא ישיב אפו עד כלותם 'His fury shall not end until they

27. E. Vogt, '"Peace among Men of God's Good Pleasure" Lk 2.14', in K. Stendahl (ed.), *The Scrolls and the New Testament* (New York: Crossroad, 2nd edn, 1992), pp. 114-17; G.W.E. Nickelsburg, 'The Qumranic Transformation of a Cosmological and Eschatological Tradition (1QH 4:29-40)', in J. Trebolle Barrera and L. Vegas Montaner (eds.), *Proceedings of the International Congress on the Dead Sea Scrolls, Madrid, 18-21 March 1991* (Leiden: E.J. Brill, 1992), pp. 649-59. Nickelsburg notes that both *1 En.* 1.8 and 1QH[a] 4.31 uses the terms 'mercy' and 'pleasure', and sees them dependent on a common tradition.

28. Cf. C. Newson, 'The Sage in the Literature of Qumran', in J.G. Gammie and L.G. Perdue (eds.), *The Sage in Israel and the Ancient Near East* (Winona Lake, IN: Eisenbrauns, 1990), pp. 373-82; 'The maskil is able to draw upon his

are utterly consumed'; 1QS 10.19-20 ואפי לוא אשיב מאנשי עולה 'my wrath shall not turn from the men of falsehood'.

Lines 12-14: God has established the remnant community as the promised eternal plant, the holy ones (the elect) are called by His name, He has opened a fountain of insight for them. The idea of a remnant community is frequent in *1 Enoch* and sectarian writings. It is also found in 4Q390 (4QPs.-Moses) 1.10 'But I will cause to remain from among them a remnant (והשארתי פלטים מהם), in orde[r] that they will not be an[nihil[a]ted by My wrath [and by [My] fa[ce] (being) hidden'.[29]

Line 12: וכול הנקרא לשמו קודש[י]ם. The elect are called by God's name, and thus qualified as holy. A related statement is 11Q14 (11Q-Blessings) 1-2.14 ושם קודשו נקרא עליכם. Cf. also the designation of the end-time community in 1QM 14.12 ואנו עם קודשכה; 4Q243 (4QpsDan[a] ar) 4.2 which probably should be reconstructed בעדנא] דנה יתכנשון קריאי קׄ[דישין (cf. קדי[שׁ]ין in line 4 of the same fragment) 'in]that[period] will gather those called h[oly ones'; and 4Q245 (4QpsDan[c] ar) 2.5 קׄ[דיש]א[ת]א ויתובון 'the h]oly ones, and they will return'. 4QFlor 3.4 possibly relates to the same motif: one can read כיא קדושי שם and translate 'but only those holy of (the) name/ those who are named holy' (Dupont–Sommer, Lohse, the present text adds weight to this option), or alternatively כיא קדושו שם 'for His holy ones are there' (Maier, Brooke, Dimant).[30]

The words עם כול קצים refer to the division of (salvation) history into periods, a central feature of sectarian theology, which also is related to the Enochic *Animal Apocalypse* and *Apocalypse of Weeks*.

special knowledge of the heavenly realm and by reciting its wonders offers protection to the community' (p. 381).

29. D. Dimant, 'The Seventy Weeks Chronology (Dan 9,24-27) in the Light of New Qumran Findings', in van der Woude (ed.), *The Book of Daniel in the Light of New Findings*, pp. 57-76. Dimant notes that this Moses apocryphon, written at the latest by the mid-first century BCE, combines terminology and ideas from sectarian literature (especially CD) and from the pseudepigrapha, primarily *Jubilees*.

30. In the second option the suffix of קדושו is read as plural, cf. E. Qimron, *The Hebrew of the Dead Sea Scrolls* (Atlanta, GA: Scholars Press, 1986), p. 59. On the interpretation of this phrase, see A. Steudel, *Der Midrasch zur Eschatologie aus der Qumrangemeinde (4QMidrEschat[a.b])* (Leiden: E.J. Brill, 1994), p. 43; G.J. Brooke, *Exegesis at Qumran: 4QFlorilegium in its Jewish Context* (Sheffield: Sheffield Academic Press, 1985), pp. 103-107.

4QInstruction reflects an early stage of this sectarian view of history.[31] פארה (line 13) is a 'bough, shoot, sprout' (of a tree). This line plays with the two different meanings of the root פאר, as פאר 'glory' is associated with מטעת עולם 'the eternal planting' in Isaiah 60–61. The phrase מטעת עולם is found in 1QS 8.5-6; 11.8; 1QH[a] 6.15; 8.6 (the planting concept is reflected throughout this hodayah, cf. also CD 1.7 מטעת שרש), and slightly different in the pre-sectarian *Book of Enoch: 1 En.* 10.16 (a planting of rightousness and truth); 84.6 (a planting with eternal seed); 93.5 (the planting of righteousness for ever); 93.10 (the eternal, righteous planting), cf. also *Jub.* 1.16/36.6 'a planting of righteousness'. The primary biblical source for this phrase is Isa. 60.21 ועמך כלם צדיקים לעולם יירשו ארץ נצר מטעו מעשה ידיו להתפאר, cf. also Isa. 61.3 וקרא להם אילי הצדק מטע יהוה להתפאר, and the tree of Eden in Ezekiel 31. The phrase מטעת עולם is found also in 4Q423 1–2. ובמטע...] מואס? [הרע יודע הטוב 7 'and in a planting [... rejecting(?)]the evil and knowing the good'.

A phrase similar to כול נוחלי ארץ (line 14), נוחלי אמת, is found in 4Q418 55.6. Cf. Ps. 37.11 וענוים יירשו־ארץ where the meaning of יירשו־ארץ, 'will inherit the land', is life on this side, not in the hereafter. In Isa. 60.21 the sentence צדיקים לעולם יירשו ארץ refers to the eschato-logical promise. In *1 Enoch*, QL, Matthew and the Mishnah, 'to inherit the earth' has an eschatological meaning. So also in our text, which is a promise of the world to come. Cf. *1 En.* 5.7 on the eternal life of the righteous 'for the chosen there will be light and joy and peace and they will inherit the earth'; CD 1.7-8 לירוש את ארצו 'to inherit His land'; 8.14-15 (=Deut. 9.5) לרשת את הגוים האלה 'to possess these nations'; Mt. 5.4 μακάριοι οἱ πραεῖς, ὅτι αὐτοὶ κληρονομήσουσιν τὴν γῆν 'Blessed are the meek, for they will inherit the earth'; *m. Sanh.* 10.1 כל־ישראל יש להם חלק לעולם הבא שנאמר ועמך כולם צדיקים לעולם יירשו ארץ נצר מטעי מעשה ידי להתפאר 'All Israelites have a share in the world to come, for it is written, Your people also shall be all righteous, they shall inherit the land for ever, the branch of My plant-ing, the work of My hands that I may be glorified'; *m. Kidd.* 1.10 כל־העושה מצוה אחת מטיבין לו ומאריכין לו ימיו ונוחל את־הארץ 'If a man performs but a single commandment it shall be well with him and he shall have length of days and shall inherit the land'. Also, *m. Sanh.*

---

31. Cf. esp. 4Q416 frag. 1; 4Q418 frgs. 123 (see text below); 161. See Elgvin, 'Early Essene Eschatology'.

connects the promise of inheriting the earth with the planting of Isaiah 60–61, as do lines 13-14 in our text.[32]

Similar to the Enochic books, *4QInstruction* does not ascribe to the remnant community a clearly-defined role in history as do later sectarian writings, although the designation 'eternal planting' indicates that the community is the nucleus of the future-restored Israel. In sectarian parlance, the 'planting', a tiny plant which will grow into a large tree which will cover the earth (Isa. 60.21, 61.3; Ezek. 31), refers to the group of the elect, now few, but destined to rule the world in the future.[33] The community behind *4QInstruction* sees itself as the remnant and nucleus of Israel which represents a fulfilment of the prophesies in Isaiah 59–61.[34] Similar to 4QpPs[a], it draws upon Psalm 37; Prov. 2.21-22 and passages from Trito-Isaiah for its teaching on the end-time; the ungodly will be annihilated, the pious will inherit the land.[35]

---

32. Cf. note 18.

33. 1QS 8.5-6; 11.8; CD 1.7; 1QH[a] 6.15; 8.4-26, cf. *1 En.* 10.16; 84.6; 93.5, 10; *Jub.* 1.16; 36.6. On the imagery of the eternal plant in QL and rabbinic tradition, see J. Licht, 'The Plant Eternal and the People of Divine Deliverance' (Hebrew), in C. Rabin and Y. Yadin (eds.), *Essays on the Dead Sea Scrolls in Memory of E.L. Sukenik* (Jerusalem: Hekhal ha-Sefer, 1961), pp. 1-27; D. Flusser, 'He has planted it [i.e. the Law] as eternal life in our midst' (Hebrew), *Tarbiz* 58 (1988–89), pp. 147-53; D. Dimant, 'Qumran Sectarian Literature', in M.E. Stone (ed.), *Jewish Writings of the Second Temple Period: Apochrypha, Pseudepigrapha, Qumran Sectarian Writings, Philo, Josephus* (CRINT; Assen: Van Gorcum, 1984), pp. 483-550, p. 539.

34. 4Q417 1.1.10-11 rephrases Isa. 61.3 and borrows עולם שמחת from Isa. 61.7: 'Gaze upon the mystery to come, understand the birth-times of salvation and know who will inherit glory and corruption. Will not[garland be given for their ashes] and eternal joy for their sorrow?' A similar use of this biblical verse is found in 1QH[a] 18.15. Isaiah chs. 59–61 played an important role for the sectarians, and the same is reflected in *4QInstruction*. The sectarians saw themselves as מטעת עולם 'the eternal plant' of 60.21; 61.3 (1QS 11.8; 1QH[a] 6.15; 4Q418 81.13; 4Q423 1-2.7), they are the righteous who will walk in 'eternal light' (60.20, cf. *1 En.* 92.4; 4Q418 69.14; 1QS 4.8; 1QH[a] 12.15). They are the שבי פשע 'the penitents' of 59.20 (cf. CD 2.5) who long to see 'the coming of the redeemer to Zion' (59.20). They are the עניים 'the poor ones' of 61.1 that mourned for Zion and have a glorious future (ענו and אביון are common self-designations of the sectarians, *4QInstruction* prefers אביון). Cf. N. Wieder, *The Judean Scrolls and Karaism* (London: East and West Library, 1962), pp. 125-26.

35. Cf. D. Michel, 'Weisheit und Apokalyptik', in van der Woude (ed.), *The Book of Daniel in the Light of New Findings*, pp. 413-34.

The community is not described as a spiritual temple, and one does not encounter a hierarchically-structured community. The remnant community is not connected to 'the renewed covenant' or to a specific historical situation as in CD. There are no indications that the community or the individual are connected to a specific charismatic leader.

The passage discussed above describes the elect in Solomonic and royal ('firstborn') categories. In *4QInstruction*, one encounters a 'realized eschatology' that perceives the enlightened, to whom God's mysteries have been revealed, as partaker of God's knowledge. The enlightened community shares the glory of Adam[36] and the wisdom of Solomon. 'Royal wisdom' might be a key word in *4QInstruction*'s interpretation of biblical traditions which now are related to the individual: the royal categories in which Adam is described (Genesis 1–2, Psalm 8),[37] the wisdom of David (2 Sam. 14.17, 20) and Solomon (1 Kgs 3-4), wisdom as a messianic quality (Isa. 11.2; Jer. 23.5), Wisdom regarded as royal (Prov. 8.23),[38] Wisdom bestowing upon her disciple a beautiful crown (Prov. 4.9).[39] *4QInstruction* addresses the elect, who has received royal wisdom from God, and therefore is called a

36. On Adam-traditions attributed to the elect in *4QInstruction*, see Elgvin, 'Wisdom, Revelation, and Eschatology'.

37. In the ancient Near East, the king's wisdom corresponds to the wisdom of Primeval Man: G. Widengren, 'Det sakrala kungadömet bland öst- och västsemiter', *Religion och Bibel* 2 (1943), pp. 49-75; Aa. Bentzen, *Det sakrale kongedømme: Bemærkninger i en løbende diskussion om de gammeltestamentlige salmer* (Copenhagen: Gads forlag, 1945), pp. 123-26; H. Ringgren, *Word and Wisdom: Studies in the Hypostatization of Divine Qualities and Functions of the Ancient Near East* (Lund: H. Ohlssons, 1947), p. 143.

38. Cf. H. Ringgren's translation, 'I was installed from everlasting, From the beginning, at the origin of the earth', *Word and Wisdom,* pp. 99-102, 141-43.

39. Also Ezek. 28; Prov. 8.14-16 and Sap. Sol. 4.20-24; 6.20-21 testify to a persistent Israelite belief in the connection between wisdom and royalty. Cf. N.W. Porteous, 'Royal Wisdom', in M. Noth and D.W. Thomas (eds.), *Wisdom in Israel and in the Ancient Near East* (Leiden: E.J. Brill, 1969), pp. 247-61; Ringgren, *Word and Wisdom*, pp. 141-43; I. Engnell, *Studies in Divine Kingship in the Ancient Near East* (Uppsala: Almqvist & Wiksell, 1943), pp. 25-31. The comment of J. Smith is fitting: 'Apocalypticism is Wisdom lacking a royal court and patron and therefore it surfaces during the period of Late Antiquity not as a response to religious persecution but as an expression of the trauma of the cessation of native kingship', in 'Wisdom and Apocalyptic', *Map is not Territory: Studies in the History of Religions* (Leiden: E.J. Brill, 1978), pp. 66-87 (86).

firstborn son of God.[40] It is possibly not incidental that no saying about a future messianic ruler is preserved from *4QInstruction*: it would be difficult to find a prominent place for such a figure in this democratized messianism. In traditional ancient Near Eastern wisdom, the figure of the sacred king empowered with divine wisdom played a central role. The Israelite adaptation of this motif is reshaped in *4QInstruction*.

3. *Wisdom and Revelation*

4QInstruction does not reflect the developed philosophical dualism of the Two-Spirit Treatise in 1QS 3-4 and the *War Scroll*. Dualistic concepts, however, do appear—more in the discourses than in the sections with practical admonition, cf. especially the eschatological discourse of 4Q416 frag. 1 and 4Q418 frag. 81: God has separated the elect from 'the spirit of all flesh' and given him his spiritual inheritance. Hence he shall separate from all (or: from everyone) hated by God, 4Q418 81.1-3 (see text above), cf. 1QS 1.3-11; 9.16-23. This ethical dualism is reflected in the pairs *truth and evil, wisdom and folly*: when he meditates on the mystery to be, the elect 'will know truth and evil, wisdom [and fol]ly', 4Q417 2.1.8-9. The eschatological discourse of 4Q416 frag. 1 discerns 'the sons of evil' from 'the sons of truth'. There comes a day of judgment on all iniquity, and the period of truth shall be completed. God will overcome the evil powers opposing Him. The extant fragments do not mention any demonic prince that rules the spirits of men, an idea we encounter for the first time in *Jubilees* (Belial, 1.20; Mastema, chs. 48–49) and which recurs in the sectarian writings (cf. 1QS 1.18, 23-24; 2.19 and the Two-Spirit Treatise; CD 5.18; 19.14; 1QH[a] 3.28-29; 1QM 13.4, 11-12; 18.1.[41]

40. Similar traditions are found in Sirach and Sap. Sol.: While Sirach attributes royal categories to the Torah (24.4, 11-12), he also portrays Wisdom bestowing royal ornaments upon her disciple (6.29-31; 15.5-6). According to Sap. Sol. 5.16 the righteous shall receive kingship and crown from the hand of the Lord. Cf. also Jas 1.12; Rev. 3.21.

41. Cf. Collins, 'Was the Dead Sea Sect an Apocalyptic Movement?', pp. 42-43; Dimant, 'Qumran Sectarian Literature', p. 493. If מֹמֹשֶ]לֶת רשעה is correctly reconstructed in 4Q418 212.1/4Q416 1.10, a cosmic dualism with a supernatural power of evil opposed to God is evident. The *Book of Mysteries* which is closely related to *4QInstruction*, refers to such powers: 'and all the adherents of the mysteries of evil are to be no more', 1Q27 1.1.7.

a. *Apocalyptic Motifs*

4QInstruction lacks a number of the central characteristics of apocalyptic literature,[42] and should not be counted as an apocalyptic book *per se*. The wisdom of this book is not revealed through angels or a sage from Israel's early history,[43] and the revelations are not transmitted within a narrative framework. Visions or auditions are probably not a central feature in the revelation of divine wisdom.[44] Different from Daniel, dreams and their interpretation are not mentioned at all.

Apocalyptic motifs, however, are to be found in *4QInstruction*, as in Qumran sectarian writings. Similar to the main sectarian writings, we find an eschatological understanding of history and its periods (but not a detailed apocalyptic view of history). The theme of esoteric divine wisdom revealed to the elect is central. Similar to *1 Enoch*, the reception of wisdom is constitutive of salvation and life eternal. The word pair *raz* and *galah*, frequent in Daniel, indicates some kind of esoteric

42. Stegemann characterizes apocalypses as literary works that claim to be divine revelations. He adds the following criteria: (1) the main theological *locus* of the work is presented as divinely revealed, (2) the problem of authority is solved by immediate accesss to the will of heaven; (3) the book is usually ascribed to a sage from Israel's history; (4) the contact between man and heaven is attained by vision, audition or an ascent to heaven; (5) the right understanding of what is seen or heard is provided by a heavenly mediator; (6) the heavenly knowledge is characterized as 'hidden' or 'secrets'; (7) innovative teachings deal with doctrine (calendar, dualism, determinism), the meaning of history, cosmology, angelology or future salvation; (8) revelations are transmitted within a narrative framework; (9) the apocalypses reflect specific educational levels (priests, teachers) and (10) a situation of religious crisis, (11) and have as their aim to bring divine order into a disordered world; (12) the authors viewed the writing of apocalypses as the best way of achieving their aim; Stegemann, 'Die Bedeutung der Qumranfunde für die Erforschung der Apokalyptik', in D. Hellholm (ed.), *Apocalypticism in the Mediterranean World and the Near East* (Tübingen: J.C.B. Mohr, 1983), pp. 495-530. On the characteristics of apocalypses, see also J.J. Collins, 'Introduction: Towards the Morphology of a Genre', *Semeia* 14 (1979), pp. 1-20.

43. The eschatological discourse 4Q416 frag. 1, however, states that to Noah were revealed the secrets about the endtime; 'He made known to Noah [the end] which is to come', 4Q416 1.3/4Q418 201.1, cf. *1 En.* 10.1-2. Further, לאנוש in 4Q417 2.18 can be interpreted both as 'to mankind' and 'to Enosh' (see below).

44. Cf., however, the designation of the *Book of Hagi* as הזון ההגי, 4Q417 1.1.18. Some lines below (line 24) we find the admonition כול הזון דע, but it is not clear to what kind of visions this line refers.

knowledge which cannot be attained by Israelites in general.[45] A heavenly book written in God's presence is essential for obtaining wisdom and for the right understanding of history. The composition has a hortatory character and a clear interest in the afterlife. In its understanding of world and man, *4QInstruction* is determined more by apocalypticism than by traditional Wisdom.

Nickelsburg has noted the number of apocalyptic terms in 1QS 11.3-9: 'revelation in the form of enlightening and seeing; the mystery to come; the fount of righteousness, knowledge hidden from humans; the dwelling place of glory; standing in the presence of the holy ones; the sons of heaven'.[46] All these concepts seem to be inherited from *4QInstruction*, which moulds traditional wisdom within an apocalyptic framework.[47] Also other terms from *4QInstruction* recur in this passage in 1QS 11: 'inheriting an everlasting possession', 'eternal planting'.

b. *The Mystery to Come*

The enlightened reader, to whom the end-time mysteries of God have been revealed, is repeatedly admonished to continue to reflect on these mysteries and his eschatological hope. The text achieves its persuasiveness by referring to the spiritual inheritance of the elect (through the community he has experienced God's blessings) and to the *raz nihyeh*. The author does not present his own instruction as inspired.[48] *Raz nihyeh* and the *Book of Hagi*, however, have divine origin. The addressee is exhorted to meditate on *raz nihyeh*, which must be a well-known concept for him. This meditation is likely connected to the study of both biblical and more sectarian books.

45. Also Sirach asserts that wisdom is a gift bestowed by God only on those who love him, 1.10; 39.1-8; cf. A.A. Di Lella, 'The Meaning of Wisdom in Ben Sira', in Perdue, Scott and Wiseman (eds.), *In Search of Wisdom,* pp. 133-48. The apocalyptic motifs of *4QInstruction*, however, sets it apart from Sirach. In its thinking of wisdom and revelation Sap. Sol. occupies a position between traditional wisdom and the apocalyptic writings: G.W.E. Nickelsburg, 'Wisdom and Apocalypticism in Early Judaism: Some Points for Discussion', *SBLSP* (1994), pp. 715-32.

46. Nickelsburg, 'Wisdom and Apocalypticism', p. 724.

47. Michel, 'Weisheit und Apokalyptik', pp. 413-34.

48. Cf. CD 1 and 1QS 8, which attribute revelation to the community, but do not claim themselves to be pieces of such revelation; Nickelsburg, '*1 Enoch* and Qumran Origins', pp. 342-43.

Raz nihyeh is the central theological concept in *4QInstruction*, occur-
ing 23 times. It also occurs in 4Q413,[49] 1Q/4QMyst and 1QS 11.3-4. In
the Bible, רז 'mystery' occurs only in the Aramaic part of Daniel (9
times). Six of the references connect רז with the verb גלה 'reveal': God
can reveal secrets to his elect. רז is a central phrase in the vocabulary of
the Qumran community for the mysteries or secrets of God, see, for
example, 1QH[a] 1.11; 8.5-6, 11; 9.23; 12.13, 20; רזי פלא 'wonderful
mysteries', 1QS 4.6; 9.18; 11.5; 1QH[a] 1.21; 2.13; 7.27; 11.10. It is
often used about the knowledge of God and his ways, which now is
revealed to the members of the community. רז is common in 1Q/
4QMyst (12 occurrences), and is also found in our text: 4Q417 2.1.27
כי משכיל התבונן ברזיכה 'the knowledgeable shall look into your
mysteries'; 4Q417 2.1.3, 15; 4Q418 219. 2 פלא (י)רז; 4Q418 177 7a
דע רזיו.

1QS.11.3-4 refers to *raz nihyeh*: כי ממקור דעתו פתח אורו ובנפלאותיו
הביטה עיני ואורת לבבי בר[ז] נהיה והוא עולם משען ימיני 'He let his light
shine from the source of His knowledge. My eye has beheld His wonders, and the light of my heart the mystery to come. The everlasting
Being is the support of my right hand.' Wernberg-Møller and Licht
discuss the meaning and temporal aspect of *raz nihyeh* in 1QS 11 in
light of 1QS 3.15 and CD 2.10. Wernberg-Møller translates 1QS 11.3-4
'my heart has beheld the secret of what happens and will happen for
ever'. Both he and Licht interpret רז נהיה and the following words עולם
והוא as parallel terms. *Raz nihyeh* is for Licht the mystery of the universe, the mystery that gives the rules of the universe (of what has
come into being, נהיה), and possibly the mystery of the future. The
author of 1QS knows the rules of the universe, also those secrets of
God's world which now are revealed to the community.[50] For Lange,
raz nihyeh is the pre-existent sapiential order of creation, which is

---

49. 4Q413 4-5 (emended): כאשר גלה אל [אוזן מבינים ברז נהיה 'as God opened
the ears of those who understand to the mystery to come'. The small fragment
4Q413 demonstrates many similarities to *4QInstruction*, cf. Elgvin, 'Admonition
Texts', pp. 183, 185; E. Qimron, 'A Work concerning Divine Providence: 4Q413',
in Z. Zevit, S. Gitin and M. Sokoloff (eds.), *Solving Riddles and Untying Knots:
Biblical, Epigraphic, and Semitic Studies in Honor of Jonas C. Greenfield* (Winona
Lake, IN: Eisenbrauns, 1995), pp. 191-202.

50. P. Wernberg-Møller, *The Manual of Discipline: Translated and Annotated
with an Introduction* (Leiden: E.J. Brill, 1957), pp. 38, 68, 151; J. Licht, *The Rule
Scroll: A Scroll from the Wilderness of Judaea. 1QS. 1QSa. 1QSb. Text, Introduction and Commentary* (Hebrew; Jerusalem: Bialik Institute, 1965), pp. 90, 228.

embodied in the Torah.[51] *Raz nihyeh* is found twice in 1Q/4QMyst (1Q27 1.3, 4 = 4Q300 3.4). Milik translates *raz niyheh* in 1Q26 and 1Q27 'le mystère futur', the mystery to come.[52]

The most frequent context of this phrase in *4QInstruction* is הגה/הדרוש/קח/הבט ברז נהיה 'Meditate/search/gaze into the mystery to come' (7 times), and אשר גלה (אל) אוזנכה (אוזן מבינים) ברז נהיה 'as He opened your ear (the ear of those who understand) to the mystery to come' (8 times). The enlightened shall continue to gaze into God's mysteries; יום ולילה הגה ברז נהיה ודרוש תמיד ואז תדע אמת 'Meditate day and night on the mystery to come. Search always <the Scriptures>, and then you will know truth', 4Q417 2.1.8.[53] God has revealed his secrets to the men of the community, cf. CD 3.13-14. God's revelation gives knowledge:...הבט ברז נהיה ואז תדע 'Gaze into the mystery to come, and then you will know...' The phrases ודע/ואז תדע/ואז תבין 'and then you will know/understand' recur in this context.

Milik's proposal to understand *raz nihyeh* as 'the future mystery' is attractive. The use of the phrase in *4QInstruction*, however, makes a futural meaning of *nihyeh* difficult. נהיה probably plays both on the *Nip'al* perfect (nihyah) and the participle (nihyeh) of היה. The perfect points to God's mysterious deeds in the past, the participle to the (eschatological) mystery which is coming into being, the unfolding mystery. The expression וכול נהיה עולם 'everything that ever came into being', 4Q418.69.6, clearly points to a meaning of נהיה in the past tense. 4Q298 1.3.9-10 has a similar phrase where תביטו is used for looking back into the past: בעבור תבינו בקץ עולמות ובקד[מ]וניות תביטו לדעת 'so that you understand the era of eternity and look into the things of the past, to know...' As said above, *4QInstruction* often uses

51. A. Lange, *Weisheit und Prädestination: Weisheitliche Urordnung und Prä-destination in der Textfunden von Qumran* (Leiden: E.J. Brill, 1995), pp. 45-120. For a summary, see 'Wisdom and Predestination in the Dead Sea Scrolls', *DSD* 2 (1995), pp. 340-54.

52. DJD, I, pp. 102-104.

53. For the admonition to meditate day and night on God's mysteries, cf. Josh. 1.8; Pss. 1.2; 119.55, 62, 147-48; 1QHᵃ 13.5-6. A close parallel is found in the prayer for the chatechumens in the fourth-century Apostolic Constitutions 8.2.6: 'and reveal to them the Gospel of His Messiah, give them illumination and understanding, instruct them in the knowledge of God, teach them His commands and His ordinances, implant in them His pure and saving fear, open the ears of their hearts that they may exercise themselves in His law day and night'. I am indebted to M. Weinfeld for the last reference.

this same verb, הבּיט, in connection with *raz nihyeh*. 4Q418 123.2.2-8 (see below) seems to indicate the use of נהיה as a participle.

4QInstruction takes *raz nihyeh* as a starting point for instructing the enlightened how he shall 'walk' (התחלך) in his everyday life. The analogy to a central parenetic theme in the New Testament epistles is not farfetched; 'you are called and saved/raised up with Christ, walk therefore according to your calling'.[54]

A fragmentarily-preserved passage connects *raz nihyeh* with the preordained periods of history:

קצו אשר [...] כול הנהיה בה למה היה ומה יהיה ב°[...] למבוא שנים ומוצא קצים[...]
[בי]לדה [...] ל°°[אלה]כ בכול בהביטכה מבין ו[אתה] נהיה[ברז מבינים אוזן אל גלה
[...] קצו[יהם עם מעשיכה שקול
עוו[ן ישפ]ט [...] כי מאד השמר לכה ⁹פקד

²at the coming of the years and the going of the periods [...] ³everything that is in it with what came into being and what will be [...] ⁴its period, as God opened the ear of those who understand for the mystery to be[...⁵and] you that understand when you meditate on all these things [...⁶in] her [ha]nd is balanced your deeds with [their] times[...] ⁷He will visitate upon you. So, take care, for[...⁸He will jud]ge evil [(4Q418 123.2.2-8).

This passage indicates that the word נהיה in the phrase *raz nihyeh* is a *Nip'al* participle of *haya*, as כול הנהיה (participle of *haya*) occurs in line 3 and רז נהיה in line 4. The coming and going of the day is a well-known theme in QL; cf. 1QS 10; 1QHª 12; 4QMystª 5 1-4. In this text, the same terminology is used about the passing of the periods of history. Lines 2-3 speak about what has happened and will happen within the periods of history; according to lines 4-5 the elect has been revealed these secrets of God, and is admonished to continue to meditate upon them. CD 2.7-13 speaks similarly about God's foreknowledge of the periods of history and their contents, his foreknowledge of the deeds of the unrighteous and his establishing an elect remnant to whom he reveals his truth. In lines 5-6, we encounter the preordained ways of the elect. *4QInstruction* shares the sectarian view of double predestination; cf. CD 2.7-10.

4Q417 1.1.10-12 relates *raz nihyeh* to מולדי ישע, the birth-times (origins) of salvation and to inheriting eternal glory: הבט ברז נהיה

54. Cf., e.g. Col. 3.1-17.

וקח מולדי ישע[55] ודע מי נוחל כבוד וע[ו]ל הלוא[ינתן פאר לאפריהמה] ולאבליהמה שמחת עולם 'Gaze upon the mystery to come, understand the birth-times of salvation and know who will inherit glory and corruption. Will not[a garland be given for their ashes] and eternal joy for their sorrow?' The message is: when you study God's mysterious plan of redemption, you will understand the pangs of salvation—the secrets about the endtime—and through this you will know who will inherit glory (namely, the elect) and who corruption (namely, the sons of the pit).[56] Similar passages which urge the man of understanding to meditate upon God's mysteries and through this to gain knowledge are found in 4Q417 2.1.2-8 and 4Q416 2.3.12-15.

4Q417 2.1.5-11 connects *raz nihyeh* with God's creation of woman: 'then you will see]what was and what comes into being with what[will b]e, in all [the periods of eternity...look upon]deed and d[eed, day and]night meditate on the mystery to] come, and search always. Then you will know truth and evil, wisdom [and fol]ly. Understand the deeds of men in all their ways with their destiny in all the periods of eternity and the eternal visitation. Then you will discern between [go]od and [evil in their]deed[s,] for the God of knowledge is the foundation of truth. With the mystery to come He distinguished the woman <from the man>, her deeds with their de[stinies] and for all their[,]her inclination and the reign of her deeds for a[l]l her[...]'

It follows from these passages that *raz nihyeh* is a comprehensive word for God's mysterious plan for creation and history, his plan for man and for redemption of the elect. It is 'salvation history' in a wider meaning. These mysteries are revealed to the elect. Cf. *1 En.* 93.10, where God reveals his secrets to the elect at the completion of the age of evil: 'there shall be chosen the elect ones of righteousness from the

55. The sentence ישע מולדי וקח is parallel to נהיה ברז הבט. ישע מולדי can be interpreted as 'birth-times/birth-pangs/origins of salvation'; cf. 4Q416 2.2.9 דרוש מולדיו; and 1QHᵃ 12.7-8 where עת מולדי carries the meaning 'beginnings of the set times'. On the word מולד see also DJD, I, p. 104.

56. It is tempting to connect this passage (and the concept of נהיה רז) with the role of the Teacher of Righteousness who revealed the hidden eschatological meaning of the Scriptures to the sect; cf. 1QpHab 7.1-14 (especially lines 12-14 כיא כול קצי אל יבואו לתכונם כאשר חקק לה[ם] ברזי ערמתו 'for all the periods of God will come in their order, as He ordained for them in the mysteries of His wisdom'). If *4QInstruction* is presectarian, it seems to reflect much of the 'theology of the Teacher' present in the movement *before* his appearance, cf. CD 1.11.

eternal plant of righteousness, to whom shall be given sevenfold instruction concerning all His flock'.

Lange is probably right when he sees *raz nihyeh* as the pre-existent sapiential order of creation. But his assertion that this author identifies the mystery with the Mosaic Torah cannot be upheld. *Raz nihyeh*, 'the mystery to come', should be understood against the background of the biblical and early Jewish concept of divine Wisdom, חכמה (Proverbs 1–9, see esp. Prov. 3.19; 8.23-31; Job 28, cf. Sir. 1.1-20 and 24).

The poem on Wisdom in Bar. 3.9–4.4 interprets the tradition from Proverbs, Job and Sirach. There is no agreement on the dating of this poem. Steck has recently argued that the book of Baruch is a literary unit deriving from 163–62 BCE.[57] If this controversial dating holds true, the compilation of Baruch would be very close in time to that of *4QInstruction*.

Similar to Proverbs, Baruch exhorts Israel to 'learn where knowledge is!' (3.14). Like Job 28 he states that men did not 'find the way to where she lives, or enter her treasure house' (3.15). 'No one knows the way to her, no one can discover the path she treads' (3.31). Finally he concludes not far from Sirach: God alone grasps the whole way of knowledge. He has found Wisdom and conveyed her to Israel as the book of the commandments of the Law, which can be seized and understood by the people of Israel alone (3.37–4.4). Neither the giants nor the Gentiles have grasped Wisdom, which has only been revealed to the elect people, God's beloved servant. Through the Torah, Israel knows Lady Wisdom. Unlike Sirach, Baruch does not see Wisdom as penetrating the world and ruling the peoples. Wisdom is, however, related to the omnipresent ways of the Creator (3.29-35). But Harrelson overstates his case when he asserts that in this poem 'Torah arises out of the

---

57. O.H. Steck, *Das apokryphe Baruchbuch: Studien zu Rezeption und Konzentration 'kanonischer' Überlieferung* (Göttingen: Vandenhoeck & Ruprecht, 1993), pp. 253-303. Most modern scholars place the redaction of Baruch and the origin of this poem in the late second or the first century BCE (after Sirach, but before the Wisdom of Solomon), without drawing so precise conclusions as Steck: D.G. Burke, *The Poetry of Baruch: A Reconstruction and Analysis of the Original Hebrew Text of Baruch 3.9–5.9* (Chico, CA: Scholars Press, 1982), pp. 26-32; W. Harrelson, 'Wisdom Hidden and Revealed according to Baruch (Baruch 3.9–4.4)', in E. Ulrich, J.W. Wright, R.P. Carroll and P.R. Davies (eds.), *Priests, Prophets and Scribes* (Sheffield: Sheffield Academic Press, 1992), pp. 158-71; cf. Steck, *Das apokryphe Baruchbuch*, pp. 285-303.

mystery of Creation itself'.[58] The connection of Wisdom and Torah in Sirach and Baruch draws upon Deut. 4.6-8, which equates wisdom and understanding with the commandments of the Law.[59] The Law gives Israel a wisdom higher than that of the Gentiles.

The apocalyptic streams from *1 Enoch* onwards interpret and transform the tradition of divine wisdom. Seen in eschatological light, the statements of Job. 28.20-21 that wisdom 'is hidden (נעלמה) and concealed (נסתרה) from the eyes of every living thing', and Deut. 29.28 'the hidden things (הנסתרות) belong to the Lord our God, but the revealed things (הנגלות) belong to us', are not sufficient any more.[60] The secrets of God are not revealed to all Israel through the Torah. These secrets were given to the sages of early biblical history, and are again revealed to the elect of the end-time community: at the completion of the seventh week 'there shall be elected the elect ones of righteousness from the eternal plant of righteousness, to whom shall be given sevenfold instruction concerning all his flock' (*1 En.* 93.10). The expectation of the approaching end and the perception of Israel, in general, as disobedient caused the apocalyptic circles to reinterpret biblical promises about God's end-time renewal of his people: the promised renewal will be for the elect circles only (= the 'remnant' of the prophets, Mic. 4.7; 5.6-7; Jer. 23.3; 31.7). These promises were connected to the traditions about divine wisdom. The Wisdom from on high (which was described in Proverbs and Job) is now revealed to the elect ones. Therefore *4QInstruction* can view the wisdom of Adam before he sinned as well as the wisdom that God gave Solomon as *typoi* of the eschatological gift of understanding which is conveyed to the elect. The connection between

---

58. Harrington, 'Wisdom Hidden and Revealed', p. 159.

59. M. Küchler, *Frühjüdische Weisheitstraditionen* (Göttingen: Vandenhoeck & Ruprecht, 1979), pp. 36-37; M. Hengel, *Judentum und Hellenismus* (Tübingen: J.C.B. Mohr, 1969), pp. 275-92.

60. According to (the unemended text of) Job 4.12-20; 5.1, 8; 6.10; 15.2-16, Job has received supernatural revelation from 'holy beings' (angels). For the correct interpretation of these verses, see H. Torczyner, *Das Buch Hiob* (Vienna: R. Lövit Verlag, 1920); H.L. Ginsberg, 'Job the Patient and the Impatient', *SVT* 17 (1968), pp. 87-111; M. Weinfeld, '"Reed-wall! hear me"—Leak of Information from the Divine Council', *Beer-Sheva* III: *Linguistic Studies in Memory of Moshe Held* (Hebrew; Beersheva: University of Ben Gurion; Jerusalem: Magnes Press, 1988), pp. 63-68.

the revelation of divine mysteries and salvation is an important *novum* by the apocalyptists.[61]

The *Epistle of Enoch* is a main source for the compiler of *4QInstruction*. *Raz nihyeh*, the central revelatory concept in this composition, is identical with the 'sevenfold instruction' which will be given to the righteous elect from the eternal plant of righteousness; *1 En.* 93.10. The designation of the sevenfold instruction = divine wisdom as '*raz*' or '*raz nihyeh*' could be an innovation by our author. The word *raz*, 'mystery', enters the Jewish and apocalyptic tradition through the book of Daniel (cf. the use of *raz* in Sir. 8.18 and 12.11 רז כמגלה). Our author could be influenced directly by the use of *raz* in Daniel; alternatively, both books could derive from related circles which characterized divine mysteries with this Aramaic word.

In my view, *4QInstruction* is one of the main sources for the theology of revelation of the Qumran covenanters.[62] *4QInstruction* characterizes God's secrets as 'the hidden things of His thought', which are revealed to the elect which has proper understanding; ובכושר מבינות נודֹ[ע נס]תֹרי מחשבתו, 4Q417 2.1.13-14 (see context below). Sectarian writings use the same terminology: CD 3.13-14 לגלות להם נסתרות, 1QS 5.11 לדעת את הנסתרות, 5Q513 (5QSectarian Rule) 1.11 להו]דֹ֯יע נסתר]ות. In the sectarian view, the Bible contained both 'clear laws' (נגלות) and 'hidden laws' (נסתרות). The latter could be discovered through the covenanters' careful searching in the Scriptures. According to Qimron and Strugnell, הבין נסתרות (cf. the word מבינות in this context in *4QInstruction*) means to understand God's secrets through the study of Scripture.[63] I think that the sectarian 'understanding of the hidden things' goes beyond inspired biblical exegesis. This concept included the esoteric understanding of the times, the knowledge that one lives in the days of the end-time, as well as access to esoteric books like the Hagi.

61. I. Gruenwald, *Apocalyptic and Merkavah Mysticism* (Leiden: E.J. Brill, 1980), pp. 3-28.
62. The pre-sectarian hymn 11QPs[a] 154 refers to the revelation of God's wisdom in a less sectarian fashion; כי להודיע כבוד יהוה נתנה חוכמה ולספר רוב מעשיו נודעה לאדם 'For to make known the glory of the Lord is Wisdom given, and for recounting His many deeds she is revealed to man' (11QPs[a] 154.5-6).
63. DJD, X, p. 132.

The word רז only occurs a few times in talmudic literature,[64] and seems to have been censored by the rabbis because of its sectarian and apocalyptic connotations. In contrast to the admonition to meditate on the hidden mysteries, rabbinic literature warns against engaging in such speculations.[65]

3. *The Book of Torah and the Book of Hagi*

A lengthy discourse on the meditation on God's mysteries is located in the middle of the book (4Q417 2.1.13-21). This passage is crucial for grasping the author's thinking about revelation.

ובכושר מבינות נוד[ע נס]תרי	13
מחשבתו עם התהלכ[ו] ת[מ]י[ם בכול מ[ע]שיו אלה שחר תמיד והתבונן [בכו]ל	14
תוצאותהמה ואז תדע בכבוד ע[ו]לם ע[ם רזי פלאו וגבורות מעשיו ואתה	15
מבין רוש פעלתכה בזכרון הע[ת] כ[י] בא חרות ה"חוק{"חוק}ים} וחקוק כול הפקודה	16
כי חרות מחוקק לאל על כול עול[ת] בני שית וספר זכרון כתוב לפניו	17
לשמרי דברו והואה חזון ההג' וספר זכרון וינחילה לאנוש עם עם רוח כ[י]א	18
כתבנית קדושים יצרו ועוד לוא נתן הגוי לרוח בשר כי לא ידע בין	19
[ט]ו[ב] לרע כמשפט [ר]וחו *vacat* ואתה בן מבין הבט *vac* ברז נהיה ודע	20
[בנחל]ת כול חי והתהלכו בפקודת[ה] מ[עשי א][ל]	21

[13]...and in a proper understanding he will kn[ow the hid]den things [14]of His thought when he walks in [p]erfecti[on in all]his d[ee]ds. Seek

64. One occurrence is the late text Pirqe Avot 6.1 ומגלין לו רזי תורה 'the secrets of Torah are revealed to him'. I am indebted to B.Z. Wacholder for this observation.

65. *m. Hagigah* 2.1 'The forbidden degrees may not be expounded before three persons, nor the story of creation before two, nor the chariot before one alone, unless he is a sage that understands of his own knowledge. Whosoever gives his mind to four things it were better for him if he had not come into the world—what is above? what is beneath? what was beforetime? and what will be hereafter', *b. Hagigah* 11b; *y. Hagigah* 2.1. See S.E. Loewenstam, 'On an Alleged Gnostic Element in Mishnah Hagigah 2.1', in M. Haran (ed.), *J. Kaufmann Festschrift* (Hebrew; Jerusalem: Magnes Press, 1960), pp. 112-21. We note that the mishnah uses the words חכם ומבין מדעתו היה for those who are allowed to discuss lofty matters in private. The root *byn* which implies contemplating and revealing mysteries (cf. Dan. 9.2 בינתי בספרים) is common in *4QInstruction*: מבין is the designation for the enlightened addresssee; he is admonished to contemplate (התבונן) on *raz nihyeh*, his understanding is designated מבינה, מבינות and נבונות. Cf. M. Weinfeld, 'You Will Find Favour...in the Sight of God and Man (Proverbs 3.4): The History of an Idea', *EI* 16 (1982), pp. 93-99 (Hebrew).

them always, and look [at al]l [15]their outcome. Then you will have
knowledge of [eterna]l glory [wi]th the mysteries of His wonder and
His mighty deeds. And you, [16]understand the poverty of your deed
when you remember the ti[me. For] the engraved law has come,
inscribed is every commandment,[66] [17]for the engraved is decreed by
God for all the iniquity(?) of the sons of perdition. And the Book of
Memory was written before Him [18]for those who keep His word. It is
the Vision of Hagi and a Book of Memory. He gave it as inheritance to
man with a spiritual people, for He fashioned it as a [19]model for the holy
ones. He had not before given Hagi to the spirit of flesh, for he could
not discern between [20][goo]d and evil with the judgment of his [sp]irit.
And you, a disciple of a man of understanding, gaze on the mystery to
come, learn [21][the inheritan]ce of all living, that they should walk
according to the visitation of the dee[ds of G]od[(4Q417 2.1.11-18).

Lines 14-16: meditate on the deeds of God and their consequences,[67]
remember that you live in the end-time. 'Then you will have knowledge of [everlasti]ng glory [wi]th the mysteries of His wonder':
already now the elect will know eternal glory, a good example of a
realized eschatology. The phrase כבוד עולם (line 15) occurs also in
1QH[a] 13.6, where it refers to God's glory from eternal time. In our text,
כבוד עולם refers to the future bliss, of which the elect has already got a
taste. The phrase רזי פלא (line 15) occurs in CD 3.18, 1QS 9.18, 1QH[a]
2.13, 4.27-28.

Lines 16-20: the mention of the (present) eschatological time, בזכרון
הْעֵֽ]ת, leads over to a passage on the *Book of Law* and the *Book of Hagi*.
In contrast to Wacholder and Abegg, I see these as two separate books.
According to lines 16-17, the law (of Moses) has been engraved[68] and

66. פקודה can be translated 'commandment', 'visitation', or 'destiny'.
67. תוצא[ותמה could mean 'their origin' or 'their consequences/outcome'. In
BH תוצאות means 'exits', 'deliverances' and more frequently 'end-points of a
bordering line'. In QL the word occurs only in the sapiential material: twice in the
Book of Mysteries; 1QMyst 1.1.12=4QMyst[a] 1.4; 4QMyst[a] 1.7 (where Schiffman
translates תו]צאותם 'that which results from them', DJD XX, p. 36); 4Q426 7.1;
twice in 4Q420/421 (4QWays of Righteousness, 4Q421 1.2.15, 3.1); and our text
which is the only case where the context for the word is preserved. Here תו]צאותמה
refer to God's mysteries. The addressee is admonished to meditate on these
mysteries and reflect on 'their outcome', what derives from them. The word
probably carries the same meaning in the other sapiential works.
68. The phrase חוק חרות appears three times in 1QS 10. Further, 1QH[a] 1.23-
24 uses many of the phrases of lines 16-17 in a somewhat different context:

given to all the people of Israel, revealing their iniquity.[69] The author contrasts the Mosaic Torah which was *engraved* (חרות, cf. Exod. 32.16) by God for all the iniquity of the sons of perdition, with the heavenly *Book of Hagi* (= the *Book of Memory*)[70] which was *written* in God's presence and revealed only to the elect.[71]

The elect, 'those who keep His word', are a 'spiritual people'[72] (line 18), and qualified as 'holy ones' (line 19). God fashioned the *Book of Hagi* as a model for the life of the elect (for תבנית as 'image/model' cf. Exod. 29.9, 40; 4Q286 1.2.6; 4Q301 2.5), it is instruction for the members of the community.

The passage on the Hagi is followed by an exhortation to the knowledgeable man (lines 20-29): he shall study God's mysteries (probably including a study of the Hagi) and their relevance for all the living. He shall 'know every vision' and keep away from evil.

חקוק לפניכה בחרת זכרון לכול קצי נצה הכול 'all things are graven before You with a stylus of remembrance for everlasting ages': the deeds of men as well as the appointed times of the years in history are engraved before God with the graving-tool of remembrance. The similarity of the phrases indicates a common milieu of origin or some kind of dependency between these texts. Cf. also 1QM 12.2-3 on the book of names (of the angels as well as the elect?) and God who engraves the favours of His blessings with the graving-tool of life (חרט חיים). Two further sectarian texts deal with the periods of history which will come as God has decided, 1QpHab 7.13-14 קץ לקצו והוא חרות על; 4Q180 1.3 כאשר חקק לה[ם] ברזי ערמתו לוחות.

69. If the reading עוֹלָה is correct, the Law is seen as revealing the sin of the people of Israel (=the sons of perdition) in general; cf. Rom. 4.15; 5.20; Gal. 3.

70. For the designation the *Book of Memory*, cf. Mal. 3.16 about the book written in heaven: ויכתב ספר זכרון לפניו ליראי יהוה. In Malachi the book of memory was written about (l^e) those fearing the Lord. In our text the same preposition l^e means either 'for those who keep His word' or 'regarding those who keep His word'. In the first case the elect are the recipients of the *Book of Hagi*, in the second case the Hagi refers to them, the future remnant.

71. Cf. the two contrasting *nomoi* in Rom. 8.2, the lifegiving *nomos* of the spirit and the *nomos* of sin and death.

72. Lange's proposal, that עם רוח 'a spiritual people' in Qumran should designate primeval angels, is not convincing. In *4QInstruction* רוח usually has the meaning 'human spirit/mind', 4Q416 2.2.6 speaks of רוח קודשכה (the only possible use of רוח for angels is 4Q418 76.3 וֹרוחי קודשׁ[). For related expressions cf. 4Q372 (4QapocrJoseph^b) 13.2 [°מ רוח עמי אֶת[; 11QMelch 2.25 משיח הרו[ח 'the one anointed with the spirit'; 4Q270 (4QD^e) 9.2.14 משיחי רוח הקדש 'those anointed with the spirit of holiness'. It is likely that עם רוח has the same meaning as אל עם and (כה)עם קודש in 1QM 1.5; 12.1; 14.12.

Lines 16-20 are open to contrasting interpretations: according to
Wacholder's understanding of this passage, the heavenly *Book of Hagi*
(= the engraved law, lines 16-17) was given to the sage Seth and by
him to Enosh who kept it secret (understanding in line 16 'He <= Seth>
bequeathed it to Enosh'). In the present time, the Hagi can be studied
by the members of the Qumran sect.[73]

Lange understands this passage somewhat differently: the sons of
Seth are the evil generation, contemporary with the righteous Enosh.[74]
The 'spiritual people', 'the holy ones' and 'those who keep His word'
are designations for angels. The *Book of Hagi*, a heavenly book first
revealed to Enosh (and now transmitted to the teacher of *4QInstruc-
tion*), embodies the sapiential order of creation (*raz nihyeh*) and refers
to a pre-existent heavenly form of the Torah. The passage merges the
Mosaic Torah ('the engraved law') with the pre-existent divine order
described in the heavenly *Book of Hagi*, similar to *Ber. R.* 1.1.[75]

As argued above, it gives more sense to see in this passage a contrast
between the Mosaic Torah, which was '*engraved* by God for all the
iniquity of the sons of perdition', and that of the heavenly *Book of
Hagi*, which was *written* in God's presence and given as an eschatological inheritance only to the spiritual community of the last days. The
phrase, 'the holy ones' is here (as in 4Q418 81.12, see text above) a
designation for the members of the community, as is 'those who keep
His word'.[76] בני שית are the evil generations of past and present.[77] אנוש

73. *A Preliminary Edition, Fascicle Two*, p. xiii.

74. Support for this interpretation can be found in early traditions about the
wicked contemporaries of Enosh; *Ber. R.* 2.3; 5.1, 5; 23.6-7; *Lev. R.* 23.3; *Num. R.*
5.3; *Tanḥ Ber.* 26; *Mek. Bahodesh* 6.34; *3 En.* 3–8. See L. Ginzberg, *The Legends
of the Jews* (Philadelphia: Jewish Publication Society, 1968), I, pp. 122-24, V,
pp. 150-57.

75. Lange, *Weisheit und Prädestination,* p. 89: 'Inhalt dieses Buches ist die
präexistente Ordnung von Sein und Welt, welche die Schöpfungsordnung, die
Aufteilung der Wirklichkeit in Gut und Böse, Weisheit und Torheit, Wahrheit und
Frevel, Geist des Fleisches und Volk des Geistes und die sich in der Thora
artikulierende ethische Ordnung der Welt <= raz nihyeh> enthält'.

76. Lange's proposal, that שמרי דברו 'those who keep His word' are primeval
angels, is difficult. In 4Q418 81.8 our author uses the same phrase on the elect
(= שמרי מצותי of Exod. 20.6, see text above). *4QInstruction* calls the angels שמים
בני (and in the hymnic context of 4Q418 81, קודשים, see above).

77. בני שית should probably be interpreted as 'the sons of perdition', not as 'the
sons of (the sage) Seth'. Cf. Num. 24.17 (quoted in 4QTest 1.13); the star of Jacob

should be translated as 'man/mankind', as regularly in QL.[78] The sentence וינחילה לאנוש refers to God's bequeathing the Hagi and eschatological salvation to the elect community,[79] not to the sage Enosh (as in the interpretation of Wacholder and Lange).

The *Book of Hagi* is known from two early sectarian works: CD 10.6, 13.2, 14.7-8 decree that both the ten judges of the community and the priest of the *minyan* shall know this book well, מבונן בספר ההגי. 1QSa

---

will crush the skulls of כל־בני־שת, which in the biblical text must mean a neighbouring tribe, and Lam. 3.47 where שאת carries the meaning 'perdition'. CD 8.18-20 interpretes Num. 24.17 on the Interpreter of the Law and the Prince of the Community, when the latter arises he will crush all the sons of Seth. It is likely that both CD 7 and our text interpreted שת of Num. 24.17 in light of Lam. 3.47 and saw 'the sons of Seth' as a synonym for 'the sons of iniquity'. The proposal that the Law (or the heavenly book) was concerned only with the sins of the primeval generation of Enosh instead of the ungodly in general, is not convincing. The word before בני שית is partly erased, but can be read as עַוְלָת 'iniquity'. If this reading is correct, the Law is seen as revealing the sin of the people of Israel in general; cf. Rom 4.15; 5.20; Gal. 3.

78. אנוש always carries the meaning 'man/mankind' where it occurs in QL, although the sage Enosh must have been mentioned in a lacuna in 4Q369 (4QPrayer of Enosh). אנוש occurs three more times in *4QInstruction*, always with the meaning 'man': 4Q418 55.11 הכאנוש הם כי יעצל ובן אדם כי ידמה 'Are they <not> like men—for he is lazy, and <like> a son of man—for he is silent?'; 4Q418 77.3 אדם ואז תבין במשפט אנוש ומשקל['then you will understand the judgment upon mankind and the testing of[man'; 4Q416 4.11-12 רבה קנאת אנוש 'great is the zeal of man'. Conclusive for the translation 'man' and not 'Enosh' in our text is the parallell to our passage in 1QS 11.5-6 where the secrets of God are revealed to the elect, but withhold from אנוש, mankind in general: בהוא עולם הביטה עיני תושיה אשר נסתרה מאנוש דעה ומזמת ערמה מבני אדם 'my eye has gazed on that which is eternal; on wisdom concealed from man, on knowledge and wise design <hidden> from the sons of men'.

Further, early Jewish sources that deal with the biblical sage do not view Enosh as the receiver of divine revelation: 'Enosh was viewed as an important antediluvian figure in Jewish circles, at least as far back as the second century B.C.E. In most of these sources, however, his name is only cited as part of a 'chain' of such righteous antediluvians', S.D. Fraade, *Enosh and his Generation: Pre-Israelite Hero and History in Postbiblical Interpretation* (Chico, CA: Scholars Press, 1984), p. 27. Also the immediate context speaks for the meaning 'man': the revelation to אנוש is connected to a 'spiritual people', which must refer to a community in the present, not to the age of Enosh. Both in 1QS 11 and our text the heavenly wisdom is only given to the elect community among mankind.

79. On this meaning of the root נחל see n. 18.

1.6-8 states that the members of the community shall be taught the *Book of Hagi* from their youth, as well as learning the laws of the covenant. The identity of the *Book of Hagi* has been hotly debated among scholars. It has been proposed that the *Book of Hagi* is identical with the Pentateuch[80] (or Bible), an option which should be discarded in light of this text. Other scholars have voiced the opinion that the *Book of Hagi* was the code of sectarian halakhah,[81] with the *Temple Scroll* as one option. According to our text, Hagi is a book with

80. So, recently, Schiffman and Stegemann following Wieder, Rabinowitz and Licht: L.H. Schiffman, *The Halakhah at Qumran* (Leiden: E.J. Brill, 1975), p. 44 n. 144; *idem, Law, Custom and Messianism in the Dead Sea Sect* (Hebrew; Jerusalem: Merkaz Shazar, 1993), pp. 63, 70 (on p. 158, however, he equates the *Book of Hagi* with the whole Bible); Stegemann, *Die Essener,* p. 162; Wieder, *The Judean Scrolls and Karaism,* pp. 215-51; Licht, *The Rule Scroll,* pp. 255-56; I. Rabinowitz, 'The Qumran Author's *spr hhgw/y*', *JNES* 20 (1961), pp. 109-14. Rabinowitz sees the *Book of Hagi* as 'a generic designation for all the books which were regarded by the Qumran writers as Holy Writ,' including the Pentateuch, the prophets and an unknown number of other writings (pp. 113-4). Wieder points to the use of the noun *hegeh* to signify the act of reading the Law and the *Shema',* and sees *hege* synonymous with *miqra*, 'reading', an appellation for the Bible. For him the *Book of Hagi* is the whole Bible.

81. So Ginzberg, Rabin, Goshen-Gottstein, Honeyman, Yadin, Baumgarten and Davies. L. Ginzberg, *An Unknown Jewish Sect* (New York: The Jewish Theological Seminary of America, 1976), pp. 49-50, bases his conclusion an the use of הגה for 'explaining words of Torah' in rabbinic literature: ספר ההגו' is nothing other than "the book of interpretations", that is, the authoritative interpretation of Scripture as given by our sect, accordingly a kind of "sectarian Mishnah"'. C. Rabin, *The Zadokite Documents* (Oxford: Clarendon Press, 1954), p. 50, sees Hagi as an etymological substitute for *mishnah*, and refers to *Gen. R.* 49.2, where הגא is 'working out new *halakhah*'. According to A.M. Honeyman, 'Note on a Teacher and a Book', *JJS* 4 (1953), pp. 131-32, 'it is justifiable to regard *hagu* as the type of study and exegesis characteristic of the Zadokite sectaries and to translate the title of their autoritative work as "book of expositition, study and interpretation"'; M. Goshen-Gottstein, '"Sefer-Hagu": The End of a Puzzle', *VT* 8 (1958), pp. 286-88, suggests that 'the Sefer Hahege contained basic commandments and customs of the sect'. J.M. Baumgarten, *Studies in Qumran Law* (Leiden: E.J. Brill, 1977), p. 16 n. 13, sees this book as a sectarian, written *Mishnah*; so also P.R. Davies, 'The Temple Scroll and the Damascus Document', in G.J. Brooke (ed.), *Temple Scroll Studies* (Sheffield: Sheffield Academic Press, 1989), pp. 201-10. If Stegemann is right in his suggestion that the Qumran version of CD was the final *Mishnah* of the Essenes (*Die Essener,* pp. 164-67), CD would be a natural candidate for the *Book of Hagi* for those who see the Hagi as the code of secterian halakha. Y. Yadin discusses the

instruction that ordinary man ('flesh') could not comprehend, but only 'a spiritual people'. The eschatological outpouring of the Holy Spirit in the community (cf. CD 2.13; 1Q34[bis] 3.2.5-7), promised by the biblical prophets, enables the members to comprehend the teaching of the Hagi.

I would like to suggest that the contents of this book are less halakhic and more concerned with 'salvation history', that it provides the basic keys to understand the times (cf. בזכרון הֹעֹ]ת 'when you remember the time', 4Q417 2.1.16): that the present age is the eschatological one promised in the Scriptures, and the Essene(-to-be?) congregation, the end-time community. The frequent admonition in *4QInstruction* 'to meditate (הגה) on the mystery to come' fits well with this understanding of the *Book of Hagi*. The name ספר ההגי means the book of *meditation* or *interpretation*; the book provided the right (eschatological) interpretation of the Scriptures.[82] This book was among 'the books of the sect', which, according to Josephus, every novice swore to preserve carefully (see *Wars* 2.142). Some scriptural verses possibly suggested the name ספר ההגי: Josh. 1.8, where Joshua is admonished to meditate, והגית, on 'this book of law'; Ps. 1.2 ובתורתו יהגה יומם ולילה, Ps. 77.13 והגיתי בכל־פעלך; cf. also the use of the verb in 1QH[a] 11.21. Further, the mention of the *Book of Hagi* is a strong indication of some kind of sectarian provenance for *4QInstruction*; the work could be related to the pre-sectarian community reflected in the earlier strata of CD.[83]

---

possibility that the *Temple Scroll* might be the *Book of Hagi*, without drawing clear conclusions: *The Temple Scroll* (Jerusalem: Israel Exploration Society, 1983), I, pp. 393-97.

82. Honeyman, 'Note on a Teacher and a Book', p. 132, notes that the term הגה is used only thrice in the Mishnah, and never on formal study of the law, it 'would almost appear as if the literature of normative Judaism avoided the term'. The frequent sectarian use of the word הגה both in the *Book of Hagi* and in the admonitions to meditate on God's mysteries, could explain this caution of the rabbis. An old wisdom text from the Geniza preserves the saying אשרי אדם מצא חכמה ויהגה בתורת ייי 'Blessed is the man who finds wisdom and meditates on the Torah of the Lord'.

83. Cf. Davies, *The Damascus Covenant*. P.R. Callaway, *The History of the Qumran Community: An Investigation* (Sheffield: Sheffield Academic Press, 1988), p. 98, notes that some expressions in the Laws of CD (משכיל, מושב, ספר ההגו) never occur in the Admonition. The Laws belong to an older stratum of CD than the Admonition; cf. M.A. Knibb, 'The Place of the Damascus Document', in *Methods of Investigation of the Dead Sea Scrolls* (see n.1), pp. 149-62. Knibb proposes a pre-Teacher date for the Laws, around the middle of the second century BCE. If Stegemann is correct in his understanding of 1QSa as the oldest community

According to our passage, the *Book of Hagi* is identical with the heavenly book inscribed before God. The imagery of the heavenly book, in which God has recorded the righteous (or the preordained history of the world) is an old Sumerian theme that is adopted in biblical and Jewish tradition.[84] The heavenly book of knowledge, which is only revealed to a restricted circle, is an idea found in pre-sectarian literature known in Qumran such as *1 Enoch* and *Jubilees*.

Since *4QInstruction* draws upon the Enoch tradition, the description of the heavenly tablets in *1 Enoch* might illuminate the understanding of the contents of the Hagi. On the heavenly tablets are inscribed divine mysteries (103.2 μυστήριον, 106.19 [רזי] מריא) which are revealed to Enoch; their content is predictions.[85] Apart from one occurrence in the later *Book of Similitudes* (47.3), the heavenly tablets are mentioned once in the *Animal Apocalypse* (81.1-2) and thrice in the *Apocalypse of Weeks/Epistle of Enoch* (93.2-3; 103.2-3; 106.19–107.1). In 81.1-2, the tablets contain the deeds of men until the last days; in 103.2-3, the ultimate lot of the righteous and the unjust; in 93.2-3 and 106.19–107.1, the secrets of history until the righteous remnant will arise. On this Enochic background it seems probable that the Hagi is an apocalyptic, visionary book that reveals salvation history from creation to the last days. The Hagi could in fact be a part of the *Enoch* literature; the

rule of the Essenes (*Die Essener*, pp. 159-62), we have references to the *Book of Hagi* only from the earliest strata of Essene literature. This has implications for the discussion of the origins of *4QInstruction*.

84. The most important biblical references to the heavenly book are Exod. 32.32-33; Isa. 4.3; Mal. 3.16; Pss. 69.29; 139.16; Dan. 7.10; 10.21; 12.1. From the post-biblical tradition can be mentioned *Jub.* 30.19-23; *1 En.* 47.3; 103.2; *Apoc. Zeph.* 3.15–4.13; 14.5; 4Q504 (4QDibHamᵃ) 1-2 recto 6.14 כול הכתוב בספר החיים; 1QHᵃ 1.23-24; 4Q180 3 והוא חרות על לוחות; Lk. 10.20; Phil. 4.3; Heb. 12.23; Rev. 3.5; 13.8. See G. Widengren, 'The Ascension of the Apostle and the Heavenly Book', *Acta Universitatis Upsaliensis* 7 (1950), pp. 7-115; L. Koep, *Das himmlische Buch in Antike und Christentum: Eine religionsgeschichtliche Untersuchung zur altchristlichen Bildersprache* (Bonn: P. Hanstein, 1952), pp. 3-27; F. Nötscher, 'Himmlische Bücher und Schicksalsglaube in Qumran', *RevQ* 3 (1958–59), pp. 405-11; S. Paul, 'Heavenly Tablets and the Book of Life', *JANES* 5 (1973), pp. 335-49.

85. Cf. H. Kvanvig, *Roots of Apocalyptic: The Mesopotamian Background of the Enoch Figure and the Son of Man* (Neukirchen–Vluyn: Neukirchener Verlag, 1988), pp. 76-79.

Apocalypse of Weeks and/or *Animal Apocalypse*, which both are designated as visions.[86]

I propose that the double reference to 'the Book of Hagi' and 'the laws of the covenant/the foundations of the covenant' in 1QSa 1.7 and CD 10.6 refer to two kinds of sectarian instruction: the Hagi conveys the knowledge of one's whereabouts in salvation history, while 'the laws of the covenant' refer to the halakhic rules of the Community (including, but not confined to the Mosaic law).

Apocalyptic literature often appeals to some pre-Mosaic sage as authority for the 'truths' they convey. *4QInstruction* mentions only Noah (4Q416 1.3/4Q418 201.1 'He made known to Noah [the end] which is to come')—and not Enoch—as receiver of divine revelation about the end-time, but one might conjecture that Enoch was mentioned in one of the lacunae in the eschatological discourse in 4Q416 6-8. If so, Enoch and Noah were portrayed as sages to whom were shown the mysteries of the end-times (נסתרות, רז נהיה), which now are revealed to the community of the eternal planting through the *Book of Hagi*.[87]

4. *Eschatology*

In its apocalyptic eschatology, *4QInstruction* is a close relative of *1 Enoch*, *Jubilees* and the main sectarian writings, and it differs from a

---

86. 11Q14 (11QSerekh hamilhama) 5.1 refers to the *Book of Hagi*; משפ[טי הגוי הנב[ונים]? 'the command]ments of Haguy, the discer[ning ones(?)'. So does 4Q491 (4QM^a) 11.1.21]ה[שמיעו בהגיא רנה 'M]ake heard the Hagi, delight'. Cf. M.G. Abegg, '4Q471: A Case of Mistaken Identity?', in C. Reeves and J. Kampen (eds.), *Pursuing the Text* (Festschrift B.Z. Wacholder; Sheffield: Sheffield Academic Press, 1994), pp. 136-47. S. Ballaban has called attention to a reference to the Hagi in a mediaeval manuscript (see 'The Enigma of the Lost Second Temple Literature: Routes of Discovery' [Phd dissertation, Hebrew Union College], pp. 134-41). This text, which shows signs of rabbinic reworking, has apparent links to QL. The superscription סודות הללו נעתקו מספר הגו 'These secrets have been copied from the Book of Hagu' introduces a messianic chronology based on Dan. 12 and other Scriptures. This reference supports the understanding of the Hagi proposed here.

87. According to *1 En.* 82.1 and 92.1 (4QEn^g ar 1.2.22) Enoch transmitted the books of knowledge to Methuselah. *Jub.* 7.38 records a chain of transmission from Enoch through Methuselah and Lamech to Noah. Cf. F. García Martínez, '*Qumran and Apocalyptic Studies on the Aramaic Texts from Qumran* (Leiden: E.J. Brill, 1992), p. 20. The sectarian work 5Q13 (5QSectarian Rule) mentions both Enoch (frag. 3), God's election of Noah (ובנוח רציתה, frag. 1 line 7) and the revelation of the hidden things (נסתר[ות], להו]ד'יע, frag. 1 line 11; אל [שי במעש'ב להבין, frag. 1 line 9).

more biblically-oriented restoration eschatology as represented by the *Words of the Luminaries*.[88] The eschatological understanding of history and its periods, which are among the mysteries of God revealed to the elect, unites *4QInstruction* with both *1 Enoch* and sectarian literature.[89] In the present period, God has chosen to reveal the mysteries of history and the eschaton to the elect. God's judgment will put an end to רשעה קץ 'the period of evil'.

4QInstruction has a clear conviction of the coming judgment and salvation, but there are no clear signs of a tense *Naherwartung*.[90] Similar to sectarian writings, *4QInstruction* describes the end-time judgment of the cosmos with separation between the righteous and the evil ones. The eschatological discourses in 4Q416 frag. 1 and 4Q418 frag. 69 have close parallels in 1QS 4.6-14; CD 2.5-10; 1QH^a 3.29-36; 4QAmram^f ar 1-2.2.4-10,[91] and fit Hippolytus's description of the eschatological teachings of the Essenes.[92]

---

88. Cf. Collins, 'Was the Dead Sea Sect an Apocalyptic Movement?', p. 44.

89. See esp. 4Q417 1.1.10-12; 4Q416 frag. 1; 4Q417 2.1.12-14; 4Q418 frag. 69; 4Q418 123.2.2-5. Cf. Dimant's characteristic of Qumran eschatology: 'the sequence of periods is enigmatic and mysterious, and therefore is designated by the term "the mysteries of God" (רזי אל). Only the knowledge of these mysteries enables a true understanding of the historical process, its direction and its approaching End', in 'Qumran Sectarian Literature', p. 536; S. Talmon, 'Waiting for the Messiah: The Conceptual Universe of the Qumran Covenanters', in S. Talmons, *The World of Qumran from Within* (Jerusalem: Magnes Press; Leiden: E.J. Brill, 1989), pp. 273-300.

90. The earliest Enoch literature, the *Book of Watchers* and the *Astronomical Book* as well as *Jubilees* are more concerned with the inevitability of the judgment than its proximity, while the *Epistle of Enoch* expects an imminent judgment. Cf. Collins, 'Was the Dead Sea Sect an Apocalyptic Movement?', p. 33; G.W.E. Nickelsburg, 'The Apocalyptic Construction of Reality of *1 Enoch*', in J.J. Collins and J.H. Charlesworth (eds.), *Mysteries and Revelations: Apocalyptic Studies since the Uppsala Colloquium* (Sheffield: Sheffield Academic Press, 1991), pp. 51-64.

91. This eschatological passage from 4QAmram^f ar (4Q548 frag. 1) displays 'sectarian terminology' ('sons of truth', 'sons of light', 'sons of darkness'). E. Puech, who dates the composition of the Visions of Amram to c. 200 BCE, remarks that 'the attribution of this manuscript to Visions of Amram is not certain, only probable', 'Messianism, Resurrection, and Eschatology at Qumran and in the New Testament', in Ulrich and VanderKam (eds.), *The Community of the Renewed Covenant*, pp. 235-56 (247 n. 33). If it does belong to the Visions of Amram, this manuscript could have been reworked by a sectarian writer. Judged from its sectarian vocabulary a date around 200 BCE does not seem probable. The only option

None of the eschatological passages of *4QInstruction* mentions any restoration of Zion or the people of the twelve tribes, a Davidic king or any other eschatological figure.[93] There is no eschatological war between the sons of light and the sons of darkness, as in the *War Scroll*, 4QPseudo-Daniel and 4QNew Jerusalem.[94] As in the main sectarian writings, the eschatology of *4QInstruction* is not centred around a messianic figure, but around an eschatological community; it displays a 'collective messianism'.[95]

This composition displays a *realized eschatology*: the hope for the eschaton is combined with the knowledge that salvation is a present reality, as is fellowship with God and participation in his mysteries. The elect has access to the hidden mysteries of God: when he meditates on the deeds of God and their consequenses, when he understands the times, he will have knowledge of eternal glory and God's wondrous mysteries. Salvation is present; already the elect have knowledge of eternal glory. The same consciousness of partaking of the eschatological salvation is known from major sectarian documents.[96]

would be to ascribe to this manuscript the invention of the terms 'sons of light' and 'sons of darkness', and postulate a later adoption of these terms from 4QAmram[f] ar by the sectarians.

92. *Refutatio* 22: 'They acknowledge both that the flesh will rise again, and that it will be immortal, in the same manner as the soul is already imperishable. And they maintain that the soul, when separated in the present life, (departs) into one place, which is well ventilated and lightsome, where, they say, it rests until judgment…Now they affirm that there will be both a judgment and a coflagration of the universe, and that the wicked will be eternally punished'. M. Smith noted that on this point Hippolytus's description is more 'Jewish' and probably more reliable than the parallel account in *Bellum*, 'The Description of the Essenes in Josephus and the Philosophumena', *HUCA* 29 (1958), pp. 273-313.

93. A similar eschatology can be found, e.g. in *1 En*, *T. Moses* and Sap. Sol. The related *Book of Mysteries* is more national and less sectarian than *4QInstruction*, as it refers both to a king and to the people of Israel, 4Q299 10.1-3; 11.2; 62.3; 64.1-2. The idea of the restoration of Zion is prominent in the eschatological psalms in Sir. 36.1-17; *Pss. Sol.* 11.3-8; 11QPs[a]Zion.

94. Puech, 'Messianism, Resurrection, and Eschatology', p. 247.

95. A phrase coined by A. Caquot, 'Le Messianisme Qumrânien', in M. Delcor (ed.), *Qumrân: Sa piété, sa théologie et son milieu* (Leuven: Leuven University Press, 1978), pp. 231-47 (231). Cf. Dimant, 'Qumran Sectarian Literature', p. 538.

96. Cf. H-W. Kuhn's characterization of the *Hodayot* with the words 'Enderwartung und Gegenwärtiges Heil', in *Enderwartung und gegenwärtiges Heil: Untersuchungen zu den Gemeindeliedern von Qumran mit einem Anhang über*

5. *Concluding remarks*

4QInstruction seems to have exercized considerable influence in the framing of sectarian thought and terminology, especially with regard to Essene theology relating to creation order, eschatology, the remnant community, and revelation of God's wisdom to the elect. *4QInstruction* represents a bridge between the apocalyptic *Enoch* literature and the clearly-defined sectarian community. If this preliminary conclusion is correct, Stegemann's assertion that in the early Essene community eschatology was of secondary importance compared with Torah observance can hardly be sustained.[97] The evidence of *4QInstruction* rather supports the positions held by Licht, Cross and Hengel: that the Dead Sea Community developed from the apocalyptic streams in second-century Judaism.[98]

The lack of connections between *4QInstruction* on the one hand, and MMT and priestly sectarian traditions on the other, does indicate that the sectarian movement represents a merger between two different streams: a lay community that fostered the apocalyptic and dualistic traditions of *1 Enoch* and *4QInstruction*, and a priestly group that brought with it Zadokite temple traditions and the wish to structure hierarchically the new community.[*]

Eschatologie und Gegenwart in der Verkündigung Jesu (Göttingen: Vandenhoeck & Ruprecht, 1966), and C. Newsom's comment on 1QS; 'the separation and purification characteristic of the eschatological age are already embodied in the language of the community's discourse. To speak such a language is an implicit claim to participate already in eschatological reality', in 'Apocalyptic and the Discourse of the Qumran Community', *JNES* 49 (1990), pp. 135-44 (141).

97. Stegemann, 'Die Bedeutung der Qumranfunde', p. 523. The same would be true of P.R. Davies's assertion that cosmic dualism was a secondary development of the sect well after the time of the Teacher, in 'Eschatology at Qumran', *JBL* 104 (1985), pp. 39-55.

98. J. Licht, 'The Plant Eternal'; F.M. Cross, *The Ancient Library of Qumran and Modern Biblical Studies* (Minneapolis: Fortress Press, 3rd edn, 1995), pp. 89-93, 143-70; Hengel, *Judentum und Hellenismus*, pp. 319-463. See also F. García Martínez, 'Qumran Origins and Early History: A Groningen Hypothesis', *Folio Orientalia* 25 (1988), pp. 113-36; J. Trebolle Barrera and F. García Martínez, *The People of the Dead Sea Scrolls: Their Literature, Social Organisation and Religious Beliefs* (Leiden: E.J. Brill, 1995), pp. 70-96.

*   I am indebted to the Research Council of Norway for financial support. For a fuller discussion with some revised conclusions, see my dissertation 'An Analysis of *4QInstruction*' (The Hebrew University of Jerusalem, 1997).

THE ISAIAH SCROLL AND THE COMPOSITION
OF THE BOOK OF ISAIAH

Jesper Høgenhaven

It is far from surprising that the complete Isaiah manuscript which turned up in 1947 among the original 'Dead Sea Scrolls'—the manuscript that was soon labeled 'the great Isaiah Scroll' or simply 'the Isaiah Scroll' ('1QIsa')—gained a central position in the early debate on the Qumran manuscripts and their significance for the study of Old Testament texts. Here, all of a sudden, the scholarly world was presented with a manuscript containing the well-known Hebrew text of the Book of Isaiah in a version roughly a millennium older than the familiar Massoretic text.[1] However, the esteem given to the *Isaiah Scroll* on account of its age was soon to be replaced by a rather more critical, or even sceptical, assessment of its text-critical value and importance. To gain an impression of the way scholarly attitudes to the *Isaiah Scroll* as a textual witness did indeed change in the course of the following years, one need only compare the 1951 Kittel edition of *Biblia Hebraica*, in which all significant variants in the *Scroll* are noted in a special apparatus, with the 1968 *Biblia Hebraica Stuttgartensia*, in which a rather meagre selection of *Isaiah Scroll* variants have found their modest place in the standard apparatus.[2]

A role of no small importance for this change of attitude was played by the work of Harry S. Orlinsky, who through the first half of the

---

1. There are two editions of the Isaiah scroll: M. Burrows, J.C. Trever and W.H. Brownlee, *The Dead Sea Scrolls of St. Mark's Monastery*, I (New Haven: Yale University Press, 1950), and *Scrolls from Qumran Cave. I. From photographs by J.C. Trever* (Jerusalem: Israel Exploration Society, 1972), with the original colour photos.

2. A. Alt, O. Eissfeldt and P. Kahle, *Biblia Hebraica* (Stuttgart: Deutsche Bibelgesellschaft, 7th edn, 1951), *Biblia Hebraica Stuttgartensia* (Stuttgart: Deutsche Bibelgesellschaft, 1968).

1950s published a series of articles, all marked by scholarly acuteness and solid learning.[3] In these *Studies in the St Mark's Isaiah Scroll*, as Orlinsky's articles were superscribed, he points convincingly to a number of demonstrably secondary readings in the scroll. The Isaiah manuscript soon suffered the fate of being labeled a 'vulgar text', and being vulgar is indeed no recommendation—among manuscripts at any rate. The learned world, then, came to view this manuscript as a textual witness which was unreliable in details and which was really important in an indirect manner because of its overall similarity to the Massoretic text. Through this basic similarity the scroll was seen as supporting the idea of the Massoretic text as old and reliable, while little importance was generally ascribed to its own peculiar readings.[4]

This more or less outspokenly negative attitude to the *Isaiah Scroll* among scholars is probably one of the reasons why interest in this manuscript among text historians soon seemed to diminish markedly, although the scroll had for some years been the object of intensive study and discussion. Another reason is, of course, the fact that new manuscripts were found at Qumran during the following years, increasing siginificantly the extent of Old Testament material, including manuscripts and fragments that were considered older than the *Isaiah Scroll* and which soon came to take over the central position in the debate on Qumran and textual criticism.

Any person who is genuinely interested in the specific textual character of the *Isaiah Scroll* may, however, have recourse to some of the thorough investigations that have in fact been carried out. In M. Martin's work, *The Scribal Character of the Dead Sea Scrolls*, from 1958, a great number of acute observations of the external peculiarities and orthographic practices of the original Dead Sea manuscripts, including the *Isaiah Scroll*, may be found.[5] Another thorough work dealing with the linguistic character of the Isaiah manuscript is E.Y. Kutscher's, *The Language and Linguistic Character of the Isaiah Scroll*, posthumously

3.   H.M. Orlinsky, 'Studies in the St. Mark's Isaiah Scroll', *JBL* 69 (1950), pp. 149-66; *JNES* 11 (1952), pp. 153-56; *JJS* 2 (1950–51), pp. 151-54; *JQR* 45 (1952–53), pp. 329-40; *IEJ* 4 (1954), pp. 5-8; *HUCA* 25 (1954), pp. 85-92.

4.   I have previously pointed out this tendency in my article 'The First Isaiah Scroll from Qumran (1QIsa) and the Massoretic Text: Some Reflections with Special Regard to Isaiah 1–12', *JSOT* 28 (1984), pp. 17-35.

5.   M. Martin, *The Scribal Character of the Dead Sea Scrolls*, I-II (Leuven: Peeters, 1958).

published in English in 1974.[6] Although in itself an excellent work marked by the profound learning of its author, Kutscher's book clearly betrays a certain predisposition to view the text of the *Isaiah Scroll* as representing a deviation from the standard set by the Massoretic tradition. In this sense, Kutscher's work also bears witness to the influence exercised by the 'vulgar text' label attached to the *Isaiah Scroll*. The expression 'vulgar text' is also found in the brief presentation of the scroll in E. Würthwein's manual, *Der Text des Alten Testaments*.[7] Among studies of the scroll and its character as a document, mention should also be made of Curt Kuhl's concise study published in *VT* in 1952.[8] These investigations actually form a solid basis for further study of the manuscript, although, as far as I can see, much of this study still remains to be done.

The way in which a text is divided and presented is, of course, an element of the greatest importance for the interpretation of the text involved. Dividing is, indeed, interpreting. An example of this is the suggestive, not to say seductive, manner in which the text of the Old Testament prophetic books is presented in the *BHS*. Without any support in the manuscripts on which the edition claims to be based, certain passages are here marked out as poetic and printed as short stanzas each beginning a new line, whereas other parts of the same prophetic book are presented as prose with all lines simply filled out. In some cases, parts of the same passage or, indeed, of the same verse, are marked as poetry and prose, respectively, and the text is accordingly split up. The result of all this is that the reader is left with a visual impression that seems to support a particular idea of how the text of the prophetic book came into being. This, of course, is the idea that the point of departure was the kernel of poetic utterances by the historical prophet, a kernel that was subsequently expanded by means of prose additions or frame texts. In some cases, such literary-critical theories are even expressed in the text-critical apparatus in the form of remarks like *probabiliter additum* or the like.

---

6. E.Y. Kutscher, *The Language and Linguistic Background of the Isaiah Scroll (1QIsa)* (STDJ, 6; Leiden: E.J. Brill, 1974).

7. E. Würthwein, *Der Text des Alten Testaments: Eine Einführung in die Biblia Hebraica* (Stuttgart: Mohr Siebeck, 4th edn, 1973), p. 36.

8. C. Kuhl, 'Schreibereigentümlichkeiten: Bemerkungen zur Jesajarolle', *VT* 2 (1952), pp. 307-33.

In 1953 Hans Bardtke published a study of the textual divisions in the *Isaiah Scroll*, viewing these divisions as an early stage leading to the division into *perashot* known from the Massoretic tradition.[9] The *Scroll* exhibits several ways of marking a division of the text. In some cases, a division is obtained by leaving the remaining part of a line empty at the end of a paragraph. In other cases, the division is marked only by means of a considerable space between words within the same line. And finally, the manuscript contains a number of marginal annotations in the form of various signs, some of which would seem to mark paragraphs, while others are more probably to be viewed as marking out certain parts of the text. A comparison with the italicization of certain passages, judged to be of central importance, in modern Bible editions has been suggested.

The textual division thus exhibited by the *Isaiah Scroll* has a lot in common with the division known from the Massoretic text, but there are also a number of differences. Much the same thing can be said about the *Scroll* in relation to the LXX traditon.

In this sense, the *Isaiah Scroll* is an important witness, not only through its actual variants but also through the way it presents and organizes the very text preserved in its columns, to the history of transmission of the Book of Isaiah. Furthermore, I should like to suggest that the *Isaiah Scroll* is a document of some significance, not only for the history of the text of the book of Isaiah, but also for our possible knowledge of the composition and purpose of that book. First of all, the existence of the scroll preserving the text of the entire literary unit, which we are used to calling the book of Isaiah, provides us with evidence that this text was extant as a literary unit as early as the end of the second century BCE, supposing, of course, that the current dating of the scroll is valid.[10] The manuscript does to all extents amd purposes comprise the familiar text of Isaiah, and it may thus be considered as proven that the composition of this book was concluded at the beginning of the Maccabean era. The proof for this rests not only upon the indirect witness of the LXX tradition, but also upon the direct evidence of an extant Hebrew manuscript. Certain theories of literary criticism

9.   H. Bardtke, 'Die Parascheneinteilung der Jesajarolle I von Qumran', in *Festschrift F. Dornseiff* (Leipzig, 1953), pp. 32-75.

10.   On the problems of dating the Qumran manuscripts, see the recent summary in H. Stegemann, *Die Essener, Qumran, Johannes der Täufer and Jesus: Ein Sachbuch* (Freiburg: Herder, 1994 [1993]), pp. 20-22.

relating to the book of Isaiah that have been advanced during the years can, in other words, be shown to be in the wrong.[11] The earliest extant shape of the book of Isaiah shows a literary form and extent practically identical to what is known from later manuscripts. In other words, any theory that views the book as the result of a compilation or combination of different and originally independent literary units such as First Isaiah, Second Isaiah, and, possibly, Third Isaiah, each of which is supposed to have once formed a prophetic book with a history of its own, remains purely theory which cannot be based upon external textual evidence of any sort.

It is obvious, nevertheless, to anyone studying the book of Isaiah that the structure and genre of this book presents an intricate problem. This problem is, of course, exactly what gave rise to literary-critical attempts at viewing the book as a composite unit. The questions concerning the composition, structure and literary genre of the book of Isaiah are closely related to a series of general questions concerning the Old Testament prophetic literature at large. As is a well-known fact, the question of the sort of literature we are dealing with here has reappeared on the agenda of biblical scholarship. We may, indeed, speak of a new orientation in prophetic studies, called forward by an increasing awareness of the insufficiency of traditional viewpoints, seing, basically, the prophetic writings as the products of a long process with the original prophetic proclamation as the historical starting-point, followed by a number of redactional additions and expansions.[12]

Now, as far as the book of Isaiah is concerned, the fact that the earliest extant textual witnesses, including the Hebrew text of the *Isaiah Scroll*, present us with the substantially familiar and intriguing

11. This would be true of B. Duhm's theory, which places the final redaction of Isaiah in the Hasmonean period. See B. Duhm, *Das Buch Jesaja übersetzt und erklärt* (Göttinger Handkommentar zum Alten Testament, 3.1, Göttingen: Vandenhoeck & Ruprecht, 4th edn, 1922), pp. 21-22.

12. An impression of recent tendencies in prophetic studies may be gained from H.M. Barstad, 'No Prophets?: Recent Developments in Biblical Prophetic Research and Ancient Near Eastern Prophecy', *JSOT* 57 (1993), pp. 39-60. See, also, F.E. Deist, 'The Prophets: Are We Heading for a Paradigm Switch?', in *Prophet und Prophetenbuch: Festschrift für Otto Kaiser zum 65. Geburtstag* (BZAW, 185; Berlin: W. de Gruyter, 1989), pp. 1-18, and, much more concisely, N.P. Lemche, 'The God of Hosea', in *Priests, Prophets and Scribes: Essays on the Formation and Heritage of Second Temple Judaism in Honour of Joseph Blenkinsopp* (JSOTSup, 149; Sheffield: Sheffield Academic Press, 1994), pp. 241-57.

literary structure also known from the Massoretic Bible, does lend support to the view that biblical exegesis has to take this structure seriously as a given fact. This is the literary unit with which we have to deal. We may in general terms describe the Old Testament prophetic writings, as they present themselves to us, as collections of relatively short literary units, cast more or less in poetic form, of which many—although not all—are formally characterized as divine oracles. As a rule, these collections are set within a more or less extensive narrative framework which in its shortest form only relates the name and origins of a certain prophetic figure.

This description could indeed be said to fit the book of Isaiah, but then a significant reservation would have to be made. Beginning from the section of the book which in the tradition current since the Christian Middle Ages is called chapter 40, the section that according to the historico-critical tradition forms the opening of Second Isaiah, the book of Isaiah contains not a single narrative text, properly speaking, not a single superscription connecting the text with, say, the prophet Isaiah, or with any named or unnamed prophetic figure or with any figure of real or fictive history. This is true of the *Isaiah Scroll*, of the Massoretic text and of the LXX. Though not often noted or commented upon in biblical commentaries, this is in fact one of the most conspicuous literary division markers between chs. 1–39 and 40–66. There can be no doubt at all, in other words, that a new section within the whole of the book begins with what we call ch. 40. This section is marked accordingly in the *Isaiah Scroll* both with the normal paragraph division and with a marginal sign. A similar sign is found at the beginning of ch. 36, the opening of the longest single narrative unit in the Book of Isaiah, chs. 36–39.[13]

The literary and theological genre of the book of Isaiah would seem, then, to merit renewed consideration. A few observations, mostly of a formal nature, on the text of ch. 40 may perhaps give a hint as to the direction that such considerations could possibly take. Isaiah 40 opens with words characterized as a divine oracle or as words of Yahweh

---

13. The sign in question, which looks roughly like a short horizontal line with a circle or semi-circle on top, is found at the following places: 35.10/36.1; 39.8/40.1; 41.13/41.14; 44.28/45.1; 52.6/52.7; 59.21; 60.1. In all cases it is possible to argue that the function of the sign may have been that of marking a theologically important text-division, or the beginning of a new significant section, but the original meaning of the marginal signs remains basically unknown.

(vv. 1-2), an utterance that emphasizes the contrast between a 'then' and a 'now', depicting the present as a time of consolation for the people of Yahweh or for Zion, a time of which the significance and impact is determined by the fact that the sins of Yahweh's people have been requited. Then a series of scenes follows. Without any introduction or explanation, the text presents us with the notion of a voice crying (*qol qore*), speaking of the way to be prepared for Yahweh (vv. 3-5), and subsequently we hear of a voice commanding somebody, a prophet or a receiver of revelation at any rate, to proclaim the word of God as the enduring power, as opposed to the transitoriness of man (vv. 6-8). Again the scene changes with no explanation given, and we hear the exhortation directed to Sion's herald of good tidings who is to proclaim the coming of Yahweh (vv. 9-11).

We may state the purpose or function of this section as that of characterizing the text that follows as revelatory literature. This is a rather vague term, chosen on purpose, so as not to use the term 'apocalyptic', although I believe that the opening section of Isaiah 40 would indeed come very close to fitting the formal definition of an 'apocalypse' offered by Adela Yarbro Collins in the *Anchor Bible Dictionary*. 'Apocalypse', according to Collins, may be defined as 'a genre of revelatory literature with a narrative framework, in which a revelation is mediated by an otherworldly being to a human recipient',[14] although here the narrative element is almost non-existent or implicit, and the otherworldly being is the 'voice'. Sticking, then, at least for the time being, to the notion of 'revelatory literature', we may note the widespread use in Isaiah 40–66 of the oracle form with the well-known quotation formula, and I may add that, in this section of the book, this gives the impression of being above all a literary form or a stylistic device that does not establish or seek to establish any connection between the passages marked as oracles and any 'prophetic' setting or situation such as the ones found in Isaiah 1–39 and in many other places in the Old Testament. The visionary nature of Isaiah 40 and the air of mystery and secrecy that dominates this text forces us, as already indicated, to look for parallels within apocalyptic literature. The parallel that immediately suggests itself is, of course, the book of Daniel, in

14. A.Y. Collins, 'Apocalypses and Apocalypticism', *ABD*, I, pp. 279-92 (279). Collins here quotes J.J.Collins, 'Introduction: Towards the Morphology of a Genre', in *idem* (ed.), *Apocalypse: The Morphology of a Genre, Semeia* 14 (1979), pp. 1-20 (9).

which visions of the future follow a narrative concerned with a figure from Israel's past to whom the revelations are then ascribed.

In fact, it is doubtful whether the importance of the genre of Daniel has been sufficiently appreciated and exploited as a possible model for studying the prophetic writings of the Old Testament. All critical scholars are somehow of the opinion that the book of Daniel was written to be exactly what it was always taken to be—a book of revelation ascribed to a recipient fictitiously placed in the past, and speaking with divine authority about the future; a future which, for the author and for the originally-intended readers of the book, is in fact the frightening and bewildering present.

This does not, indeed, seem very far removed from the way the prophetic writings were used and interpreted in the earliest tradition for which we possess historical knowledge. This of course takes us back again to the library of Qumran. The finding of a great number of manuscripts and fragments of prophetic writings shows how this literature was preserved and cherished by Jewish circles at that time. The exegetical works—the *pesharim*—indicate that the prophets were believed to have received revelations long ago, their words being, however, primarily if not exclusively directed to future generations. To the prophets, God had in the past revealed the secrets about the things to come. Such is the earliest interpretation of the prophetic books that can be documented. Should we perhaps not at least allow for the possibility that the perspective of their authors may actually have been more or less the same?

THE SPIRIT IN HUMAN BEINGS IN SOME QUMRAN NON-BIBLICAL TEXTS

Robert W. Kvalvaag

1. *Introduction*

The term רוּחַ is very common in Qumran sectarian literature; the most thorough study of the subject so far lists 233 occurrences of רוּחַ in the non-biblical scrolls published until 1988.[1] The term most frequently appears in the sense 'human spirit', and it therefore plays a significant role in the anthropology of the sect.[2] There are two points I want to make in this paper: first, to show that according to the sectarians, the spirit or spirits within each human being determines his or her whole existence, both within and outside the community: it reveals what kind of person one is before one enters the community, it is the decisive factor when one is about to enter the community, it is the subject of cleansing and recreation as one enters the community, and it determines one's rank within the community; and, secondly, to point out that there is not one consistent pneumatology in the Qumran sectarian literature: important texts like the *Community Rule*, on the one hand, and the *Hodayot*, on the other, describe the spirit or spirits in humans differently, each employing its own distinctive terminology and its own distinctive ideas.

2. *The Origin and Tasks of the Spirit in Human Beings*

The origin and tasks of the spirit or spirits in human beings is an important theme in both the *Community Rule* and in the *Hodayot*. As far as

---

1. A.E. Sekki, *The Meaning of ruah at Qumran* (SBLDS, 110; Atlanta, GA: Scholars Press, 1989).
2. According to Sekki, *The Meaning of ruah*, רוּחַ is found 97 times as the spirit of man, 58 times in the sense angel/demon, 35 times as the spirit of God, 27

the origin of the spirit is concerned, the *Hodayot* uses a different vocabulary from the *Two Spirit Treatise* of the *Rule* and vice versa. The *Hodayot* emphasize that God has created one spirit in each human, while basic to the *Two Spirit Treatise* are the two spirits God has designed for each human being.

a. *The Predestined Spirits in the Two Spirit Treatise*
The *Two Spirit Treatise*, 1QS 3.13–4.26, begins with the purpose of instructing the sectarians regarding the nature of all human beings.[3] The introduction to the *Two Spirit Treatise* says that 'It is for the Master to instruct and teach all the Sons of Light concerning the nature (תולדות)[4] of all the sons of man[5] with respect to all the kinds of their spirits with their distinctions[6] (לכול מיני רוחותם באותותם)', 1QS 3.13-14.[7]

According to the *Two Spirit Treatise* human beings are not controlled either by the spirit of truth or by the spirit of injustice; they are rather thought to be influenced by both spirits at the same time. The author is, in other words, aware of the necessity to explain the mixed character

times meaning wind, and then there are 16 occurrences of the term in the *Two Spirit Treatise*, 1QS 3.13–4.26.

3.   Unless otherwise indicated, the English translation of Qumran sectarian literature in this paper is taken from F. García Martínez, *The Dead Sea Scrolls Translated: The Qumran Texts in Epistles* (trans. W.G.E. Watson; Leiden: E.J. Brill, 1994).

4.   The word תולדות is sometimes tranlated 'history' in 1QS 3.13, e.g. by García Martínez, *The Dead Sea Scrolls Translated*, but this is rejected by J.H. Charlesworth, *The Dead Sea Scrolls: Hebrew, Aramaic and Greek Texts with English Translations*. I. *Rule of the Community and Related Documents* (Tübingen: J.C.B. Mohr, 1994). J.H. Charlesworth also translates תולדות as 'nature' in 1QS 4.15, 'In these [the two spirits] are the natures of all the sons of man'. The use of the word תולדות together with the word מין, 'kind' or 'species', and the reference to the purpose of the creation of humans in 1QS 3.17, suggests that there are several allusions to the creation-narrative of Gen. 1 in the first part of the *Two Spirit Treatise*, cf. M.A. Knibb, *The Qumran Community* (Cambridge Commentaries on Writings of the Jewish and Christian World 200 BC to AD 200, 2; Cambridge: Cambridge University Press, 1987), p. 96.

5.   In a note, Charlesworth, *The Dead Sea Scrolls* p. 15 n. 59, explains that כול בני איש, 'all the children of men', in this text means all humankind.

6.   García Martínez, *The Dead Sea Scrolls Translated*, translates מיני רוחותם לכול at the beginning of 3.14 as 'concerning the ranks of their spirits'.

7.   The translation of 1QS 3.13-14, is from Charlesworth, *The Dead Sea Scrolls*.

(תולדות) of human beings and in particular the admixture of evil in those who belong to the spirit of truth.[8] The nature (תולדות) of every human being is ruled by the two spirits (1QS 4.15),[9] and each human being thus belongs to both the sphere of light and the sphere of darkness by his or her very nature; the nature of humans is determined by whether a person's portion (נחלה) in the two spheres is great or small (1QS 4.16).[10] Humans are affected by different spirits, and their behaviour is determined by whichever spirit is predominant in them. There is, in other words, no clear line of demarcation between the two groups of humans. What finally resolves the fate of each human being is 'the spirit that is in him [at the time of] the visitation' (1QS 4.26).

The question of the creation of humans and the origin of the spirit is touched upon in 1QS 3.17. According to this text, God created humans to rule the world: 'He created the human for the dominion of the world, designing for him (שום לו) the two spirits,[11] in which to walk until the appointed time for his visitation, namely the spirits of truth and deceit'.

This doctrine of the two spirits in 1QS 3.13–4.26 thus involves a problem of consistency: if the two spirits are to be regarded as influencing each individual, struggling in the hearts of *each human*, 4.23, how

8.   P. Wernberg-Møller, 'A Reconsideration of the Two Spirits in the Rule of the Community', *RevQ* 11 (1961), pp. 413-41 (425), thinks that תולדות in 3.19 also should be translated 'characters, dispositions, minds', and that תולדות thus is synonymous with רוח. Most scholars disagree with Wernberg-Møller on this issue, and translate, e.g., 'fountain' (Vermes, *The Dead Sea Scrolls in English* [Sheffield: JSOT Press, 3rd edn., 1987], p. 65).

9.   That is how 1QS 4.15 is translated by Vermes. According to García Martínez, *The Dead Sea Scrolls Translated*, p. 7, 1QS 4.15 says that 'In these [the two spirits], lies the history of all men'.

10.   Several scholars have pointed out that there are interesting points of contact between Gnosticism and Qumran. The Gnostic idea of 'know your divine self' as essential to salvation is matched in Qumran by the emphasis on ignorance as man's point of departure and knowledge as the final goal. An important task for humans in this world is to find out who they really are. The lot of the sectarian 'is to search all his life, by his own action and by divine illuminating grace, in order to discover to which part he belongs, Light or Darkness', D. Dimant, 'Qumran Sectarian Literature', in M.E. Stone (ed), *Jewish Writings of the Second Temple Period* (CRINT, 2; Philadelphia: Fortress Press, 1984), p. 538.

11.   The translation is from Charlesworth, *The Dead Sea Scrolls*, p. 15. Vermes translates 'has appointed for him two spirits', instead of 'placed within him' (García Martínez, *The Dead Sea Scrolls Translated*). The Hebrew לו (not בו) seems to favour 'for' instead of 'within'.

can they simultaneously give rise to two sharply-distinguished groups of humanity?[12] However, this cosmic and psychological dualism may be understood as different aspects of the same basic dualism. This consistency is reflected in the terminology employed; the term רוּחַ designates both domains: it both denotes a cosmic entity, an angel, and a human quality, the spirit within each human being.

The implications of 1QS 4.26 are of such significance that the whole text is worth quoting. God 'has given them', that is, the two spirits, 'as a legacy to the sons of men (וינחילן לבני איש), so that they know good [and evil] (לדעת טוב [ורע]), so they decide the lot of every living being (להפיל גורלות לכול חי),[13] in compliance with the spirit there is in him [at the time] of the visitation'.

1QS 3.13–4.26 contains several references to the first chapters of Genesis. The expression 'that they know good [and evil]' in 4.26 is obviously a reference to the account of creation in the opening chapters of the Hebrew Bible, in this case to Gen. 3.5. The big difference between 1QS 4.26 and Gen. 3.5 lies in the fact that while knowledge in Gen. 3.5 is a result of the fall, knowledge of good [and evil] in 1QS 4.26 has its origin in God's creative act. The two spirits, both created by God, have been given to *all* humans, so that they may know good and evil, and that the destiny of *all* the living may be according to the spirit within them at the time of the visitation.[14] According to this text,

---

12. Cf. the comment by A.R.C. Leaney, *The Rule of Qumran and its Meaning* (NTL; London: SCM Press, 1966), p. 37: 'Perhaps there is here an example of thinking which at the logical level is confused; and the reason for this confusion is that the writer is not clear whether he wishes to teach that man as such is a combination of a good and bad spirit or that mankind is divisible into the good (arising from light) and the bad (arising from darkness)'. P. von der Osten-Sacken, *Gott und Belial* (SUNT, 6; Göttingen: Vandenhoeck & Ruprecht, 1969) tried to solve this problem by maintaining that 1QS 3.13–4.26 is not a literary unit; he found three distinct stages in its production.

13. H. Stegemann, 'Zu Textbestand und Grundgedanken von 1QS III, 13-IV, 26', *RevQ* 49–52 (1988), pp. 95-131, thinks the lacunae after טוב includes more than just ורע. Stegemann offers the following *Ergänzungsvorschlag*: 'damit sie [den Unterschied zwischen] Gut [und Böse] zu erkennen vermögen. [Denn] Go]tt selbst läßt die Lose ergehen für jeglichen Lebendigen, (טוב [ורע כיא א[ל יפיל לדעת
(גורלות לכול חי'.

14. Cf. Wernberg-Møller, 'Rule of the Community', p. 434, where he speaks of the 'universal aspect' of this text.

knowledge is not a negative consequence resulting from the fall, but attainable for all human beings because of the spirit(s) within them.[15] According to the final words of the *Treatise of the Two Spirits*, all human beings are born with a certain spiritual discernment; the decisive issue is which of the two spirits in a person is the strongest, determining his or her existence, when the determined end or renewal of creation comes.

b. *The Creation of the Spirit in the Hodayot*

The origin of the spirit is also described in several *Hodayot*. The vocabulary, however, is different from the vocabulary of the *Two Spirit Treatise*. As has been noted above, the latter text differs from the Hodayot because according to this text God has designed or appointed two spirits for every human being, while the *Hodayot* focuses upon the creation of the one spirit in humans.[16] What has traditionally been enumerated as the first *Hodaya* is a good example.[17]

The first *Hodaya* is a composition about creation. God is portrayed as creator, having a purpose for each of his creatures. He has created and ordered the universe and humankind. The creator also has a predetermined plan for his creation and for humans.[18]

1QH 1 is saturated with spirit-language: three times the creation of the spirit is mentioned, twice related to יצר, in 1QH 1.8-9 and 15, and once related to ברא, in 1.27-28. According to 1QH 1.9-10, God has

---

15. Stegemann, 'Textbestand und Grundgedanken', pp. 119-120, maintains that the *Erkenntnisfähigkeit* of all humans according to 1QS 4.26 is a kind of Qumran 'know yourself'-ability, enabling each human to understand to what kind of category, i.e. the portions of light or darkness, he or she belongs to.

16. E.H. Merrill, *Qumran and Predestination: A Theological Study of the Thanksgiving Hymns* (STDJ, 8; Leiden: E.J. Brill, 1975), p. 28, claims that predestination is *the* basic theme of 1QH. Merrill maintains that the doctrine of the two spirits is important in 1QH, even though he found that '1QH 14:11-12 appears to be the only passage where the two spirits are clearly mentioned'.

Several scholars, e.g. M. Hengel, *Judaism and Hellenism* (London: SCM Press, 1974), II, p. 156 n. 794, thinks the רוחות in 1QH 14.11 refer to angelic beings.

17. The enumeration of the *Hodayot* in this paper does not follow García Martínez's edition, *The Dead Sea Scrolls Translated*, but is the traditional one found, e.g. in Lohse and Vermes.

18. There is a strong emphasis upon predetermination in the first part of this psalm: 'In your wisdom you es[tablished] eternal [. . .]; and before creating them you know all their deeds, for ever and ever. [. . .] [Without you] nothing is done, and nothing is known without your will' (1QH 1.7-8).

fashioned every spirit, he has ordered the heavenly part of the universe by creating the heavenly spirits. The reference might very well be to the stars, represented as spirits or personal beings: the stars follow exactly the courses prescribed for them by God, and the regular precision of their movements is among the mysteries of God's creation.[19]

The text continues by describing earthly creation, including the establishment of humans and the creation of the human spirit: 'To the spirit of man which you have formed in the world (לרוח אדם אשר יצרת בתבל לכול ימי עולם), [You have given dominion over the works of your hands][20] [ותתנם לממשלה]', 1QH 1.15.

Although the restoration of the text quoted here is generally accepted by scholars, the text is quite corrupt, and one ought therefore to proceed with caution. The text deals with the creation of the human spirit, but the context in which this statement occurs, is lost. If the restored text is correct, it combines the idea of the spirit of humans with the idea of human beings as the image of God. This notion is also present in the *Two Spirit Treatise*, where the concept of man as *imago Dei* is connected to the conception of the שתי רוחות appointed for man to walk in until the time of God's visitation (1QS 3.17-18). In the context of the teaching on the two spirits, 1QS 3.13–4.26 says that God created human beings to govern the world (לממשלת תבל).

In 1QH 1.27-28, the creation of the spirit occurs in a context that explains the ability of humans to express themselves through speech:

> You created breath on the tongue (אתה בראתה רוח בלשון), you know its words, You instituted the fruit of the lips, before they came to be; you placed a rhythm for words, and a cadence to the puff of breath from the lips (ומבע רוח שפתים במדה). You make the rhythms emerge by their

19. The meaning of the expression אתה יצרתה כול רוח in 1QH 1.9 is controversial. H.-W. Kuhn, *Enderwartung und gegenwärtiges Heil* (SUNT, 4; Göttingen: Vandenhoeck & Ruprecht, 1966), pp. 124-25, maintains that 'every spirit' refers to 'every human spirit' in the sense 'predestined being of humans'. Sekki, *The Meaning of ruah*, pp. 168-69, thinks that רוח in this case refers to the angels. My interpretation follows that of Hengel, *Judaism and Hellenism*, I, p. 234, and II, p. 157 n. 806. Hengel, II, p. 154 n. 780, also points out that there are a number of analogies to Cleanthes's *Hymn to Zeus* in 1QH 1. According to Hengel, this shows how closely the philosophical monotheism of the Greeks and the Jewish belief in creation approached one another despite their fundamental differences.

20. García Martínez's translation (*The Dead Sea Scrolls Translated*) 'So that the spirit of man rules over the world', is strange and hard to substantiate from the Hebrew text. My translation is almost identical with that of Vermes.

mysteries and the puffs of breaths by their measures (ומבעי רוחות
לחשבונם), to declare your glory and tell your wonders, in the deeds of
your truth and your just judgments, to praise your name through the
mouth of all (בפה כול).[21] And they will know you by their intellect
(יודעיכה לפי שכלם),[22] and they will bless you for [everlasting] centuries' (1QH 1.27-31).

There are at least three features of this text that requires further comment. The first is the creation of breath or spirit for the tongue.[23] 1QH
1.27-29 seems to reflect an interpretation of Gen. 2.7 that emphasizes
the breath or spirit in humans as that faculty which enables human
beings to speak and communicate verbally.[24] By giving breath to

---

21. The great majority of scholars translate 1QH 1.31 as does García Martínez,
The Dead Sea Scrolls Translated. The translations of T. Gaster, *The Dead Sea
Scriptures* (New York: Doubleday, 1956); J. Maier, *Die Texte vom Toten Meer*. I.
Übersetzung (Munich: Reinhardt, 1960); S. Holm-Nielsen, *Hodayot, Psalms from
Qumran* (Acta Theologica Danica, 2; Aarhus: Universitets-forlaget, 1960);
M. Mansoor, *The Thanksgiving Hymns* (STDJ, 3; Leiden: E.J. Brill, 1961); and
G. Vermes are almost identical with that of García Martínez, *The Dead Sea Scrolls
Translated*.

22. The relationship between the first part of 1QH 1.31, 'to praise your name
through the mouth of all', and the following 'And they will know you by their
intellect', is somewhat controversial.

E. Lohse finishes the sentence after יודעיכה, so that the connection between
'know' and 'intellect' is lost. According to Lohse's punctuation the text states that
God's name might be praised 'durch den Mund aller, die dich kennen. Gemäß ihrer
Einsicht sollen sie dich preisen in alle E[wigkeit]'. Lohse was followed by
R. Bergmeier and H. Pabst in 'Ein Lied von der Erschaffung der Sprache: Sinn und
Aufbau von 1 Q Hodayot I, 27-31', *RevQ* 19 (1965), pp. 435-39. Bergemeier and
Pabst argued that the last sequence of this text, 1.30-31, describes the praise of God
in the community and not by the mouth of all humans, because if the latter is
implied 'ergibt sich der für die Theologie der Qumrangemeinde ungeheuerliche
Satz, daß alle Menschen Gott erkennen können'.

23. Both Holm-Nielsen, *Hodayot*, and Mansoor, *The Thanksgiving Hymns*,
translate 'spirit' in 1.28.

24. The Targums interpreted the נשמה of Gen. 2.7 as רוח ממללא, 'spirit of
speech', or 'ability to speak'. A similar expression, which also probably alludes to
Gen. 2.7, occurs in *1 En.* 84.1, 'Then I raised up my hands in righteousness and
blessed the Holy and Great One; and I spoke with the breath of my mouth and the
tongue of flesh which God has made for the children of the flesh, the people, so that
they should speak with it; he gave them the breath and the mouth so that they
should speak with it.'

humans, God has created speech so that human beings might be able to praise him, and he knows its contents even before the words are uttered.

The second feature that requires explanation is the expression 'and they will know you by their intellect'. The term שכל, 'understanding', seems to connote 'spirit' in several 1QH contexts.[25] This probably happens in 1QH 1.31, where the expression לפי שכלם parallels the oft-occurring expression לפי רוחום (cf. 1QS 2.20 and 9.14). In 1QH 1.31, then, the psalmist asks that *all* humans might know God according to their creaturely-given understanding/spirit. The underlying idea is probably here, as in 1QS, that human beings know God according to the quality of their spirit, which is equated with understanding; compare the somewhat similar idea that all humans can know good and evil if they are ruled by the spirit of truth (1QS 4.26).[26]

---

25. This also happens in CD 10.9-10. This text is part of the rule for the judges of the Congregation, and the rule concludes by saying that no man over sixty shall hold office as judge of the congregation, for because man sinned 'his days were shortened, and because of God's wrath against the inhabitants of the earth he decided to remove knowledge, דעתם, from them before they completed their days'.

The text quoted in CD 10.9-10 is taken from *Jub.* 23.11, a text that again refers to Gen. 6.3. The point is that the רוח of Gen. 6.3 has become *knowledge* in *Jub.* 23.11, דעת in CD 10.10. The author of the *Damascus Rule* thus refers to the human spirit as the ability to judge and understand. No man over the age of sixty is permitted to hold office as judge of the congregation, because the human spirit within the judge which enables him to know and understand is soon going to depart from him, for even he, the judge, is no more than flesh.

26. The relationship between שכל and רוח is also expressed in 1QH 12.22-23. This text deals with entrance into the community, the term נגש, used in 12.23, is often regarded by scholars to be terminus technicus for entrance into the eschatological יחד. (Cf. Kuhn, *Enderwartung und gegenwärtiges Heil*, p. 112 n. 3). According to the translation of Vermes, 1QH 12.22-23 says that men are admitted (נגש) into the community '*in accordance with their understanding*' (ולפי [ ] כשכלם). (García Martínez, *The Dead Sea Scrolls Translated*, does not translate נגש in the sense 'admit' here; according to his translation the passage reads: 'And to the extent of their intellect you let them improve' [נגש]). In other words, those who seek to become members of the community are not totally void of understanding, they are able to enter precisely because they have a certain insight or spirit. (On this, cf. Mansoor, *The Thanksgiving Hymns*). And this measure of spirit or understanding that they already possess determines their initial rank and position in the covenant community. This aspect is emphasized by me since it is often overlooked by scholarship. Scholars are of course perfectly right in stressing the fact that entering the community means receiving wisdom, 'the opening of knowledge', 1QH 12.13. A

The third feature that is particularly interesting about this psalm is its universality. The first *Hodaya* is a creation-psalm; the intention is to praise God for his universal righteousness and creative activity. He has created all humans with a spirit (1.15), and this makes it possible for human beings to express themselves so that they can tell of God's glory and recount his wonders (1.27-30).[27] Because *all* humans are created with spirit, the author requests in 1.30-31 that God's name might be praised by the mouth of *all*, 'so that they may know Thee according to their understanding, and bless Thee forever'.[28]

The universalistic claims of this psalm correspond to the anthropology of some of the pre-sectaraian literature from Qumran, in which all humans are described as equipped with understanding and knowledge.[29] 1QH 1 is one of the few *Hodayot* in which there are no references to an elect group or to a specific community, or to entrance into that community.[30] The author of this *Hodaya* is a righteous individual who expresses his views on God's sovereignty. God has created both macrocosmos and microcosmos: from the great heavenly bodies to the sounds uttered by humans when they speak. The author of 1QH 1

body of hidden knowledge is revealed to those who enter the covenant, 1QS 8.11-12.

27. Except for the word 'constantly', Gaster, *The Dead Sea Scriptures*, p. 19, is right when he says that 'in the *Book of Hymns* the idea is affirmed constantly that every man is endowed at birth with the charisma of knowledge and discernment'.

28. Vermes's translation. S.J. Tanzer, 'The Sages at Qumran: Wisdom in the Hodayot' (Dissertation, Harvard University, 1987), p. 34, thinks 1QH 1.27b-31a either is a disguised exhortation to the righteous to use the insight which God has given them in order to proclaim God's glory, or it may also be understood as a disclaimer of any merit for human beings as they sing God's praises.

29. Cf. esp. 'The Words of the Luminaries', 4Q508 frag. 8, and 'Sapiental Work A', 4Q423 5.

30. Cf. Holm-Nielsen, *Hodayot*, p. 30. The only exception might be the last occurrence of רוח in this text:

> And you, in your compassion,
> and in the vastness of your mercy,
> have strengthened the spirit of man before his miseries
> (חזקתה רוח אנוש לפני נגע)', 1.31-32.

Although the notion of cleansing appears later on in the text (1.33), this cleansing is not connected with the operation of the Holy Spirit. Instead 1.32 mentions the strengthening of the human spirit לפני נגע, literally 'before the scourge'. This expression does not refer to entrance into the community, but to persecution.

stands before God first and foremost as a creature before his creator, and one of his main points is to emphasize how everything depends upon God and his sustenance: the stars in their circuits, human beings in their sinfulness, the spirit within humans and the puff of breath passing out from human lips.[31]

3. *The Examination of the Spirit before Entering the Community*

The discussion above, with respect to the origin or creation of the spirit in humans, reveals that according to the sectarians *all humans* were regarded as either created with one spirit or as possessing two spirits which both have their origin with God. I shall now proceed to look at some texts describing the central role of the spirit in each human as he approaches the community to join the covenant. Since the sectarians believed in a double division of humankind into Sons of Light and Sons of Darkness, not everyone was entitled to join the sect. Strict measures of selection, in which the novices had to prove their sagacity and moral perfection, were applied. In addition, the sectarians also used 'objective' criteria in order to detect the true nature of the novice. The horoscopes found at Qumran are important in this context, because it is probable that they were used as criteria by the help of which the leaders of the sect could discover the true nature of the novice.

a. *The Community Rule: Determining the Quality of the Spirit*
The *Community Rule* places great emphasis on the 'quality' of each person's spirit, because the spirit each human has within determines what kind of person he or she is.[32] The examination of each human's רוח is an important feature of the *Community Rule*. The first time this takes place is when a novice is to enter the Covenant: his spirit is then to be examined with respect to his understanding and practice of the

---

31. This aspect is noted by B. Nitzan, *Qumran Prayer and Religious Poetry* (STDJ, 12; Leiden: E.J. Brill, 1994), p. 337.

32. Commenting upon the anthropological spirit in the Rule, E. Schweizer states that רוח in this text 'is on the way to meaning the existence of man specifically as he lives before God, i.e. the self which is set over his soul and body', *Spirit of God* (London: A. & C. Black, 1960), p. 17. Cf. also E. Schweizer, 'Gegenwart des Geistes und eschatologische Hoffnung bei Zarathustra, Spätjüdischen Gruppen, Gnostikern und den Zeugen des Neuen Testaments', in W.D. Davies and D. Daube (eds.), *The Background of the New Testament and its Eschatology* (Festschrift C.H. Dodd; Cambridge: Cambridge University Press, 1956), pp. 482-508 (493).

Law (1QS 5.20-21), 'And when someone enters the covenant...they shall test (דרש) their spirits (רוחום) in the Community [discriminating] between a man and his fellow, in respect of his insight and his deeds in law'.[33] What does the initial testing of spirit(s) imply? The last part of the text quoted explicitly states that the first examination involves finding out whether or not the novice has a basic knowledge of Torah and has been attempting to live a life in accordance with its demands.[34]

A similar procedure is described in 1QS 6.14. This text states that 'to any in Israel who freely volunteers to enrol in the council of the Community, the Instructor who is at the head of the Many shall test him with regard to his insight and his deeds' (לשכלו ולמעשיו).[35] A comparison of 1QS 6.14 with 6.17, reveals that רוח in this context probably connotes 'understanding, insight'. 1QS 6.17 describes what happens to the novice after the one year of probation has been completed: 'he must not touch the pure food of the Many while they test him about his spirit and his deeds' (לרוחו ומעשׂו).

b. *The Qumran Horoscopes: Determining the Share of the Spirit in Humans in the Houses of Light and Darkness.*
According to the Qumran horoscopes, 4Q186, the place of a person in the camp of Light or the camp of Darkness is determined by how many parts of his or her spirit belong to the camp of Light and correspondingly to the camp of Darkness. This corresponds to the idea found in 1QS 4.24-25, where a person's portion or inheritance in either of the two spirits determines the degree of righteousness or wickedness of each individual. In these horoscopes every human being is depicted as a being divided into parts of light and darkness: there are nine parts in all, and the portions of light and darkness are variously mixed. As the number is uneven, either good or evil is bound to dominate. 4Q186, 1.2.7-8,

---

33. Similar expressions occur in CD 13.11-12: 'And everyone who joins his congregation, he should examine, concerning his actions, his intelligence, his strength, his courage and his wealth; and they shall inscribe him according to his condition in the lot of light'.

34. On entrance into the community, cf. M. Newton, *The Concept of Purity at Qumran and in the Letters of Paul* (SNTSMS, 53; Cambridge: Cambridge University Press, 1985).

35. This testing of the spirits by the leaders of the Community is probably reflected in 1QH 14. 11-12, which says that 'You teach your servant [...] of the spirits of man, for corresponding to the spirits you allot them between good and evil'.

gives the following description of a largely good man born under the influence of Taurus, 'in the foot of the bull' (ברגל השור): 'His spirit consists of six (parts) in the House of Light, and three in the Pit of Darkness' (ושלוש בבור החושך רוח לו בבית האור שש). Equally important is the relationship between the morphology of certain parts of the body and the sign of the Zodiac under which one was born. In the horoscopes, physical characteristics are associated with spiritual qualities, as well as with the birthday of the individual and his Zodiacal symbol.[36]

Although 4Q186 does not mention *two spirits*, but understands *the spirit* of the individual as being conditioned by both darkness and light, this astronomical text has some interesting similarities with the *Two Spirit Treatise* in the *Community Rule*.[37] According to 1QS 3.19 the spirit of truth originates in a habitation of light (במעון אור). In 4Q186, frag. II, the spirit of the person in question is said to have six parts in the house of light (בית האור). 1QS 3.19 says that the spirit of perversity originates in a spring of darkness (וממקור חושך), and the spirit of the person described in the horoscope just referred to, has three parts in the pit of darkness (בבור החושך).[38]

4. *Entering the Community: The Cleansing and Recreation of the Spirit in Humans and the Gift of the Holy Spirit*

The novice's spirit has now been examined regarding knowledge of the law, and it has been established that his spirit has more parts or portions

36. Shortness, fatness and irregularity of the features are associated with wickedness, while their opposites reflect virtue. I. Gruenwald, *From Apocalypticism to Gnosticism* (BEATAJ, 14; Frankfurt am Main: Peter Lang, 1988), p. 86 n. 49, might be right when he says that 'the very fact that the sect had to recur to special methods of defining man's character according to the morphology of the body, in spite of the astrological implications of this method, is a clear proof that people were initially unaware of their share in either of the lots, the sons of light or the sons of darkness'.

37. According to Charlesworth, *The Dead Sea Scrolls*, the author of 1QS 10.3 must have known the scroll of astronomical lore found in Cave 4. Several scholars have argued that 1QS 10.2-5 refers to the zodiac. J.T. Milik, *The Books of Enoch: Aramaic Fragments of Qumran Cave 4* (Oxford: Oxford University Press, 1976), p. 187, argues that 1QS 10.3 speaks about constellations of the zodiac.

38. On the similarities between the Horoscopes and the *Community Rule*, cf. J.H. Charlesworth, 'John and Qumran', in J.H. Charlesworth (ed.), *John and Qumran* (London: Chapman and Hall, 1972), pp. 77-106 (86), and *idem*, 'Jewish

in the House of Light than in the House of Darkness (either 5.4, 6.3, 7.2 or 8.1). What then happens to the spirit of the novice as he enters the community? This is perhaps the point where the texts differ the most. According to the *Rule*, no change takes place in the spirit, while a radical change takes place according to the *Hodayot*.

a. *The Cleansing of the Human Being in the Community Rule*
When someone is about to enter the covenant, the *Community Rule* emphasizes the cleansing role of the Holy Spirit.[39] In a section dealing with those who refuse to enter the community, and who are pronounced unclean, the following statement describes what happens to those who desire to enter the covenant:

> For, by the spirit of the true counsel concerning the paths of man (כיא
> ברוח עצת אמת אל דרכי איש), all his sins are atoned so that he can
> look at the light of life. And by the spirit of holiness (ברוח קדושה),
> which links him with his truth he is cleansed of all his sins. And by the
> spirit of uprightness and of humility, (ברוח יושר וענוה), his sin is
> atoned (1QS 3.6-8).

The spirit of holiness cleansing the devout person of all his sins is no doubt the Holy Spirit.[40] In the final judgment, this purification will be

---

Interest in Astrology', *ANRW* 2.20.2, (1987), pp. 926-50 (938-40). According to Charlesworth it is unwise to conclude that the zodiacal documents represent only an extreme fringe in the Qumran Community.

39. There is no agreement among scholars as to how the sectarians thought about the Holy Spirit. F. Nötscher, *Zur theologischen Terminologie der Qumran-texte* (BBB, 10; Bonn: Hanstein, 1956), p. 42, claims that the sectarians did not regard God's spirit as a personal being distinct from God, but as an impersonal power. Similar views are maintained by F.F. Bruce, 'Holy Spirit in the Qumran Texts', *ALUOS* 6 (1966–68), pp. 49-55. Sekki, *The Meaning of ruah*, pp. 71-72, agrees with Nötscher. This view has recently been challenged by J.H. Charles-worth, 'The Dead Sea Scrolls and the Historical Jesus', in J.H. Charlesworth (ed.), *Jesus and the Dead Sea Scrolls* (New York: Doubleday, 1992), pp. 19-62. Charles-worth claims that at Qumran 'the holy spirit' was regarded as angelic and as a separate being (hypostasis). It is not the holy spirit *of* God but 'the Holy Spirit' *from* God.

40. The idea of cleansing is closely connected with entrance into the commu-nity in several *Hodayot*, e.g. in 1QH 3.20-23. This text is additionally important because it most likely shows that the sectarians not only spoke of humans as having a spirit, but as also being a spirit. In 3.21 the whole person is described as a 'corrupt spirit'; the sectarian refers to himself as a perverted person whom God has cleansed (cf. Sekki, *The Meaning of ruah*, pp. 138-39): 'You have purified the corrupt spirit

repeated, and the cleansing will then be total, because the root of evil, the spirit of falsehood within man, will then be rooted out from human flesh. In addition, God will then shed the spirit of truth upon the devout person and plunge him into the spirit of purification (1QS 4.19-22). While it is easy to identify the spirit of holiness in 1QS 3.7, as God's spirit, the two other occurrences of רוּחַ in 1QS 3.6 and 3.8 are somewhat more difficult to place within a fixed category. There seems to be a difference between 1QS 3.7 on the one hand, and 3.6 and 3.8 on the other, in the sense that 3.8 refers to an act of God while 3.6 and 3.8 refers to acts of humans. The attainment of that purity that unites human beings to God's truth can only be granted by God's Spirit, but the atonement for sin described in 1QS 3.6-7 seems to be an act of humans: the one who is about to enter the covenant makes atonement by his humble submission and by his obedience to the law of God. Only through a spiritual apprehension of how the way of humans should be properly directed can his sins be expiated (3.6), only by showing that he has a spirit of uprightness and humility can his sin be atoned (3.8). The submission and humility of the human spirit makes atonement possible, but only God, by the spirit of holiness, can purify humans and purge them of all their iniquities.[41] This cleansing prefigures the final cleansing by the spirit of holiness, which will take place in the end, a cleansing which involves the ripping out of all spirit of injustice from the innermost parts of the flesh of the sectarians (1QS 4.20-21).

(רוח נעוה טהרתה) from the great sin ... you cast eternal destiny for man (איש) with the spirits of knowledge' (1QH 3.21-22).

The phrase רוח נעוה in 1QH 3.21 is probably parallel with איש in 3.22, and it is therefore likely that both phrases refer to the whole human being. In 1QH 13.13, the author uses the expression רוח בשר, 'spirit of flesh', which probably denotes the human being as a whole, since it is parallel to ילוד אשה, 'one born of a woman' in 13.14. In 1QH 1.22 the author similarly refers to himself as רוח התועה, 'spirit of mistake' in parallelism with מבנה החטאה, 'building of sin'. For discussion of these passages, cf. esp. A.A. Anderson, 'The Use of "RUAH" in 1QS, 1QH and 1QM', *JJS* 12 (1962), pp. 293-303.

41. 1QS 9.3-5 seems to envisage the covenant community establishing a living temple as a habitation for the Holy Spirit. According to Charlesworth, 'The Historical Jesus', p. 21, the sectarians claimed that 'the Holy Spirit' had left the polluted temple in Jerusalem and accompanied them into the wilderness. There 'the Holy Spirit' dwelt in 'the house of holiness', i.e. the covenant community.

b. *The Recreation of the Spirit in Human Beings and the Gift of the Holy Spirit in the* Hodayot.

The *Community Rule* never explicitly states that entrance into the community means receiving the Holy Spirit. A very different picture emerges when one examines the relevant texts in the *Hodayot*. According to the *Rule*, a person who entered the community had to swear with a binding oath to revert to the Law of Moses (1QS 5.8). This oath is also referred to by the author of 1QH 14.17: with an oath the sectarian has enjoined his soul not to sin against God. In 15.13 this person describes what happened when he 'drew near', that is, entered the community in the following manner: 'In Thy goodwill towards [ashes Thou hast shed] Thy Holy Spirit[42] [upon me] and thus drawn me near[43] to understanding of Thee'.[44]

Another expression which is used several times to express the gift of the spirit is רוח אשר נתתה בי, 'the spirit which you have given me'. This expression occurs in 1QH 16.11-12:

> I know that no-one besides you is just. I have appeased your face (פניך ואחלה) by the spirit which you have given me ([אשר נתתה]בי[ברוח), to lavish your favour on your servant for [ever], to purify me with your holy spirit, to approach your will according to the extent of your kindness.

By the spirit which God has given (נתן) to the psalmist he implores God (חלה פני), literally, 'smooths the face of God'.[45] By imploring God by the spirit he has received, the psalmist in 1QH 16.11 asks God to purify him (טהר) by God's holy spirit and draw him near (נגש) to God by his grace. By the gift of the spirit the sectarian has received knowledge of God, and is able to seek God. According to this text, it is impossible for any human to understand the divine secrets and be purified except by God's Holy Spirit.

---

42. The expression רוח קודשכה, 'your holy spirit', occurs 6 times in 1QH, in 8.6; 9.32; 12.12; 14.13; 16.12 and 17.26.

43. The translation of this text is from G. Vermes. The verb נגש is rendered differently by García Martínez, *The Dead Sea Scrolls Translated*, who translates: 'You make me approach your intelligence'. On the usage of נגש as a terminus technicus for entrance into the eschatological יחד, cf. my n. 26.

44. The translation of this text is from G. Vermes.

45. This expression is paralleled by similar expressions from the Hebrew Bible, e.g. Ps. 77.6, where Asaph says his spirit searched for an answer from God, and Isa. 26.9, which says that 'my spirit within me earnestly seeks thee'.

What, then, do the *Hodayot* say about the human spirit in this context? There is one text in particular which is relevant regarding this
question:

> What is flesh compared to this? What creature of clay can do wonders?
> He is in sin from his maternal womb, and in guilty iniquity right to old
> age. But I know that justice does not belong to man nor the perfect path
> to the son of man. To God Most High belong all the acts of justice, and
> the path of man is not secure except by the spirit which God creates for
> him (כי אם ברוח יצר אל לו), to perfect the path of the sons of man
> so that all his creatures come to know the strength of his power and the
> extent of his compassion with all the sons of his approval (1QH 4.29-
> 33).

According to 1QH 4, there are basically two groups of people in the
world: those who deviate from God's covenant (4.19) and those who
unite together for God's covenant (4.24). The author belongs to the
council of the holy ones (4.25); his face has been brightened with God's
covenant (4.5-6). In the text quoted above, the psalmist identifies himself with the rest of humanity as a creature of clay and as sinful by
nature. The context of 1QH 4, however, is not human beings in general,
but the covenant community. A central idea of the text is that flesh, that
is, human beings, are dual beings; on the one hand, they are clay and,
on the other, they are spirit. The way of man is not established in so far
as he is flesh and clay, but this is possible because of the created spirit.
Since God's spirit in the Scrolls is never the object of a creating
activity, the creation of the spirit in 4.31 probably denotes the
Neuschöpfung or recreation of the human spirit as the outsider enters
the community. 1QH 4.31 might therefore be understood in terms of
Ezek. 36.26 as the new disposition given by God to his eschatological
people, depicted in terms of a recreation of the created spirit in the
sectarian.[46]

---

46. This is the interpretation of Sekki, *The Meaning of ruah*, p. 127. However,
several scholars argue that רוח in 4.31 denotes the spirit given to human beings in
creation, i.e. E. Sjöberg, 'Wiedergeburt und Neuschöpfung im palästinischen Judentum', *ST* 4 (1950), pp. 44-85; J. Schreiner, 'Geistbegabung in der Gemeinde von
Qumran', *BZ* 9 (1965), pp. 161-80; and E. Brandenburger, *Fleisch und Geist*
(WMANT, 29; Neukirchen–Vluyn: Neukirchener Verlag, 1968), p. 94. Kuhn, *Enderwartung und der wartiges Heil*, p. 126, thinks 1QH 4.24 denotes the predestined
spirit of the sectarian, while von der Osten-Sacken, *Gott und Belial*, pp. 137-38,
claims that this text describes the created spirit of the sectarian after it has been
cleansed by the sectarian's entry into the community.

The question we must now ask is this: in what way is the spirit in humans described *after* one has entered the covenant community?

5. *The Spirit in Humans and Life in the Community*

Although much attention is paid to the human spirit in the *Rule* also after the novice has entered the community, it seems clear from the *Rule* that no fundamental change has taken place in the spirit. The spirit is now to be tested annually in order to find out whether or not progress in insight and understanding has been made. In the *Hodayot*, the gift of the Holy Spirit gives the life of the sectarian a completely new dimension. Because of the spirit God has given to him or shed upon him, the sectarian is now able to know the divine secrets.

a. *The Testing of the Spirit within the Community According to the Community Rule*

According to the *Rule*, the spirit and deeds of those who have entered the Covenant are then to be examined every year (1QS 5.24), 'And their spirit, רוחם, and their deeds must be tested, year after year, in order to upgrade each one to the extent of his insight שכל and the perfection of his path'. This implies that each sectarian was regarded as capable of growing in spiritual maturity and insight. Rank was very important at Qumran and members were re-evaluated every year and reassigned rank according to their purity and righteousness.[47] The annual testing of the spirit means that each person's spiritual condition was subject to change from year to year. According to the *Two Spirit Treatise*, such 'flexibility' is impossible: the natures of all human beings are pre-determined, ordained by God before creation. A person's participation in the portion (נחלה) of truth and his or her corresponding participation in the realm or lot (גורל) of falsehood determines his or her whole course of life (1QS 4.24), and the eternal destiny of each human being (4.26). None can escape their predetermined lot.[48]

47. This emphasis on rank in the community, is also echoed in 1QH 9.15-16:

One man is more just than another man,
one fellow is wiser [than a fellow,]
the flesh is respected more than one made from [clay,]
one spirit is more powerful than another spirit (רוח מרוח תגבר).

48. This point is emphasized by Stegemann, 'Textbestand und Grundgedanken',

1QS 9.14 and 15 describes the tasks of the wise leader. It is his task
to

> separate and weigh (שקל) the sons of Zadok [Blank] according to their
> spirits (לפי רוחום)...he should carry out the judgment of each man in
> accordance with his spirit (כרוחו). He should include each one
> according to the purity of his hands and according to his intellect (שכלו
> לפי), promote him.

Movement through the ranks of the community depends on each member's purity and understanding of Torah. To examine someone who has already entered the covenant concerning his spirit is basically to enquire into his understanding of the Law. In this context, spirit and understanding belong together. The Qumran priestly hierarchy was in fact, organized according to the perfection of the spirit of each priest (1QS 2.20).[49] The members of the *Yachad* were ranked in a strict order, each man's position was determined annually on the basis of his רוח, that is, his spiritual character, and his deeds. An important part of the office of the Master of the Community is to be informed about the progress in understanding and insight of each community-member, because it is his task as Master 'to carry out the judgment of each man in accordance with his spirit' (1QS 9.15). Because he knows how far each member has reached in understanding, the Master is also able 'to guide them all in knowledge according to the spirit of each' (1QS 9.17-18). The kind of spirit a person has reveals the nature of that person, a person's spirit determines his character and behaviour. A man who has been a member of the community for a long time and then departs from it does so because his spirit turns away or fails (1QS 7.18).

b. *The Spirit in Humans and God's Holy Spirit in the Life of the Sectarians According to the Hodayot*
According to the *Hodayot*, God sheds his Holy Spirit upon the devout sectarian; through this gift God delights, instructs and cleanses the

esp. p. 119 and p. 128. D. Dombkowski Hopkins, 'The Qumran Community and 1Q Hodayot: A Reassessment', *RevQ* 39 (1981), pp. 323-64 (351), thinks that 1QS 3.22-24 implies an ambiguity of life for the elect: even the righteous assigned to the lot of the 'sons of light' can sin and err because the Prince of Darkness and his attendant spirits constantly battle to bring the righteous under their dominion.

49. 1QS 2.20 is part of the description of the 'Entrance into the Community'-ceremony, 1QS 1.16–3.12. This ceremony contains a curse addressed to the lot of

psalmists.[50] The following text from 1QH 12 deals with the question of how it is possible for the sectarian to know God:

> And I, the Instructor, have known you, my God, through the spirit which you gave to me (ברוח אשר נתתה בי), and I have listened loyally to your wonderful secret through your holy spirit. You have opened within me knowledge of the mystery of your wisdom, the source of your power (1QH 12.11-13).

The sectarian knows God by the spirit God has given him.[51] The coming of the Holy Spirit to the psalmist enables him to listen to God's counsel and opens up for him a treasury of spiritual knowledge. Through God's Holy Spirit, he is able to gain insight into the divine secrets; the Holy Spirit communicates revelation to the elect ones.

However, the coming of the Holy Spirit does not mean that the human spirit now completely disappears from the scene. There are several texts from the *Hodayot* where the human spirit is depicted as a source of spirituality for the sectarian. This happens in 1QH 15, a psalm using creation language to portray God's intensions for the wicked and for the righteous. God has created the just person and established him from the womb, his destiny is eternal salvation (15.14-16). God has also created the wicked and vowed them from the womb to the Day of Massacre (15.17). Every human being is predestined from birth for evil or for good, for destruction or for salvation. In this context the following statement occurs:

> What, then, is flesh, to understand [your wonders?] And how can dust direct its steps? You have fashioned the spirit (אתה יצרתה רוח) and have organised its task. From you comes the path of every living being (1QH 15.21-22).

In this text the psalmist asks two questions, and he then gives the answer. In the two questions, human beings are characterized as flesh and dust, while, in the answer, the psalmist focuses upon the human spirit. The basic message of the text is that the flesh-aspect of humans does

---

Belial, 2.5. According to this curse, the spirit of the apostate will be obliterated, 2.14.

50. 1QH 7.6-7; 9.32; 14.13 and 16.12.

51. Sekki, *The Meaning of ruah*, pp. 87-88, thinks that there is a close analogy syntactically and conceptually between the expression ברוח אשר נתתה בי and Ezek. 36.27 and 37.6. Sekki believes that the sectarians saw themselves as the eschatological heirs of Ezekiel's promise of the spirit in Ezek. 36.27.

not understand; as a creature viewed as dust, the sectarian is not able to find the way, but the sectarian knows he is more than flesh; he is spirit, too, and therefore he is able to undersand and direct his steps.[52] God has furthermore organized the task of the human spirit, fixing its activity before birth so that it is not under human control: 'I know that every spirit is fashioned[53] by your hand (ואדעה כי בידך יצר כול רוח) [and all its travail] you have established even before creating it', 15.13.[54]

In other words, according to 1QH 15, the sectarian, even after joining the community, regards his own created spirit as a source of knowledge.[55] Dust, that is, the members of the community, whose lives were predetermined from the womb (15.15) can direct their steps because of the created spirit within them.[56] There is nothing in this text which implies that the recreated human spirit is meant.

1QH 15 furthermore describes human beings as dual beings: viewed from the flesh-dust side, they are weak and ignorant; viewed from the aspect of the *created* spirit, they are capable of insight.[57] There

---

52. For a detailed study of this text, cf. Kuhn, *Enderwartung und gegenwärtiges Heil*, pp. 122-26. In Kuhn's analysis, the three terms פעולה, כון and יצר are typical in texts where רוח means the predestined being of humans. All three terms occur in 1QH 15.21-22 and in 1QH 1.8-9.

53. Vermes translates: 'I know that *the inclination* of every spirit [is in Thy hand]'.

54. García Martínez, *The Dead Sea Scrolls Translated*, translates 'even before creating *him*', thus interpreting כול רוח in the sense 'every human being'. My translation follows Vermes. The Hebrew Bible describes the creation of the spirit with the verb יצר in Zech. 12.1.

55. There seems to be agreement among scholars that 1QH 15 deals with the anthropological spirit. This is the opinion of, e.g., Kuhn, *Enderwartung und gegenwärtiges Heil*, pp. 122-26; von der Osten-Sacken, *Gott und Belial*, p. 137; H. Lichtenberger, *Studien zum Menschenbild in Texten der Qumrangemeinde* (SUNT, 15; Göttingen: Vandenhoeck & Ruprecht, 1980), pp. 69-70; and Sekki, *The Meaning of ruah*, pp. 126-27.

56. This makes 1QH 15.13 and 1QH 15.21-22 very similar to 1QH 14.31. However, the notion of predestination, which is very strong in 1QH 15, is absent from 1QH 4. Although 1QH 15 and 1QH 4 share some common vocabulary, the basic conceptual framework is different in the two texts: In 1QH 15, God's creation of the righteous takes place individually in the womb, whereas in 1QH 4, this creation probably has to do with the entrance into the community; cf. Sekki, *The Meaning of ruah*, p. 127.

57. K.G. Kuhn, 'New Light on Temptation, Sin and Flesh in the NT', in K. Stendahl (ed.), *The Scrolls and the New Testament* (London: SCM Press, 1958),

also seems to be a certain correspondence between 'the predetermined being'[58] of humans in 1QH 15 and the two predetermined spirits given to all humans according to the *Rule*. Just as humans are given different spiritual dispositions at birth (1QS 3.13–4.26), so 1QH 15 teaches that God has preordained each person's spirit and its task before birth.

6. *Summary and Conclusions*

This brief discussion of the pneumatology of some texts from the sectarian literature of the Qumran scrolls has revealed that this pneumatology contains diverse and even conflicting elements. Nor is it possible to speak about a single view of humans in Qumran sectarian literature.[59] Thus the view of human beings found in the *Two Spirit Treatise* is quite different from the view of humans found in the *Hodayot*. The most characteristic feature of the anthropology of the *Hodayot*, and one which is quite peculiar to this group of texts in the Qumran sectarian literature, is the view that humans are constituted of a duality of flesh and spirit; the flesh is base by nature, for it is susceptible to sin, while the spirit is capable of purification and re-creation. Although the sectarian receives the Holy Spirit when he enters the community, the authors of the hymns often emphasize how their own created spirit continues to play a significant role as a source of spirituality and strength.

A certain duality in humans is present also in the *Two Spirit Treatise*, but there the duality is between the different spirits, the spirits of truth and the spirits of falsehood, struggling in the hearts of humans. All in all, the *Community Rule* is much more concerned about the human spirit than the Holy Spirit, because the human spirit, as the insight of the sectarian, represents his personal and constantly evolving religious character, which also serves as the basis for his changing rank in the community.[60] It is therefore not possible to draw one harmonious

pp. 94-113, points to Mk 14.38, 'the spirit is willing, but the flesh is weak', as a text closely resembling 1QH 15.21-22.

58. Kuhn, *Enderwartung und gegenwärtiges Heil*, p. 125, calls רוח in 1QH 15.22 'das prädestinierte Sein des Menschen'.

59. I am fully aware of the point that this at least partly might be due to the different literary genres, but that alone does not explain all the differences.

60. Cf. Sekki, *The Meaning of ruah*, p. 120. Cf. also Schreiner, 'Geistbegabung in der Gemeinde von Qumran', p. 170: '"Geist" ist der Gemeinde durchaus das Herrschende und Beständige, das Wichtige, Bestimmende und Bleibende—man möchte beinahe sagen: das eigentlich Gültige am Menschen'.

picture of the human spirit in sectarian literature; rather, the different texts must be treated separately and, to a certain extent, interpreted independently of each other.[61]

61. Sekki, *The Meaning of ruah*, has been severely criticized for treating the scrolls as one homogenous body of literature, and for presenting a 'pneumatology of the sect' through a simple classification of all the instances of the word for spirit; cf. esp. M. Horgan in her review of Sekki's work in *CBQ* 54 (1992), pp. 544-46.

THE UNDERSTANDING OF COMMUNITY IN THE OLD TESTAMENT AND IN THE DEAD SEA SCROLLS

Niels Peter Lemche

1. *A Preliminary Note*

Before I start, I must make it clear that we in Old Testament studies have not really been discussing the issue of terminology relevant to this discussion and are therefore rather unprepared to distinguish between issues such as 'community', 'sect' and 'society'. I accept that the correct terminology is well-known in New Testament studies and is often used to distinguish between the community as a whole and the sectarian movements in Palestine in the first century CE, including the early Christian 'church'. In the field of Old Testament studies, such distinctions have so far been deemed unnecessary, as we have been speaking about the Israelite nation, Israelite society and the people of Israel, and not about the Israelites as a religious community—to say nothing of an Israelite sect or sectarian movement. The closest to the point is Bernhard Lang's concept of a 'Yahweh Alone Movement' being around since the eighth century BCE, and exemplified in those days by the prophetic movement.[1]

2. *Biblical Israel and the Community of the Damascus Documents: Two Sectarian Societies*

It is, however, my general plan to question the self-assuredness of Old Testament scholarship by indicating that this lack of terminological differentiation cannot be sustained by referring to the concept of the Israelites as formulated by biblical authors. This will be done in a rather

---

1. B. Lang, 'The Yahweh-Alone Movement and the Making of Jewish Monotheism', in *idem*, *Monotheism and the Prophetic Minority* (SWBAS, 1; Sheffield: Almond Press, 1983), pp. 13-59.

q1general way, as I will on this occasion only present the outline of a problem. For those who read Danish, I have a paper, recently published;[2] otherwise I ask my colleagues to await a book in English in preparation which will deal with the issue in a more comprehensive way.[3]

That the Dead Sea Scrolls including the *Damascus Document* (henceforward CD), reflect the self-understanding of a society, which by all means can be defined as a religious community—or rather a sectarian community—a self-contained unit with established boundaries to the outside world is made obvious by almost every page of the more important parts of the Qumran library. And it is certainly immaterial whether the understanding of the community in the Dead Sea Scrolls is based on an extant, living community situated at Qumran and distributed all over Palestine as maintained by Josephus and Philo, or is a reflection on hopes for a community to be, intended to exist in an ideal world rather than in the world of the present.[4]

It is especially the description of the history of Israel in the CD that creates this understanding of a religious community, which has created

2.   'Samfundsopfattelsen i GT og i Dødehavsteksterne', in Niels Hyldahl and Thomas L. Thompson (eds.), *Dødehavsteksterne og Bibelen* (Forum for Bibelsk Eksegese, 8; Copenhagen: Museum Tusculanum 1996), pp. 64-78.

3.   *The Israelites in History and Tradition* (The Library of Ancient Israel; Louisville, KY: Westminster/John Knox Press, 1998).

4.   By this I should like to indicate that, after having reread the *Manual of Discipline* (1QS) and comparative DSS, I entertain some doubts about the place of this manual. The usual interpretation seems closely connected with the theory that it was describing life at Qumran. Philo and especially Josephus do not seem to indicate any connection (which would most likely have been unknown to them), but they are speaking about an Essene community much larger than anything that could have been housed by the Qumran settlement. I acknowledge that common ground exists between the descriptions of the lives of the Essenes in Josephus and in the 1QS, but would—at least at this stage—propose that the composer of the 1QS is looking forward to a 'better' world. It is, of course, not a serious problem that a community spread out over all of Palestine should understand itself to be a small tightly interconnected group. This is exactly the attitude of quite a few modern sectarian movements, even very large ones numbering in the millions. It is, on the other hand, sometimes maintained that the community behind such writings as the CD, 1QS, or 1QM need not in light of general Jewry of their own time be considered 'sectarian', as it is difficult to indicate what was mainstream Judaism then. However, this community, in establishing boundaries between its own members and non-members, certainly thinks and acts like a sectarian society.

its own boundaries against the outside world and thereby changed its lifestyle into one of a sectarian movement. The history of the Israelite nation is viewed as one long succession of rebellions against the God of Israel and his covenant, until the moment when the 'Teacher of Righteousness' and his chosen few were spared the fate of the unfaithful and libellous multitude, after having been punished 'at the end of a period of three hundred and ninety years' from the time that they were delivered into the hands of Nebuchadnezar.[5] The crucial part of this passage in the CD runs like this:

וּבְזָכְרוֹ בְּרִית רִאשֹׁנִים הֵשְׁאִיר שְׁאֵירִית לְיִשְׂרָאֵל וְלֹא נְתָנָם לְכָלָה

However, when he remembered the covenant of the very first, he saved a remnant for Israel and did not deliver them up to destruction' (García Martínez, p. 33).

The two governing concepts are: Covenant and Remnant, as the community led by the Teacher of Righteousness is identified as a remnant of the Israelite nation, otherwise defined as an עדה 'congregation' and המון 'multitude' (CD 12.1). עדה is, however, an expression already firmly embedded in the understanding of the Israelite community as a religious congregation as found especially in the Priestly strata of the Pentateuch, whereas המון does not convey any specific meaning.[6]

Allow me to quote from the conclusions of L. Rost in his study of קהל and עדה:

5.   CD 1.5-7. Thus the restoration after the Exile is not reckoned to be a restoration at all. In fact, the perspective is that there was no exile, only an enduring punishment, from which the holy few of the Teacher of Righteousness were spared.
6.   The old translation by F.F. Hvidberg, *Menigheden af den nye Pagt i Damascus* (Copenhagen: Gad, 1928), p. 38, and commentary, p. 69 (see also p. 65) 'horde'—with a reference to, among other passages, Ps. 22.17 (other examples than the ones presented by Hvidberg could be found, e.g. Judg. 14.8: עֲדַת דְּבוֹרִים 'a swarm of Bees')—is interesting but probably cannot be sustained. The translation of CD 2.1 in Florentino García Martínez, *The Dead Sea Scrolls Translated: The Qumran Texts in English* (trans. W.G.E. Watson; Leiden: E.J. Brill, 1994), p. 33, 'against his congregation', must be a slip of the pen. The CD clearly says 'against their congregation', which is not quite the same. עדה formed—together with קהל— the theme of the well-known study by L. Rost, *Die Vorstufen von Kirche und Synagoge im Alten Testament: Eine wortgeschichtliche Untersuchung* (BWANT, 4.24; Stuttgart: Kohlhammer, 1938). That the CD uses עדה in this way cannot be a surprise, as a number of its central concepts comes from the same source, such as (in the same passage) זכר in the meaning of 'remembering a covenant' or ברית הקים for 'establishing a covenant'.

1) קהל and עדה have different meanings. קהל indicates the people assembled for religious festivals, public court sessions, military campaigns. עדה denotes the community as assembled around the אהל מועד.

2) קהל is used everywhere in Old Testament tradition; the content of עדה has been decided by the Priestly Source and will only be found in literature belonging to this source or dependant of it.

3) קהל can be applied to non-Israelites; since the original Passah in Egypt, עדה always means the community of Israel.[7]

I don't think that there can be any reasonable doubt that the outlook of the author of the CD is the use of עדה as found in the above-mentioned parts of the Torah, and that this shows that the community whose origin is narrated by the CD wanted to understand itself as a sectarian group—a 'remnant'—inside the religious community, which according to its self-interpretation already understood itself to be the Israel of the Old Testament. Biblical Israel was to this community certainly an עדה: the people of the covenant bound by the obligations laid down by the Lord at Sinai. They did not, however, have to invent their concepts. Rather, the model was presented to them already by the Old Testament itself, especially in the book of Isaiah, a collected work which was probably not finished before the late Persian/early Hellenistic Period, and, of course, one of the more popular 'biblical' books of the Qumran library.

So, I shall introduce this section by quoting Isaiah chapter 4 (vv. 3-6):

> Then those who are left in Zion, who remain in Jerusalem, every one whose survival in Jerusalem was decreed will be called holy. When the Lord washes away the filth of the women of Zion and cleanses Jerusalem from bloodstains by a spirit of judgement burning like fire, he will create a cloud of smoke by day and a bright flame of fire by night over the whole building on Mount Zion and over all her assemblies (מִקְרָאֶהָ not עדה!); for his glory will be a canopy over all, a cover giving shade by day from the heat, a refuge and shelter from storm and rain' (REB).

The passage quoted does not yet speak about a remnant (שְׁאֵרִית),[8] but the verb שאר (together with יתר) is found in v. 3. And the idea of the

---

7. Rost, *Die Vorstufen*, pp. 87-88.

8. This word only shows up in a very limited number of passages in Isaiah (14.30; 15.9; 37.4, 32; 33.17; 46.3); it is much more common in Jeremiah, however, often used without any specific meaning (about Gentiles as well as Israelites). Isaiah prefers שאר.

remnant is—as is well-known—a favourite one in Isaiah. In this connection, the famous conclusion to Isaiah 6 should of course be cited:

> Even though a tenth part of the people were to remain (the verb שאר is
> not used!), they too would be destroyed like an oak or a terebinth when
> it is felled, and only a stump remains. Its stump is a holy seed.

2. *The Old Testament and the Qumran Library*

When this paper was planned, it was my intention to question the distance often assumed between the Old Testament and the Qumran library. I will turn to this theme now, as, in the notes which follow, I will try to show that this idea of the community of Israel as a holy community (on the basis of which a still 'holier' community will arise) is in fact not very old, but rather arose in the very same period as the Qumran writings; that is, no later than the late Persian and early Hellenistic Period.[9]

In my Danish lecture on this subject,[10] I had introduced this section by pointing to the differences between the understanding of the Jewish community in the two books of Ezra and Nehemiah (or rather between the main part of both books) and the so-called 'Gedenkschrift' of Nehemiah (Neh. 1.1–7.3), which is embedded in the Ezra-literature of the Old Testament.

According to Ezra, the Israelite/Jewish community in Jerusalem already exists, although its identity is threatened by—among other things—marriages between Jews and Gentiles. However, there can be no doubt that the community is understood to be in its essence a particularistic, Jewish one, which accordingly accepts the Torah of Moses as presented to them by Ezra and which freely accepts a kind of ethnic cleansing, a topic that is not too popular nowadays.

According to the Old Testament, Ezra predates Nehemiah, but many Old Testament scholars have been clever enough to accept this claim of the Old Testament as unrealistic. In fact, it is impossible, not only because of what is written in Nehemiah's *Gedenkschrift*, but also because of the idea of society and community in this part of the book of Nehemiah. Nehemiah displays very little of the particularism of Ezra. He arrives not because of some rumors concerning the impurity and

---

9. Cf. on this my 'The Old Testament: A Hellenistic Book?', *SJOT* 7 (1993), pp. 163-93.

10. Cf. n. 2 above.

bad manners of the returned Jews, but because the city of Jerusalem is in ruins and is stricken by poverty. His mission is not to create a Jewish identity or to formulate a Law—a Torah—for this community, but to rebuild a destroyed city and bring people to live there. In fact, Nehemiah's activity may have been totally secular. Almost nothing indicates that he was interested in religious matters.

This is certainly fascinating—because it may be evidence of several things, among which (as the most important and most conspicuous) is the possibility that Judaism in the biblical sense was not yet an issue to be reckoned with in Palestine. This supports the opinion of this speaker that the cradle of Judaism was in fact not Palestine but the Babylonian *golah*, that is, not the Babylonian Exile in the narrow definition of the word, but the Jewish community in Mesopotamia that developed out of the exile.

3. *The Theses*

As a consequence, I should like to formulate some theses based on this assumption:

1) The Israel implied by the Old Testament is a Jewish society.
2) Pre-exilic Israel was not a Jewish society.
3) The Old Testament cannot—neither in part nor as a whole— be understood without its basis in a Jewish society.
4) The Israel of the Old Testament cannot have come into existence before the late Persian/early Hellenistic period.
5) The idea of 'Israel' in the Old Testament is basically the same as that found in the Dead Sea Scrolls.
6) The Old Testament may—or may not—be the origin of the idea of a religious community to be found in the Dead Sea Scrolls.

4. *The Different Israels*

Before these theses are dismissed as too 'radical' I should like to say that some Old Testament scholarship has given up the traditional rather naive historical readings of the biblical literature. We see no defense possible for a position arguing that the Old Testament sources should be treated differently from any other written source from the ancient world, be this the ancient Near East or the Graeco-Roman world.

Furthermore, we see no reason why we should not use any modern methodology deriving from general literature or sociology and used in the modern—and *post*-modern—world to deconstruct texts or to discover and explain the social production of texts or whatever issue may be at stake. The historical reading of the Old Testament literature has proven to be false, not because the Old Testament as such is a book of lies—a ridiculous conclusion forced upon us by wrong methodology—but because the history constructed on the basis of such a reading has proven to be false, simply because the results of the historical reading do not confirm with results achieved by other means, especially archaeological and sociological analysis.

Based on such observations as these, Philip R. Davies formulated his theory a couple of years ago about the existence of three different Israels:[11]

1)   The Israel of History
2)   The Israel of the Bible (Old Testament)
3)   Ancient Israel

The Israel of history is the state of Israel, known to have existed between c. 900 and 700 BCE and mentioned in the Mesha inscription[12] as well as the recently-found Bet-Dawd inscription from Tel Dan.[13] To historical Israel also belongs Mernephtah's Israel,[14] although the connection between this Israel and the Israel of Mesha's time (between c. 1200 and 850 BCE), may be difficult to trace.

Biblical Israel is the Israel of the Old Testament, that is, it is an Israel of literature, and it only exists in this literature and nowhere else.[15]

---

11. P.R. Davies, *In Search of 'Ancient Israel'* (JSOTSup, 148; Sheffield: Sheffield Academic Press, 1992). Davies's study is essentially based on the major synthesis by Thomas L. Thompson, *The Early History of the Israelite People* (SHANE, 4; Leiden: E.J. Brill, 1992).

12. KAI 181.

13. A. Biran and J. Naveh, 'An Aramaic Stele Fragment from Tel Dan', *IEJ* 43 (1993), pp. 81-98, and 'The Tel Dan Inscription: A New Fragment', *IEJ* 45 (1995), pp. 1-18. The literature on this text is already rather comprehensive and the interpretations going in many directions. For this writer's view, cf. N.P. Lemche and T.L. Thompson, 'Did Biran Kill David? The Bible in the Light of Archaeology' *JSOT* 64 (1994), 3-22.

14. Translation: *ANET*, III, p. 378.

15. To be accurate, it could also be said to exist in literature that paraphrases the Old Testament.

Ancient Israel is the Israel of the biblical scholars, that is, a product of their imagination. It only exists in the minds of biblical scholars; neither in the so-called real world nor in the Bible. It only represents, at best, a rationalistic paraphrase of the biblical text. Its claim to be identical with the Israel of history is, by all means and from any logical angle, naive and erroneous.

I am not going to waste more time on this distinction, which is a fundamental one and cannot be escaped. It can of course be refined, for example, by the argument that there are many biblical Israels: one in the Pentateuch, another in the Deuteronomistic literature, in Isaiah, in Jeremiah, and so on. This is true and important, as is also the remark that there are as many 'ancient Israels' as there are scholars around.[16]

5. *The Theses: A Commentary*

1)   Let us have a look at my first thesis: The Israel of the Old Testament is a Jewish society—or better, community.

For a starter: biblical Israel is founded on the Torah, the Law of Moses, presented to the Jews by God on Mount Sinai, as the basis of the covenant between Israel and God.

The notion of the covenant and of the Law may be different from place to place. Famous is—or should be—the difference between Deuteronomy and Exodus–Numbers: according to the Tetrateuch, the fulfilment of the requirements of the Law is the condition attached to the divine covenant, whereas in Deuteronomy, Law and covenant are separated, as the Law was first presented to Israel as a gift on the plains of Moab (Deut. 4).

Apart from that, the Jewish nation is a nation of God, his 'People of the Covenant', or to be brief: the Jewish nation is understood to be a religious community ruled by the one God, Yahweh. The argument could, however, be broadened, as it could at the same time be argued

---

16. Criticism of Davies's distinction and of this author's use of Davies can be found in K. Berge, 'Comments on Lemche's Paper', *SJOT* 8 (1994), pp. 198-205, and especially in S. Norin, 'Respons zu Lemche: 'Ist es möglich die Geschichte des alten Israels zu schreiben?', *SJOT* 8 (1994), pp. 191-97, both of which are in response to this author's 'Is it Still Possible to Write a History of Israel', *SJOT* 8 (1994), pp. 165-90. Neither Berge nor Norin, however, understand the logical importance and inescapability of Davies's position. They are arguing from a scholarly position which is no longer shared by their opponents.

that this community also shows traces of being a sectarian community, a religious sect keen on accepting rules that are only valid for itself, and keen on excluding any persons not fulfilling the requirements of the community/sect. In no way can it be argued that this community was a normal nation, an *ethnos*, although according to its self-understanding it would not be far removed from the definition of an *ethnos* (a people) in Herodotus's writings. A nation is identified by common blood, a common religion and a common language. The heavy weight on common blood given by the Old Testament genealogical speculation and exemplified in the book of Ezra is, however, peculiar to the Old Testament and not easily found in the ancient Near East. It is as if we need the Greeks to formulate the theory before it can be applied to literature.[17] The importance in the Old Testament of an exclusive religion for Israelites (Jews) need not be stressed in this place.

Probably to the surprise of some of my colleagues, I am ready to accept their claim that Julius Wellhausen was wrong when he claimed that the Prophets precede the Law. I really think that the Law (understood to be obligatory rules to be followed by the members of the Israelite/Jewish community) predates the Prophets of the Old Testament. The reason for this is, among other passages, quotations such as the one from Isaiah 4, according to which the Israel of the prophets is 'already' understood to be a small religious exclusive group—not even a community, but a sectarian group of limited extension.

2)   Pre-exilic Israel was not a Jewish society.

This is an easy one. According to the Deuteronomistic History, seconded by the prophetic literature, the Israelites of pre-exilic times were not really Jews, as they almost never fulfilled the requirement of the Covenant and the Law. Almost without exception they transgressed the commandments of the Lord and at the end forced God to forsake his people because of their idolatrous manners.

---

17. This is not to say that traces of such an understanding cannot be found in the ancient Near East, for example in Egypt, and parallels to the Greek concept of barbarians can be found also in Mesopotamian sources, but in both places the distinction between the barbarian and the non-barbarian is first and foremost a geographical distinction: people living in Egypt versus people living outside Egypt, and in Mesopotamia, between the inhabitants of the fertile plains of the Euphrates and Tigris *versus* the uncivilized inhabitants of the steppe (e.g. the *Amurru*) or of the mountains (e.g. the *Guteans*).

This picture, nourished by the books of the Old Testament, at the same time concurs well with and is in disagreement with the evidence from the pre-exilic period. There is no doubt that Yahweh was a major god in Palestine of the Iron Age, probably even the most important one. Most of the early personal names reviewed by Jeff Tigay some years ago are theophoric names based on some form of the divine name Yahweh.[18] Since such names may be considered to be personal confessions in a god of this name, it is a safe conclusion that Yahweh was an important deity to the group of people represented by these names. However, these names—and especially names from the Samarian ostraca of the eighth century—also carry other theophoric elements probably not to be identified with Yahweh. In addition, it also now seems an established fact that Yahweh was not a bachelor in those days, being accompanied (also acknowledged by the Deuteronomists)[19] by a goddess called Asherah.[20]

So the Yahweh of pre-exilic times seems to have been rather different from the Lord of the Old Testament and not yet the established single God of early Judaism, but still a member of the community of deities of the West-Semitic world.

This impression of pre-exilic religion is also corroborated by other evidence from this world, such as the iconographic evidence, consisting of examples from private cult (collected for example by Urs Winter and severely misinterpreted by the same scholar).[21]

18. Cf. J. Tigay, *You Shall Have no Other Gods* (HSS, 31; Atlanta, GA: Scholars Press, 1986).

19. Cf. 2 Kgs 23.6-7.

20. As found in the inscriptions from Kuntillet 'Ajrud and Khirbet el-Qôm. On these, cf., among the most recent contributions, Z. Meshel 'Two Aspects in the Excavations of Kuntillet 'Agrüd', in W. Dietrich and M.A. Klopfenstein (eds.), *Ein Gott Allein? JHWH-Verehrung und biblischer Monotheismus im Kontext des israelitischen und altorientalischen Religionsgeschichte* (13. Kolloquium der Schweizerischen Akademie der Geistes- und Sozialwissenschaften 1993; Freiburg: Universitätsverlag, 1994), pp. 99-104; J.M. Hadley, 'Yahweh and "His Asherah": Archaeological and Textual Evidence for the Cult of the Goddess', in Dietrich and Klopfenstein (eds.), *Ein Gott allein?*, pp. 235-68.

21. Cf. U. Winter, *Frau und Göttin: Exegetische und ikonographischen Studien zum weiblichen Gottesbild im Alten Israel und in dessen Umwelt* (OBO, 53; Freiburg: Universitätsverlag; Göttingen: Vandenhoeck & Ruprecht, 1983). Winter's conclusion seems to be exactly the opposite of the ones that his material

The Israelites of the pre-exilic period were all Ba'al-worshippers, or so it is maintained by the Old Testament itself, in spite of the fact that this was probably not true. Why, then, this sad picture of the pre-exilic ages? Probably because the exile—or rather the notion of an exile—is such a convenient idea: it creates distance and unity at one and the same time. The people of the book, the authors of the Old Testament and their audience were Jews of the assumed postexilic period. They were the remnant, the purified few who survived the holocaust of the Babylonian exile.[22] Consequently, the fathers had to die in exile, and their sons were to return in order to take into their possession their rightful inheritance, simply because they were still the sons of the departed and sinful fathers. Their inheritance still belonged to them and nobody else, in spite of the fact that the people who went into exile were only a small fraction of the whole population.

3) The Old Testament cannot be understood without this Jewish background.

This seems self-evident in light of the two former paragraphs and needs no further confirmation. The Old Testament presupposes that the punishment of the unfaithful generation has been accomplished and that a new society has arisen. Its societal outlook is the one of the Jews who had returned, or who maintained that they had returned, from Mesopotamia. It is not the one of the pre-exilic age.

4) The Israel of the Old Testament cannot have come into existence before the late Persian and Hellenistic period.

A more precise formulation would be that the Jewish community in Palestine did not originate before the late Persian and the Hellenistic period, as it can certainly not be excluded (as it is rather likely) that the roots of this society/community should be sought not in Palestine but in Mesopotamia. My main witness is Nehemiah who seems to have

---

indicates. Against his collected material, he supports the Old Testament notion of a single Israelite God. I cannot see how this view can be sustained.

22. It is immaterial that the Babylonian exile was not a holocaust and that Judeans removed from Palestine at the beginning of the sixth century BCE were settled in Mesopotamian under conditions which would soon develop beyond anything that could be achieved in Palestine. This is partly due to the fact that the basis of economic development was infinitely better in the Mesopotamia of ancient times than in stony and hilly Palestine.

known nothing about a Palestinian Jewish society. Indeed, the establishment of this society or community seems to presuppose the successful conclusion of the activity of Nehemiah. And as Nehemiah seems not to be earlier than the mid-fifth century BCE (he may be later but was certainly not earlier), we are already arriving at the later part of Persian's rule.[23] The only way to escape this conclusion would be to maintain that Nehemiah's history is fiction, whereas Ezra's story is to be believed: hardly a valid observation from a historian's point of view.

5-6)   The idea of Israel in the Old Testament and in the Dead Sea Scrolls is solidly identical, and the Old Testament may—or may not—reflect the origin of the idea of a religious community as found in the Dead Sea Scrolls.

It is obvious that the ideas of Israel as a religious organization (be it a religious community or a sectarian group) to be found in the Old Testament and in the Dead Sea Scrolls, are comparable if not identical. It is also likely that the idea of the holy seed (so to speak, the remnant of the remnant) which forms the basis of the sectarian (and here there can be no doubt: it is truly sectarian) self-interpretation of the writings of the Qumran library is of the same vintage as Isaiah's talk about the remnants of Israel, as is also the talk about punishment and destruction in Isaiah and comparable literature as well as in the Qumran writings, including also the eschatological parts such as the *War Scroll*.[24] Therefore, the conclusion is hardly to be escaped that some parts of the biblical literature lie behind the formulation of a communal self-definition in the Dead Sea Scrolls, not merely the book of Isaiah, but (as is known from the commentaries found at Qumran) the prophetic books in general. However, it is also obvious that such Qumran writings followed the pattern laid out in the biblical literature, by maintaining that their

23. There is no reason to pay attention to the claims of Ezra. As I have shown in another place, Ezra is probably a totally spurious figure: a person without a family and without a history (there is really no argument that may determine the date of his arrival in Jerusalem, be it in mid-fifth century BCE, around 400 BCE or in the mid-fourth century), and also without a book of his own, or, rather, endowed with too many books and fragments. See my 'Ezra and the Pentateuch', to be published in T.L. Thompson (ed.), *Changing Perspectives in Biblical Interpretation* (The Copenhagen International Seminar; Sheffield: Sheffield Academic Press, forthcoming).

24. In this connection, comparable parts of Isaiah should not be forgotten, such as the so-called 'little Apocalypse' in Isa. 24-27, always assumed to be very late.

adversaries belonged to Israel, although it is an Israel that still has to be punished. Here they accepted the prophetic model: an idolatrous and unfaithful Israel, which sinned against the Lord, the God of Israel. Only after the purification can the sectarian movement behind the Dead Sea Scrolls stand forth as the true Israel prepared to inherit the land. The model is clear, at least to the author of the CD: an exile is needed before the end can come, and if we cannot find somebody to carry us into exile (another 'Nebuchadnezar'—were they disappointed by some-body, perhaps Epiphanes?), we will have to invent one for ourselves, we will have to leave the country and move to some other place (*in casu* 'Damascus') as part of the purification process. The interesting aspect of this could be the remembrance that exile and Judaism are tightly interwoven, and that Palestine, the Promised Land, can only be won by the purified few. This is a concept which is not forgotten by the authors of the Dead Sea Scrolls. Here they are truly in accordance with the writers of the biblical literature.

THE HISTORY OF THE QUMRAN COMMUNITY
IN THE LIGHT OF RECENTLY AVAILABLE TEXTS

Florentino García Martínez

The topic I have been given[1] is 'The History of the Qumran Community'. This title implies as a starting point that there has been a Qumran Community. I fully agree with this starting point, and I do not think it is necessary to discuss here the theories that deny all connection between the scrolls and the people who lived in the Khirbet, such as the theory of Norman Golb who postulates that the scrolls come from different libraries of Jerusalem and that they represent the literature of the whole of the Judaism of the time.[2] I think I refuted long ago the arguments put

---

1. Paper read at the Copenhagen Qumran Seminar. I have kept the form of the oral presentation, adding only some bibliographical references. I want to thank the organizers of the Seminar for the most congenial atmosphere in Schaeffergården, all the participants for the animated and fruitful discussions, and especially Professor T.L. Thompson for the revision of my English text.

2. Among the various presentations of his hypothesis, I can list: N. Golb, 'The Problem of Origin and Identification of the Dead Sea Scrolls', *Proceedings of the American Philosophical Society* 124 (1980), pp. 1-24; 'Who Hid the Dead Sea Scrolls?', *BA* 28 (1987), pp. 68-82; 'Les manuscrits de la mer Morte: Une nouvelle approche du problème de leur origine', *Annales ESC* (1985), pp. 1133-49; 'Who Wrote the Dead Sea Scrolls?', *The Sciences* (1987), pp. 40-49; 'The Dead Sea Scrolls: A New Perspective', *American Scholar* 58 (1989), pp. 177-207; 'Khirbet Qumran and the Manuscripts of Judaean Wilderness: Observations on the Logic of their Investigation', *JNES* 49 (1990), pp. 103-14; 'Die Entdeckungen in der Wüste Judäas—neue Erklärungsversuche', in J.B. Bauer *et al.* (eds.), *Qumran: Ein Symposion* (Grazer Theologische Studien, 15; Graz: Institut für ökumenische Theologie und Patrologie, 1993), pp. 87-116; 'Khirbet Qumran and the Manuscripts Finds of the Judaean Wilderness', in M.O Wise *et al.* (eds.), *Methods of Investigation of the Dead Sea Scrolls and the Khirbet Qumran Site: Present Realities and Future Prospects* (Annales of the New York Academy of Sciences, 722; New York: New York Academy of Sciences, 1994), pp. 51-70.

forth by Golb in his first series of articles,[3] and I have failed to discover any new solid piece of evidence to support his theory in his latest book, *Who Wrote the Dead Sea Scrolls?*.[4] Suffice it to say that Golb's theory fails to explain the archaeological facts (such as the unprotected water supply, the presence of the cemeteries and so on), it is not compatible with the absence of compositions to which could be ascribed a pharisaic origin, and it does not explain the homogeneous character of the collection as a whole or of the collection of each cave in spite of the diversity of compositions there included. In the words of Geza Vermes: 'The soft underbelly of the Jerusalem hypothesis is revealed, apart from the patent weakness of the archaeological interpretation, for Qumran is not a fortress, by the composition of the manuscript collection itself, definitely pointing towards a *sectarian* library'.[5]

I do not think it necessary either to discuss the widely-publicized theories of R. Eisenman[6] and B. Thiering.[7] The chronological framework that these theories require has been completely disproved by the two latest Carbon 14 analyses of the manuscripts done with the Accelerator Mass Spectometry, the one done by the Institut für Mittelenergiephysik of Zurich and published in 1991,[8] and the one done by the Arizona Accelerator Mass Spectrometer Facility of the University of Arizona, Tucson, which will shortly be published, and which contained not only a larger number of samples but samples taken from historically

3.   F. García Martínez and A.S. van der Woude, 'A 'Groningen' Hypothesis of Qumran Origins and Early History', in F. García Martínez (ed.), *The Texts of Qumran and the History of the Community. III. The History of the Community* (Paris: Gabalda, 1990), pp. 521-41 [= *RevQ* 14.56 (1990), pp. 521-41].

4.   N. Golb, *Who Wrote the Dead Sea Scrolls? The Search for the Secret of the Qumran Manuscripts* (New York: Charles Scribner's Sons, 1995).

5.   G. Vermes, *The Dead Sea Scrolls: Qumran in Perspective* (London: SCM Press, rev. edn, 1994), p. 21.

6.   R. Eisenman, *Maccabees, Zadokites, Christians and Qumran* (Leiden: E.J. Brill, 1983) and *James the Just in the Habakkuk Pesher* (Leiden: E.J. Brill, 1986).

7.   B.E. Thiering, *Redating the Teacher of Righteousness* (Australian and New Zealand Studies in Theology; Sydney: Theological Explorations, 1979), *The Gospels and Qumran* (Sydney: Theological Explorations, 1981), *The Qumran Origins and the Christian Church* (Sydney: Theological Explorations, 1983), and *Jesus the Man: A New Interpretation of the Dead Sea Scrolls* (New York: Doubleday, 1992).

8.   G. Bonani, *et al.*, 'Radiocarbon Dating of the Dead Sea Scrolls', *'Atiqot* 20 (1991), pp. 27-32.

more sensitive manuscripts such as 1QpHab, 4QpPsal[a], 4QSerek[d] and 4QDamascus[a,b].

In my opinion, only four hypothesis need to be considered: three that in one way or another connect the community of Qumran with the Essenes, and a fourth that connects the community with the Sadducees.

The first is the old hypothesis that simply identifies the community of Qumran with the Essenes; it was put forth first by Sukenik,[9] was developed by Dupont-Sommer[10] and Geza Vermes,[11] and adopted and established by Milik[12] and Cross.[13] At present it has entered the standard text-books and is so well known and firmly established that many have forgotten that it is, and remains, a simple hypothesis. I will call this hypothesis the 'traditional Essene hypothesis'.

The second is the so-called 'Groningen hypothesis',[14] which recognizes the many elements in common between the Qumran community and the Essenes as described in the classical sources, but at the same time takes seriously the sensible differences between these two entities. This hypothesis considers the Qumran community as a break-away group from the Essenes, the result of a split motivated by the refusal of the majority of the Essenes to accept the halakhic and ideological positions put forth by the Teacher of Righteousness as result of his conviction of having received by revelation the correct interpretation of the biblical text. In this way, this hypothesis tries to account for the

9.   E.L. Sukenik, *Megillot Genuzot I* (Jerusalem: Mosad Bialik, 1948), pp. 16-17.

10. Dupont-Sommer, A., *Les écrits esséniens découverts près de la Mer Morte* (Paris: Payot, 4th edn, 1983), pp. 349-68.

11. In his various publications on the topic, since his dissertation of 1953, 'Les manuscrits du désert de Juda'. The most recent presentation of Vermes's views can be found in *The Dead Sea Scrolls*, pp. 100-41.

12. J.T. Milik, *Ten Years of Discovery in the Wilderness of Judaea* (trans. J. Strugnell; London: SCM Press, 2nd edn, 1963), pp. 80-98.

13. F.M. Cross, *The Ancient Library of Qumran* (Sheffield: Sheffield Academic Press, 3rd edn, 1994), pp. 54-87.

14. F. García Martínez, 'Orígenes del movimiento esenio y orígenes de la secta qumránica: Pistas para una solución', in V. Collado Bertomeu and V. Vilar Hueso, *II Simposio Bíblico Español* (Valencia-Córdoba: Fundación Biblica Española, 1987), pp. 527-56; F. García Martínez, 'Qumran Origins and Early History: A "Groningen Hypothesis"', *Folia Orientalia* 25 (1989), pp.113-36; F. García Martínez and A.S. van der Woude, 'A "Groningen" Hypothesis of Qumran Origins and Early History', *RevQ* 14.56 (1990), pp. 521-41.

similarities with the parent group (the Essenes) as well as for the differences with it that result from the acceptance of the halakhic positions of the Teacher of Righteousness.

The third theory is the Essene hypothesis as 'revised and augmented' by Harmut Stegemann,[15] which considers the Qumran Essenes as the main Jewish Union in late Second Temple times and which sees the Essenes' Qumran settlement as 'a study centre for all members, wherever they usually lived'. In Stegemann's own words:

> The final conclusion of this study is that the Essenes were indeed the main Jewish Union of late Second Temple times. They were founded about 150 BCE by a former high priest of the temple in Jerusalem. He was traditionally-minded in every respect, and he was disposed to include all Israel in his Union. Regrettably, what he could accomplish was limited in his times by unfavourable political circumstances and by rival religious groups. Nevertheless, the Essenes became spiritually the leading group of Palestinian Judaism in their times, after more than a century of their existence praised by contemporary Jewish authors as 'the best of all Jews'. In this way they became a very impressive model of the privileges of a mainly Torah-oriented Judaism for all times (p. 165).

The fourth hypothesis postulates a Sadducean origin for the Qumran sect.[16] Basing his argument on the undeniable Sadducean character of some of the halakhot of MMT, Schiffman claims a Sadducean Zadokite origin for the Qumran sect. He does not claim 'that the Dead Sea sect as we know it is Sadducean, only that its origins and the roots of its halakhic tradition lie in the Sadducean Zadokite priesthood'. In the view of Schiffman, the Hasmonean priests imposed Pharisaic views on

---

15. H. Stegemann, 'The Qumran Essenes: Local Members of the Main Jewish Union in Late Second Temple Times', in J. Trebolle Barrera and L. Vegas Montaner (eds.), *The Madrid Qumran Congress* (STDJ, 11.1; Leiden: E.J. Brill, 1992), pp. 83-166, and *idem, Die Essener, Qumran, Johannes der Täufer und Jesus: Ein Sachbuch* (Freiburg: Herder, 1993) [all quotations are taken from the English article].

16. L.H. Schiffman, 'Miqsat Ma'śe ha-Torah and the Temple Scroll', *RevQ* 14.56 (1990), pp. 435-57; *idem*, 'The New Halakhic Letter (4QMMT) and the Origins of the Dead Sea Sect', *BA* 53 (1990), pp. 64-73; *idem*, 'The Sadducean Origins of the Dead Sea Scroll Sect' in H. Shanks (ed.), *Understanding the Dead Sea Scrolls* (New York: Random House, 1992), pp. 35-49; *idem, Reclaiming the Dead Sea Scrolls* (Philadelphia: Jewish Publication Society, 1994), pp. 83-95 (89) [quotations are taken from this latest book].

the Temple community; a group of pious Sadducees protested the impo-
sition and formed a sectarian group which seceded from participation in
the ritual of the Jerusalem Temple. In the words of Schiffman:

> The earliest members of the sect must have been Sadducees unwilling to
> accept the status quo in the aftermath of the Maccabean revolt. The
> Maccabees, by replacing the Zadokite high priesthood with their own,
> reduced the Zadokites to a subsidiary position for as long as Hasmonean
> rule lasted (pp. 87-88)...After they failed in their initial attempts, exem-
> plified in the *Halakhic Letter*, to reconcile and win over the Hasmonean
> and the remaining Jerusalem Sadducees to their own system of Temple
> practice, the Qumran Zadokites gradually developed the sectarian men-
> tality of the despised, rejected, and abandoned outcast. Accordingly,
> they began to look upon themselves as the true Israel, condemning and
> despising all others (pp. 88-89)...they still were leaderless until, at some
> point, the Teacher of Righteousness arose to lead them. It was he who
> gave the sect shape and direction. Eventually he led the group from its
> Sadducean origins toward its intensely apocalyptic, sectarian mentality
> and toward the many beliefs that differentiated the sect from the Sad-
> ducees (p. 95).

I assume that all these hypotheses are well known, and that everyone is
able to weigh the arguments put forth in their defense. I do not think it
will be useful to indulge in polemics, to discuss these arguments yet
again, or to evaluate the pros and cons of each one of these hypotheses
one by one.

I intend to follow here another way suggested some years ago by
Timothy Lim.[17] At the end of an article in which he analyzes both the
theory of N. Golb and the 'Groningen Hypothesis', Lim concludes:

> This article has sought to examine the state of the question by way of
> assessing two important hypotheses, but it has proven impossible to take
> into account the newly released material. It will be of great interest to
> see which elements will withstand the test of time and the demands of
> the new evidence (p. 466).

To my knowledge, this has not yet been realized. H. Stegemann, who
knows well all this material, thinks that:

> Unfortunately, very little of this additional material does much to enrich
> our knowledge of the Essenes much more than Philo, Josephus, and the
> Qumran scrolls published so far have already done (p. 165).

---

17. T.H. Lim, 'The Qumran Scrolls: Two Hypotheses', *SR* 21 (1992), pp. 455-
66.

It is obvious that I do not fully agree with Stegemann, and I think the test proposed by Lim could be fruitfully applied. My intention here is precisely to begin this application, and to assess the four selected theories in view of the newly-released material. Put differently, I intend to examine which of these four theories is the most congruent with the evidence now available. Of course, I cannot review all the documents in the time I have at my disposition. I will therefore concentrate on those documents that appear to be the most promising for shedding some light on the problem, namely: 4QMMT; 4QDamascus; 4QSerek-Damascus and the different Calendars.

1.

I think we should start with the Calendars and Priestly Rosters, not only because they reveal one of the weakest spots in some of the theories (Stegemann, for example, recognizes the Calendar as the first *problem* in his reconstruction) but because we encounter the same *solar* calendar in two of the most important texts that have recently become accessible: 4QMMT[a] and 4QS[e] (4Q259). If we leave out for the moment the two calendars just mentioned (4Q394 and 4Q259), we have 15 manuscripts in Cave 4 which contain the remains of eight (or nine) calendrical compositions that are clearly different one from another. These have been designated 4QCalendar[a-h] and listed under the Q numbers 4Q320–330.[18]

These compositions are of different sorts: some of them are intended to synchronize the dates of the widely-used *lunar* calendar with the *solar* calendar which these texts consider the right one. Others are intended to synchronize the *solar* calendar with a six-year cycle of the 24 priestly courses which do weekly service in the Temple. Yet others are intended to record which priestly course is in service at the beginning of each month of the cycle, or at the beginning of each season, or at the end of each season, or in which priestly course each sabbath of the year falls, or in which priestly course the Passover falls. Others are festal calendars that indicate in which priestly course fall the traditional Old Testament feasts, or some special feast envisioned, for example, in

18. The different numbers resulting from my count and the Q numbers are the result of later subdivision of some of the material of the original plates: 4Q320 and 4Q329 have been divided into two different manuscripts, and 4Q324 into four.

the *Temple Scroll*, fall. Finally, others are intended to record the date within this system on which historical events occurred.

These eight calendars are not only different because of their contents. They can also be distinguished on the basis of their different literary forms, and even on the basis of their different scribal characteristics. Some of them [4Q320, 4Q321–321a and 4Q325] are well-written copies of complex literary compositions with various clearly distinct parts; others [4Q328–329, 4Q329a and 4Q330] seem to be simple lists, something like our pocket calendars; some others [at least three or four of the six copies of Calendar C] have been carelessly written in a semi-cursive script, or have other writing on the back, which indicates that they are probably autograph copies intended for personal use. It will be useful here to provide a very short description of each of these different compositions.[19]

4QCalendar A (4Q320), formed of small leather bands and possibly written at the end of the second century BCE, contains three clearly different sections: the first offers a synchronism of the *solar* calendar of 364 days represented by the priestly courses with a *lunar* calendar of 354 days during a cycle of three years; the synchronism is shown indicating with numbers which day of the solar month corresponds to the last day of the lunar months of either 29 or 30 days. It also shows in which priestly course this correspondence occurs. The second section is very fragmentary, but seems to compose a jubilee cycle in which the roster of priests on duty at the end of each month was schematically listed. The third section is a festal calendar covering a six-year cycle, indicating on which day of the week of which priestly course the well-known feasts of the Old Testament fall.

4QCalendar B (4Q321–321a). The first and better preserved copy of this composition (4Q321) has been copied in a manuscript of small dimensions with only eight or nine line per column, written in a beautiful Herodian hand dating from the turn of the era.[20] It contains two

---

19. The Hebrew text is now easily available in the first volume of B.Z. Wacholder and M.G. Abegg, *A Preliminary Edition of the Unpublished Dead Sea Scrolls: The Hebrew and Aramaic Texts from Cave Four: Fascicle One* (Washington: Biblical Archaeology Society, 1991), pp. 60-101. The only complete translation I know is in Dutch, in F. García Martínez and A.S. van der Woude, *De rollen van de Dode Zee: Ingeleid in het Nederlands vertaald* (Kampen: Kok, 1995), II, pp. 463-94.

20. This manuscript was published in 1991 (see S. Talmon and I. Knohl, 'A

clearly different parts. The first offers a synchronism of the *solar* calendar with the *lunar* calendar and with the priestly courses, using two key days of the lunar month: the new moon designated with the previously-unknown word *dwqh* and the full moon, for which no especial name is used. The second part notes which priestly course is on duty at the beginning of each month during the six-year cycle, and in which priestly course the main feast falls without indicating in which day of the week this happens.

4QCalendar C^{a-f} (4Q322–324). Although the designation used implies we have here six copies of the same composition, I am rather inclined to consider them as six compositions of the same type and literary genre because there are no overlaps either in the calendrical data or in historical allusions. As has been said previously, four of these manuscripts seem to be personal copies, a designation that could possibly also apply to the other two copies: the one written on papyrus (4Q324b) and the one written in the so-called 'Cryptic writing' (4Q324c). These compositions are characterized by using the priestly rosters as a calendrical element in order to indicate when certain historical facts happened. The historical allusions (facts and/or names) are not like those of the pesharim, which have been completely theologized. Nor are they like the historical allusions of later compositions such as the *Meggilat Ta'anit*, which serve as the bases for annual celebrations. The preserved fragments offer no value judgments concerning the events mentioned. They simply record when something happened. The fragmentary nature of the remains palpably reduces their usefulness for historical reconstruction. The only thing we can say is that these *calendars* (or rather *annali*) chronicle the facts of the years preceding the conquest of Jerusalem by Pompey, as the names of all the

---

Calendrical Scroll from Qumran Cave IV: Mish B^a [4Q321]', *Tarbiz* 60 [1991], pp. 505-21 [Hebrew]) and has been the subject of various studies: M. Albani, 'Die lunaren Zyklen im 364-Tage-Festkalender von 4QMischmerot/4QS^{d}', *Forschungstelle Judentum: Mitteilungen und Beiträge* 4 (1992), pp. 3-47; C. Martone, 'Un calendario proveniente da Qumran recentemente publicato', *Henoch* 16 (1994), pp. 49-75; M.O. Wise, 'Observations on New Calendrical Texts from Qumran' in *idem, Thunder in Gemini* (JSPSup, 15; Sheffield: JSOT Press, 1994), pp. 222-32; M.O. Wise, 'Second Thoughts on *dwq* and the Qumran Synchronistic Calendars' in J.C. Reeves and J. Kampen (eds.), *Pursuing the Text: Studies in Honor of Ben Zion Wacholder on the Occasion of his Seventieth Birthday* (JSOTSup, 184; Sheffield: Sheffield Academic Press, 1994), pp. 98-120.

protagonists mentioned correspond to known important figures of the period from Alexandra Salome until Aemilius Scaurus.

4QCalendar D (4Q325) is similar to one of the parts of the Calendars A and B, in which the priestly course is indicated wherein the sabbaths and some feasts fall. The difference is that the feasts recorded are apparently only the pentecostal feasts of firstlings, the feast of the new barley (*sheorim*), the new wheat, wine, oil (reconstructed) and wood.

4QCalendar E^{a-b} (4Q326–327) is very similar to 4QCalendar D, in which there is a record of the dates of the sabbaths and feasts. The different is that apparently in these calendars these dates are not related to the priestly courses. The second of these calendars (4Q327) is well known because the editors of 4QMMT have published it as part of one of the copies of MMT (4Q394).[21]

4QCalendar F^{a-b} (4Q328–329) records which priestly courses are on duty at the beginning of each year and at the beginning of each month (4Q328) that starts a new season (*t^{e}qufah*) of the same six-year cycle, or (4Q329) at the end of the month in which each season begins.

4QCalendar G (4Q239a) is a simple sheet which records on which priestly course Passover falls in each year of the cycle.

4QCalendar H (4Q330) is so fragmentary that it is impossible to ascertain the type of calendar used.

These are the calendrical materials now available. What can we conclude from these materials regarding our problem? To which of the four hypotheses do they lend more support?

We can start by noting that the use of the priestly courses as a principle of reckoning the time indicates the strong priestly roots of these calendars and of the people who used them. This fact is congruent with all four theories, as all of them underline the importance of the priestly component of the community and the continued strong interest in cultic matters even after the break with the Temple of Jerusalem. But the fact that these priestly courses are used as the frame of a *solar* calendar of 364 days and that all the calendars found are *solar* calendars seem to be compatible only with the Groningen Hypothesis.

The descriptions have shown that not one of the calendars found can be considered as representing the *lunar* calendar followed by other Jews and used in the temple cult. This is not exactly the situation one

21. Which it is not, as I think I have proved in 'Dos Notas sobre 4QMMT', *RevQ* 16.62 (1993), pp. 293-97.

would expect if the scrolls were brought from the different libraries of Jerusalem and represented the whole of the literature of the period; a fact which underlines the homogeneity of the collection and its 'sectarian' character, and further disqualifies Golb's hypothesis.

It also disqualifies the 'traditional Essene' hypothesis and the hypothesis of the 'Essene Union' in so far as in the classical descriptions of the Essenes there is no hint at all that they followed a different calendar from the rest of the people.[22] This is a well-known objection to these theories, and remains a main obstacle to the simple identification of the community of the Scrolls with the Essenes as known from the classical sources in spite of the desperate efforts of Stegemann[23] to minimize the force of the argument.

The same argument even more clearly disqualifies the Sadducean hypothesis. It is true that we have even less information on the Sadducees than we have on the Essenes, but the complete silence of the rabbinical writings on the issue is certainly significant. After all, we know of several cases of alternating Sadducean and Pharisaic dominance in the Temple, and on none of these occasions is the calendar problem brought to the fore.

Besides, our calendars offer us a concrete proof that they are not congruent with the Sadducean hypothesis. The feast of the first fruits of barley is clearly fixed on the 26th of the first month, a Sunday, and is considered the starting point for counting the dates of the other pentecostal festivals. These calendars differ on this detail from the position taken by the Boetusians (or Sadducees) as shown by *m. Men.* 10.3, according to which the Sadduceans held that the festival was to be celebrated the day after the first sabbath following Passover, and not (as in these calendars) on the day following the first sabbath after the whole festival. This example, by the way, is extremely interesting: it show that both the Boetusians and the community of Qumran (on the evidence of the *Temple Scroll*) interpreted *shabbat* in the biblical expression *mimmohorat hashshabbat* (of Lev. 23.11 and 15) in the same manner (as opposed to the Pharisees). For the Pharisees, *shabbat* would mean 'a day of rest' and they fixed the feast of the 'Omer on the 16th of Nisan, after the 'day of rest' that was the first day of Passover (the 15th

22. These descriptions are easily available in G. Vermes and M.D. Goodman (eds.), *The Essenes According to the Classical Sources* (Oxford Centre Textbooks, 1; Sheffield: JSOT Press, 1989).
23. 'The Qumran Essenes', pp. 114-22.

of Nisan). For the Boetusians and the community of Qumran, *shabbat* means 'Saturday', and *mimmohorat hashshabbat* thus means Sunday. But the different dates postulated for the festival by the Boetusians and by the calendars of the community clearly show that a common interpretative tradition on halakhic matter does not necessarily mean that the two groups arrived at the same conclusion, and even less, of course, that the two groups are identical.

Another interesting point is that the people who wrote and used these calendars knew that others followed a different calendar, and they accordingly tried to synchronize both. Nevertheless, they present their own calendar as a matter of fact. There is no hint of polemic in the way these calendars are presented, not even regarding the ones which synchronize the *solar* with the *lunar* calendar. We are far from a situation like the one found in *Jubilees*, which strongly advocates one calendar and condemns in no uncertain terms anyone who does not follow it. Nothing of the sort is found in these 4Q Calendars. The polemics that necessarily relate to the adoption of a different calendar seem to be forgotten. It seems to me that although this fact does not disqualify any of the hypotheses under consideration, it is nevertheless less congruent with 'Main Union Essenes' of Stegemann's hypothesis than with the other theories, in so far as it is easier to understand such a lack of polemics in a situation of isolation than in a situation of continuous interaction and contact.

As far as can be ascertained, the events recorded in the calendars with historical allusions do not refer to the inner history of the group, but to the political and military history of Palestine. Therefore, they seem to be of no help in reconstructing the history of the community. If anything at all can be concluded from these limited references, it is that all the persons named seem to belong to the period between Alexandra Salome and Pompey. This could mean that the Antiochean crisis, that is of such importance to both the 'traditional Essene hypothesis' and the new revised Essene hypothesis of Stegemann, was not very important to the writers of these calendars, a situation that would be more congruent with the Groningen hypothesis, which clearly separates the origins of the community from the Antiochean crisis, and rather locates the move to Qumran at the end of the second century BCE.

II

The second document I wanted to examine is the *Miqsat Ma'aśe ha-torah*, fully available since last summer[24] and considered to be the point of departure for the 'Sadducean' hypothesis.[25]

As is well known, this document has been fragmentarily preserved in six different manuscripts (4Q394–399) which (thanks to overlapping) have been put together in a 'composite text'. This composite has been generally accepted, although the precise location of one sizeable fragment remains a matter of dispute, even between the two editors of the composite: Qimron and Strugnell.[26]

The document, whose introduction has been lost, consists of two or perhaps three sections with distinct contents: a calendarical, legal and hortatory section. It seems clear that the legal and hortatory sections are structurally united and form a whole as parts of the same original composition. Both are written in the same style, with the same opposition between the 'we' and the 'you', and both have a sort of inclusion between the beginning and the end (lines 4 and 113 of the 'composite text') with strictly parallel sentences.

It is less certain that the first part, the calendar, was originally part of the same composition. In Strugnell's opinion[27] it is not as polemical as the other parts; it is not addressed to any 'opponents' and it is only attested in one of the copies (4Q394) and not in another (4Q395),

24. E. Qimron and J. Strugnell, *Qumran Cave 4. V. Miqsat Ma'aśe ha-Torah* (DJD, 10; Oxford: Clarendon Press, 1994) (all quotations are taken from this edition).

25. Although, in fact, the revival of the old Sadducean hypothesis goes back to the publication of the *Temple Scroll* in which are reflected two of the controversies about purity between Sadducees and Pharisees recorded in the Mishnah; see J.M. Baumgarten, 'The Pharisaic-Sadducean Controversies about Purity and the Qumran Texts', *JJS* 31 (1980), pp. 157-70.

26. See Appendix 2 (pp. 201-202), 'Additional Textual Observations on 4QMMT' by E. Qimron, and Appendix 3 (pp. 203-206), 'Additional Observations on 4QMMT' by J. Strugnell. Strugnell has voiced his criticism even before the official publication of the book; see J. Strugnell, 'MMT: Second Thoughts on a Forthcoming Edition', in E. Ulrich and J. VanderKam (eds.), *The Community of the Renewed Covenant: The Notre Dame Symposium on the Dead Sea Scrolls* (Christianity and Judaism in Antiquity Series, 10; Notre Dame: University of Notre Dame Press, 1994), pp. 57-73.

27. Qimron and Strugnell, *Qumran Cave 4*, p. 203.

which seems, however, to preserve the beginning of the composition. The limited text that has survived (only the fragmentary remnants of three lines have been preserved), the facts that the manuscript with the remains of the calendar seems to be the oldest of all the copies of MMT, and the absence of an introduction to the composition as a whole, do not allow us, in my opinion, to exclude the calendar as an original part of the composition, as one of the key elements of the composition, and as one of the elements in which the 'we' group of the composition has separated itself from the others. Furthermore, it was, in fact, included in one of the copies of the composition, in much the same way as a calendar had been included in one of the copies of 4QS. We are at the least entitled to conclude that the group who wrote the composition and who continued to copy it, had accepted and had followed this *solar* calendar of 364 days.

The legal part of the composition is consistently redacted in a plural form. It offers itself as the expression of the halakhic positions, not of a single individual, but of a group which speaks of itself in the plural 'we'. This group thinks in a different way than another group which is always referred to in the third person plural, 'they', and which, in the hortatory section, is identified as 'the majority of the people'. This group is clearly different from those addressed by the composition, to whom the document refers in the legal section, with the use of the second person plural, 'you'. However, in the hortatory sections of the document, we find a curious mix of singular and plural forms. Although we find one example of the plural you-form, referring to the addressee, the addressee of this section is normally referred to in the singular you-form, a person who apparently occupied a pre-eminent position.

This use of 'we', 'you' and 'they' underlines the programmatic character of the composition as well as its polemical nature. The group which exposes its ideas in the document (the 'we' group, to use Qimron's terminology)[28] has apparently broken with another (larger) group (the 'they' group) which is understood to interpret some legal precepts wrongly. The 'we' group address its composition not to this dissenting group, but to yet another group (the 'you' group) and its leader (the singular 'you').

The hortatory section makes it clear that the 'we' group expects to win the 'you' group over to its side, so that in the end the 'you' group

28. Qimron and Strugnell, *Qumran Cave 4*, p. 175.

will recognize that the halakhic positions defended by the 'we' group are indeed the correct ones, as opposed to the positions of the 'they' group. The reasons given are, on the one hand, that the 'you' group knows the probity of the 'we' group and, on the other hand that the 'you' group has enough knowledge of Scripture to be able to recognize that the legal interpretations proposed by the 'we' group are the right ones. This means that the interpretations of the 'we' and 'you' groups are not very distant from one another, and that the existing differences between the 'we' and the 'you' group (which are never spelled out in the text) are judged to be easily bridged over.

It is interesting to note the assumption of the text that this recourse to Scripture will lead the 'you' group not only to appreciate the correctness of the halakhic interpretations of the 'we' group, but also that its interpretation of sacred history is the correct one, that the accomplishment of the blessings and curses shows that the present time is to be understood as 'the last days', and, accordingly, that in this period, it is necessary to be protected from Belial. For our purposes, the most interesting question connected with this fascinating document is the identification of the three groups. Everybody agrees that the 'they' group must be the Pharisees, an identification which does not need to occupy us here.

It is obvious that the 'we' group is related to, or identical with, the Qumran community. The just-mentioned theological ideas of the hortatory section are common to the Qumran writings. Even more telling is the huge number of halakhic positions which deviate from traditional halakhah but agree with halakhic positions known to us thanks to 11QTemple and the *Damascus Document*.[29] For example: the eating of offerings on the same day as the sacrifice, the selection of hides, the understanding of the foetus as distinct from the mother, the tithes for herd and flock, the process of purification of lepers and the impurity of the human bones.

It is equally obvious that some of the halakhic positions defended in the composition are positions taken by the Sadducees in their polemic

---

29. First summarized by Y. Sussmann, 'The History of Halakha and the Dead Sea Scrolls: Preliminary Talmudic Observations on *Miqsat ma'aśe ha-torah* (4QMMT)', *Tarbiz* 59 (1989–90), pp. 11-76 (Hebrew) (partially translated into English and published as Appendix 1 in Qimron and Strugnell, *Qumran Cave 4*, pp. 179-200), and studied in detail by E. Qimron in the chapter 'The Halakha', in Qimron and Strugnell, *Qumran Cave 4*, pp. 123-77.

against the Pharisees. The two most clear and telling examples adduced by Schiffman are the discussion as to the purity of those preparing the cow (the red-heifer) for the purification offering and the discussion on the purity of the liquid streams (the pouring of liquids from one vessel to another).[30] In these two cases we have specific information in rabbinic texts (in *m. Para* 3.7 and in *m. Yadayim* 4.7, respectively) about the positions of the Sadducees and the Pharisees, and there is no doubt that the halakhic position of the 'we' group in these cases agrees with the halakhic position that has been attributed to the Sadducees, while the opposite position of the 'they' group agrees with that attributed to the Pharisees.

On other halakhot also adduced by Schiffman as proof of the Sadducean character of the halakhah of MMT,[31] the particularly 'Sadducean' character is less clear or has been disputed.[32] I think that the following sweeping conclusion drawn by Sussmann is unwarranted:

> Thus, I would venture to say that those of the sect's halakhot which are not explicitly identified by the rabbinic sources as Sadducean may be assumed to be such, since these rulings were followed by the members of the sect, whose halakhic views are otherwise known to be Sadducean (p. 196).

Nevertheless, MMT clearly favours at first sight the hypothesis of Sadducean origins for the Community, although, in my opinion, it remains short of having been proven for the following reasons:

1) The identity of a few halakhic positions should not be confounded with the identity of two groups. Two different groups can perfectly easily have in common some halakhic traditions. The 'we' and the 'you' groups of MMT, which are presented as distinct, nevertheless apparently share the same halakhic traditions, although these are opposed to the traditions of the 'they' group. Of course, there is no reason why two groups should disagree in everything. In this particular case, the opposite should be expected. After all, the Qumran community uses the

30. L.H. Schiffman, 'Pharisaic and Sadducean Halakhah in Light of the Dead Sea Scrolls: The Case of the Tevul Yom', *DSD* 1 (1994), pp. 285-99.

31. See the works cited in n. 16.

32. For example, in a series of articles published collected and edited by Z.J. Kapera, *Qumran Cave Four: Special Report: 4QMMT* (Krakow: Enigma, 1991); Davies, 'Sadducees in the Dead Sea Scrolls?', pp. 85-94; Eisenman, 'A Response to Schiffman on MMT', pp. 95-104; VanderKam, 'The Qumran Residents: Essenes not Sadduccees!', pp. 105-108.

self-designation 'sons of Zadok', referring to its priestly ancestry, while the Sadducees seem to derive their name from Zadok.

2) It seems difficult to reconcile the few indications about the Sadducees known from rabbinic writings with the more elaborate descriptions of the Sadducees that are provided by Josephus and the New Testament. This has led even the defenders of the Sadducean hypothesis to distinguish between different types of Sadducees: those described by Josephus and the ones described in the Mishnah. It is clear that the ideological tenets of the Sadducees as described by Josephus contradict several of the most characteristic tenets of the Qumran writings. As VanderKam says:[33]

> Perhaps, for the sake of clarity in English, we could use *Zadokians* for the people to whom the Mishna refers. They may have been very much like the Essenes or even identical with them. That they were Sadducees of the type known from the New Testament and Josephus is obviously wrong.

3) A serious obstacle to the Sadducean hypothesis is formed by the presence of the remnants of the *solar* calendar in at least one of the manuscripts. This obstacle becomes a stumbling block if, as I think, the calendar of the original composition is one of the elements that separates this 'we' group from 'the majority of the people'[34] or from 'the council (or multitude) of the congregation' (as Wacholder and Abegg prefer to reconstruct the sentence).[35] As I have mentioned in the previous section, this last argument also holds against the 'Essene' hypothesis in both of its forms, and strongly supports the 'Groningen hypothesis'.

An important element in deciding which of these three hypotheses best supports the new data of MMT is the understanding of MMT as a Qumranic or a pre-Qumranic document. As is well known, the editors of the texts disagree on this issue. Qimron,[36] bluntly asserts that it is a

33. J.C. VanderKam, *The Dead Sea Scrolls Today* (Grand Rapids: Eerdmans, 1994), p. 95.

34. According to the reconstruction of the editors, Qimron and Strugnell, *Qumran Cave 4*, p. 59

35. B.Z. Wacholder and M.G. Abegg, *A Preliminary Edition of the Unpublished Dead Sea Scrolls: The Hebrew and Aramaic Texts from Cave Four: Fascicle Three* (Washington: Biblical Archaeology Society, 1995), pp. xxiv-xxv and p. 287.

36. Qimron and Strugnell, *Qumran Cave 4*, p. 175

Qumran text; Strugnell[37] considers a pre-Qumranic setting for the document more likely.

A Qumranic setting would appear congruent with the traditional 'Essene' hypothesis. The 'we' group would be the Essenes, who address the document, in the words of Cross:[38]

> to a leader and group admired for wisdom and understanding by the authors. This is most easily understood as a collateral line of Zadokite priests who have not joined the Essene community and its priests of the Zadokite house.

But the problem with this interpretation is very similar to the problem of the Sadducean interpretation: the difficulty of reconciling the profile of the 'we' group as reflected in MMT with what Josephus tell us about the Essenes.

I have addressed the issue of the Qumranic or pre-Qumranic setting of MMT in my contribution to the late SBL meeting in Chicago,[39] and my conclusion was that of the two topics I had discussed (the expressions *'aharit hayamim* and *ma'aśe ha-torah*), one pointed to a pre-Qumranic setting for the composition while the other did not demand a Qumranic setting for it. This makes a pre-Qumranic setting most likely indeed, on the condition, however, that this pre-Qumranic setting is understood as related to the future Qumran community. Otherwise the elements noted to be held in common with other Qumranic writings would remain without explanation. And this is precisely the understanding of the document as put forward by the 'Groningen Hypothesis'. This hypothesis considers 4QMMT as having originated within the formative period of the Qumran community, when the group, which in its later context we call the Qumran community, had already been formed, had adopted the calendar, and was following the halakhah we know from other Qumran compositions. The group had then also started to develop some of the characteristic theological ideas that we meet in a much more developed form in these same Qumranic compositions, but it had not yet occupied the Qumran settlement.

---

37. Qimron and Strugnell, *Qumran Cave 4*, pp. 114-21,

38. F.M. Cross, *The Ancient Library of Qumran* (Sheffield: Sheffield Academic Press, 3rd edn, 1995), p. 185.

39. F. García Martínez, '4QMMT in a Qumran Context', in J. Kampen and M.J. Bernstein (eds.), *Reading 4QMMT: New Perspectives on Qumran Law and History* (SBL Symposium Series, 2; Atlanta: Scholars Press, 1996), pp. 15-27.

III

The third document I want to examine is the *Damascus Document*, because the 4Q copies now available in preliminary transcriptions in the first volume of Wacholder and Abegg[37] have greatly modified our understanding of the original composition as a whole. On the basis of content, the original composition can now easily be divided into three different parts: 1) An extended admonition directed to the members of the group that forms an introduction to the subsequent laws. 2) A compendium of legal norms, some of them of biblical origin, others representing the halakhic interpretation of biblical laws followed within the group, and yet other specific norms which apply to the life of the group. 3) A collection of sectarian rules (for the meetings of the camps, for the Inspector and for the Many) followed by a penal code, which regulates the infractions of the community discipline and the process of expulsion of the sinner, and which is concluded by the ceremony of expulsion from the community.

1) The first part, the initial admonition, is a long exposition on the history of salvation in which the history of the group is embedded: the result without any doubt of a long redactional process. It is best known by the two copies of the Cairo Genizah. The new fragments add only a call to the sons of light to separate from 'those who move the boundary', to listen to the voice of Moses and to remain faithful to all the precepts, especially 'not advancing or delaying their festivals' (4QD[b]). If fragment 9 of 4QD[e] is to be placed at this point, as it seems to me,[38] this introduction will have contained a list of sins that reappear later on in the specific laws: sexual offenses (including improper use of one's wife), tithes, the money of ransom for their souls, skin diseases, and so forth. These new elements do not substantially change the understanding of the old Admonition known from the copies of the Cairo

---

37. Quoted in n. 19. All references to the 4Q manuscripts are taken from this preliminary edition. The references to the Genizah copies are taken from the edition of E. Qimron and M. Broshi (eds.), *The Damascus Document Reconsidered* (Jerusalem: Israel Exploration Society, 1992).

38. Because it ends with the beginning of a discourse in the first person, strictly parallel to the beginning of the other three discourses of the admonition, 4QD[e] 9.2.19-20: 'And now, listen to me all you who know justice and fulfil the law. I shall give you paths of life, but the ways of the pit I shall open for the wicked and their deeds.'

Genizah, but prove at least that the opinions of those who have considered the Admonition and the Laws to be two independent and
unrelated compositions were wrong.

2) The new fragments have shed much more light on the second part
of the composition. They have not only proved that the original order
was severely truncated in the Genizah copy, but also that the extension
and variety of this section is not well represented in this copy. Basically, this second part is a collection of legal lore, globally ordered by
themes, and sometimes even provided with rubrics which determine
their contents. But we do not find a systematic treatise of sectarian
halakha or an exposition of biblical laws in the order in which they
appear in the biblical text. Indeed, we are confronted with an anthology
of legal norms extracted from different collections of halakhic materials
in which laws intended for all Israel are mixed with norms intended to
regulate the life of sectarian assemblies in the cities or in the camps, or
to regulate the conduct of sectarian functionaries.

Sometimes it is possible to fathom the reason for putting together
different norms. For example, the reference to the oath of the covenant
has motivated the insertion of the norms that regulate entrance into the
group. The norms on the testimony before judges have motivated the
inclusion of the rules for the judges of the community. The prohibition
of sacrifices gives the possibility to include other prescriptions concerning the temple and the city of the temple. But in many other cases, it
seems impossible to ascertain the reason of the sequence for the laws in
the compendium.

The themes that can be recognized putting together the elements fur-
nished by the copies of Cave 4 with CD A are the following, and
appear in this order (I indicate only the main topics and mention only
the manuscript in which the norms are better preserved): norms against
cheating your fellow communitarians, about women and the selection
of a wife (D^c 1.1); norms about tithes, sacrifices of pagans and the
metals used by them (D^c 1.2); norms about unfaithful women and bitter
waters (D^e 8); norms about the disqualification of priests (D^b 6.1-2);
norms about skin diseases and child birth (D^b 9.1-2); norms about wines
and other produce of the fields (D^b 12-13); norms about oaths (CD A
15); instruction for the entrance into the covenant (CD A 15-16); norms
about oaths of women (CD A 16); about the freewill-offerings (CD A
16); about reproof and witnesses (CD A 9); norms about judges in the
congregation and about purification with water (CD A 10); norms about

the sabbath (CD A 10-11); about relations with Gentiles (CD A 12) and dietary and purity norms (CD A 12).

3) The third part (which begins in CD A 12.19 with the heading: 'Rule for the assembly of the cities of Israel') is more homogeneous and contains sectarian legislation: a rule for the assembly of the camps (CD A 12.23–13.7); for the Inspector of the camps (13.7–14.2); for the session of all the camps, determining the 'priest who is named at the head of the many' and the 'Inspector who is over all the camps' (CD A 14.3-12); norms to provide for the needs of the 'many' (CD A 14.12-18); a penal code which defines the punishments for the transgressions of the community discipline and which is partially parallel to the penal code of 1QS, but adds other transgressions, which are punished by expulsion from the community (D^b 18.4 and D^e 11.1). This third part (and the whole composition) ends with a description of the ceremony of exclusion of unfaithful members, a ceremony which is to be celebrated in the third month (D^b 18.5 and D^e 11.2).

This short summary shows the enormous richness of the new fragments of the *Damascus Document* and the potential they have to modify our understanding of the history of the Community. It also makes clear that it is impossible to deal with all of them in the available space. I will concentrate on one topic: the penal code that had not been preserved in the Genizah copies.

This penal code is in part parallel to the penal code of 1QS, although some of the penalties imposed for the same transgressions of community discipline are different in both forms of the penal code. Also, this penal code mentions some transgressions which are punished by expulsion that are not mentioned in 1QS, and which throw new light on the community discipline, such as committing a sexual offence with one's wife, despising the communal law, or murmuring against 'the fathers of the assembly'.[39]

But to fully understand these differences and their implications for the history of the community, I should mention first another composition (4Q265) in which the same penal code appears: a composition known under the title *4QSerek Damascus*.[40] This composition has been

---

39. But the offence of murmuring against 'the mothers' merits only a 10-day punishment.

40. Partially published and studied by J. Baumgarten, 'The Cave 4 Versions of the Qumran Penal Code', *JJS* 43 (1992), pp. 268-76. The full Hebrew text of the fragments can be found in Wacholder and Abegg, *Fascicle Three*, pp. 72-78.

preserved in only one copy, a manuscript from the end of the first century BCE. From the 25 fragments assigned to this manuscript, only four are of such a size as to allow one to draw some conclusions about their contents.

In spite of the small amount of material preserved, it is clear that the composition is a combination of the *Serek* and the *Damascus Document*. This is shown by the common elements, as well as by the differences from both compositions. For example, by the remains of a procedure of entrance into the community, which seems very close to the procedure of 1QS 6, insofar as several years are involved and the questioning is done by the 'many', but is not the same we find in CD. Similar also to 1QS 8.1 is the specification of 4QSD that the council of the community has to be formed by 15 members. On the contrary, however, frag. 2 is very similar to the sabbath code of CD, although not completely identical. For example: in both documents, it is forbidden to extract an animal which has fallen in the water. However, while CD A 11.16-17 forbids using a rope or other tool for helping a person who has fallen into the water, 4QSD allows throwing him his garment and lifting him out with it. Also different is the limit that an animal should walk on the sabbath: 2000 cubits in 4QSD against only 1000 cubits in CD A 11.5-6.

The penitential code is found in frag. 1. Its most notable characteristic is that the punishment takes the form of temporary expulsion *and* deprivation of half of the food ration, an element which is otherwise only mentioned once in the penal code of 1QS (on 6.25), and which is *completely absent* from the penal code of 4QD, which mentions temporary expulsion and temporary punishment, without specifying which sort of punishment is foreseen, but indicating that the punishment (whatever it may be) is always shorter than the temporary expulsion.

It is obvious that the three forms of the penal code are closely related. The similarities and the differences can be explained according to different theoretical models. The three depend on a common source: a penal code unknown to us, which is modified to apply it to the needs of the community to which it is addressed. One of the penal codes is the source used by the redactor of the other two. They represent three successive phases of the same code. Furthermore, if the development model is the more likely, it will be necessary to be precise as to the direction in which this development has occurred. This requires establishing which is the older form of the penal code, as well as whether the development is directed from a more lenient to a more rigorous form of penal code or from the more rigorous to a more lenient. Once we have established which of the penal codes is the oldest, we should weigh the possibility that at some point in the long redactional history of the compositions, the penal code could have been modified under the influence of a code which had originated at a later date.

In order to assess which one of these theoretical possibilities is the more likely, it is necessary to analyze three factors: the offences reported in the three codes (which ones present in one code are missing in the others, as well as why they are missing); the penalties imposed for the same offence in each code, the differences between the penalties and the reasons behind these differences; and the differences that appear (as scribal corrections) in 1QS which modify the penalties recorded for some offenses.

The model I am using at the moment is the one in which both 4QD and 1QS are dependent on a common source (a penal code belonging to the parent movement of the Qumran sect) and according to which 4QSD knows both 4QD and 1QS and modifies them in the direction of a more lenient position.

It is obvious that the code of 1QS is the more rigorous of all three codes regarding the length of the penalties imposed and, in at least one case, the type of penalty (food deprivation). It is equally obvious that the penal code of 4QD includes a series of offenses that lead to expulsion. These offences are not included in 1QS. Similarly, this penal code applies to a community of married men and women (consider the expulsion for sexual offenses with one's wife, but also norms for selecting wives, a selection which requires the approval of the Inspector) and in which the 'fathers' and the 'mothers' are persons of unequal authority. It seems equally obvious that 4QSD can only apply to a community in which the members share the food they take. This sort of punishment seems to be the development of a tendency started in 1QS.

Which of the four hypotheses sketched out above is the most congruent with this penal code? As far as it implies a closely-structured community, it does not seem to lend any support to the Sadducean hypothesis. On the contrary; the fact that the penal code of 4QD does not mention the deprivation of food as a form of punishment certainly does not favour the 'Essene' hypothesis, which considers 'common meals' as one of the closer parallels of the Qumran community with the Essenes as described in the classical sources. If my model for explaining the relationships between the different forms of the penal code can be accepted, it would support the 'Groningen hypothesis'.

In summary I do not think the Sadducean hypothesis can be maintained in the light of the new evidence, nor do I think that this evidence recommends the revised and augmented 'Essene' hypothesis that has been put forward by H. Stegemann. The question as to whether the teacher-group consisted of Essenes or a break-away group from the Essenes remains the key question for the explanation of the history of the Community. And I think the evidence now available clearly points to the fact that the teacher-group was not formed of Essenes that we know from our classical sources, but was rather a break-away group from this parent Essene movement, as it is understood in the Groningen Hypothesis.

In an article published in 1990 I summarized the understanding of the origins of the Qumran community in this way:[41]

> The study of this material [the writings of the pre-Qumran formation period] allows us to conclude that the fundamental disputes within the Essene movement during the formative period of the sect were centred on the question of the calendar and the subsequent organization of the festive cycle, and on a particular way of understanding the biblical prescriptions relating to the temple, the cult and the purity of persons and things. This particular halakhah is rooted in the Teacher of Righteousness's consciousness of having received by divine revelation the correct interpretation of the biblical text, an interpretation which is thus inspired and prescriptive, and the acceptance by some members of the community of this interpretation as a revelation. The rejection of this interpretation and of the particular halakhah deriving from it by the rest of the members of the Essene movement would end by making it impossible for them to stay together.

It is my conviction that the texts which have been recently made available confirm the understanding of the history of the Qumran community suggested by the 'Groningen Hypothesis' more than by any other of the four hypotheses considered here.

---

41. García Martínez and van der Woude, 'A "Groningen" Hypothesis of Qumran Origins and Early History', p. 538.

THE USE OF OLD TESTAMENT QUOTATIONS
IN THE QUMRAN COMMUNITY RULE[1]

Sarianna Metso

The existence of differences between the twelve copies of the *Community Rule* found in Qumran Caves 1, 4 and 5 is what one would antici-pate. After all, the manuscripts 1QS, 4QS[a-j] and 5Q11 were transmitted over a period of more than one hundred years. Somewhat surprising, however, is the fact that some of these differences are related to the use of Old Testament citations. Quite naturally, the citations which appear in the manuscript 1QS were a subject of study long before the material from Cave 4 was available to the vast majority of scholars.[2] These studies, such as those of Fitzmyer in 1961 and Vermes in 1989, include not only 1QS but other Qumranic rule texts (CD, 1QM) as well, and they mainly deal with the technique, that is, the exegetical principles involved in the use of these quotations and the classification of different ways of using the citations in the texts.[3] The availability of the Cave 4 material has opened up a new perspective of particular interest to the

1.   This paper is related to my doctoral dissertation which is shortly to be sub-mitted to the University of Helsinki. The work deals with the redaction history of the *Community Rule* and is based on a literary-critical analysis of the complete material of this document found in Qumran Caves 1, 4 and 5.
2.   Transcriptions of Cave 4 material of the *Community Rule* presented in this paper are by the author, but it may be noted that the Cave 4 fragments of the *Community Rule* have recently been published by E. Qimron, 'Cave IV Fragments (4Q255–264 = 4QS MSS A–J)', in J.H. Charlesworth (ed.), *The Dead Sea Scrolls: Hebrew, Aramaic, and Greek Texts with English Translations*. I. *Rule of the Com-munity and Related Documents* (Tübingen: J.C.B. Mohr [Paul Siebeck]; Louisville, KY: Westminster/John Knox Press, 1994), pp. 53-102.

[3] 3.   J.A. Fitzmyer, 'The Use of Explicit Old Testament Quotations in Qumran Literature and in the New Testament', *NTS* 7 (1961), pp. 297-333; G. Vermes, 'Biblical Proof-Texts in Qumran Literature', *JSS* 34.2 (1989), pp. 493-508. See also, e.g., P. Wernberg-Møller, 'Some Reflections on the Biblical Material in the

present writer, namely, that of the role of these citations in the redactional process of the *Community Rule*.

In what follows, I shall focus on three manuscripts in particular: 1QS, 4QS^b and 4QS^d. The best-preserved copy of the *Community Rule*, 1QS, is Hasmonean and has been dated to 100–75 BCE. The manuscripts 4QS^b and 4QS^d, on the other hand, are Herodian and can be dated to 30–1 BCE.[4] Both 4QS^b and 4QS^d give a form of the text shorter than that of 1QS. Moreover, the text of 4QS^b is practically identical with that of 4QS^d. The manuscripts even look alike: both of them are carefully written on well-prepared skins which have columns of about the same, rather small, size. There is only one clear difference between these two manuscripts from Cave 4: whereas 4QS^b includes part of the text from all sections of the *Community Rule*, 4QS^d does not—and did not even in its original form—contain any parallel to columns 1QS 1–4 (liturgical and theological sections). The text beginning with the parallel to 1QS 5.1 (regulations for community life) was most likely also the beginning of the whole manuscript of 4QS^d, since the right margin of column 1 in fragment 4QS^d 1 is unusually wide and bears no marks of stitching.

The *Community Rule* alludes to the Old Testament almost constantly. Old Testament phrases and expressions have been worked into the very fabric of the text without being designated as citations. This kind of style, familiar from other Qumranic texts, and from the New Testament as well, involves implicit exegesis and is due to thorough acquaintance with and reverent meditation upon the Old Testament.[5] Isolated explicit Old Testament citations introduced by specific formulas are far less frequent in the *Community Rule*. In 1QS there are only three of them and, quite astonishingly, they are entirely lacking in 4QS^{b,d}.

Before moving on to consider concrete examples of citations in the *Community Rule*, it needs to be emphasized that when discussing the so-called rule-texts (1QS, CD, 1QM) we are dealing with writings very different from the exegetical texts belonging to the interpretative genre,

---

Manual of Discipline', *ST* 9 (1956), pp. 40-66; S.D. Fraade, 'Interpretative Authority in the Studying Community at Qumran', *JJS* 144.1, (1993), pp. 46-69.

4.   The paleographical datings of 4QS^{b,d} first became known to me through personal consultation with H. Stegemann and A. Steudel in Göttingen. These datings have been recently confirmed by F.M. Cross, 'Paleographical Dates of the Manuscripts', in Charlesworth (ed.), *The Dead Sea Scrolls*, I, p. 57.

5.   Fitzmyer, 'The Use of Explicit Old Testament Quotations', pp. 298-99.

which includes such thematic midrashim as 4QMidrEschat (4Q174+ 177) and 11QMelchizedek, on the one hand, and the pesharim commentaries on complete biblical books, on the other hand. Whereas these writings display a clearly recognizable structure and take the citation as a starting-point for the interpretation, the structure in the rule-texts varies, and citations are used rather to support or illustrate an argument. Very often a citation acts as a kind of proof-text. Within the Qumran writings, the rule-texts (1QS, CD, 1QM), which combine citations into a prose narrative, come closest to the way the citations are used in the New Testament.

1. *Cases of Old Testament Citations in the* Community Rule

Two Old Testament citations are to be found in 1QS column 5, which begins a collection of rules for community life.[6] A passage commencing in line 7 speaks about the oath to be taken by those desiring to become members of the community. They were to bind themselves to the law of Moses (1QS 5.7b-10a) and to separate themselves from the men of injustice (1QS 5.10b-20a). In 1QS 5.7 the passage has a clear title: 'These are their rules of conduct, according to all these statutes, when they are admitted to the community' (ואלה תכון דרכיהם על כול החוקים האלה בהאספם ליחד) while 4QS[b,d] lacks such a title and begins with the words 'Everyone who joins the council of the community' (כול הבא לעצת היחד). A brief glimpse of the two versions of 1QS and 4QS reveals that the text of 1QS is more than twice as long as that of 4QS[b,d].

Quotation of Exodus 23.7

1QS 5.13b-16a:

13bאל יבוא במים לגעת בטהרת אנשי הקודש כיא לוא יטהרו14 כי אם שבו

מרעתם כיא טמא בכול עוברי דברו ואשר לוא יוחד עמו בעבודתו ובהונו

פן ישיאנו15 עוון אשמה כיא ירחק ממנו בכול דבר כיא כן כתוב מכול

דבר שקר תרחק ואשר לוא ישוב איש מאנשי16 היחד על פיהם לכול תורה

ומשפט

---

6.   See the translation in the Excursus.

4QS^b frag. 5, 8b-10a:

^{8b}[ואשר לוא יגעו לטהרת אנשי]^9 הקודש <u>ואל יוכל אתו ביחד</u> ואשר ל[וא

ישיב איש מאנשי היחד על פיהם]^{10a} לכול תורה ומשפט

4QS^d frag. 1 1.7b-9a:

^{7b}ואשר לא יגעו לטהרת אנשי ^{8} [הקוד]ש <u>ואל יוכל אתו בי[ו]נהד</u> ואשר לא

ישיב א[י]ש מאנשי היחד על פיהם לכל]^{9a} [תורה] ומשפט

In 1QS 5.13b-15a there is a section that is entirely lacking in 4QS^{b,d}. If we follow the end of line 7 and the beginning of line 8 in 4QS^d, which is better preserved than 4QS^b, we shall see that the words 'They shall not touch the purity of the men of holiness' (ואשר לא יגעו לטהרת אנשי [הקודש]) here provide a loose parallel to 1QS 5.13: 'He shall not enter the waters in order to touch the purity of the men of holiness' (אל יבוא במים לגעת לטהרת אנשי הקודש). The sentences begin somewhat differently, but apart from the preposition the words לטהרת אנשי הקודש (4QS^{b,d}) and בטהותרה אנשי הקודש are identical. These words occur in 4QS^{b,d}, followed by the sentence, 'He shall not eat with him within the community' (ואל יוכל אתו ביחד), which has nothing corresponding to it in 1QS. To be quite accurate, a similar kind of sentence does occur a little later in 1QS 5.16, but it appears in 4QS^{b,d} also. Thus, the prohibition against eating with a man of injustice occurs twice in 4QS^{b,d}, which makes one wonder whether the first occurrence is the result of an error (יוכל—ייחד; however, the verb יוכל appears in both 4QS^b and 4QS^d). Instead of the sentence ואל יוכל אתו ביחד, 1QS has a long passage which includes a biblical citation: 'No-one shall join with him (i.e. with a man of injustice) with regard to his work or his wealth lest he burden him with iniquity and guilt. But he shall keep away from him in everything, for thus it is written, "You shall keep away from everything false".' The sentence following the citation in 1QS, 'No one of the men of the community shall answer...' (ואשר לוא ישוב איש מאנשי היחד), is also attested in 4QS^{b,d}.

In this passage the basic statement of the oath to separate oneself from outsiders is clarified and confirmed with biblical proof-texts—Lev. 22.16 and Exod. 23.7. The former is an allusion (cf. Lev. 22.16(-15) ולא...והשיאו אותם עון אשמה), but the latter is a direct quotation. There is an introductory formula, כיא כן כתוב, which is followed by the citation, מכול דבר שקר תרחק. Interestingly, the citation is in a form that corresponds with the Septuagint rather than with the Masoretic text. The indefinite pronoun כול is missing in the Masoretic text (מדבר־שקר תרחק), but has an equivalent in the Septuagint (ἀπὸ παντὸς ῥήματος ἀδίκου). It is likely that the biblical manuscript used by the author contained this short word as a variant reading. Actually, Exod. 23.7 has to do with justice in lawsuits, but here—typically for Qumranic exegesis—it has been disconnected from its original context and applied to an entirely different matter. The catchwords here are רחק and דבר. The latter occurs not only immediately before the citation formula, but also earlier in line 14, in the third of the sentences starting with the conjunction כיא (note that there are five such sentences beginning with the conjunction כיא following one another).

Quotation of Isaiah 2.22

1QS 5.16b-19a:

16b ואשר לוא יוכל מהונם כול ולוא ישתה ולוא יקח מידם כול מאומה 17 אשר
לוא במחיר כאשר כתוב חדלו לכם מן האדם אשר נשמה באפו כיא במה נחשב
הואה כיא 18 כול אשר לוא נחשבו בבריתו להבדיל אותם ואת כול אשר להם
ולוא ישען איש הקודש על כול מעשי 19a הבל כי הבל כול אשר לוא ידעו את
בריתו

4QSb frag. 5, 10b-12a:

10b ואל יואכל 11 איש מא[נשי הקודש]   ולא ישענו על כול 12a מעשי
ההבל כי הבל כו[ל אשר לוא י]דעו את בריתו

4QSd frag. 1, col 1. 9b-11a:

9b ואל יואכל איש מאנשי הקדש 10 [ ]   [ל]   [°] ולא*ישנעו על [כל מע]שי
ההבל כי הבל כל אשר] לא ידעו 11a את בריתו

(*Scribal error, corr. ישענו.)

The next direct quotation occurring in 1QS is in lines 16b-18, and again it is lacking in 4QSb,d. In line 9 of 4QSd the words ואל יואכל correspond to the words ואשר לוא יוכל in 1QS 5.16. In 4QSd they are followed by the phrase איש מאנשי הקדש, which is lacking in 1QS. Then there is a gap of about three words in 4QSd, followed by the words ולא ישנעו על ('They shall not rely on'; note the scribal error in the verb, corr. ישענו) which correspond to the words ולוא ישען איש הקודש על ('No man of holiness shall rely on') in line 18 of 1QS. No matter what the missing words in the gap were, it is clear that the whole of the passage 1QS 5.16b-18b, with the citation from Isa. 2.22, was not included in the text of 4QS[b,d].[7] The missing passage, beginning with ואשר לוא יוכל, reads in full: 'No one shall eat or drink anything of their property, or take anything at all from their hand except for payment, as it is written, "Have no more to do with man in whose nostrils is breath, for what is he worth?" For all those who are not counted in his covenant, they and everything that belongs to them are to be kept separate.'

The passage continues the prohibition on contact with the men of injustice, apparently with a concern to preserve the ritual purity of the community. The formula preceding the citation is here different from the one in the previous passage. Instead of כיא כן כתוב, the text reads כאשר כתוב. The citation is in a form identical with the Masoretic text except for the form of the personal pronoun הואה. 1QIsa[a] uses the shorter form הוא, but chooses the longer form לכמה, which, however, in 1QS occurs as לכם. The quotation is followed by an interpretative comment. Note that in the context of the previous citation such an expository element is completely lacking. Obviously, the writer played with the verb נחשב, 'be accounted, be esteemed' and twisted its sense to bear the meaning 'being reckoned in the community' (cf. the occurrence of the same verb in 1QS 5.11). In the text of Isaiah, this verse counsels the people to cease trusting in the proud person, for in the day of God's judgment, human pride will be humbled. Isaiah's prophecy has been given a totally different point of reference.

Quotation of Isaiah 40.3

1QS 8.12b-16a:

12b ובהיות אלה ליחד בישראל 13 בתכונים האלה יבדלו מתוך מושב *הנשי העול
ללכת למדבר לפנות שם את דרך הואהא 14 כאשר כתוב במדבר פנו
דרך ···· ישרו בערבה מסלה לאלוהינו 15 היאה מדרש התורה [אשר] צוה
ביד מושה לעשות ככול הנגלה עת בעת 16a וכאשר גלו הנביאים ברוח קודשו

4QSd frag. 2, 1.6b-8a:

6b ובהיות אלה] בישראל [יבדלו מ]תוך מושב 7 אנשי העול ללכת למדבר
לפנות שם את דרך האמת (?) היאה מדרש התור]ה אשר צוה ביו]ד מושה לע[שות
כל] הנגלה 8a עת בעת וכאשר גלו הנביאים ברוח קודשו

(*Scribal error, corr. אנשי.)

7.   This verse is in 1QIsa[a] and in the MT, but that verse is a later addition, not yet in the Septuagint tradition.

The third of the biblical quotations occurring in the *Community Rule* is
to be found in 1QS column 8, in a section which contains a threefold
occurrence of the words בהיות אלה בישראל ('When these exist in
Israel'). The passage has been highly debated among scholars. Some
commentators suppose sectizn 1QS 8-9 to refer to the time of the founding of the community and consider that it represents a sort of 'Manifesto' or 'programme of the community'.[8] Professor Stegemann, on the
other hand, argues that the whole of the section of columns 8 and 9
consists of secondary additions.[9] My view of the matter is largely based
on the evidence of manuscript 4QS[e].[10] This manuscript lacks a long

8. E.g. E.F. Sutcliffe, 'The First Fifteen Members of the Qumran Community:
A Note on 1QS 8:1 ff.', *JSS* 4 (1959), pp. 134-38; A.R.C. Leaney, *The Rule of
Qumran and its Meaning* (The New Testament Library; London: SCM Press;
Philadelphia: Westminster Press, 1966), pp. 112, 115, 211; J. Murphy-O'Connor,
'La genèse littéraire de la Règle de la Communauté', *RB* 76 (1969), pp. 528-49
(529); J. Pouilly, *La Règle de la Communauté: Son evolution littéraire* (Cahiers de
la Revue Biblique, 17; Paris: J. Gabalda, 1976), p. 15; C. Dohmen, 'Zur Gründung
der Gemeinde von Qumran (1QS VIII–IX)', *RevQ* 11 (1982), pp. 81-86; M.A.
Knibb, *The Qumran Community* (Cambridge Commentaries on Writings of the
Jewish and Christian World 200 BC to AD 200, 2; Cambridge: Cambridge
University Press, 1987), p. 129. For recent discussion on the passage, see G.J.
Brooke, 'Isaiah 40,3 and the Wilderness Community', in G.J. Brooke and F. García
Martínez (eds.), *New Qumran Texts and Studies: Proceedings of the First Meeting
of the International Organization for Qumran Studies* (STDJ, 15; Leiden: E.J. Brill,
1992), pp. 117-32; U. Glessmer, *The Otot-Texts (4Q319) and the Problem of Inter-
calations in the Context of the 364-Day Calendar* (Qumran-Studien: Schriften des
Institutum Judaicum Delitzschianum, 4; Göttingen: Vandenhoeck & Ruprecht,
1996), pp. 125-164.
9. H. Stegemann, *Die Essener, Qumran, Johannes der Täufer und Jesus: Ein
Sachbuch* (Spektrum, 4249; Freiburg: Herder, 1994), pp. 158-59.
10. J.T. Milik ('Le travail d'édition des fragments manuscrits de Qumran', *RB*
63 [1956], pp. 60-62) dates the manuscript to the second half of the second century,
but F.M. Cross states in his recent list of the dates of the 4QS manuscripts that
4QS[e] was written about 50–52 BCE. In his Haskell lectures (*The Ancient Library of
Qumran and Modern Biblical Studies: The Haskell Lectures* [London: Gerald
Duckworth, 1958], p. 58) Cross stated that 4QS[e] was written at the beginning of the
first century BCE, but apparently he was not talking about the same manuscript. P.S.
Alexander overlooked my comment '...it remains unclear whether he [Cross] is
actually talking about the same manuscript, for he refers to 4QS[e] as being a papyrus', when he referred to my article 'The Primary Results of the Reconstruction
of 4QS[e]', *JJS* 44 (1993), pp. 303-308, esp. p. 303 n. 1. Alexander writes: 'Metso,
JJS 44 (1993), p. 303 n. 1 has been misled by a change of siglum into claiming also

passage providing a parallel to 1QS 8.15b–9.11, and indeed, there are good grounds to presume that the passage is a secondary insertion.[11] But there still remains a section corresponding to 1QS 8.1-10. In the light of 4QS^e it seems that the section parallel to 1QS 8.1-10 formed an introductory passage for the following sections with regulations addressed to the wise leader. Although these regulations for the wise leader may be of early origin, I no longer think it appropriate to speak of a manifesto, but simply of an introduction that is comparable to two other introductions in 1QS, namely to those at the beginning of columns 1 and 5.

Whatever the correct interpretation of the section, it is clear that it once again discusses the theme of separation from the men of injustice. There is no preserved parallel to this text in 4QS^b, and a fragment in 4QS^d has preserved only a part from the left edge of a column, which, nevertheless, allows a comparison with the text in 1QS. This column of 4QS^d, to which the fragment belongs, had 15-18 words per line. Leaving out the orthographical differences, the text seems in lines 1-5 to follow 1QS rather closely (the superlinear words in 1QS 8.9-11 were apparently in the text of 4QS^d). In the middle of line 6, however, from the sentence beginning with the words בהיות אלה בישראל ('When these exist in Israel') onwards, the text begins to differ. The words ליחד ('as a community') and בתכונים האלה ('in accordance with these rules') written above the line in 1QS 8.12 and 13 are lacking in line 6, and the gap at the beginning of line 7 has room for only about ten words, while in 1QS there are twenty. Obviously, some of the text of 1QS 8.13-15 was not included in 4QS^d, and filling up the gap with the rest of the sentence, which begins with the words בהיות אלה בישראל, reveals that the missing part was the citation from Isa. 40.3.

The text of 4QS^d thus reads as follows: 'When these exist [in Israel], they shall separate themselves fr[om the settlement] of the men of [injustice and shall go into the wilderness to prepare there the way of him. This is the study of the la]w which he commanded through [Moses, that they should d]o all [that has been revealed] from ti[me to time and in accordance with what the prophets revealed by his holy spirit].' An alternative reading for 'the way of him' is attested in 4QS^e, which has

---

Cross in support of a very early date for 4QS^e'. P.S. Alexander, 'The Redaction History of Serekh-HaYahad: A Proposal', *RQ* 17 (1996), pp. 437-55 (445 n. 17).

11. I have discussed this question in 'The Primary Results', pp. 303-308.

'the way of truth' (דרך האמת) instead of the syntactically difficult personal pronoun הואה. It is interesting that both writers avoided the use of
the name 'Yahweh' in this way. The more extensive version of 1QS has
the phrases 'as a community' and 'in accordance with these rules' added
above lines 12 and 13, to be read after the words 'When these exist in
Israel', and the citation of Isa. 40.3 follows the words 'to prepare there
the way of him'. The text of 1QS reads: 'When these exist as a community in Israel in accordance with these rules, they shall separate themselves from the settlement of the men of injustice and shall go into the
wilderness to prepare there the way of him, as it is written: "In the wilderness prepare the way of ···· make level in the desert a highway for
our God". This (way) is the study of the law w[hich] he commanded
through Moses, that they should act in accordance with all that has been
revealed from time to time and in accordance with what the prophets
revealed by his holy spirit.'

The introductory formula appears in the form of כאשר כתוב as earlier
in 1QS 5.17. The citation במדבר פנו דרך ···· ישרו בערבה מסלה לאלוהינו
omits the words קול קורא, which appear at the beginning of the verse
in the Masoretic text, and instead of the tetragrammaton, the scribe of
1QS has marked four dots. The use of four dots instead of the tetragrammaton is also attested elsewhere in the scrolls (e.g. in 4QTest and
4QTanh). In some cases the name of God, out of reverence, is written
in paleo-Hebrew script instead of in the square characters. The manuscript 4QS^d, in fact, provides two examples of the latter in the parallels
to 1QS 9.25 and 9.9 (4QS^d 2 3.9 and 2 4.8). The manuscript 1QIsa^a has
a small variant from the Masoretic text: instead of ישרו, 1QIsa^a reads
וישרו. In the book of Isaiah, this verse belongs to the Deuteroisaianic
book of Consolation of Israel. Yahweh intends to place himself at the
head of his people and lead them to freedom from exile across the
desert, as he did at the exodus from Egypt into the Promised Land. But
the Qumranic writer disregards the historical context, and uses the verse
to provide a motive for the community's withdrawal into the desert
to live a life of perfection in accordance with the Law. The same verse
from Isaiah is also used in the New Testament with reference to John
the Baptist by all four evangelists (Mt. 3.3; Mk 1.3; Lk. 3.4-6; Jn 1.23).
There the purpose of the verse is to explain John's presence in the
desert. The way in which the evangelists have detached the verse from
its original context and accommodated it into a new environment is
very similar to the one we find in the *Community Rule*.

2. *The Question as to the More Original Version*

In order to solve the question of which of the two versions is more original—the longer one with the quotations represented by 1QS or the
shorter one of 4QS[b,d]—the possible motivation for lengthening or short-
ening the text needs, in particular, to be discovered. A broader comparison between the text of 1QS with its parallels in 4QS[b,d] reveals that not
only are the citations absent in 4QS[b,d], but also other passages, individual words and phrases are missing. In some places, writers have chosen
different wordings. The title at the beginning of 1QS 5, for example, is
different from the one in 4QS[b,d]; while 4QS[b,d] uses the technical term
הרבים, 1QS renders a long phrase involving the sons of Zadok, that is,
the priests, and the men of the community; in some places, 4QS[b,d]
appears to lack words like 'the community' (היחד) and 'the eternal covenant' (ברית עולם). The words and phrases that are present in 1QS but
missing in the version of 4QS[b,d] have the nature of either strengthening
the self-understanding of the community or of providing a scriptural
justification for the community's regulations. In my opinion, inserting
theologically significant words into the text is natural, whereas omitting
them is very difficult to explain. Omission of part of the text usually
comes into question only when the text is out of date, for example, or
when it contains elements which are considered somehow questionable.
Compared to 4QS[b,d], the text of 1QS gains more authority when the
community's own regulations attain a biblical legitimization.

One may still ask, however, whether the citations could not have been
omitted because they were considered self-evident. It has to be borne in
mind that in two cases out of three the writer has assumed that when
a biblical passage is directly quoted, it does not entirely convey the
sensus plenior, the hidden inner meaning of Scripture. It needs to be
interpreted and applied specifically to the teaching of the community.[12]

---

12. This is clearly the case in 1QS 5.16b-19a, where the expository element
'For all those who are not counted in his covenant, they and everything that belongs
to them are to be kept separate' has been brought into the text by the redactor. In
1QS 8.12b-16a, the reminiscence of Isa. 40.3 was obvious even before inserting the
direct quotation, and the expository element 'This (way) is the study of the law
w[hich] he commanded through Moses, that they should act in accordance with all
that has been revealed from time to time and in accordance with what the prophets
revealed by his holy spirit' was already part of the original text. See below, the end
of the next passage in this article.

Even with an interpretative explanation, the connection between a regulation and the citation supporting it appears, at least to the modern reader, very arbitrary. And even though someone may have wished to abbreviate the text by omitting the citations, it remains to be explained why terms like 'the community' (היחד) and 'the eternal covenant' (ברית עולם), which are important for the self-understanding of the community, were excluded.

A further argument supporting the view that the shorter version is the more original[13] can be adduced by the observation that in the version of 4QS[b,d] the text runs smoothly without any breaks in the line of thought, whereas in 1QS the natural flow of the text is interrupted. In the middle of line 13 of 1QS 5, the third person plural, referring to the men of injustice, changes to the singular, although the theme of separation remains the same. After the quotation of Exod. 23.7 in line 15b, plural forms are again used of the wicked. It is difficult to see the written passage (1QS 5.13b-15a) as referring to a person joining the community. The passage seems rather to refer to one of the men of injustice, or to a person whose conversion is insincere. Some commentators suspected that this passage was an interpolation even before the material from Cave 4 was available.[14] The thought which is interrupted at the end of line 13 continues at the end of line 15. The syntax of the passage 1QS 5.13b-15a is also very peculiar, for the particle כיא appears there five times. Moreover, the idea of interpolation is further supported by the fact that an interval has been left in the middle of line 13, and there is a paragraphus in the margin. A glance at the version of 4QS[b,d] reveals that the problem with the number (sg.–pl.) does not come up at all in 4QS[b,d], for the passage 1QS 5.13b-15a is missing, as well as the preceding passage in the plural form in 5.11b-13a. The second passage, containing a citation which is lacking in 4QS[b,d], seems to be better adjusted to its context, but it may be noted that line 18 actually only repeats what is said previously in lines 10b-11a. The third citation in

---

13. G. Vermes earlier stated in his remarks on the 4QS[b,d] parallels of 1QS 5: 'At a preliminary guess, it can already be surmised that 1QS is more likely to be an expanded edition of the Cave 4 texts than 4QS an abridgement of 1QS', 'Preliminary Remarks on Unpublished Fragments of the Community Rule from Qumran Cave 4', *JJS* 42.2 (1991), pp. 250-55.

14. Murphy-O'Connor, 'La genèse littéraire', p. 546; Knibb, *The Qumran Community*, p. 110.

1QS 8 seems to fit the context quite well, too, but the sentence preceding the citation formula has so many words in common with the citation of Isa. 40.3 that one may speak of an implicit citation. It was later inserted as an explicit citation into the text.

3. *Conclusions*

The text of 1QS seems to have gone through a redaction, the purpose of which was to provide scriptural legitimization for the regulations of the community, as well as to strengthen the community's self-understanding. Perhaps—this is my tentative suggestion—at the time that the proof-texts were added, enthusiasm within the community had begun to show signs of waning and the need for separation was being questioned. Therefore, the strict rules had to be justified by allusions to the Scriptures.

A parallel phenomenon to the one we find in relation to 1QS and 4QS^{b,d} can be found in the New Testament. In order to point out the emphases Matthew wished to convey to his readers, he expanded the text of Mark with Old Testament quotations (*Reflexionszitate*, see, e.g., Mk 1.21/Mt. 4.13-16; Mk 3.7-11/Mt. 12.15-21; Mk 11.7/Mt. 21.4-5). Here, too, we find that the later version contains scriptural quotations, while the earlier one lacks them.

Both 4QS^b and 4QS^d, which can be dated to the last third of the last century BCE, are paleographically several decades later than 1QS, which was written 100–75 BCE. Since the 4QS manuscripts, nevertheless, represent a more original text, it is clear that 1QS and 4QS^{b,d} cannot be directly dependent on each other or even belong to the same textual family. There must have been a split in the textual tradition at a very early stage, about 100 BCE, or even earlier.

Why the community continued copying the shorter text, even though a more extensive version represented by 1QS was available, remains an open question. Of course, the text of Mark was also further transmitted during the time when the text of Matthew already existed. But the *Community Rule* as a legislative document represents a very different type of text from the Synoptic Gospels. It seems that there were several legitimate versions of the *Community Rule* co-existing,[15] and that the

15. E.P. Sanders already paid attention to the problem of contradicting regulations in the *Community Rule* while discussing the two different penal codes in 1QS 8.16b-20 and 8.20–9.2: 'Theological disparities can be accommodated, but the

relation between a written document (the *Community Rule*) and actual life in an Essene community has so far been seen too directly and in too uncomplicated a manner.

Excursus: Translation of the Sections of the Community Rule Containing Biblical Citations[16]

1QS 5.1-20:

(1) *This is the rule for the men of the community*[17] who willingly offer themselves to turn back from all evil and to hold fast to all that he has commanded *as his will*.[18]

They shall separate themselves from the congregation (2) of the men of injustice and shall form a community in respect of the law and of wealth. They shall be answerable *to the sons of Zadok, the priests who keep the covenant, and to the multitude of the men* (3) *of the community who hold fast to the covenant; on their word the decision shall be taken*[19] on any matter having to do with the law, with wealth, *or with justice.*[20] *Together*[21] they shall practise *truth and*[22] humility, (4) righteousness and justice, kindly love and circumspection in all their ways. Let no man walk in the stubbornness of his heart so as to go astray *after his heart* (5) *and his eyes and the thought of his inclination! Rather they shall circumcise in the community the foreskin of their inclination and of their stiff neck*[23] that they may lay a foundation of truth for Israel, for the community *of the eternal covenant.* (6) *They shall make expiation*[24] for all those who willingly offer themselves to holiness in Aaron and to the house of truth in Israel, and for those who join them in community. *In lawsuits and judgments* (7) *they shall declare guilty all those who transgress the statutes.*

halakhah on a given point cannot be two different things at once' (*Paul and Palestinian Judaism: A Comparison of Patterns of Religion* [London: SCM Press, 1977], p. 325). On the question, see also P.R. Davies, 'Redaction and Sectarianism in the Qumran Scrolls', in F. Garciá Martínez, A. Hilhorst and C.J. Labuschagne (eds.), *The Scriptures and the Scrolls: Studies in Honour of A.S.Van Der Woude on the Occasion of his 65th Birthday* (VTSup, 44; Leiden: E.J. Brill, 1992), pp. 152-63.

16. Except for the italics and the footnotes, the translation follows that of Knibb, *The Qumran Community*, pp. 104-35.

17. 4QS[b,d]: 'This is the teaching for the wise leader concerning the men of the Torah'.

18. Lacking in 4QS[b,d].

19. 4QS[b,d]: 'to the authority of the Many'.

20. Lacking in 4QS[b,d].

21. Lacking in 4QS[b,d].

22. Lacking in 4QS[b,d].

23. Lacking in 4QS[b,d].

24. Lacking in 4QS[b,d].

These are their rules of conduct, according to all these statutes, when they are admitted to the community.[25]

Everyone who joins the council of the community (8) *shall enter into the covenant of God in the presence of all those who willingly offer themselves.*[26] He shall undertake by a *binding*[27] oath to return to the law of Moses with all his (9) heart and soul, *following all that he has commanded,*[28] and in accordance with all that has been revealed from it *to the sons of Zadok, the priests who keep the covenant and seek his will, and to the multitude of the men of their covenant* (10) *who together willingly offer themselves for his truth and to walk according to his will.*

He shall undertake by the covenant[29] to separate himself from all the men of injustice *who walk* (11) *in the way of wickedness. For they are not counted in his covenant because they have not sought or consulted him about his statutes in order to know the hidden things in which they have guiltily gone astray,* (12) *whereas with regard to the things revealed they have acted presumptuously, arousing anger for judgement and for taking vengeance by the curses of the covenant to bring upon themselves mighty acts of judgement* (13) *leading to eternal destruction without a remnant.*[30]

He shall not enter the waters in order to[31] touch the purity of the men of holiness, *for men are not purified* (14) *unless they turn from their evil; for he remains unclean amongst all the transgressors of his word. No one shall join with him with regard to his work or his wealth lest he burden him* (15) *with iniquity and guilt. But he shall keep away from him in everything, for thus it is written, 'You shall keep away from everything false'.*[32] No one of the men of the community shall answer (16) to their authority with regard to any law or decision.[33] No one shall eat *or drink anything of their property, or take anything at all from their hand,* (17) *except for payment, as it is written, 'Have no more to do with man in whose nostrils is breath, for what is he worth?' For* (18) *all those who are not counted in his covenant, they and everything that belongs to them are to be kept separate.*[34] No man of holiness shall rely on any deeds (19) of vanity, for vanity are all those who do not know his covenant. He will destroy from the earth all those who spurn his word: all their deeds are impure (20) before him, and all their wealth unclean.

25. Lacking in 4QS[b,d].
26. Lacking in 4QS[b,d].
27. Lacking in 4QS[b,d].
28. Lacking in 4QS[b,d].
29. 4QS[b,d]: 'to the multitude of the council of the men of the community'.
30. Lacking in 4QS[b,d].
31. 4QS[b,d]: 'They shall not...'.
32. Lacking in 4QS[b] and 4QS[d], which read instead: 'He shall not eat with him within the community'.
33. 4QS[b,d]: plus about three words (not preserved).
34. Lacking in 4QS[b,d].

1QS 8.1-16:

(1)[35] In the council of the community (there shall be) twelve men and three priests, perfect in all that has been revealed from the whole (2) law, that they may practise truth, righteousness, justice, kindly love, and circumspection one towards another; (3) that they may preserve faithfulness in the land by a constant mind and a broken spirit; that they may pay for iniquity by the practice of justice (4) and (the endurance of) the distress of affliction; and that they may walk with all men according to the standard of truth and the rule of the time.

When these exist in Israel, (5) the council of the community shall be established in truth as an eternal plant, a holy house for Israel and a most holy assembly (6) for Aaron, witnesses of truth for the judgement and chosen by the will (of God), that they may make expiation for the land and pay (7) the wicked their reward. It shall be the tested wall, the precious corner-stone, whose foundations shall neither (8) shake nor stir from their place. (It shall be) a most holy dwelling (9) for Aaron, with eternal knowledge of the covenant of justice, and shall offer a soothing odour; and (it shall be) a house of perfection and truth in Israel (10) that they may establish the covenant according to the eternal statutes. And they shall be accepted to make expiation for the land and to determine the judgement of wickedness; and there shall be no more injustice.

When these have been established in the fundamental principles of the community for two years in perfection of way, (11) they shall be set apart as holy within the council of the men of the community. And nothing which was hidden from Israel, but found by the man (12) who studies shall he hide from these through fear of an apostate spirit.

When these exist as *a community*[36] in Israel (13) *in accordance with these rules*,[37] they shall separate themselves from the settlement of the men of injustice and shall go into the wilderness to prepare there the way of him, (14) *as it is written: 'In the wilderness prepare the way of* · · · · *make level in the desert a highway for our God'.*[38] (15) This (way) is the study of the law w[hich] he commanded through Moses, that they should act in accordance with all that has been revealed from time to time (16) and in accordance with what the prophets revealed by his holy spirit.

35. No parallel preserved to 1QS 8.1-6 in 4QS.
36. Lacking in 4QS^d (no parallel preserved in 4QS^b).
37. Lacking in 4QS^d (no parallel preserved in 4QS^b).
38. Lacking in 4QS^d (no parallel preserved in 4QS^b).

QUMRAN AND LXX

Staffan Olofsson

The main theme here is 'Qumran and canon', thus the questions mainly concern text development, text tradition and textual criticism; it is the texts themselves that are in focus. My particular subject is Qumran and LXX; the relations between Qumran and the Septuagint are interesting and have been treated on many occasions.[1] But this paper is limited to questions concerning the *Vorlage* of the Septuagint.

My own field of research is not really the Qumran texts, nor even the biblical scrolls from Qumran, but rather the translation technique of the LXX. On the other hand, I have an interest in the biblical Qumran texts since they have an obvious bearing on the question of translation technique. Because in order to say something specific about the translation technique one has to recognize which Hebrew text the translators had in front of them. But it is also the other way around; the so-called *Vorlage* on which the translators made their version cannot be detected if you have not studied the technique of a specific translator.[2] I would in fact emphasize that the translation technique is the starting point for questions concerning the *Vorlage*.[3]

---

1.   One may, for example, mention the international symposium on the 'Septuagint and its Relation to the Dead Sea Scrolls and Other Writings' in Manchester 30 July to 2 August 1990.

2.   See the discussion in S. Olofsson, *The LXX Version* (ConBOT, 30; Stockholm: Almqvist & Wiksell International, 1990), pp. 65-70.

3.   By translation technique, I refer to the way the translator rendered his Hebrew *Vorlage*, the term does not in itself imply a conscious philosophy of translation. On the other hand, translation technique cannot be discussed in isolation from questions regarding background, theology and competence of the translator. Most of the translators of the Old Greek did not have a conscious theory of translation that they applied in their work. The Septuagint was, after all, a pioneer work of huge dimensions without precedent in the Greek world. See, e.g. the description in Olofsson, *LXX Version*, pp. 5-6.

In order to retrovert the Greek text to a *Vorlage* different from the MT, one must pose questions concerning the competence, theology and technique of the translator. For example: what is his knowledge of Hebrew and how did he interpret specific words? Did he chose freely between different Greek synonyms in the rendering of a Hebrew word? How closely did he reflect the grammatical choices in the Hebrew text? Did he, as a rule, follow the word order of his *Vorlage* or was he independent from it? What was his relation to his *Vorlage* as regards the number of words, that is, the so-called one-to-one relation? How did he translate idiomatic phrases? Did the translator try to reflect the etymology of the Hebrew words?[4] One only has to take a look at modern translations in order to see different modes of translation exemplified. But while the translation techniques within modern translations are consistent, this is not at all the case with the LXX. Rather, the LXX can be described as a combination of all different kinds of translations and paraphrases, from the most literal to the paraphrastic. Thus the experience from one translation unit (usually a book) cannot be applied to any other unit in the LXX. In fact, the study of the methods of translation in the translation units in the LXX is the pivotal point not only for the *Vorlage* of the translation but also as regards the Old Greek, that is, the original translation.[5] See for example, Pietersma who emphasizes 'the ever present need for the critic to be thoroughly acquainted with

4. For the typology of the literal translation technique, see esp. J. Barr, 'The Typology of Literalism in Ancient Biblical Translations' (MSU, 15; Göttingen: Vandenhoeck & Ruprecht, 1979), pp. 279-325, and E. Tov, *The Text-Critical Use of the Septuagint in Biblical Research* (Jerusalem Biblical Studies, 3; Jerusalem: Simor, 1981), pp. 57-60.

5. See, e.g. the method of A. Pietersma used in his discussions of the Old Greek in the Psalter. See, e.g. the following articles of A. Pietersma, 'Ra 2110 (P. Bodmer XXIV) and the Text of the Greek Psalter', in D. Fraenkel, U. Quast and J.W. Wevers (eds.), *Studien zur Septuaginta: Robert Hanhart zu Ehren* (MSU, 20; Göttingen: Vandenhoeck & Ruprecht, 1990), pp. 262-86; *idem*, 'David in the Greek Psalms', *VT* 30 (1980), pp. 213-26; *idem*, 'Proto-Lucian and the Greek Psalter', *VT* 28 (1978), pp. 66-72; *idem*, 'The Greek Psalter: A Question of Methodology and Syntax', *VT* 26 (1976), pp. 60-69; *idem*, *Two Manuscripts of the Greek Psalter in the Chester Beatty Library Dublin* (AnBib, 77; Rome: Biblical Institute Press, 1978); *idem*, 'Articulation in the Greek Psalms: The Evidence of Papyrus Bodmer XXIV', in G.J. Norton and S. Pisano (eds.), *Tradition of the Text: Studies Offered to Dominique Barthélemy in Celebration of his 70th Birthday* (OBO, 109; Göttingen: Vandenhoeck & Ruprecht, 1991), pp. 184-202.

the style and translation techniques of the translator whose work he is attempting to reconstruct'.[6]

Other versions, and especially Hebrew texts, deriving from around the turn of the Christian era or earlier, can confirm the suggestion of a different *Vorlage* from MT already suspected by the investigation of the translation technique, and they may indicate by themselves differences in *Vorlage* which could otherwise easily be interpreted as expressions of interpretation or translation technique. The Hebrew text behind the LXX is of great importance for all works of textual criticism, which is, for example, clearly shown by the text-critical choices in modern Bible translations. In fact, LXX is the most important single source for textual emendations in our critical editions of the Hebrew Bible, as well as in the modern translations. Furthermore, the Qumran biblical texts have a bearing on the question of the *Vorlage* of the LXX.

Few will deny that the Dead Sea Scrolls have had a tremendous impact on the evaluation of the textual history of the Old Testament text, not least the relation between LXX and its Hebrew *Vorlage*.[7] Scholars, like J. Wellhausen and G.R. Driver, from the late nineteenth and early twentieth centuries, emphasized the value of LXX for textual criticism of the Hebrew text. Circumstances after World War I, however, favoured scholars with a more negative attitude toward LXX vis-à-vis the received Hebrew text. But the discovery of the Dead Sea Scrolls in the 1940s forced scholars 'to turn back to the Septuagint as a reliable witness to the Hebrew text whence it derived'.[8] Of course, many mistakes were made. For example, 'much uncritical enthusiasm was expressed for LXX text of Isaiah and its alleged derivation from a Hebrew text virtually identical with that of the first, complete Isaiah Scroll (designated 1QIs[a]) when it was made public first in part and then in whole'.[9] But as a whole, many emendations on the basis of LXX in the

6.   Pietersma , 'Greek Psalter', p. 60.

7.   See, e.g., E. Tov, 'The Contribution of the Qumran Scrolls to the Understanding of the LXX', in G.J. Brooke and B. Lindars (eds.), *Septuagint, Scrolls and Cognate Writings: Papers Presented to the International Symposium on the Septuagint and its Relation to the Dead Sea Scrolls and Other Writings (Manchester 1990)* (Septuagint and Cognate Studies, 33; Atlanta, GA: Scholars Press, 1992), pp. 11-47 (12-13).

8.   H.M. Orlinsky, 'The Septuagint and its Hebrew Text', in *The Cambridge History of Judaism* (Cambridge: Cambridge University Press, 1989), II, p. 534-62 (552).

9.   Orlinsky, 'The Septuagint and its Hebrew Text', p. 552.

last part of the twentieth century have been verified by the Qumran texts. In fact, the whole procedure of retroversion has received massive support from the Dead Sea Scrolls.[10] This is true also for the book of Psalms.

The choice regarding the texts to be discussed is mainly based on my own interest in the book of Psalms, but I also think that the importance of Qumran MSS can easily be demonstrated by Qumran Psalter MSS. The variation between LXX and MT in the book of Psalms is especially related to details, thus illustrating the ordinary situation in this regard; most Qumran scrolls are close or fairly close to MT. Jeremiah, where LXX is one sixth shorter than MT and has a different arrangement of the overall composition, is an exception rather than the rule. LXX is in this case to be regarded as an edition of the book prior to the more expanded edition in MT. This can be illustrated by Qumran material, since the short edition of LXX is now evidenced by 4QJer[b], and the expanded edition by 4QJer[a,c]. Thus the revised form found in MT is at least from 200 BCE, the date of 4QJer[a].[11]

I have chosen to present LXX readings which are also found in 11QPs[a] as an illustration to questions concerning the *Vorlage* of LXX.[12] The choice of 11QPs[a] is perhaps somewhat arbitrary, since at least 36 fragments from different MSS of the book of Psalms have been found in Qumran.[13] Arguments in favour of the use of 11QPs[a] are, however, easy to find. It is presented in a critical edition in the DJD series,[14] and is of a substantial size, in contrast to the small unedited fragments found in Qumran Cave 4. 11QPs[a] is, according to Sanders, to be dated from the first half of the first century CE. Even though, in my view, it is not really contemporary with the *Vorlage* of LXX Psalms it is in fact earlier than all the extant LXX mss of the Psalter. It is difficult to give

10. Tov, 'Contribution', pp. 12-13.

11. Regarding the date of 4QJer[a] see, e.g. E. Tov, '4QJer[a]: A Preliminary Edition', *Textus* 17 (1994), pp. 1-41 (8).

12. Cf. also J. Cook, 'On the Relationship between 11QPs-a and the Septuagint on the Basis of the Computerized Data Base Computer Assisted Qumran Project', in Brooke and Lindars (eds.), *Septuagint, Scrolls and Cognate Writings*, pp. 107-30.

13. J.C. VanderKam, *The Dead Sea Scrolls Today* (Grand Rapids: Eerdmans, 1994), p. 30.

14. J.A. Sanders, *The Psalms Scroll from Qumran Cave 11* (DJD, 4; Oxford: Clarendon Press, 1965).

an exact date for the LXX translation; I myself would favour a date in the second century BCE.[15]

The authors of *La Bible grecque des septante* attempted to connect the translation of individual books to specific localities,[16] but the result must be considered uncertain. The translation of the Psalter has been associated with Palestine by H.-J. Venetz on the basis of certain points of contact with the so-called kaige-group, which has been shown, through the studies of Barthélemy, to be at home in Palestine.[17] Oliver Munnich, on the other hand, has convincingly pointed out the weakness in Venetz's analysis. The not infrequent translation of כִּי as καὶ γάρ (not καίγε) and the occurrence of βαρὶς or πυργόβαρις, words which, according to Jerome, occur only on Palestinian soil, are by themselves not sufficient indicators for connecting the Psalter text with the kaige-group.[18] Nevertheless, a Palestinian locale for the translation is possible.

If the translation uses a Palestinian hermeneutic tradition, or was at home in Palestine, this would strengthen the employment of elements in 11QPs[a] reflecting the *Vorlage* of LXX Psalms on certain points. No

15. Regarding the date of the translation of the book of Psalms, an early date in the second century BCE seems to be favoured in, e.g. G. Dorival, M. Harl and O. Munnich, *La Bible grecque des septante du Judaïsme Hellénistique au christianisme Ancien* (Editions de CERF—Editions de CNRS, 1988), p. 111; O. Munnich, 'La Septante des Psaumes et le groupe *kaige*', *VT* 33 (1983), pp. 75-89; J. Schaper, 'Der Septuaginta-Psalter als Dokument jüdischer Eschatologie', in M. Hengel, A.M. Schwemer (eds.), *Die Septuaginta zwischen Judentum und Christentum* (WUNT, 72; Tübingen: J.C.B. Mohr [Paul Siebeck], 1994), pp. 38-61 (60-61); while A. van der Kooij seems to argue for a date in the first century BCE in his article, 'On the Place of Origin of the Old Greek of Psalms', *VT* 33 (1983), pp. 67-74 (73).

16. Thus the Pentateuch, Judges, 1–2 Samuel, 1–2 Kings, 1–2 Chronicles, *3 Maccabees*, Proverbs, Job, Psalms of Solomon, Sirach, the Twelve Prophets, Jeremiah, Baruch, the Letter of Jeremiah and Ezekiel are all assigned to Egypt, while Ruth, Esther, Qoheleth and Lamentations are placed in Palestine; see Dorival, Harl and Munnich, *La Bible grecque des septante*, pp. 101-109. Occasionally a scholar names Antioch (2 Macc., *4 Macc.*) or Leontopolis (Isa.) as possible origins, pp. 102-104.

17. H.-J. Venetz, *Die Quinta des Psalteriums: Ein Beitrag zur Septuaginta- und Hexaplaforschung* (Hildesheim: Gerstenberg, 1974).

18. See Munnich, 'La Septante des Psaumes', pp. 80-83. I have not seen the arguments of J. Schaper supporting Venetz and van der Kooij concerning the origin of the Psalter. See the reference in Schaper, 'Der Septuaginta-Psalter', p. 61 n. 67.

LXX texts from the Psalter have been detected in Qumran, even though MSS from the Pentateuch as well as a fragment from the epistle of Jeremiah were found in Cave 4 in Qumran. Furthermore, a steadily increasing number of Hebrew MSS from Qumran have been discovered. None of them are identical, and they contain variations of the kind we easily find in the old versions of the Old Testament, not least LXX. This has enhanced the probability that small deviations from MT in LXX reflect Hebrew texts somewhat differently from MT rather than illustrate the theology or interpretation of the translator. See the evaluation of R. Hanhart, who emphasizes that 'As a matter of first principle the Greek translation must be considered as a faithful rendering of the original as far as content and form is concerned, a rendering exact even in grammatical and syntactical details like those involving parataxis, the article and the pronouns'.[19] This is not least the case for a book as literal as LXX Psalms. For example, Galen Marquis has in a recent article even argued that when it is possible to retrovert an inverted phrase in LXX Psalms it could be used as an indication of a *Vorlage* with the word order of the Greek text, since the deviations from the word order of the Hebrew in LXX are few in the Psalter.[20] That is perhaps to go too far, but I have argued in an article published in *SJOT* that not a few of the inversions in LXX Psalms in fact reflect a different Hebrew *Vorlage*.

I am not primarily interested in text-critical decisions regarding the oldest text; rather, my question relates to where LXX can be adduced as a textual witness at all, that is, where it reflects a text variant from MT. My question is basically: when are we allowed to reconstruct a *Vorlage* different from MT on the basis of grammatical minutiae?[21] This is a question sometimes posed in LXX literature, but no definite answers seem to be found.[22] But as a matter of fact such retroversions are often made in modern editions of the MT, that is, *BHK* and *BHS*. Moreover, the question is whether retroversions can be made on the basis of an in-

19. R. Hanhart, 'The Translation of the Septuagint in Light of Earlier Tradition and Subsequent Influences', in Brooke and Lindars (eds.), *Septuagint, Scrolls and Cognate Writings*, pp. 339-79 (341).

20. G. Marquis, 'Word Order as a Criterion for the Evaluation of Translation Technique and the Evaluation of Word-Order Variants as Exemplified in LXX-Ezekiel', *Textus* 13 (1986), pp. 59-84 (67).

21. In fact, it is harder to know when to retrovert from LXX than to decide the exact wording of the retroversion. See, e.g. Tov, *Text-Critical Use*, p. 73.

22. See, e.g. Tov, *Text-Critical Use*, pp. 114-16.

vestigation of interpretation and translation technique alone, or whether they ought to be supported by Hebrew text material or at least other versions of the Old Testament.

I will not take up the questions regarding the understanding of 11QPs[a] as an edition of the Hebrew Psalter, different from the one in MT, or as a liturgical composition, since I am dealing with differences in detail rather than with composition, even though the overall composition may have a bearing on the evaluation that certain details in LXX different from MT are based on a *Vorlage* identical with 11QPs[a].

Of course I am aware of the uncertainty concerning the Old Greek text, especially since we have no pre-Christian MSS to the Septuagint book of Psalms, but one can at least take for granted that such a text once existed.[23] My discussion is based on the text of Rahlfs in the Göttingen edition[24] and the text of MT according to *BHS*. Therefore, as a matter of convention, MT is used as the basis of the comparison. Even though Rahlfs's text cannot be equated with the Old Greek, it is an eclectic text based on the experiences of the eminent LXX scholar. New MSS which were not at Rahlfs's disposal have turned up, the most important being perhaps 2149, 2150, 2110 (P. Bodmer XXIV).[25] Investigations of translation technique have also yielded some significant results that could be used for new evaluations concerning the Old Greek. But I would rather suggest that the Old Greek is not far from the critical text we have in the Göttingen edition. New textual finds can, of course, change the picture considerably. That I am inclined to presuppose a different *Vorlage* behind the variants in LXX, which are supported by 11QPs[a], and often also by old versions, is easily seen in my comments on the concrete texts.[26] Other possibilities cannot of course

23. See, e.g. O. Munnich, 'Indices d'une Septante originelle dans le Psautier grec', *Bib* 63 (1982), pp. 406-16.

24. A. Rahlfs (ed.), *Psalmi cum Odis* (Septuaginta, Vetus Testamentum Graecum Auctoritate Academiae Scientiarum Gottingensis editum, 10; Göttingen: Vandenhoeck & Ruprecht, 1931).

25. P. Bodmer XXIV (Rahlfs 2110) is a manuscript of the third or fourth century CE (or even second century) containing approximately Pss. 17–118, and a member of Rahlfs's Upper Egyptian text group and in fact a better witness to the Upper Egyptian text than the MSS which Rahlfs had at his disposal. See D. Barthélemy, 'Le Psautier grec et le papyrus Bodmer XXIV', *RTP*, 3rd series 19 (1969), pp. 106-10; Pietersma, 'P. Bodmer XXIV', p. 265. Other important MSS are 2149, 2150 from the fourth century CE. See further Pietersma, *Two Manuscripts*.

26. Regarding the suggestion of a different *Vorlage* from MT in LXX Psalms in

be ruled out, since agreements in minutiae may be coincidental. The small contextual changes, such as in number, pronouns, particles and verbal forms, which the two sources sometimes have in common, could have developed independently.

Regarding the use of 11QPs[a] as the basis for retroversions, a question of principle could be addressed. Must a Hebrew text in its overall composition and in textual details be closer to LXX than to MT to be used as *Vorlage* of LXX variants? It is my belief that not only 'septuagintal scrolls', that is, scrolls that are closer to LXX than to any other textual tradition, can be used for supporting a *Vorlage* of LXX differing from MT. Furthermore, the term 'septuagintal scroll' is confusing, since LXX as a whole is not based on a Hebrew text with specific textual characteristics.[27] In order to ascertain the closeness of a certain Qumran scroll to a LXX book, one must also be clear over the methodology of such an evaluation. In the words of E. Tov:

> As a rule, the determining of the relation between the LXX and the scrolls does not take into consideration the originality of the readings... if the LXX and a scroll agree in a presumed common secondary reading (often an error), such an agreement may point to a very close connection between the two... With regard to the shared original readings, if two texts share a reading which probably is original, while the corrupted reading is found in another source, the closeness reflected by the presumably original shared reading is less significant, since it is natural for any two texts to share original readings.[28]

Even though the verdict that a certain reading is original is far from certain one could suggest that at least the following variants in my material common to LXX and 11QPs[a] are original readings: Ps. 145.5, 13. Cf. also 119.49 and 145.15, where limited support from 11QPs[a] can be found.

---

general terms see P.W. Flint, *The Dead Sea Psalms Scrolls and the Book of Psalms* (Leiden: E.J. Brill, 1997), pp. 236, 249, regarding specific passages under consideration, see the comments concerning Ps 119.49, 125.4; 139.19 on pp. 233-236. Cf. in this connection the comment of J. Barr: 'it remains the general probability that, where there are textual variations, one of which provides a direct and fairly literal path from the original to the translated text, while the other can only be a free, indirect or dubiously related connection, the direct path does result from literal translation, 'Typology', p. 285.

27. Tov, 'Contribution', pp. 40-42.
28. Tov, 'Contribution', pp. 24-25.

The book of Psalms in LXX version is in many respects a strictly literal translation. Thus the possibility for differences reflecting a Hebrew text is much greater in this book than in, for example, Isaiah. I will give some examples of deviations from MT in 11QPs[a], which are reflected in the LXX version, complemented by a few facts and my own evaluation. The translation of MT is, as a rule, taken from NRSV and the translation of LXX has the vocabulary of NRSV as its point of departure. The translations are thus idiomatic rather than literal, although the differences between MT and LXX under discussion are clearly marked; they are in the cursive.

Quantitative Differences between LXX, 11QPs[a] and MT

Psalm 145.13

מַלְכוּתְךָ מַלְכוּת כָּל־עֹלָמִים וּמֶמְשֶׁלְתְּךָ בְּכָל־דּוֹר וָדוֹר:

Your kingdom is an everlasting kingdom,
and your dominion endures throughout all generations.

ἡ βασιλεία σου βασιλεία πάντων τῶν αἰώνων,
καὶ ἡ δεσποτεία σου ἐν πάσῃ γενεᾷ καὶ γενεᾷ.
πιστὸς κύριος ἐν τοῖς λόγοις αὐτοῦ
καὶ ὅσιος ἐν πᾶσι τοῖς ἔργοις αὐτοῦ.

Your kingdom is an everlasting kingdom,
and your dominion endures throughout all generations.
The Lord is faithful in his words
and holy in all his works.

11QPs[a]. נאמן אלוהים בדבריו וחסיד בכל מעשיו + ς´ E´ Σ Θ A´ MT וָדוֹר:
See also LXX Vulg PR Syr.[29] The נ-stroph in this acrostic psalm is missing in MT but present in 11QPs[a] and in old versions. LXX is reconstructed as נֶאֱמָן יְהוָה בְּכָל־דְּבָרָיו וְחָסִיד בְּכָל־מַעֲשָׂיו, both in *BHK* and *BHS*, and regarded as the original Hebrew text. But בְּכָל was hardly in the *Vorlage* of LXX.

Comment: The rendering in LXX is evidently based on a *Vorlage* identical with 11QPs[a], except for the name of God (יְהוָה or אֱלֹהִים).

---

29. The נ-stroph is also found in MS 142 in Kennicott, but it is probably based on a retranslation from the Greek. For this suggestion, I am indebted to Professor E. Tov. κύριος in LXX reflects יהוה rather than אלהים.

Psalm 119.68

טוֹב־אַתָּה וּמֵטִיב לַמְּדֵנִי חֻקֶּיךָ:

You are good and do good;

teach me your statutes.

χρηστὸς εἶ σύ, κύριε, καὶ ἐν τῇ χρηστότητί σου

δίδαξόν με τὰ δικαιώματά σου.

You are good, *O Lord*,

and teach me your statutes in your goodness.

> MT κύριε אֲדוֹנִי 11QPsᵃ LXX PR (= *Le Psautier romain et les autres ancien psautiers latins* ed. Dom Robert Weber, 1953), Syr (= *The Peshitta Psalter*, ed. by William Emery Barnes, 1904)

In *BHS* it is noted that LXX and Peshitta support κύριε, while it is not even mentioned in *BHK*. There are no specific reasons for introducing it into the LXX text. No other occurrences of the phrase טוֹב־אַתָּה appear in the Psalms and where it can be found (Judg. 11.25; 1 Sam. 29.6, 9), it is not followed by אֲדֹנָי or יְהוָה. In fact, neither טוֹב אַתָּה יְהוָה nor טוֹב אַתָּה אֲדֹנָי occur in MT. κύριε is missing in Sa Ga Augᵘᵃʳ. אֲדֹנָי is supported by Peshitta and Latin Psalters. The existence of אֲדוֹנִי in 11QPsᵃ mirrors the Hebrew *Vorlage* of LXX. Although making implicit participators explicit is a common translation technique,[30] it seldom occurs in the book of Psalms.[31] The LXX Psalms is a very literal translation, not least as concerns quantitative relations, and if we can show a Hebrew text with this variant, it is probably the *Vorlage* of LXX.

Comment: The rendering in LXX is evidently based on a *Vorlage* identical with 11QPsᵃ אֲדוֹנִי or with יהוה.

---

30. See, e.g. the examples adduced by Jan de Waard concerning Ruth in 'Translation Techniques Used by the Greek Translators of Ruth', *Bib* 54 (1973), pp. 499-515.

31. κύριος could perhaps be regarded as an exception to this rule since it occurs more than 30 times in the Psalter without counterpart in MT: 2.12; 5.11; 7.7; 22.32; 25.21; 31.20; 35.18, 23; 40.17; 44.27; 48.12; 51.20; 55.24; 79.9; 80.8; 84.6; 88.3; 94.19; 97.10; 98.1; 102.26; 103.11; 119.7, 68, 85, 93, 97, 168; 136.23; 138.1; 139.13; 142.8; 143.8; 145.13; 147.1. Some texts are disputed; perhaps the Old Greek was identical with MT in, e.g. 87(88).3; 93(94).19; 118(119).7. See Pietersma, 'P. Bodmer XXIV', p. 283. In most cases, however, I would argue that a different *Vorlage* is reflected.

Conjunctions

Psalm 139.19

אִם־תִּקְטֹל אֱלוֹהַּ רָשָׁע וְאַנְשֵׁי דָמִים סוּרוּ מֶנִּי׃

O that you would kill the wicked, O God,
and that the bloodthirsty would depart from me —
ἐὰν ἀποκτείνῃς ἁμαρτωλούς, ὁ θεός,
ἄνδρες αἱμάτων, ἐκκλίνατε ἀπ᾽ ἐμοῦ.
Surely you will slay the wicked, O God,
depart from me you bloodthirsty men

וְאַנְשֵׁי MT   ἄνδρες אנשי 11QPsᵃ LXX Σ PR PIH

In *BHK* אַנְשֵׁי is suggested as the *Vorlage* of LXX Symmachus and
Hieronymus. Cf. *BHS om cop.*

Comment: The rendering in LXX is probably based on a *Vorlage* identical with 11QPsᵃ אנשי.

Lexical Deviation

Psalm 129.3

עַל־גַּבִּי חָרְשׁוּ חֹרְשִׁים הֶאֱרִיכוּ לְמַעֲנוֹתָם׃

The *plowers* plowed on my back;
they made their furrows long.
ἐπὶ τοῦ νώτου μου ἐτέκταινον οἱ ἁμαρτωλοί,
ἐμάκρυναν τὴν ἀνομίαν αὐτῶν·
The *sinners* wrought on my back;
they prolonged their iniquity.

חֹרְשִׁים MT ᾽Α Σ et rel   οἱ ἁμαρτωλοί רשעים 11QPsᵃ LXX Vulg PR

חָרַשׁ in the meaning 'plow' occurs in qal in Deut. 22.10; Judg. 14.18;
1 Sam. 8.12; 1 Kgs 19.19; Hos. 10.11, 13; Amos 6.12; 9.13; Ps. 129.3;
Job 1.14; Prov. 20.4 and in niphal, Jer. 26.18; Mic. 3.12. It is usually
understood by the translators; it is rendered by ἀροτριᾶν in Deut.
22.10; 1 Kgs 19.19; Job 1.14; 4.8; Isa. 28.24; Jer. 26.18; Mic. 3.12,
while in Hos. 10.11, 13 and Amos 6.12 חָרַשׁ is interpreted as 'to be
silent', i.e., II חָרַשׁ, in Amos 9.13 it is rendered by ἀλοητός 'threshing,

threshingtime', in 1 Sam. 8.12 and Prov. 20.4 the rendering is based on a different *Vorlage*, but it never has ἁμαρτωλός as equivalent. It is true that חָרַשׁ is sometimes misunderstood and לְמַעֲנוֹתָם is probably read as לְעֲוֹנוֹתָם (*BHS*), but most of the LXX translators were familiar with חָרַשׁ in the meaning 'to plow'.

In *BHS* LXX is retroverted to הָרְשָׁעִים. In *BHK* it is not even registered!

Comment: The rendering in LXX is evidently based on a *Vorlage* identical with 11QPsª רשעים or with the suggested *Vorlage* in *BHS* הָרְשָׁעִים.

Grammatical Differences between LXX, 11QPsª and MT
Numerus (Sing-Plural) and Suffixes

Psalm 119.49
זְכֹר־דָּבָר לְעַבְדֶּךָ עַל אֲשֶׁר יִחַלְתָּנִי׃
Remember *a word* to your servant
in which you have made me to hope.
μνήσθητι τὸν λόγον σου τῷ δούλῳ σου, ᾧ ἐπήλπισάς με.
Remember *your word* to your servant
in which you have made me hope.

דָּבָר MT ’A PIH (= *Sancti Hieronymi Psalterium Iuxta Hebraeos*, ed. Dom Henri de Sainte Marie, 1954) Targ (cf. Vulg) τοὺς λόγους σου דבריכה 11QPsª LXXˡᵘᶜ Θ O´, דברך τὸν λόγον σου LXX Vulg PR Syr Most modern versions make the same change as a translation technique, e.g., NRSV 'your word to your servant'.

Comment: The LXX may reflect a *Vorlage* דברך, while 11QPsª evidences a variant with a second singular suffix with 'word' in the plural, דבריכה, which is reflected by some lucianic MSS *L* Tht.

Psalm 132.18
אוֹיְבָיו אַלְבִּישׁ בֹּשֶׁת וְעָלָיו יָצִיץ נִזְרוֹ׃
His enemies I will clothe with disgrace,
but on him, *his crown* will gleam (lit. flourish).
τοὺς ἐχθροὺς αὐτοῦ ἐνδύσω αἰσχύνην,
ἐπὶ δὲ αὐτὸν ἐξανθήσει τὸ ἁγίασμά μου.
His enemies I will clothe with disgrace,
but on him shall *my holiness* flourish.

נִזְרוֹ MT   τὸ ἁγίασμά μου LXX Vulg PR Syr. 11QPsᵃ may reflect MT
נזרו, but ו is uncertain.

LXX and Peshitta are retroverted to נִזְרִי in *BHK*. Cf. Ps. 89.40 נִזְרוֹ —
τὸ ἁγίασμα αὐτοῦ. Otherwise ἁγίασμα except in 132.8 is a rendering
of קֹדֶשׁ with cognates in LXX Psalms, 78.54, 69; 93.5; 96.6; 114.2. *BHS*
notes that LXX and Peshitta have a suffix in first singular rather than
third singular in MT.

Comment: The LXX is reflecting a *Vorlage* נזרי which is also supported
by Peshitta. The reading in 11QPsᵃ is uncertain.

Psalm 125.4
הֵיטִיבָה יְהוָה לַטּוֹבִים וְלִישָׁרִים בְּלִבּוֹתָם׃
Do good, O LORD, to those who are good,
and to those who are upright *in their hearts*!
ἀγάθυνον, κύριε, τοῖς ἀγαθοῖς
καὶ τοῖς εὐθέσι τῇ καρδίᾳ·
Do good, O LORD, to those who are good,
and to those who are upright *in heart*!

בְּלִבּוֹתָם MT τῇ καρδίᾳ בלב 11QPsᵃ 4QPsᵉ LXX Lat

The phrase לִישָׁרִים בְּלֵב, with or without suffix, is not evidenced
otherwise by the Hebrew Bible, but לְיִשְׁרֵי־לֵב in Ps. 36.11; 97.11 is
translated by τοῖς εὐθέσι τῇ καρδίᾳ, and the same is true for לְבָרֵי לֵבָב
in 73.1. In 7.11 יִשְׁרֵי־לֵב is translated by τοὺς εὐθεῖς τῇ καρδίᾳ, and in
32.11; 64.11 and 94.15 by οἱ εὐθεῖς τῇ καρδίᾳ, and לְיִשְׁרֵי־לֵב by τοὺς
εὐθεῖς τῇ καρδίᾳ in 11.2. In *BHK*, *BHS* no suggestion of a different
Vorlage is made.

Comment: Either the translator has been influenced by the renderings of
the phrase elsewhere in the Psalter or the equivalent reflects a different
Vorlage, בלב, evidenced by 11QPsᵃ and 4QPsᵉ.

Psalm 119.105
נֵר־לְרַגְלִי דְבָרֶךָ וְאוֹר לִנְתִיבָתִי
Your word is a lamp to my feet
and a light to *my path*.

λύχνος τοῖς ποσίν μου ὁ λόγος σου
καὶ φῶς ταῖς τρίβοις μου.
Your word is a lamp to my feet
and a light to *my paths*.

לִנְתִיבָתִי MT ταῖς τρίβοις μου לנתיבותי 11QPsª LXX Vulg PR Syr

Cf. *BHK*, where LXX and Peshitta is retroverted to לִנְתִיבוֹתָי, and *BHS* where the plural of LXX and Peshitta is noted.

Comment: The LXX is probably reflecting a *Vorlage* נתיבותי evidenced by 11QPsª.

Psalm 142.5
הַבֵּיט יָמִין וּרְאֵה וְאֵין־לִי מַכִּיר
אָבַד מָנוֹס מִמֶּנִּי אֵין דּוֹרֵשׁ לְנַפְשִׁי׃
Look on my right hand *and see* —
there is no one who takes notice of me;
no refuge remains to me,
no one cares for me.
κατενόουν εἰς τὰ δεξιὰ καὶ ἐπέβλεπον,
ὅτι οὐκ ἦν ὁ ἐπιγινώσκων με·
ἀπώλετο φυγὴ ἀπ' ἐμοῦ,
καὶ οὐκ ἔστιν ὁ ἐκζητῶν τὴν ψυχήν μου.
I looked on my right hand and *I saw* that
there was no one who took notice of me;
refuge failed me,
and there is no one who cares for me.

הַבֵּיט יָמִין וּרְאֵה MT κατενόουν εἰς τὰ δεξιὰ καὶ ἐπέβλεπον
אביטה ימין ואראה 11QPsª LXX Vulg PR Targ Syr

Without reference to 11QPsª VB could be interpreted as reflecting a translation technique similar to that of RSV 'I look to the right and watch'. No suggestion regarding a different *Vorlage* is made in *BHK* or *BHS*.

Comment: The LXX is probably reflecting a *Vorlage* אביטה ימין ואראה evidenced by 11QPsª.

Psalm 144.5

יְהוָה הַט־שָׁמֶיךָ וְתֵרֵד גַּע בֶּהָרִים וְיֶעֱשָׁנוּ׃

Bow your heavens, O LORD, and *you shall come down*;
touch the mountains so that they smoke.

κύριε, κλῖνον οὐρανούς σου *καὶ κατάβηθι*,
ἅψαι τῶν ὀρέων, καὶ καπνισθήσονται·

Bow your heavens, O LORD, *and come down*;
touch the mountains so that they smoke.

וְתֵרֵד MT καὶ κατάβηθι ורד 11QPs[a] LXX Vulg PR

κατάβηθι is nearly always a rendering of רֵד in LXX, Exod. 19.24; 32.7;
Deut. 9.12; Judg. 7.9, 10; 1 Sam. 23.4; 2 Sam. 11.8; 1 Kgs 18.44;
21.18; 2 Kgs 1.15; Jer. 22.1, רְדָה Gen. 45.9; 2 Kgs 1.9, 11. or רְדִי Is
47.1; Jer. 48.18. In Jer. 18.2 καὶ κατάβηθι corresponds to וְיָרַדְתָּ and in
Ezek. 32.21 to יָרְדוּ. In Ezek. 31.18 וְהוֹרַדְתָּ seems to be rendered by
κατάβηθι καὶ καταβιβάσθητι and in Exod. 32.34; 2 Kgs 9.32 κατάβηθι
occurs without corresponding text in MT.

Without reference to 11QPs[a], the rendering in LXX could be regarded
as a translation technique similar to that of RSV: 'and come down'. No
suggestion regarding a different *Vorlage* is made in *BHK* or *BHS*.

Comment: The LXX probably reflects a *Vorlage* ורד evidenced by
11QPs[a].

Verb/Noun

Psalm 145.5

הֲדַר כְּבוֹד הוֹדֶךָ וְדִבְרֵי נִפְלְאוֹתֶיךָ אָשִׂיחָה׃

On the glorious splendor of your majesty,
and on *your wondrous works*, I will meditate.

τὴν μεγαλοπρέπειαν τῆς δόξης τῆς ἁγιωσύνης σου *λαλήσουσιν*
καὶ τὰ θαυμάσιά σου διηγήσονται.

On the majesty of the splendor of your holiness *they shall speak*;
and they shall tell of *your wonders*.

וְדִבְרֵי MT λαλήσουσιν ידברו 11QPs[a] LXX Vulg PR

נִפְלְאוֹתֶיךָ MT καὶ τὰ θαυμάσιά σου ונפלאותיכה 11QPsᵃ LXX Vulg PR. That λαλήσουσιν reflects יֵדַבְּרוּ is also suggested in *BHK* and *BHS* with reference to LXX and Peshitta.[32] Even the conjunction could reflect a Hebrew ו as is evident from 11QPsᵃ. This is, of course, not suggested in *BHK*, *BHS* on the basis of translations. דִּבְרֵי occurs 11x in the Psalter: 7.1; 18.1; 22.2; 35.20; 36.4; 52.6; 65.4; 105.27; 109.3; 137.3; 145.5, and it is otherwise always rendered by λόγος or ῥῆμα. The difference between י and ו in the Qumran scrolls is generally so small that they were seldom copied accurately.

Comment: The LXX is probably reflecting a *Vorlage* with ידברו and ונפלאותיכה evidenced by 11QPsᵃ.

Personal Pronoun

Psalm 145.16
פּוֹתֵחַ אֶת־יָדֶךָ וּמַשְׂבִּיעַ לְכָל־חַי רָצוֹן:
Opening your hand,
satisfying the desire of every living thing.
ἀνοίγεις σὺ τὴν χεῖρά σου
καὶ ἐμπιπλᾷς πᾶν ζῷον εὐδοκίας.
You open your hand,
and fill every living thing with pleasure.

> MT σὺ אתה אם 11QPsᵃ LXX Vulg PR Syr

The rendering in LXX could be regarded as a translation technique similar to that of RSV: 'You open your hand'. 11QPsᵃ has אתה אם but it is more probable that LXX reflects אַתָּה־יָדֶךָ (*BHK*) or אַתָּ־יָדֶךָ (*BHS*).

Comment: The rendering in LXX is probably based on a *Vorlage* including אַתָּה as in 11QPsᵃ.

Deviations with ו can Reflect a Vorlage Different from MT

See the following examples from 11QPsᵃ:

32. See also, e.g. F.W. Mozley, *The Psalter of the Church: The Psalms Compared with the Hebrew, with Various Notes* (Cambridge: Cambridge University Press, 1905), p. 188.

248 Qumran between the Old and New Testaments

Ps. 102.27 כַּלְּבוּשׁ καὶ ὡσεὶ περιβόλαιον וכלבוש 11QPs[a] LXX Lat Syr.
(*BHS* G 𝔊 S pr cop). καὶ is missing in La[G].

Ps. 119.163 תּוֹרָתְךָ τὸν δὲ νόμον σου ותורתך 11QPs[a] (*BHS* pc Mss 𝔊S
וְתוֹ׳)

Ps. 122.7 שַׁלְוָה καὶ εὐθηνία ושלוה 11QPs[a] (*BHK* LXX וְשַׁלְוָה, *BHS* nonn
Mss 𝔊S וְשׁ׳)

Ps. 135.18 כֹּל καὶ πάντες וכל 11QPs[a] Ken LXX Vulg PR Syr (*BHK*
mss וְכֹל, *BHS* nonn Mss 𝔊𝔊S וְכֹל)

Ps. 139.19 וְאַנְשֵׁי ἄνδρες אנשי 11QPs[a] LXX Σ PR PIH (*BHK* > ו 𝔊, Hier,
BHS 𝔊 σ´ Hier om copula)

Ps. 145.5 נִפְלְאֹתֶיךָ καὶ τὰ θαυμάσιά σου ונפלאותיכה 11QPs[a] LXX
Vulg PR

Although *BHS* is generally more reluctant than *BHK* to retranslate from
the LXX deviations in relation to MT, small differences as regards singular and plural, omission or addition of conjunctions are, as we have
seen, often noted as *Vorlage* variants in *BHS* in the book of Psalms.
11QPs[a] has often confirmed suggestions made in *BHS* regarding a different *Vorlage*, and, furthermore, Qumran texts have made it probable
that other differences, which are not recorded in *BHK* or *BHS* are based
on the Hebrew *Vorlage*, rather than on the translation technique. This
cannot, of course, be generalized to suggest that most differences in any
other book are based on the Hebrew.

THE ARCHAEOLOGY OF KHIRBET QUMRAN

Allan Rosengren Petersen

1. *Introduction*

The reason that the subject 'The Archaeology of Khirbet Qumran' is on the programme of this conference is that the Dead Sea Scrolls were seen relatively soon after their discovery in connection with Khirbet Qumran. It has been believed that—with the possible exception of the *Copper Scroll*—the Dead Sea Scrolls were written at Qumran and belonged to the Essenes, a Jewish sect that lived there.

It has been questioned by some scholars, however, whether the Dead Sea Scrolls stem from Qumran at all. That is one of the reasons for discussing the archaeology of Qumran in this context. Furthermore, if we may conclude that the Dead Sea Scrolls were written or even produced at Qumran, how and to what extent can archaeology contribute to our knowledge of the people behind the scrolls?

What I want to say consists of three parts: first, I want to say something concerning de Vaux's methods and excavation techniques. Secondly, I shall present a few criticisms of de Vaux. Finally, I shall present my own views on the matter. What I shall not give is a thorough description of the various occupational phases at Khirbet Qumran. The standard paradigm or standard interpretation of the ruins, as presented by de Vaux in his Schweich Lecture, is, I presume, well known.

2. *On Methods and Excavation Technologies*

Tell el-Far'ah (ancient Tirza) in the Central Hill country was excavated during nine seasons from 1946 to 1960 by R. de Vaux. In this case, de Vaux produced a very 'biblical' interpretation: an incomplete palace was interpreted as the palace that had been abandoned by Omri when he moved his residence from Tirza to Samaria. Furthermore, de Vaux thought he was able to detect how the settlement had evolved from an egalitarian society in the early Iron Age to a city divided into rich and poor quarters, thus providing the material background for the social criticism of the prophets. Unfortunately, de Vaux never finished the final report himself. This report has, however, been completed by Alain Chambon.[1]

In his detailed review of the final report, McClellan has proposed some alternative interpretations, assigning various buildings to other strata than what de Vaux did. 'The consequences of these proposed changes are that there is no reliable evidence for an unfinished palace that might be attributed to Omri, nor is there evidence for a widening socioeconomic gap between rich and poor at Tell el-Far'ah (N).'[2] The reason this reinterpretation is possible is, of course, that Tell el-Far'ah 'was excavated prior to the wide adoption of stricter stratigraphic controls of the Kenyon-Wheeler system'.[3] Instead, 'stratigraphic assignments are based on typological differences in the pottery and objects or on design considerations of the architectural plans'.[4]

Though the final report on Khirbet Qumran is as yet unpublished, there is reason to believe that this site, which was excavated at the same time as Tell el-Far'ah, was excavated according to more or less the same excavation techniques. There are two major problems involved. First, there is the question of method. Secondly, there is the problem of excavating a site in the light of ancient texts. In the first case (Tell el-Far'ah) the Old Testament served as a kind of 'guide-book' or key to interpretation; in the second case (Khirbet Qumran) the Dead Sea Texts served this purpose. For instance, de Vaux wanted to push the beginning of period 1*a* back to the middle of the second century BCE, because he had the idea that Jonathan was referred to in the Dead Sea Texts. Other examples are the interpretation of various rooms and installations in the Qumran settlement, such as the scriptorium, the refectory, the various ritual baths, and so on.

1. A. Chambon, *Tell el-Far'ah I: L'âge du fer, éditions recherche sur les civilisations, mémoire no 31* (Paris: Gabalda, 1984).
2. T.L. McClellan, review of *Tell el-Far'ah I: L'âge du fer*, by A. Chambon, in *BASOR* 267 (1987), pp 84-86.
3. McClellan, review, p. 85.
4. McClellan, review.

As with Tell el-Far'ah, de Vaux never published the final excavation report concerning Khirbet Qumran. Roland de Vaux died in 1971. From 1986 to the beginning of the 1990s a team of scientists worked 'to make available a complete publication of the archaeological data'[5] under the direction of Robert Donceel. Recently, however, the work has been taken over by the archaeological director of the Ecole Biblique, Jean-Baptiste Humbert. The work in question has encountered a number of difficulties. Some of the difficulties are in connection with the coins discovered on the site. According to R. Donceel, a very large percentage of the coins found at Khirbet Qumran have disappeared.[6] Also, a number of lamps have disappeared—and, of course, almost invariably some of the most beautiful and most complete.[7] Statistics are relatively easy to present. It is much more difficult to assess the damage caused by the absence of an excavation report in terms of lacking evidence for the occupational sequence proposed by de Vaux. Thus Humbert has been able to produce an occupational sequence which differs significantly from what de Vaux suggested. I shall return to Humbert's interpretation shortly.

3. *Critics of de Vaux*

In recent years, critics of de Vaux have presented alternative interpretations of the archaeological data from Khirbet Qumran. Some of these views will be presented here. The first two (Golb and Donceel) are what can best be termed revisionist views: there is no reason to believe that Khirbet Qumran was the mother-house of the Essenes and that the Dead Sea Scrolls originated here. Humbert holds a kind of middle position: he does accept the Essene theory, but he does so with some modifications and reinterpretations. I have also included a review of a recent

---

5.   R. Donceel, 'Reprise des travaux de publication des fouilles au Khirbet Qumran', *RB* 99 (1992), pp. 557-73 (557).

6.   The total number of coins registered in the inventory is 1, 231 coins and fragments from Qumran itself and 144 from 'Ain Feshkha, though the exact number is difficult to estimate. Some coins have disintegrated during cleansing, whereas other pieces of metal originally thought of as coins and registered as such have proven to be mere pieces of metal. More important, however, is the fact that a large number of coins have disappeared. After cleansing the coins, 691 coins remained. The team working on the final publication have been able to find only 196 of these!

7.   Donceel, 'Reprise', p. 561.

book by Stegemann, although he is not a critic of de Vaux. Stegemann's view represents a development of the traditional Essene theory and he has put forward some interesting observations that are worth discussing in this context.

On a number of occasions, Norman Golb has challenged the traditional view of Qumran as the community residence of an Essene sect.[8] In short, Golb's thesis is that Khirbet Qumran was a military stronghold and that the Dead Sea Scrolls originated in Jerusalem. In Golb's opinion, the Qumran-Essene theory stems from the order in which the Dead Sea Scrolls were found. If they had been found in a different order (for instance, beginning with the Masada fragments and then perhaps the Murabba'at scrolls) scholars would have interpreted the whole lot differently and the Jerusalem theory (the theory that the Dead Sea Scrolls originate in Jerusalem—Golb's theory) would have been the predominant view among scholars.[9]

One of the things that puzzles Golb is that the Essenes, who according to Philo were a peace-loving people, could have occupied *and defended* a strategic site in the Judaean wilderness before and during the First Revolt. Khirbet Qumran, or so Golb claims, is well-suited for a fortress. Furthermore, the khirbeh was destroyed through violent military action. The walls of period II were mined through, according to F.M. Cross.[10] Golb thinks that this does not correspond with the description of the Essenes as a peace-loving sect. Golb quotes Philo, who says that among the Essenes one could not find 'any maker of arrows, spears, swords, helmets, corselets, or shields, any maker of arms or war-engines etc...'[11] Philo obviously had great esteem for the Essenes.[12] When reading his account as a historian, one must distinguish between

---

8.   N. Golb, 'Who Hid the Dead Sea Scrolls?' *BA* 48 (1985), pp. 68-82; *idem,* 'The Dead Sea Scrolls: A New Perspective,' *The American Scholar* 58 (1989), pp. 177-207; *idem,* 'Khirbet Qumran and the Manuscripts of the Judaean Wilderness: Observations on the Logic of their Investigation,' *JNES* 49 (1990), pp. 103-14.

9.   Cf. Golb's hypothetical reconstruction of events if the order of discoveries had been reversed in, 'Who Hid the Dead Sea Scrolls?', pp. 80-81.

10.   Quoted by Golb, 'Khirbet Qumran', p. 107.

11.   Quoted from Golb, 'Khirbet Qumran', p. 107.

12.   On Philo's account of the Essenes, cf. P. Bilde's presentation in this volume, 'The Essenes of Philo and Josephus'.

what we can (reasonably) know about the Essenes and the superlatives that an adoring Philo might attribute to them. Actually, Josephus reports that the Essenes bore defensive weapons while traveling.[13] Now, how a group of Essenes in the wilderness of Judaea would react when faced with Roman soldiers a few decades after Philo's death could hardly be predicted by Philo. Thus Philo's account on the peace-loving Essenes need not be an obstacle for the Essene theory. Besides, it is interesting to see how classical authors are often quoted uncritically on events of the past whereas nowadays the biblical texts are sifted much more carefully when the attempt is made to extract historical information (at least by a number of scholars).

Another example of this 'classical fundamentalism' is Golb's understanding of Pliny's words that the Essenes lived among the palm trees, *socia palmarum*.[14] Does this mean that the Essenes lived in a remote place, where you would expect to find nothing but palm trees, or does it imply that the Essenes lived in a grove of palm trees and that—if investigations were to prove that palm trees did not exist at Khirbet Qumran in antiquity—the Essenes could not possibly have inhabited this place? Golb seems to adhere to the last view. He thinks that the 'fully developed site with many interesting architectural features' is 'somewhat in contrast with the statement of Pliny that the Essenes lived among the palm trees'.[15] It is not. The only company the residents of Khirbet Qumran would have had is the surrounding vegetation.

Golb believes that the Murabba'at scrolls make it necessary to raise questions about the Dead Sea Scrolls. To him, the discovery of the Murabba'at manuscripts 'proved that the Jews had taken care to preserve their personal documents in antiquity and that these were capable of survival in the Judean wilderness'.[16] This, according to Golb, raises the question: '[I]f the scrolls were originally located at the Qumran settlement, and if they were all gathered up in haste from the so-called scriptorium and elsewhere at the site when the Essenes learned of the Romans' approach, how could original documents such as letters and

13. *War* 2.125. Also quoted by Golb, 'Khirbet Qumran', p. 107.
14. *Hist. Nat.* 5.15.73.
15. Golb, 'Who Hid the Dead Sea Scrolls?', p. 70.
16. Golb, 'Who Hid the Dead Sea Scrolls?', p. 74.

legal deeds have been so meticulously excluded from storage in the caves?'.[17] Golb suggests that the Dead Sea Scrolls were brought from Jerusalem shortly after the fall of Galilee. 'Once the manuscript finds of Qumran are seen in this light, there is no longer any need to question the absence of documentary materials, such as letters and legal texts, at the Qumran caves: One would not normally expect to find such documents among collections of literary scrolls—that is, libraries—removed far from their original home.'[18] Does this mean that one would expect letters to be among the scrolls of a library, if it is removed to a place *close* to its original home? 'Furthermore, as Josephus informs us, the archives of Jerusalem were burned by a faction of Jewish zealots in August of AD 66.'[19] How is it that Golb supposes that at Jerusalem libraries of literary texts and archives of administrative texts were kept separately, whereas at Qumran the two necessarily must have been kept together? Anyway, if the Dead Sea Scrolls represent a library (or many libraries), libraries of purely literary texts did exist at that time. The lack of private letters or more official administrative texts is as hard or as easy to explain, whether the scrolls originated in Jerusalem or in Qumran.

In Golb's theory, the people behind the Dead Sea Scrolls hid the scrolls with the aid of inhabitants of the Dead Sea region.[20] Why would they do that? Why would they not prefer absolute secrecy? After all, the vast number of caves in the north-western part of the Dead Sea area makes it hard to understand why people from Jerusalem would go all the way to the shores of the Dead Sea with scrolls when other caves closer to Jerusalem could easily have given shelter to the scrolls.[21] Golb presumably feels compelled to write this because the ceramic jars in which some of the scrolls were stored were identical to jars found in Khirbet Qumran and were in all likelihood produced here. So, in Golb's

---

17. Golb, 'Who Hid the Dead Sea Scrolls?', p. 75; cf. Golb, 'The Dead Sea Scrolls', p. 194.

18. Golb, 'Who Hid the Dead Sea Scrolls?', p. 80.

19. Golb, 'Who Hid the Dead Sea Scrolls?', p. 80.

20. Golb, 'Who Hid the Dead Sea Scrolls?', p. 81.

21. A map showing the vast number of caves in the north-western area of the Dead Sea can be seen in Golb, 'Who Hid the Dead Sea Scrolls?', p. 73. It will be noticed that quite a few caves are nearer to Jerusalem than the rather isolated Qumran-caves.

theory, inhabitants of Jerusalem brought literary scrolls to a distant military outpost, where they bought jars to store the scrolls in, and with the help of people in the region (whoever they were), hid the scrolls in caves near the Dead Sea, thus sharing their secret with—as it seems— as many people as possible. One cannot say that things could not possibly have happened the way Golb suspects, but on the other hand, Golb's theory is certainly not the easiest solution. Golb has, however, pointed to one thing that is worth bearing in mind. Not all the scrolls need to stem from only one place.

Pauline Donceel-Voûte and Robert Donceel, who had been in charge of the final publication of the Qumran excavation until a few years ago, have presented the hypothesis that the Qumran buildings are a villa— possibly with some perfume-manufacturing going on as well—or a kind of small winter-palace comparable to Herod's winter-palace near Jericho. There is some evidence to support this view; for instance, some column drums and bases. However, the vast cemetery and unpleasant location speaks against this hypothesis. Recently, Jean-Baptiste Humbert from the Ecole Biblique has taken over the final excavation report. 'Damit dürfte der Villen-Spuk ein Ende haben' ('And that should be the end of the Villa phantom'), as Stegemann categorically puts it.[22] Now, the Donceels are 100 per cent revisionists—they reject the standard paradigm altogether. J.-B. Humbert, who is now working on the final publication on the archaeology of Khirbet Qumran, has reconciled the villa-features of the khirbeh with the Essene theory. So the 'Villen-Spuk', the villa-ghost, is not quite dead yet.

What Humbert suggests is that in the earlist Hellenistic phase (phase 1*a*), Khirbet Qumran was a Hasmonean villa. This hypothesis is built on the previously-mentioned luxurious features of Khirbet Qumran and on the observation that there is a roadway leading from Qumran to Hyrcania (a Hasmonean fortress some 10 km from Qumran in the direction of Jerusalem) and from there to Jerusalem. In some places, this road is paved, and is thus not just an ordinary path. In Humbert's view this is no coincidence—there must have been a closer connection between the two. Furthermore, as Humbert puts it, the Essenes detested the Hasmoneans and Hasmonean customs. Therefore, they would have

---

22. H. Stegemann, *Die Essener, Qumran, Johannes der Täufer und Jesus: Ein Sachbuch* (Freiburg: Herder, 1993), p. 98.

rejected the money of the Hasmoneans. Consequently, all coins issued by the Hasmoneans found in Qumran must be attributed to the inhabitants of the place before the coming of the Essenes. Now, I find that argument dubious. If I detested a person, I would not thereby despise his money!

In his description of the life of the Judaean aristocracy, Humbert describes the Dead Sea area as an exotic paradise in winter and springtime. The Dead Sea area was to the princes of Judah what the Nile or the Euphrates was to the Ptolemaic and Seleucid kings. I have never been to Qumran during wintertime, so I would not know—but, instinctively, I find the description exaggerated. According to Josephus, Hyrcania was destroyed during the reign of Herod the Great, rebuilt and used as a prison. In this situation, according to Humbert, Qumran probably ceased to be dependent on Hyrcania. That was the end of phase 1*a* in de Vaux's terminology and the beginning of the Essene settlement, in Humbert's reconstruction.

Humbert suggests that the northern enclosure is to be interpreted as '[u]ne cour aux sacrifices', a sacrificial courtyard (see plate below).[23] The *miqveh* (locus 138) in the north-western area is a later addition. The original sacrificial court must have had a western wall going from locus 123 to locus 136. What Humbert thinks is that the altar was placed against this 'mur fantôme', as Humbert himself calls it—this phantom-wall, of which there are no traces.[24] The key to the interpretation of the Essene settlement is the cult.[25] As is almost always the case with cultic interpretations, almost anything can be interpreted as having had a cultic/religious significance. This is true in archaeology as well as in literary studies.

A relatively recent book on Qumran and the Dead Sea Scrolls is Stegemann's *Die Essener, Qumran, Johannes der Täufer und Jesus: Ein Sachbuch*. Stegemann's book is a very good *Sachbuch* that contains some interesting new observations and interpretations. On the whole, Stegemann supports de Vaux's interpretation. Qumran was inhabited by Essenes. However, Stegemann does produce some new and interesting ideas. On the basis of an analysis of possible functions of various

23. This plate is reproduced at the end of the paper.
24. J.-B. Humbert, 'L'espace sacré à Qumrân: Propositions pour l'archéologie', *RB* 101 (1994), pp. 161-214 (187).
25. Humbert, 'L'espace sacré à Qumran', p. 162.

workshops at Qumran and of the buildings at 'Ain Feshka, Stegemann arrives at the following conclusion as to the plan and function of the building-complex, as such: it was to serve the production of scrolls, including the preparation of the leather. The actual study of the texts was very much part of the work necessary to produce new scrolls.[26] Dye-works had to be placed away from the residential quarters of towns and villages because of their 'penetranten Gestank'.[27] Stegemann's interpretation thus forms a neat contrast to the pleasant odour of the perfume-factory theory!

The production of books would provide books for all the Essene congregations in the country (the Essene party had 4000 members according to Josephus).[28] Compared to the circumstances of book-production in our day, Qumran and 'Ain Feshka was 'nichts anderes als die Einrichtung eines Verlagshauses' ('nothing but the establishment of a publishing house').[29] One of the very good things about Stegemann's publishing-company hypothesis is that it is based on the study of the scrolls as archaeological material rather than as texts. According to Stegemann, the Qumran library comprised about 1000 volumes. Where was this vast material produced? What kind of installations are needed to produce this amount of parchment? Where would we find such installations? These are the kinds of questions Stegemann asks when studying the scrolls as scrolls, setting aside for a moment, as it were, the study of the scrolls as texts.

4. *Conclusion*

Did the Dead Sea Scrolls originate in Qumran? In my view, three things are important in this connection: first, the proximity of at least some of the caves to the Qumran settlement. The depositing of scrolls

26. Stegemann, *Die Essener*, p. 78: 'Dieses Baukonzept zeigt eine klare Schwerpunktsetzung. Es ging um die *Herstellung* von Schriftrollen samt allen Vorstadien der Ledergewinnung und der weiteren Lederbearbeitung. Nur in zweiter Linie ging es auch um das *Studium* dieser Schriftrollen im Rahmen des religiösen Lebens der Beteiligten. Aber auch das Studium diente in Qumran nicht zuletzt dem Vertrautwerden der Schriftrollenkopisten mit den Texten, die sie berufsmäßig übertragen mußten.'

27. Stegemann, *Die Essener*, p. 78.

28. Stegemann, *Die Essener*, p. 194.

29. Stegemann, *Die Essener*, p. 82.

in the caves close to the Qumran settlement could not have taken place without the knowledge of the people living there. Secondly, the correspondence between the pottery found in the caves and the Qumran pottery of phases I and II: even though the Qumran types of ceramics are no longer considered typical of Khirbet Qumran only, I do believe that no parallels to the special jars in which some of the scrolls were placed have yet been found. Thirdly, the inkwells. The inkwells, I think, are slightly overlooked. Inkwells are relatively rare in excavations. The finding of *inkwells* in a desert area is a most extraordinary thing. Khairy has made a study of inkwells of the Roman period from Jordan.[30] In order to have sufficient material for comparison, Khairy uses material from Roman sites in Germany. I think this fact testifies to the rarity of the objects.

These are the purely archaeological arguments that one might present in favour of the theory that the Dead Sea Scrolls originate in Qumran. In addition to this, one could mention Pliny's account on the Essenes, but that is another kind of argument which I will not deal with at the moment.

I believe that there is sufficient evidence to sustain the theory that the Dead Sea Scrolls (or at least a large number of them) originated in Khirbet Qumran. And if the Dead Sea Scrolls are Essene writings, well, then the settlement at Khirbet Qumran could be termed an Essene settlement. But then Qumran need not have served the same purpose during all phases of occupation. And Qumran need not have served only one purpose at a time. If Stegemann is correct that Qumran was a place of book-production, at least two products were then produced at Qumran: scrolls and pottery. One should not forget that a substantial stock of ceramics was found at Khirbet Qumran—more than 700 bowls —that was what the archaeologists found in just one spot. Now, if the final excavation report shows that there is substantial reason to suppose that the manufacture of perfume also took place at Qumran, this is not a serious blow to the Essene theory. One does not exclude the other.

I think it is fair to say that in these years, Qumran and Dead Sea Scrolls studies are at a new beginning. How are we to pursue these studies? The history of research has shown that doing archaeology in the light of ancient texts is a very dubious matter. What is needed in the

---

30. Nabil I. Khairy, 'Inkwells of the Roman Period from Jordan', *Levant XII* (1980), pp. 155-62.

study of Khirbet Qumran and in the study of the Dead Sea Scrolls is to separate the study of the scrolls *as texts* from the study of Khirbet Qumran. The study of the scrolls *as scrolls*, however (i.e. as parchment or papyrus with ink on it), is an integral part of the archaeological study of the Qumran area and cannot be separated from this. Let me give one example: the ink on some, if not all, of the scrolls tallies with the ink found in the inkwells at Khirbet Qumran. This could be incidental. But it is an example of how one can study the Dead Sea Scrolls as scrolls. Similarly, neutron-activation analysis could determine whether the clay used for the pottery found in the caves is identical to the clay used for the pottery found in the khirbeh. Another example is Stegemann's publishing-company hypothesis. One of the very good things about it is that it is based on the study of the scrolls as scrolls, that is, as archaeological material.

However, reconstructing the history of the Essene Sect from the Dead Sea Texts and trying to make this reconstruction fit the archaeological data is a very dubious project. Could I suggest that we apply the term 'The Dead Sea Texts' when we talk about the scrolls as texts, and the term 'The Dead Sea Scrolls' when we talk about the scrolls as scrolls, as documents from antiquity. I think that relatively few of us have ever had a chance to study the Dead Sea Scrolls—whereas all of us, I presume, have studied the Dead Sea Texts. I think Khirbet Qumran should occupy a less important place in our minds. If Stegemann's hypothesis that Khirbet Qumran is a 'Verlaghaus' is accepted, then it follows—as Stegemann also clearly states—that Khirbet Qumran is not the central Essene place of worship. In other words, it is not a temple or anything of the kind. The 4000 Essenes that Josephus tells us about lived elsewhere. Qumran does not comprise the entire Essene movement. The texts were copied at Qumran, but they were not intended to be used in Qumran only. And this should have some effect on our way of speaking about things. Take, for instance, the title of this volume: Qumran between the Old and the New Testaments. Is that a good title? Think about it: an ancient ruin between two collections of texts? Could I suggest that we focus on writings, for instance, and speak of the Dead Sea Texts and the Old and the New Testament—or maybe even better, that we focus on religious movements and speak about ancient Judaism, the Essene movement and Christianity. Thus we would be dealing with entities that are comparable. Qumran should not be used as a synonym for the Dead Sea Texts.

'THE ARCHAEOLOGY OF KHIRBET QUMRAN'

Humbert's reconstruction of Khirbet Qumran, 'niveau 3'. From J.-B. Humbert: 'L'espace sacré à Qumran: Propositions pour l'archéologie', *RB* 101 (1994), pp. 161-214. Published by permission.

4QTESTIMONIA AND BIBLE COMPOSITION: A COPENHAGEN LEGO HYPOTHESIS

Thomas L. Thompson

In the formation of the Old Testament, it is not so much clear that we are dealing with ancient traditions as that we are dealing with—from the very first compositions that we know—traditions that have been presented and are understood as ancient. The long-standing separation of scholarship in our field between those who are engaged in the relatively hard science of lower criticism and those in the very soft, theologically-driven, speculation of higher criticism has helped us to avoid some of the implications of this observation, and has allowed many higher critics a security and self-confidence that is not properly ours. Transmission, as we all know, whether oral or written, transposes. Our traditions, as we first know them in the Dead Sea Scrolls, are specifically—from the historical perspective of the Hellenistic period and from our perspective of the texts as artifacts—not so much ancient as textual manifestations of Hellenistic and Greco-Roman traditions that relate, at best, to what is only known as a past that has been narrated or transmitted. The referents of these texts do not in fact carry us into a tradition earlier than that implied by the conglomerate of the extant texts themselves.

The richness and variety found among the Qumran texts, I believe, not only open up many alternative explanatory possibilities for biblical composition, they also present us with concrete examples of those processes that are involved in the creation and transmission of books and other texts in this part of the ancient world. In many ways, Qumran provides us with our field's Serbo-Croation singer of tales,[1] with the help

---

1. Here I refer to the Serbo-Croatian singer who was studied in the 1930s by M. Parry and later by his student, A.B. Lord. See, esp., A.B. Lord, *The Singer of Tales* (Harvard Studies in Comparative Literature, 24; Cambridge, MA: Harvard University Press, 1960).

of which analogy we might not only test hypotheses from the perspective of antique patterns of composition, but we might also expand the quantity and testifiable variance of material that is now available to higher criticism. The Qumran collection offers us our extra-biblical and archaeological evidence: that external control that has always been absent to biblical composition theory. With Qumran, we have an entry into the actual world of text-making, tradition composition and transmission.

I am afraid our approach is going to have to be radical in more than one way. Once we have begun dealing with compositional issues involving specific texts that existed prior to the formation and redaction of individual biblical books, we are going to have to deal with such materials in a very different context than that of a hypothetical final or canonical text of any specific book, as has been the usual practice. I hope you will agree with me in the course of this presentation that a specific book of the Bible in its so-called final form—whether it is Isaiah (the 36- or the 66-chapter version), Genesis or Psalms—is not a terribly productive focal point for biblical composition theory. Sinaiticus and Vaticanus—and we certainly cannot speak intelligently about final or canonical form in any earlier period—surely are far too late to serve as direct witnesses to issues of composition. Unlike some modern books, the significant units of biblical tradition do not seem to have been organized along a single trajectory. Final forms do not render us with a satisfactory vantage point for viewing the process of historical composition. This is true whatever our theological needs.

The Dead Sea texts make it both possible and necessary to understand our texts before the process of tradition formation was completed. They present us with sources, drafts and versions of what, at a much later date, came to be recognized as biblical tradition. In themselves, however—in their own historical contingency—they are not biblical, but independent of such a final form and significance. These scrolls and text fragments reflect literary contexts not only logically but empirically prior to any scholarly-constructed biblical world. The implications of this seem worth exploring, however briefly.

To some extent we need to return to some of the problems of tradition history, but we are not required to fall into the trap of discussing texts we do not have. If we should find ourselves talking about phenomena such as the wilderness tradition, we need to avoid prejudicing our discussion by thinking too specifically from the familiar perspective of the canonical Exodus/Numbers tradition. In the context of the Hellenistic world of our texts, it is not yet clear that this specific variant of the wilderness tradition had yet taken pride of place. Before we are finished, we will have many reasons for doubting that this particular variant was historically primary. We also need to adopt some of the old-fashioned strategies of formalism and comparative literature. We need to develop spectra of techniques, metaphors and genres, and approach them from at least three perspectives: (1) structural and technical characteristics (so, for example, beginnings, endings, transitions, inclusions, settings, the mixing of genres, and so on); (2) the themes and literarily-referential motifs of our texts: stories out of time, wilderness, exodus, exile, preserving the law, saving, guiding, providing, murmuring, backsliding, fall from grace, and so on; and (3) formalistic criteria and taxonomies, both small and large.

To some extent, the individual books of the extant or final text seem to have been at times strikingly arbitrary products of collection techniques—here, I think especially of Obadiah and Joel, but also of Exodus and Isaiah—rather than the result of coherent, conceptual or ideological productions that mark such books as offering to their implied readers an intellectual matrix of interpretation. What appears to have been present in the collective process of tradition creation seems reflected rather in efforts to collect and propose variable expressions and explorations of themes and ideas. These sorely need analysis to make them clear.

We have a large number of texts from the caves of the Dead Sea that lead me to question the sharp distinction that we have made between the process of text transmission and their composition. I am here thinking of the many segmentary blocks of very brief compositions that have been recognized as variants of Bible texts or as resembling or being nearly identical to passages that are found in the Bible. Yet, other Dead Sea texts are unlikely derivatives from biblical texts. I also doubt that we can any longer speak intelligently about identifying specific texts as either expansions or abbreviations of biblical texts simply on the basis of their being larger or smaller forms of our canonical versions. Certainly the widespread mixing—not only at Qumran but in so-called intertestamental literature—of biblical and non-biblical texts requires that we entertain the question of whether our authors and collectors understood what a biblical text was. It is not apparent.

The frequent association in the Qumran texts of multiple small text segments and fragments does not always accomplish complete coherence nor does it always reflect what we might understand as sense or sound reason. Rather, often partially motif- or theme-dependent analogies have been used in the manner of a coupling principle.

I have taken 4QTestimonia as my model because this particular Qumran text not only puts together several Pentateuch-like segments or text units of the sort that we find scattered throughout Exodus, Leviticus, Numbers and Deuteronomy, but 4QTestimonia also has, in addition, its own unique text segment. 4QTestimonia has a clear and sufficient leitmotif and orders itself in the form of successive divine utterances and predictions, and possibly selects text blocks that have potential messianic-like overtones, but it is not so obvious that the text creates an interpretation or signification of the segments as collected. I think it doubtful that this text implies the self-conscious secondary qualities of the sort that is so apparent in the *targumim*. Thematically, a contrast between a promise regarding a good prophet, like Moses, and the man from Belial or the like, stands at the center of our text. Moses, Baalam ben Peor, Levi and Jacob are all positive heroes comparable to those we find in the Bible. But I am uncertain that 4QTestimonia has actually used these texts from their biblical contexts, or whether such so-called biblical segments, in fact, had been used from within other independent contexts, comparable to the way 1 Samuel and 1 Chronicles are dependent on an independent context.

4QTestimonia's first sentence resembles Deut. 5.28-29. In the Bible's text, however, the words of the people are spoken to Moses. In the segment from Qumran, it is Yahweh who has been addressed. Nevertheless, this does not appear to be either a tendentious or a contextually relevant change, as in both cases the segments' settings are wholly comparable. If the variation is not entirely arbitrary, one might suggest that the received texts are both independently derived from a common stream of tradition.

The second sentence of 4QTestimonia resembles Deut. 18.18-19, rendering a succession of text as in the Samaritan's version of Exod. 20.21 and comparable to fragment 6 of 4Q158. In this sentence, 4QTestimonia presents a text that is a nearly verbatim rendition of Deuteronomy's, except that 4QTestimonia—with a flexibility common to so many transmission variants—introduces the word 'prophet' somewhat earlier in the narration than does Deuteronomy.

With the third segment, 4QTestimonia has its own introductory clause that only resembles that of Num. 24.15a. Here, again, one needs to ask whether this is the result of arbitrariness or whether it is reflective of an independent source. I would suggest that the source of this passage was the same for both the biblical and the Qumran text, and tentatively would conclude that one or both of the respective authors acted arbitrarily.

The fourth segment is identical to Deut. 33.8-11. The fifth segment of this text, however, offers a surprise. Here, even though the biblical and the Qumran texts are very similar to each other, the comparable text of Josh. 6.26 is integrally bound to the story of Jericho's fall, while 4QTestimonia has nothing at all to do with this particular narration or this particular fortress. Nevertheless, the segment of 4QTestimonia does not have any independent entry to its story variant. It speaks rather of the songs of Joshua, of destiny and thanksgiving in the manner we are familiar with from the songs of Qumran. Instead of Joshua's 'Jericho', we read in our Qumran text: 'this town', and Jerusalem is now clearly our text's reference. Similarly, instead of Joshua's 'youngest', the Qumran text reads 'your Benjaminite', which is a referent to the well-known story of Joseph. After such variations, the Qumran text goes its own way, at least in its description of Jerusalem's destiny-determining evil and hatefulness,[2] while Joshua 6 closes more simply with Joshua's oath. Not only are the first three segments of the text provided without commentary, but I also doubt that we can follow Brooke here in seeing this segment as evidence of midrashic interpretation of Bible texts cited. Only the prior assumption of dependence and citation supports such a reading. This segment of 4QTestimonia shows rather that the text has its own independent significance and referent. How then, might one explain the synoptic similarities?

Particularly instructive is the observation that 4QTestimonia is not a fragment of a larger text, but rather a complete, albeit damaged, composition in its own right. One needs to seek an interpretation of it as a whole composition, for its form is neither accidental nor arbitrary. There are, of course, many possible explanations regarding its origin. Has the author of 4QTestimonia used biblical texts as a basis for writing his own? Or should we perhaps understand 4QTestimonia as a variant biblical-like tradition which had failed to make a canon, as its comparable segments did in the Samaritan and Massoretic Pentateuchs?

2.   It is precisely here, however, that 4QTestimonia echoes the psalter's well-known congruence of curses and thanks related to the metaphor of walking in the path of the torah or of righteousness.

Did the biblical texts in their many variations originally derive from just such texts as 4QTestimonia? Or are we to entertain yet other possibilities?

We find problems comparable to those of 4QTestimonia in 4QFlorilegia, which plays with the Bible texts in the manner of targums, but without an accompanying biblical recitation. Selected text segments are thematically ordered in terms of the 'house of David' and are markedly theological in their signification. We should not neglect to ask whether we might far better see in the florilegia a type of targum on texts such as 4QTestimonia! 4QFlorilegia, in the manner of 4QTestimonia, references text segments similar to what we find in 2 Sam. 7.10, Isa. 8.11 and especially Ezek. 44.10, but which are significantly different from their massoretic variants, so that one might better think of a type of 4QTestimonia, rather than a Bible text, as its *Grundtext*. This suggests that texts like 4QTestimonia were understood as worthy of interpretation.

There are a large variety of such texts among the Dead Sea scroll. The variants at Qumran of this kind of text have a large range. Interesting are those which have been described as 'expansions'.[3] 4Q158 is particularly surprising in that this text, although resembling the Esau/Jacob story of Gen. 32.25-33, is a complete story and it is the Genesis narration that breaks off uncompleted between verses 29 and 30. Similarly, Genesis (perhaps to be understood as a shortened form of a story like 4Q158?) speaks of a blessing, but fails to actually give it! Should we perhaps understand the florilegia as theological traditions comparable to those we find in the Bible?

There are reasons to believe that we should think further about the composition of biblical texts: not only concerning whether one or other of such text and text fragments from Qumran may well represent an earlier witness than the text we have in the Bible, but also whether the composition of biblical texts, including those of the Pentateuch, ought better to be understood as a process common to these texts as well, specifically involving the question of tradition transmission as one of composition's primary functions, rather than, for example, that of creative narration. Compositions similar to these that I have discussed from Qumran are also frequently found elsewhere. For example, Deut. 34.10 immediately follows 18.18 not only at Qumran but in the Syriac

---

3.   So, 4Q364–65.

peshitta as well. Differences or variants in the form, as well as in the contexts of segments of the tradition, are ubiquitous. In the Testimony of Judah, it is particularly interesting to observe that the sons of Judah descend immediately from Judah's son Shelah and not—as in Genesis 38 and the book of Ruth—from Judah himself. Is the Tamar story unknown? Or do we have a wholly independent tradition reflected here?

It is clear that our biblical traditions are still undergoing significant compositional type changes at the close of the second century BCE and even later. It is also obvious that we can no longer claim that this type of text, as we have found in the Qumran caves, is simply commentary on biblical literature. The historiographies of Isaiah 36–39, 2 Chronicles 29–32 and 2 Kgs 18.1–20.21 present us with independent variants of a tradition, with Isaiah and 2 Kings dependent on the same source. Apart from 2 Kings 20 and Isaiah 38, these three texts are identical. Isaiah 38 not only transmits Hezekiah's monologue but the previous story is also transmitted in a variant form. However, the specification of Hezekiah's sickness in Isaiah 38, 21 is not very firmly anchored to its context of Hezekiah's deathbed scene in Isa. 38.1–6 and it is also not to be found in the story as presented in 2 Kings. Since both Isaiah and 2 Kings close at the same point, they might well be understood as variants that have used different sources that are quite distant from the story of Hezekiah as it is found in 2 Chronicles.

A biblical book in its final form is not very useful for questions of composition, since final forms of texts are rather the foundations for explaining a text's transmission, its quality, its importance. I mean that if one speaks of final form, one is talking about a reference to the implied reader. Such questions regarding the final form of our text belong properly to 'reader response' and reception criticism. They can hardly help us if we wish to investigate the historical process of our texts' composition!

It is equally clear that in the analysis of form and genre, form-criticism of any acceptable question is ever undermined by its inability to deal with the problem of *Sitz im Leben*. Literary forms and genres are the creations and representations of authors. They are neither very tightly linked with a text's purpose nor with the decisive and determining techniques of authorship that are important for meaning, intention and compositional process, with the many different methods, patterns, motifs, themes and play that drive creative works. Authorial identity, form and genre, intention and purpose, *Tendenz* and ideology are secondary products. In art, music and literature of this type, composition is driven by a spectrum of changing variables and by the many possibilities offered by motifs and themes of a work's small unities and complexes rather than by the prospect of some completed whole which in the process of the work can only offer a provisional concept or vision that is not to be determined until after the work is completed.

The subtitle of my paper, 'A Copenhagen Lego Hypothesis', takes its departure from the observation of what one might define as 'the smallest units of the tradition that have the ability to persist and to recur in variable forms'. The definition is borrowed from classic formalism, but it is less abstract than formalism's 'motif' or 'plot-motif'. That is why I try to evoke the very physical sense of the—at least in Denmark— ubiquitous lego-block. Within a given tradition continuum, transmission of such units is quite concrete, sometimes involving verbatim and nearly identical variants of a tradition block or segment. This is irrespective of genre or literary typology, and is determinative of tradition building, affecting both the smallest and largest units of tradition.

All biblical genres are what might be described as segmented genres; that is, they are complex units of tradition that are composed of multiple smaller segments of material. In a quite substantial way, larger tradition units are created through the joining or selecting of smaller units. In biblical poetry, for example, it is commonplace to recognize that the independent quality and mobility of a poem's segments can be easily exchanged as they take part in one or many psalms and songs. I list only three examples, but almost the whole of the psalter and all songs in narratives are implicated: (1) the 'son of God' motif as we find it in Ps. 2.7 is directly echoed in Ps. 89.26-27, 2 Sam. 7.14-16 and 1 Chron. 17.12 and finds a more developed form in Ps. 132.11. (2) The pattern of the introduction to the oracle which is placed in David's mouth at his death in 2 Sam. 23.1 is not only echoed in the introduction to Balaam's oracle of Num. 24.3-4, but also again in vv. 15-16 where it is internally expanded with the addition of another segment. (3) The aetiological creation of an Asaph song at David's direction in 1 Chronicles 16, integrating into the context of 1 Chronicles' story variants of four psalm segments of three non-Asaph songs of the psalter.[4] This text I will discuss below.

---

4.   1 Chron. 16.7-36; Ps. 105.1-15; Ps. 96.1-13; Ps. 106, 1.47-48.

We find this same compositional technique in the production of many of the songs that have been collected under the structures that are called prophetic books. For example, we have a long song about the Moabites in two variant forms. We find one in Jeremiah 48 as a saying of Yahweh in the context of a series of such divine utterances against various enemies of Israel. The second is in Isaiah 15 and 16. Here, again, the context is that of a series of divine sayings: in this case by Yahweh Sebaot. In the Isaiah use of this song material, the content is richer than in Jeremiah, but nevertheless only superficially integrated into the narration of the prophet's life. The song is called an oracle here: a prophetic utterance. Somewhat inconsequently we are told at the song's closure that this was a word of Yahweh, which had been uttered against Moab in the past. Why? On the basis of Isaiah, we cannot know. However, the variant passage in Jeremiah reads: 'In the end I will restore the destiny of Moab'. In the closure of Isa. 16.1-5, which also reads somewhat inconsequently in context, we find the basis for Jeremiah's optimism about Moab's future: 'When the oppressor is no more, destruction has ceased, and marauders have vanished from the land, then a throne shall be established in steadfast love in the tent of David. On it shall sit in truth a ruler who seeks justice and who is swift to do what is right.' This small block or text-segment is not to be explained as a gloss. I would rather suggest that this lego-block has been intentially integrated with reference to Jeremiah as a saving grace against the murderous lions establishing the destiny of the remnant of the land pronounced in Isa. 15.9b. We find recurrently such text-segments echoing the motif of saving grace as thematic counterpoints to prohecies of doom, and we must conclude that such is their proper context. We also constantly find such short segments of text being set in multiple variant biblical contexts throughout the prophetic books, as, for example, in the verbatim variants dealing with Yahweh's *tora* and Zion in Isa. 2.2-4 and Mic. 4.1-4. Only the context is different; nevertheless, both passages are fully and successfully contextualized. The Isaiah variant presents the utterance as a vision of the saving word over Jerusalem *and Judah*, while in Micah the saving word is bound to an utterance against Israel and closes with the motif—echoing the theology of Ezra 1.3— that the saving grace of Israel's God will now come out from Jerusalem. It is clear that Micah's collected series of sayings holds together implicitly independent utterances, creating, as it were, a form of text collage.

As might be expected, substantial structural variants, which are in their content and language as far apart as, for example, the Judah/ Tamar story is from Ruth, also occur frequently in poetry. Some are essentially thematic variants, such as the utterances against Edom that we find in Obad. 1.1-9 and Jer. 49.7-22. To protect us from the temptation of offering a historical explanation of this type of variant, we should focus on the closure of the Jeremiah saying in vv. 21-22, which has a nearly verbatim variant in the very next chapter (50.44-46) but this time presented as an oracle not against Edom but now against Babylon. In this, we have not only a brilliant integration of a single saying with utterances both against Edom and Babylon, we also have a form of significance-building expansion or abbreviation. In reality we are presented with two distinct transmissions of one and the same tradition segment.

The techniques involved in the compositon of wisdom literature resemble those of poetry. In the genre of wisdom couplets, we typically find as the building blocks for Weisheitssprüche sentences and half-sentences that can travel and that can be used in a variety of ways. For example, in Prov. 13.19 we read: 'A desire fulfilled is sweet to the soul; but to turn away from evil is an abomination to the foolish'. Each half of this couplet can be used in different contexts and be paired with other tradition segments in a comparably satisfying matching. Further, collections of such traditional couplets offer multiple contexts for the very same proverb, as is the case for Prov. 20.16 and 27.13, where this proverb about surety for strangers, built through the parallelism of two closely variant segments, finds itself both in a miscellaneous collection of maxims and in a collection of admonitions and wisdom presented as those of a teacher in the style of Amenemope. These variants can be complex and rich. The couplets of Prov. 22.28 and 23.10 present us with the opening segment: 'Do not remove the ancient marker', which is completed by two variant closures playing on the verbal motif of 'father': 'which your fathers have set' and alternatively: 'or enter the fields of the fatherless', and in this variance rendering radically different signification. While this opening segment echoes a proverb of the Amenemope admonitions, it is also found in Deut. 19.14—in a very close variant of the Proverbs 22 couplet, in its manifestation as a 'law' of Moses: 'Do not remove your neighbor's marker; which the men of old have set', a 'legal' motif, which in a poem of Hosea is referenced as an analogue of lawless Judah: 'The princes of Judah have become like those who remove the marker' (Hos. 5.10). Such an economy of composition is one of the central causative factors reflected in the close formal proximity of biblical traditions presented as songs and those offered as wisdom. In both Job 7.17 and Ps. 8.5 we find the famous interrogatory entrance: 'What is a person?'. Job completes the query not only by completing the entry segment with 'that you make so much of one', and coupling it with 'and that you pay attention to one', a couplet in itself capable of a positive orientation, but Job expands the parallelism with the contextualizing closure: 'that you visit one every morning and test one every morning'. Psalm 8, however, offers the variant query: 'that you are mindful of one', and closes the couplet with the matching segment: 'or the son of man that you care for him', and then—also expanding—parallels this block with the splendid: 'Yet you have made him a little less than Elohim and have crowned him with glory and honor'. We find this tradition block yet again in Ps. 144.3-4 with, not only the interogatory expansion comparable to psalm 8: 'O Yahweh, what is a person that you would know one, or the son of man that you would think of him', but also the responsory expansion that closes this segment of the song by answering—and this we should mark well—the unexpanded query, 'A person is like a breath, whose days are like a passing shadow'. Thematically, the segment in Job and these two tradition blocks in the book of Psalms belong to the same literary and intellectual discussion. So, too, does the thematically similar variant in the expansive variant in Eliphaz's speech of Job 4.17-19 ('Can a mortal man be righteous before God, etc.?') as well as his briefer version which we find in Job 15.14 ('What is man that he can be clean, or he that is born of a woman that he can be righteous') as well as perhaps the far more distant variant in Job 15.16 ('How much less one who is abominable and corrupt, a person who drinks iniquity like water').

One text reflecting a type of variant often described in terms of expansion and paraphrase is found in the tradition blocks of Job 21.14-16 and 22.17-18. Only a half-sentence is rendered verbatim in both variants: 'They say to God: let us alone!' In Job 22, this segment is completed with 'What can the almighty do to us', to form a single statement. In 21, ch. 22's statement (beginning with 'They say to God: let us alone') is expanded with: 'We do not want knowledge of your ways'—or just as easily understood as abbreviated by deleting 'What can the almighty do to us'—to render: 'What is the almighty that we should serve him and what is our profit in praying to him?'. It is exactly at this point, however, that a discussion in terms of expansion and abbreviation explains nothing, as at this point the seemingly obviously abbreviated tradition block in ch. 22 now expands itself: 'the counsel of the wicked is far from me; the righteous see it and are glad, etc.'

This technique of creating texts is also found, as we are all aware, in the collections of laws and cultic regulations of the Pentateuch, entertaining a wide range of variants. We find casuistic law sayings, such as those we find in the so-called covenant code of Exod. 20.22 to 23.33—with a wide range of variants in cuneiform monumental inscriptions such as the Hammurapi stele, a mixture of casuistic sayings with narrative apodictic forms as in Deuteronomy 12–26, as well as in the didactic forms of blessings and curses as in Deuteronomy 27–28. Naturally, we also have the famous story variants of Exod. 20.1-17, Exodus 34, Leviticus 19 and Deuteronomy 5–6. A rich store of examples is also found among the cultic regulations. We might profitably compare Exodus 29's treatment of priestly ordination with that of Leviticus 8. Exodus 29.38-42's text for the daily burnt offering has its closest variant in Numbers, but it also shows up in a new context in Ezekiel's variant of 46.13-15. Exodus 23's cultic calendar is a tradition segment that has life also in four different contexts: once again in Exodus, in ch. 34, and in Leviticus 23 and Deuteronomy 16.

I can hardly hope to discuss all the ways that the stories of the Old Testament use this kind of composition technique but I would like to take three examples which are very interesting.

(1) 1 Chron. 16.7-36 writes a new Asaph song. It is built on the basis of four segments of three different canonical songs (none of which, I might add are Asaph songs). Verses 8-22 of 1 Chronicles 16 are derived from Ps. 105.1-15; vv. 23-33 come from Ps. 96.1-13 and vv. 34-36 come possibly from the beginning and certainly from the end of Psalm 106. It is interesting that in bringing together Psalm 106 vv. 1 and 47, 1 Chronicles creates a three-fold command as closure: 'Give Thanks...; Say "deliver us"...; Blessed be Yahweh...', rendering a much more sophisticated and significant ending for its Psalm than had existed for Psalm 106. In addition, 1 Chron. 16.36b: 'Then all the people said "Amen" and praised Yahweh', is far better used to anchor the song to Chronicle's story than as a kind of psalmic responsory as it is used in Psalm 106. In discussing 1 Chronicles 16, one must also think of that great song: 'Yahweh is my rock, my Burg and my salvation', which we find in David's mouth in 2 Samuel 22 and possibly

dependently in Psalm 18. We should also think of David's unique deathbed song of 2 Sam. 23.1-7, that has been attracted to the salvation song because of its 'rock' and 'Burg' motifs.

The integration of the Chronicles and Samuels songs into their narratives is remarkable. The prose introduction in 2 Sam. 22.1: 'David addressed the words of this song to Yahweh, etc.' is also found in a close variant in the untypical prose introduction to Psalm 18. Moreover, when we note that Psalm 18's entry: 'I love you, Oh Yahweh, my strength', is absent in Samuel, it becomes difficult to see the book of Psalms as 2 Samuels' source. Further, not only are none of the Psalms that 1 Cronicles uses themselves Asaph songs, but there is also a significant conceptual variance between Ps. 105.5-6 and 1 Chron. 16.12-13. The book of Psalms reads: 'Remember the wonderful works that he has done; remember his miracles and the judgements he has made, you descendents of Abraham his servant, children of Jacob, his chosen'. The variant statement in 1 Chronicles, however, reads instead of Abraham: 'you descendents of Israel his servant!' This, of course, is according to the central understanding of Abraham as *Aber hamon*: the father of many peoples, a concept which plays a central role in the late integrating theophany of Genesis 17, but is hardly integrated into the primary Abraham chain narrative, which rather understands Abraham as quintessentially Israel's.[5] Given that the psalm of Chronicles is also fully integrated both in its entry and closure into 1 Chronicles' story of David, I would recommend that we entertain a view of 1 Chronicles 16 as reflecting a *typical* act of biblical composition: a reuse of traditional materials in a new context for new purposes.

(2) Compare 2 Chron. 7.3-6 with its variant in 2 Chron. 5.11b-14, set in the time of Solomon, but comparing it to David's time. This block of tradition reiterates the giving of thanks to Yahweh 'for his steadfast love endures for ever'. We are here faced with a text-segment which can hardly be explained in any other way than as a kind of narrative lego-block of tradition. This observation, I think, appears conclusive when we look at the word *beyadam* in 2 Chron. 7.6d, which the RSV renders 'opposite them'. Unlike ch. 5, 2 Chronicles 7—though also set in Solomon's time—looks back to a comparable tradition-segment

---

5. T.L. Thompson, *The Origin Tradition of Ancient Israel* (JSOTSup, 55; (Sheffield: JSOT Press, 1987).

from David's time: 'The priests stood at their posts; the Levites also, with the instruments for music to the Yahweh which King David had made for giving thanks to Yahweh—for his steadfast love endures for ever—whenever David offers praises by their ministry: *opposite them* the priests sounded trumpets, and all Israel stood. At that time Solomon held a feast…' The *beyadam* has been left in the Davidic period of the text segment that had been introduced even as the context requires that the text's audience returns to the time of Solomon. With good sense, the Syriac eliminates the problem by excising the offending *beyadam*.

A comparable, but not nearly so perfect, example is found in 2 Chron. 1.1-4, the story in which Solomon, reiterating the activities of David goes up to the high place at Gibeon, 'for the tent of meeting…was there'. Verse 4 then finds it necessary to explain that David had taken the ark to 'the place prepared' and had pitched another tent in Jerusalem for it. I would suggest that this gloss comes from the compositor's own pen. Why does the tradition used here send Solomon to Gibeon when everything has been already moved to Jerusalem by David? That I think is implicit but clear. In Jewish stories, if one sets out to prepare for temple building, whether one is a David or a Solomon, one simply begins with the tent at Gibeon. 2 Chronicles 1 along with its variant of 1 Kings 3 about Solomon, and 1 Chronicles 21 with its variant in 2 Samuel 24 are simply four variant renditions of the same tradition-segment.

(3) The story variants of 1 Samuel 31, 2 Samuel 1 and 1 Chronicles 10. The problem of these narrative variants lies at the center and climax of what is often called the Succession Narrative, and the problem is that we do not have a narration here. Rather, Saul's death stops the plot entirely. Instead of a story narration, we are treated to a series of plot segment variants, which are collected successively while Saul's body and armor hang in the temple and his head rolls across the forgotten battlefield. Instead of a narrative dealing with the transition of Saul's kingdom to David's, as the scholarly world has led us to expect, we find, echoed and reiterated, a variety of narrative segments all dominated by a motif that originally had entered the narrative back in 1 Samuel 14 and 16: the fear about killing Saul as Yahweh's Messiah, which had first enduced David to take the risk of being faithful to his role as Saul's son and as Yahweh's servant. Here at the close of Saul's life this fear does in everyone who steps unto the scene as the narration recites successively a chain of variant segments concerning Saul's

death. Entirely apart from the so-called David history, we find altogether at least three and possibly five different and independent tradition segments concerning this 'event'.

In 1 Samuel 31, we have Saul and his armor-bearer. Both commit suicide. In 2 Samuel 1—which follows immediately upon the 1 Samuel's version—Saul's armor-bearer becomes an Amalekite. He knows that Saul is dead, because in this narration he says that he had killed him. The story in 1 Samuel and that in 1 Chronicles are very similar insofar as they render Saul's death, but the difference in narration is significant concerning what happened with the bodies, his armor and his head. There is certainly no doubt that we are not playing with history recounted. Nor are we dealing with the mixture of incomplete pieces of tradition gathered around one or other hero, theme or motif. These biblical texts are built from shattered shards of stories, which have been collected and organized and ordered. Such texts are hardly what we can call literature. They are rather traditions established, which give echo to and call up a forgotten past.

However much it may often help us in distinguishing and classifying texts, we also need to get away from a concentration on ideology, with its assumption of self-conscious *Tendenz*, as our primary interpretative focus. Far better, we might concentrate rather on ideation, the formation of ideas, themes and motifs within the ancient text, the nature of formulas and secondary verbal formation and how they affect and shape understanding. Unless we first can trace the process of ideation in any specific literary expression, we cannot hope to understand its *Tendenz* or its ideology. The reiteration of a tradition segment is not of itself a reiteration of the contextualized thought which once may have governed such formulas. Nevertheless, the units of tradition—through their formulaic character—create the perception of reflecting a reality that functions as an ideological referent of a text as tradition. In this respect, intertextuality is the legitimate exploration of such perceived reality. In the process of ideation, the transcendent quality of text accesses reality in a manner unavailable to event and history. It may well be a serious error of reading to continue to consider tales in the form of coherent units of tradition. We have long correctly learned to read larger units, such as the Abraham cycle, as composite—indeed segmented—wholes, freeing ourselves of the need for consistency and integrated resonance. So, too, we might approach much smaller units of the tradition; for example, 2 Samuel 1. If we read the story, we find that as we pass from story segment to story segment, each block must be comprehended out of context, where it has its integrity (asking the question about the 'Amalekite'). Even in the story's closure, the tale escapes integration, remaining fragmented, and only in the last scene do we gain any inference of the purpose or intention of the narrative as constructed: the sacred quality of Yahweh's Messiah.

Is it to be so taken for granted as to shape our very point of departure in interpretation that these text segments—when the intentionality of biblical composition is addressed—typically had any specific *Sitz im Leben* that we ought see them as songs, oracles or proverbs of the society rather than as a specific written product that has presented itself as such? Did the actual texts we have, indeed, ever have concrete political and historical referents, reflected implicitly in their contents and formulation; that is, do the segments as such—as tradition blocks—always have what we might seriously identify as an implied reader or author?

THE SIGNIFICANCE OF THE TEXTS FROM THE JUDEAN DESERT FOR THE HISTORY OF THE TEXT OF THE HEBREW BIBLE: A NEW SYNTHESIS[1]

Emanuel Tov

1. *Introduction*

In many ways, the newly discovered texts have revolutionized study of the text of not only the Hebrew Bible, but also that of the Greek. Many aspects of the transmission of the biblical text can now be illustrated by the texts from the Judean Desert, and this applies also to some aspects of the last stages of the literary growth of the biblical books. In scholarly jargon it may sound a little bombastic to speak of 'revolutionizing' the field, but I do believe that this term correctly describes the finds from the Judean Desert, especially the ones from Qumran. Some will claim that the texts found outside Qumran in Murabba'at, Naḥal Ḥever, and Masada are uninteresting, as they 'merely' confirm the medieval MT, but these texts, too, are in many ways exciting. The novel aspects relating to these texts pertain not only to new data, but also to a better understanding of the data known prior to the Qumran finds. In this paper I submit my temporary summarizing analysis, which is meant to expand and update my earlier summaries,[2] and to take into consideration the summaries of others.[3] I realize that this summary is temporary since not all the data are known or sufficiently analyzed. At the same

---

1. For bibliographical references relating to the published and unpublished documents, the reader is referred to E. Tov with the collaboration of S.J. Pfann, *Companion Volume to the Dead Sea Scrolls Microfiche Edition* (Leiden: E.J. Brill, 2nd rev. edn, 1995).

2. 'A Modern Textual Outlook Based on the Qumran Scrolls,' *HUCA* 53 (1982), pp. 11-27; 'Hebrew Biblical Manuscripts from the Judaean Desert: Their Contribution to Textual Criticism', *JJS* 39 (1988), pp. 1-37; *Textual Criticism of the Hebrew Bible* (Minneapolis: Fortress Press; Assen: Van Gorcum, 1992).

3. In chronological order: P.W. Skehan, 'Qumran, Littérature de Qumran, A.

time, most of the texts from Cave 4 have been published[4] or are known from monographs.[5] The largest groups of texts on which we lack detailed information at this stage is that of Psalms.

At the beginning of this survey, we should reflect for a moment on the overall approach to the biblical and nonbiblical scrolls from Qumran. It is probably true to say that the analysis of these texts would have been very different had the texts from Cave 4 been published prior to or simultaneously with those from Cave 1. As it happened, the texts that have been most researched are the ones that became known first, that is, 1QIsa[a] and 4QSam[a]. It is therefore not surprising that in the minds of many scholars, consciously or not, the special characteristics of the large *Isaiah Scroll* were considered to be the norm for the nature and scribal features of the Qumran texts. The impressive length of 1QIsa[a], which remains unequalled among the other finds of biblical texts, also gave much weight to that scroll. With the publication of the other texts, however, it has since become clear that this scroll is not typical of the Qumran finds. If anything, this scroll may be considered typical of the texts written in a specific orthographical and morphological style, but even this characterization is imprecise, since within this group 1QIsa[a] is

Textes bibliques' (DBSup, 9; Paris: Gabalda, 1979), pp. 805-22; F. García Martínez, 'Lista de MSS procedentes de Qumrán', *Henoch* 11 (1989), pp. 149-232; E.C. Ulrich, 'The Biblical Scrolls from Qumran Cave 4: An Overview and a Progress Report on their Publication', *RevQ* 14 (1989–90), pp. 207-28; A.S. van der Woude, 'Fünfzehn Jahre Qumranforschung (1974–1988)', *TRu* 55 (1990), pp. 245-307, esp. pp. 274-307; *TRu* 57 (1992), pp. 1-57; G.J. Brooke, 'Torah in the Qumran Scrolls', in H. Merklein *et al.* (eds.), *Bibel in jüdischer und christlicher Tradition: Festschrift für Johann Maier zum 60. Geburtstag* (BBB, 88; Bonn: Anton Hein, 1993), pp. 97-120; E. Ulrich, 'The Dead Sea Scrolls and the Biblical Text', in P.W. Flint and J.C. Vanderkam (eds.), *The Dead Sea Sea Scrolls after Fifty Years* (Leiden: E.J. Brill, 1998), pp. 79-100.

4.   For the publications of recent years, see: P.W. Skehan, E. Ulrich, and J. Sanderson (eds.), *Qumran Cave 4. IV. Palaeo-Hebrew and Greek Biblical Manuscripts* (DJD, 9; Oxford: Clarendon Press, 1992); E. Ulrich and F.M. Cross (eds.), *Qumran Cave 4. VII. Genesis to Numbers* (DJD, 12; Oxford: Clarendon Press, 1994); E. Ulrich (ed.), *Qumran Cave 4. IX. Deuteronomy–Kings* (DJD, 14; Oxford: Clarendon Press, 1995); E. Ulrich (ed.), *Qumran Cave 4. X. The Prophets* (DJD, 15; Oxford: Clarendon Press, 1994); E. Ulrich (ed.), *Qumran Cave 4. XI. Psalms to Chronicles* (DJD, 16; Oxford: Clarendon Press, forthcoming).

5.   See especially P.W. Flint, *The Dead Sea Scrolls and the Book of Psalms* (STDJ, 17; Leiden: E.J. Brill, 1997).

rather idiosyncratic with regard to its Aramaizing variants, its excessively full orthography and peculiar morphological features, and its manifold corrections.

The present survey is the first to cover all the sites in the Judean Desert, including texts found on Masada, in Naḥal Ḥever, in Murabbaʿat, and Ṣeʾelim, and it is the first to include indirect evidence embedded in nonbiblical Qumran texts.

a. *Masada, Naḥal Ḥever and Murabbaʿat*
Excavations on Masada[6] yielded two manuscripts of Leviticus,[7] one of Deuteronomy,[8] one of Ezekiel and two or three of Psalms.[9] All these texts are very close to the MT, with the sole exception that MasPs[b], is written in a special stichometric system leaving spaces after groups of two or three words at different places in the line. Both Talmon and García Martínez (see nn. 7-9) remark that there are hardly any differences between these texts and the medieval MT. Also the texts from Naḥal Ḥever (Numbers, Deuteronomy, Psalms) and Murabbaʿat are almost identical to the MT.[10] This is especially evident in the well-preserved *Minor Prophets Scroll* from Murabbaʿat (MurXII, also known as Mur 88).

The texts from these three sites are thus almost identical to the medieval consonantal text of the MT, even more so than the proto-Masoretic Qumran texts. For example, Barthélemy considers Mur12 a characteristic product of the textual standardization that took place between the two revolts and which is therefore more properly proto-Masoretic,

6. For a brief description of all the biblical fragments found at Masada, see S.Talmon in the catalogue of the Masada exhibit, *Sippurah shel Meṣadah* (Jerusalem: Israel Exploration Society, 1994), pp. 97-102; *idem, Masada VI*, forthcoming.

7. S. Talmon, 'Fragments of Two Scrolls of the Book of Leviticus from Masada', *Eretz Israel* 24 (1994), pp. 99-110 (Heb.).

8. See F. García Martínez, 'Les manuscrits du Désert de Juda et le Deutéronome', in F. García-Martínez *et al.* (eds.), *Studies in Deuteronomy in Honour of C.J. Labuschagne on the Occasion of his 65th Birthday* (Leiden: E.J. Brill, 1994), pp. 63-82, esp. pp. 75-78.

9. See S. Talmon, 'Fragments of a Psalms Scroll from Masada, MPs[b] (Masada 1103–1742)', in M. Brettler and M. Fishbane (eds.), *Minhah le-Nahum: Biblical and Other Studies Presented to Nahum M. Sarna in Honour of his 70th Birthday* (JSOTSup, 154; Sheffield: JSOT Press, 1993), pp. 318-27.

10. Partly published preliminarily by Y. Yadin in *IEJ* 11 (1961), pl. 20 and *IEJ*

so to speak, than the earlier Qumran texts of the *Minor Prophets* and of other books.[11]

b. *Qumran*
As in the past, the main sources for our knowledge of the biblical text in Qumran manuscripts remain those that contain a running biblical text, but our information about these manuscripts can now be supplemented by other sources which have not been used much in the past. The information from these sources is significant, although the amount of information embedded in them is limited. I refer to biblical quotations in the nonbiblical compositions as well as to excerpted and abbreviated biblical manuscripts. At the same time, the biblical manuscripts remain the most obvious source. The information about differences between the various Qumran documents is taken at face value, that is, as reflecting variant readings or exegesis by the scribes or authors of the nonbiblical compositions; Greenstein, on the other hand, suggested that when encountering variations in the biblical and nonbiblical texts, one's first inclination should be to assume the scribe's faulty memory.[12] This is a fresh approach which has much to recommend it, but in my view it applies only to a few instances.

2. *The Biblical Text Reflected in the Nonbiblical Compositions*

A full analysis of the biblical text in Qumran ought to include quotations from the Bible in the nonbiblical documents. By way of comparison, since the textual apparatuses of critical editions of the Hebrew Bible include references to quotations from the biblical text in rabbinic writings, and since critical editions of the LXX contain quotations of the LXX by the Church Fathers, any analysis of the text of the Bible in Qumran ought to include quotations in the nonbiblical writings. After

12 (1962), pl. 48B. For Murabba'at, see P. Benoit *et al.*, *Les grottes de Murabba'at* (DJD, 2; Oxford: Clarendon Press, 1961).

11. D. Barthélemy, *Critique textuelle de l'AT* (OBO, 50.3; Fribourg/Göttingen: Universitätsverlag/Vandenhoeck & Ruprecht, 1992), III, p. cxiii.

12. E.L. Greenstein, 'Misquotation of Scripture in the Dead Sea Scrolls', in B. Walfish (ed.), *The Frank Talmage Memorial Volume* (Haifa: Haifa University Press, 1993), pp. 71-83. A similar theory had been advanced previously by H.M. Orlinsky for 1QIsa[a]: 'Studies in the St. Mark's Isaiah Scroll', *JBL* 69 (1950), pp. 149-66, esp. p. 165.

all, through these quotations additional sources of information can be reached which add to our knowledge of the variety of biblical texts in the period under investigation. In the past, these nonbiblical texts have rarely been included in text-critical analyses, with some justification, since it is very difficult to extract from them reliable information about the biblical text quoted. These difficulties are caused by the fact that biblical quotations and stretches of biblical text are found in a great variety of compositions, each of which requires a different type of analysis. Thus the evaluation of the textual deviations reflected in the biblical quotations in these compositions differs not only from one category of composition to the other, but also from one composition to the next. The following three categories of composition are distinguished.[13]

a. *Free Quotations and Allusions*
The first category pertains to nonbiblical compositions, both sectarian and nonsectarian, which freely quote from and allude to passages in the Bible. In the case of the sectarian writings, this is understandable since the Bible held a very central position in the life of the Qumranites, so that the *Hodayot*, the *Rules*, 4QShirShabb, and sapiential compositions abound with biblical quotations. This also pertains to non-Qumranian compositions such as 4QNon-Canonical Psalms A–B (4Q380–81). Most of these quotations are free, involving changes in the biblical text and combinations of different biblical texts. As a result, these deviations from the textual witnesses of the Bible cannot be evaluated easily within the context of a text-critical discussion. That is, while there remains a slight possibility that such a deviation reflects a variant reading not known from the direct witnesses of the text, probably most deviations derive from the authors' free approach. The textual background of some compositions has been studied, but few solid conclusions have been reached.[14]

13. Excerpted and abbreviated biblical manuscripts, analyzed below as a subgroup of biblical manuscripts, are not included in this group.
14. M.H. Goshen-Gottstein, 'Bible Quotations in the Sectarian Dead Sea Scrolls', *VT* 3 (1953), pp. 79-82; J. Carmignac, 'Les citations de l'Ancien Testament dans "La guerre des fils de la lumière contre les fils des ténèbres"', *RB* 63 (1956), pp. 234-61, 375-91; M. Mansoor, 'The Thanksgiving Hymns and the Masoretic Text (II)' *RevQ* 3 (1961), pp. 387-94; J. de Waard, *A Comparative Study of the Old Testament in the Dead Sea Scrolls and in the New Testament* (Studies on the Texts

b. *Pesharim*

The pesharim are composed of quotations from the biblical text (lemmata) and their exposition (the pesher). The lemmata in the eighteen pesharim on biblical books or parts of them from Caves 1 and 4 contain long stretches of biblical text, which, when combined, would amount to biblical manuscripts, were it not that they have been preserved only fragmentarily. In addition, the exposition in the pesher itself sometimes also reflects a few additional readings differing from the biblical text on which the pesher comments.[15] For 1QpHab, 4QpNah, 4QpPs, and some sections of the pesharim on Isaiah, extensive stretches of biblical text have been preserved, while the preserved text of the other pesharim is more fragmentary. In the past the question has been raised whether the biblical text contained in and reflected by these pesharim adds to our knowledge of the biblical text. A positive answer to this question was given by the editors of textual editions who decided to incorporate readings from these pesharim in their textual apparatuses (*BHS* and *BHQ*[16] for 1QpHab and HUBP[17] for the pesharim on Isaiah). At the same time, other scholars ascribed as many non-Masoretic readings in the pesharim[18] as possible to the contextual exegesis of the authors of these pesharim.[19] However, although the biblical text of the pesharim undoubtedly reflects contextual exegesis by the authors of the pesharim,

of the Desert of Judah, 4; Leiden: E.J. Brill, 1965); G. Vermes, 'Biblical Proof Texts in Qumran Literature', *JSS* 34 (1989), pp. 493-508.

15. The relevant instances have been discussed in scattered analyses, and now also in a monograph by I. Goldberg, 'Variant Readings in the Pesher Habakkuk', *Textus* 17 (1994), pp. ט-כד (Heb.).

16. *Biblia Hebraica Quinta*, in preparation.

17. See M.H. Goshen-Gottstein, *The Hebrew University Bible: The Book of Isaiah* (Jerusalem: Magnes Press, 1995).

18. E.g. G. Molin, 'Der Habakkukkommentar von 'En Fešḥa in der alttestamentlichen Wissenschaft', *TZ* 8 (1952), pp. 340-57; G.J. Brooke, 'The Biblical Texts in the Qumran Commentaries: Scribal Errors or Exegetical Variants?' in C.A. Evans and W.F. Stinespring (eds.), *Early Jewish and Christian Exegesis: Studies in Memory of William Hugh Brownlee* (Atlanta, GA: Scholars Press, 1987), pp. 85-100 with references to earlier studies.

19. In the words of Brooke, 'The Biblical Texts', p. 87: '...that in more cases than are usually recognized the variants in the biblical texts in the Qumran commentaries have been deliberately caused by the desire of the Qumran commentator to make this text conform with his exegetical understanding'.

including a few cases of sectarian exegesis,[20] undoubtedly many of the deviating readings found in the lemmata or embedded in the exposition of the pesharim reflect ancient variants copied from the manuscript on which the pesher is based. At the same time, it is hard to determine how many of the readings that look like contextual changes were initiated by the authors of the pesharim and how many were found in their *Vorlagen*. A maximalistic approach to the amount of manuscript variation underlies the lists of presumed variant readings for 1QpHab by Brownlee[21] and for all the pesharim by Lim.[22] Thus, according to Lim (p. 90), 17 per cent of all the words of the MT of Nahum differ from the corresponding preserved segments of 4QpNah. A minimalistic approach is reflected in the views of the aforementioned scholars (n. 18) who ascribe most of the differences between the biblical text and the pesharim to the latter's exegetical changes, and very few to a presumed different underlying *Vorlage*. The number of readings of 4QpNah which, according to Lim, differ from the MT is very high indeed, but they include two problematic groups, viz., all the morphological variations and a large number of contextual changes. If all these elements were indeed inserted by the authors of the pesharim, their underlying biblical text was probably not very different from the other textual witnesses. We hardly have any criteria for deciding whether this was the case, although the mentioned sectarian changes (see n. 20) incline one to believe that the authors of the pesharim themselves inserted the alterations. But if they did not, this *Vorlage* already included the morphological variations and contextual changes, so that those manuscripts must have resembled 1QIsa[a] and similar texts. Believing that this was the case, several scholars[23] have indeed characterized the underlying text of the pesharim as 'vulgar' texts.[24]

20. The most clear-cut examples are 1QpHab 8.3 (Hab. 2.5) הון (MT: הויין); 1QpHab 11.3 (Hab. 2.15) מועדיהם (MT: מעוריהם). For an analysis of these readings, see W.H. Brownlee, *The Text of Habakkuk in the Ancient Commentary from Qumran* (JBL Monograph Series, 11; Philadelphia: Scholars Press, 1959), pp. 113-18.

21. Brownlee, *The Text of Habakkuk*.

22. T.H. Lim, Holy Scripture in the Qumran Commentaries and Pauline Texts (Oxford: Clarendon Press, 1997), chapter 4.

23. J. van der Ploeg, 'Le rouleau d'Habacuc de la grotte de 'Ain Fešha', *BiOr* 8 (1951), pp. 2-11, esp. p. 4; K. Elliger, *Studien zum Habakuk-Kommentar vom Toten Meer* (BHT, 15; Tübingen: Mohr Siebeck, 1953), p. 48; P. Kahle review of *Studien zum Habakuk-Kommentar vom Toten Meer* (BHT, 15; Tübingen: Mohr Siebeck,

c. *Rewritten Biblical Compositions*

A literary genre which is often described as a group of rewritten biblical compositions provides substantial information relevant to our knowledge of the biblical text. These rewritten biblical compositions reformulate the content of the Bible, especially of the Pentateuch, adding and omitting minor and major details, as well as changing many a word. Each composition is unique, inserting a different number of changes in the biblical text. Some compositions are very close to the biblical text, such as 4QRP (4QReworked Pentateuch)[25] and the *Temple Scroll* (especially as contained in 11QT[a]), both of which contain very long stretches that run parallel to the biblical text. In fact, 4QRP[a-e], which has been preserved well in its five different manuscripts (including 4QRP[a]=4Q158), is almost in the nature of a regular biblical manuscript to which a thin layer of exegetical changes was added. It is often very hard to recognize these exegetical changes in the mentioned compositions. This applies to compositions whose names contain the elements 'Ps(eudo)' and 'Apocr', such as 4QapocrJoseph[a-c], 4QapocrMos[a-b], 4QapocrJosh[a-b], 4QpsEzek[a-e], and 4QapocrJer A-E, as well as to 4QExposition on the Patriarchs (4Q464), and 4QparaGen-Exod (4Q422). Because of the difficult distinction in these compositions between the biblical text and the more substantial added layer of exegesis and rewriting, it is hard to incorporate the underlying biblical text in a text-critical analysis. In the case of the first-mentioned compositions, however, the underlying biblical text is recognizable so that some conclusions suggest themselves.

1953) by K.S. Elliger in *TLZ* 79 (1954), pp. 478-79 (479); S. Segert, 'Zur Habakuk-Rolle aus dem Funde vom Toten Meer VI', *Archiv Orientalni* 23 (1955), pp. 575-619 (608). These scholars probably go too far when describing the biblical quotations in the pesharim as reflecting a distinct textual recension deviating from the other textual sources. A similar conclusion was reached by M. Collin, mainly on the basis of an analysis of 1QpMic, which was characterized by him as reflecting a third recension of the biblical book, alongside the MT and LXX: 'Recherches sur l'histoire textuelle du prophète Michée', *VT* 21 (1971), pp. 281-97. This characterization was rejected by L.A. Sinclair, 'Hebrew Texts of the Qumran Micah Pesher and Textual Traditions of the Minor Prophets', *RevQ* 11 (1983), pp. 253-63.

24. For a discussion of what many scholars name 'vulgar texts', see E. Tov, *Textual Criticism*, pp. 193-97.

25. See E. Tov and S.A. White: '4QReworked Pentateuch[b-e]', in H. Attridge *et al.* in consultation with J. VanderKam, *Qumran Cave 4. VIII. Parabiblical Texts, Part 1* (DJD, 13; Oxford: Clarendon Press, 1994), pp. 187-352.

For example, there is strong evidence that at least three of the manuscripts of 4QRP (4Q158, 364 and 365 = 4QRP[a,b,c]) are close to the Sam. Pent. and hence to the so-called proto-Samaritan manuscripts.[26] A similar text is reflected in the biblical quotations in the book of *Jubilees*, although there is more evidence pertaining to the Ethiopic 'grand-daughter' translation of that book than to the fragmentary Qumran texts.[27] Also for 11QT[a] much textual evidence is available, especially for cols. 51-66. An analysis of that evidence does not show a close textual relation to any of the known textual witnesses of the Bible, and its text should probably be characterized as reflecting an independent textual tradition.[28]

Although the amount of information on the biblical text reflected in the nonbiblical compositions from Qumran is limited, these sources need to be further explored for text-critical purposes. Among other things, an attempt should be made to examine possible links between the biblical quotations in the nonbiblical Qumran texts, especially the sectarian ones, and the biblical texts found in Qumran. This is a difficult task, since it is not easy to determine on which specific biblical manuscript a quotation in a nonbiblical composition is based. Characteristic readings of the biblical texts need to be isolated in the quotations, and this is possible only when the differences between the manuscripts themselves are sufficiently distinctive. For example, in Isaiah the differences between 1QIsa[a] (sometimes agreeing with 4QIsa[c]) on the one hand and on the other hand the proto-Masoretic 1QIsa[b] and most of the Isaiah manuscripts from Cave 4 are quite distinct, as are the differences in Jeremiah between (1) 4QJer[b,d] and the LXX, (2) the Masoretic 4QJer[a,c], and (3) 2QJer. At the same time, it remains difficult to determine proximity between brief quotations from these two books in nonbiblical compositions and specific Qumran biblical manuscripts. A

26. See E. Tov, 'The Textual Status of 4Q364–367 (4QPP)', in J. Trebolle Barrera and L. Vegas Montaner (eds.), *The Madrid Qumran Congress: Proceedings of the International Congress on the Dead Sea Scrolls, Madrid, 18–21 March, 1991* (Studies on the Texts of the Desert of Judah, 11; Leiden: E.J. Brill, 1992), pp. 43-82.

27. For an analysis, see J. VanderKam, *Textual and Historical Studies in the Book of Jubilees* (HSM, 14; Missoula, MT: Scholars Press, 1977).

28. See E. Tov, 'The Temple Scroll and Old Testament Textual Criticism', *Eretz Israel* 16 (Hebrew with English summary; Jerusalem: Israel Exploration Society, 1982), pp. 100-11.

few special links between such quotations and Qumran manuscripts have been noticed, but research of this type is still in its infancy.[29]

3. *Biblical Manuscripts*

a. *Excerpted and Abbreviated Texts*
The existence of excerpted biblical texts among the Qumran manuscripts has been assumed for some time.[30] With the publication of additional texts, especially from the Pentateuch, this category has been extensively analyzed by the present author.[31] Due to the fragmentary nature of these texts, their essence is not always clear, nor is the background of the excerpting. Most excerpted texts were probably made for liturgical purposes:[32] all the *tefillin*, several manuscripts of Exodus and Deuteronomy,[33] and a very long list of Psalm texts from Caves 4 and 11 containing major transpositions, omissions and additions (e.g. 4QPs^n in which Ps. 135.12 is followed by 136.22-23).[34] The same pertains to a few manuscripts containing an abbreviated text, but the evidence for such texts is far from clear. Thus 4QExod^d (Exod. 13.15-16; 15.1) omits 13.17-22 and all of ch. 14; 4QCant^a omits 4.7–6.11, and 4QCant^b

29. See the discussion of the quotation from Deut. 33.8-11 in 4QTestim below. See further the examples listed by Tov, 'Hebrew Biblical Manuscripts', p. 34. Vermes, 'Biblical Proof Texts', mentions a few cases of difference between the MT and the text quoted in Qumran compositions, e.g. cf. 1QS, 5, line 17 לכם agreeing with the MT Isa. 2.22 differing from לכמה in 1QIsa^a; cf. also הואה with הוא in 1QIsa^a.

30. See esp. H. Stegemann, 'Weitere Stücke von 4QpPsalm 37, von 4QPatri-archal Blessings und Hinweis auf eine unedierte Handschrift aus Höhle 4Q mit Exzerpten aus dem Deuteronomium', *RevQ* 6 (1967), pp. 193-227 (217-27); Brooke, 'Torah in the Qumran Scrolls'.

31. E. Tov, 'Excerpted and Abbreviated Biblical Texts from Qumran', *RevQ* 16 (1995), pp. 581-600.

32. The background of the scrolls containing merely Deuteronomy 32 (4QDeut^q) and Ps. 119 (4QPs^{g,h} and 5QPs) is not clear.

33. 4QExod^e (Exod. 13.3-5); 4QDeut^j (Exod. 12.43-51; 13.1-5 and fragments of Deut. 5, 6, 8, 11, 30 [?], 32); 4QDeut^k (Deut. 5, 11, and 32); 4QDeut^n (Deut. 8.5-10; 5.1–6.1).

34. For details, see P.W. Flint, 'The Psalms Scrolls from the Judaean Desert: Relationships and Textual Affiliations', in G.J. Brooke with F. García Martínez (eds.), *New Qumran Texts and Studies: Proceedings of the First Meeting of the International Organization for Qumran Studies, Paris 1992* (Studies on the Texts of the Desert of Judah, 15; Leiden: E.J. Brill, 1994), pp. 31-52.

omits Cant. 3.6-8 and 4.4-7.[35] If the characterization of these texts as excerpted and abbreviated texts is correct, their major omissions and transpositions should be disregarded in the text-critical analysis, but their other details should be regarded as reflecting a regular biblical manuscript, and hence should be included in the text-critical analysis. Thus the *tefillin*, containing combinations of four different biblical texts, often agree with one of the other textual witnesses, and their readings should thus be included in the text-critical analysis of Exodus and Deuteronomy. Some of these readings agree with the Masoretic family, and others with the LXX or the Sam. Pent.; in the latter case, especially in harmonizing readings.[36] Again, other readings agree with certain Qumran scrolls.

The relevance to the text-critical analysis of some excerpted biblical manuscripts is a matter of dispute. The Qumran texts bearing biblical names are included in our analysis, even if the biblical name is somewhat misleading, such as the presumptive liturgical text which was named 11QPs[a], since the greater part of that scroll runs parallel with biblical Psalms. Certainly the *tefillin* have to be integrated in the text-critical analysis. The textual character of some excerpted texts is extremely important. Thus the first biblical text quoted in 4QTestim which combines Deut. 5.28-29 and 18.18-19 is close to the Sam. Pent. and 4QRP[a] (4Q158, of a proto-Samaritan character). At the same time, the third quotation in 4QTestim, from Deut. 33.8-11, is very close to one of the Qumran scrolls, namely 4QDeut[h], and may have been based on that scroll or a similar one.[37] These two quotations thus show that the author of 4QTestim used at least two biblical scrolls of a different character, that is, a scroll close to the Sam. Pent., namely a pre-Samaritan text and 4QDeut[h], a text close to the proto-Masoretic text. This

35. For both texts, see Tov, 'Excerpted and Abbreviated Biblical Texts', and 'Three Manuscripts (Abbreviated Texts?) of Canticles from Qumran Cave 4', in *JJS* 46 (1995), pp. 88-111.

36. See E. Eshel, '4QDeut[n]: A Text that has Undergone Harmonistic Editing', *HUCA* 62 (1991), pp. 117-54.

37. See E. Tov, 'The Contribution of the Qumran Scrolls to the Understanding of the LXX', in G.J. Brooke and B. Lindars (eds.), *Septuagint, Scrolls and Cognate Writings: Papers Presented to the International Symposium on the Septuagint and its Relations to the Dead Sea Scrolls and Other Writings* (Manchester, 1990) (Septuagint and Cognate Studies, 33; Atlanta, GA: Scholars Press, 1992), pp. 11-47, esp. pp. 31-35; J.A. Duncan, 'New Readings for the "Blessing of Moses" from Qumran', *JBL* 114 (1995), pp. 273-90.

mixture was undoubtedly unintentional, but resulted from the availability of these particular scrolls to the scribe, and probably neither he nor other authors took notice of the different textual character of the scrolls consulted.

Another feature of the excerpted and abbreviated texts is that, with the exception of some *tefillin* and *mezuzot*, none of these texts is close to the MT.[38] This indicates a certain milieu for these anthologies, whose purpose differed from that of the writing of regular Scripture texts. In any event, in the light of this analysis, the mentioned texts are included in the textual analysis in the next paragraphs.

b. *Biblical Texts*

1. *Background.* The number of biblical texts from Qumran is approximately 200, but it constantly changes with new insights into the nature of the fragments, in particular due to the separation or combination of groups of fragments—more the former than the latter, so that the number of recognized texts constantly increases. Thus, while Skehan listed 172 different scrolls in 1965,[39] the first edition of the *Companion Volume to the Microfiche Edition to the Dead Sea Scrolls* in 1993 listed 189 biblical texts,[40] slightly more than were listed a decade ago.[41] In the

38. For an analysis, see Tov, 'Excerpted and Abbreviated Biblical Texts'.

39. P.W. Skehan, 'The Biblical Scrolls from Qumran and the Text of the Old Testament', *BA* 28 (1965), pp. 87-100.

40. How uncertain we are regarding the number of texts originally deposited in the caves is shown by the number of reinforcing tabs found in Cave 8. Each reinforcing tab was probably attached to a single scroll, and unless this cave contained a leather workshop or depository, many scrolls must have decayed in this cave in which archeologists have discovered 68 reinforcing tabs, usually of coarse leather, and remains of only four different manuscripts. See J. Carswell, 'Fastenings on the Qumran Manuscripts', *DJD* 6 (Oxford: Clarendon Press, 1977), pp. 23-28 (24). At the same time, the number of scrolls identified on the basis of their handwriting is probably smaller than their number in reality, since often different scribes copied segments of the same scroll.

41. The list in Tov and Pfann, *The Dead Sea Scrolls on Microfiche*, includes the following figures: Cave 1: 15; Cave 2: 17; Cave 3: 3; Cave 4: 129; Cave 5: 7; Cave 6: 7; Cave 8: 2; Cave 11: 9. This calculation includes all the texts bearing a biblical name, even though some of them (11QPs[a] and several of the Psalms texts from Cave 4) may be in the nature of liturgical collections. At the same time, Greek biblical texts and paraphrases in any language (e.g. 4QpaleoParaJosh) are not included.

second edition of this *Companion Volume*,[42] four items were added. Temporary lists of the contents of the different fragments of biblical texts have been provided by Glessmer, Scanlin, and Ulrich.[43]

The great majority of the Hebrew biblical texts comes from Cave 4, while smaller quantities were found in Caves 1, 2, 3, 5, 6, 8, and 11. It would be beneficial if these biblical texts could be classified according to certain objective criteria, but there is hardly an objective criterion for classifying them. For one thing, the contents of each of the caves are not homogenous, with the sole exception of Cave 7 containing only Greek papyri. The main depository of texts is Cave 4, which contains copies of all the books of the Hebrew Bible, with the exception of Esther.[44] It is a significant fact that virtually all the so-called canonical books were found in this cave, which probably implies that an effort was made to store in that cave all the books that were considered authoritative at that stage, at least in certain Jewish circles, and which became authoritative at a later stage for all of Judaism. On the other hand, of the Apocrypha, and the so-called Pseudepigrapha, only a few books were represented in Cave 4 (*Tobit, Jubilees, Levi, T. Jud., T. Naph.*). Cave 4, thus, may have served as a central depository for the books of the Qumran community. Although it is hard to generalize, it is clear that a distinction should be made, subjective though it may be, between texts containing more elements that are significant for our understanding of the presumed original text of the Hebrew Bible and those that contain fewer such elements. It is probably not coincidental that most Qumran copies of the biblical books that are considered to be significant for the textual analysis of the Hebrew Bible were found in that cave. While a text like 1QIsa[a] may be important to our understanding of the textual transmission of the Bible, it contains so many

42. *Companion Volume to the The Dead Sea Scrolls Microfiche Edition* (Leiden: E.J. Brill, 2nd rev. edn, 1995). Items were added in Leviticus, Deuteronomy and Isaiah.

43. U. Glessmer, 'Liste der biblischen Texte aus Qumran', *RevQ* 16 (1993), pp. 153-92; H. Scanlin, *The Dead Sea Scrolls and Modern Translations of the Old Testament* (Wheaton: Tyndale House Publishers, 1993); E. Ulrich, 'An Index of the Passages in the Biblical Manuscripts from the Judean Desert (Genesis-Kings)', *DSD* 1 (1994), pp. 113-29; *idem*, 'An Index of the Passages in the Biblical Manuscripts from the Judean Desert (Part 2: Isaiah-Chronicles)', *DSD* 2 (1995), pp. 86-107.

44. The absence of this book should be ascribed to coincidence (destruction of the material) rather than to any other factor.

secondary features that its importance for the reconstruction of the original text of the Bible is limited. Cave 4 does contain texts of the type of 1QIsa[a], but, on the other hand, the caves other than Cave 4 hardly contain any texts which are of major significance for text-critical analysis.

2. *Texts in the Paleo-Hebrew Script.* The great majority of the Qumran texts as well as all the biblical texts from the other sites in the Judean Desert are written in the square script, and they reflect a textual variety to be elaborated upon below. A similar variety is reflected in the texts written in the paleo-Hebrew script, so that the textual character of these texts cannot serve as a key for unscrambling the riddle of the writing in this script. The biblical texts written in the paleo-Hebrew script differ from the texts written in the square script only with regard to the scribal characteristics inherent with the writing in that script and with regard to the lack of scribal intervention in them.[45]

At Qumran, fragments of 12 biblical texts written in the paleo-Hebrew script have been found as well as four nonbiblical paleo-Hebrew texts of uncertain nature:[46] 1QpaleoLev, 1QpaleoNum (same scroll as 1QpaleoLev?); 2QpaleoLev; 4QpaleoGen-Exod[l], 4QpaleoGen[m], 4QpaleoExod[m], 4QpaleoDeut[r,s], 4QpaleoJob[c]; 6QpaleoGen, 6QpaleoLev; 11QpaleoLev[a]. Three fragments (4Q124–125; 11Q22) are unidentified. 4QpaleoParaJosh, probably not a biblical text, contains parts of Joshua 21.

45. Cf. E. Ulrich, 'The Palaeo-Hebrew Biblical Manuscripts from Qumran Cave 4', in D. Dimant and L.H. Schiffman (eds.), *A Time to Prepare the Way in the Wilderness: Papers on the Qumran Scrolls by Fellows of the Institute for Advanced Studies of the Hebrew University, Jerusalem, 1989–1990* (Studies on the Texts of the Desert of Judah, 16; Leiden: E.J. Brill, 1995), pp. 103-29. On p. 129, Ulrich concludes: 'In sum, except for their script, the palaeo-Hebrew biblical manuscripts from Qumran cave 4 do not appear to form a group distinguishable from the other biblical scrolls in either physical features, date, orthography, or textual character'. The lack of scribal intervention in the paleo-Hebrew texts has been described in my article, 'The Socio-Religious Background of the Paleo-Hebrew Biblical Texts Found at Qumran', in H. Cancik and others (eds.), *Geschichte-Tradition-Reflexion, Festschrift für Martin Hengal zum 70 Geburtstag,* I (Tübingen: J.C.B. Mohr, 1996), pp. 353-74.

46. See M.D. McLean, 'The Use and Development of Palaeo-Hebrew in the Hellenistic and Roman Periods' (unpubl. dissertation, Harvard University, 1982), pp. 41-47 (University Microfilms); P.W. Skehan, E. Ulrich and J.E. Sanderson, *Qumran Cave 4.* IV. *Palaeo-Hebrew and Greek Biblical Manuscripts* (DJD, 9; Oxford: Clarendon Press, 1992).

Beyond Qumran, the two texts written on both sides of the enigmatic nonbiblical papyrus fragment found in Masada, pap paleoMas 1o (Mas1039-320) are also written in paleo-Hebrew characters.[47]

The fragments written in the paleo-Hebrew script contain only texts of the Torah and Job—note that the latter is traditionally ascribed to Moses (cf. *b. B. Bat.* 14b-15a; cf. also manuscripts and editions of the Peshitta in which Job follows the Torah). Note also that for these two quantities only Targumim were found in Qumran. The longest preserved texts written in the paleo-Hebrew script are '4QpaleoExod^m and 11QpaleoLev^a.

All texts written in the paleo-Hebrew script reflect a similar scribal approach, but the scribes often displayed their individuality in specific features.

These texts, rather than preceding the use of square script, were actually written at a relatively late period, as a natural continuation of the tradition of writing in the 'early' Hebrew script, and were concurrent with the use of the square script, as can also be proved by a paleographical examination of the paleo-Hebrew script.[48] While it is tacitly assumed by most scholars that with the revival of the paleo-Hebrew script in the Hasmonean period, texts were transformed from the square to the paleo-Hebrew script,[49] it would be more natural to assume that the habit of writing in the paleo-Hebrew script had never ceased. Elsewhere I tried to prove that the paleo-Hebrew texts from Qumran derived from the circles of the Sadducees.[50] The same article suggests that the Qumran scribes themselves were influenced by this tradition by writing the tetragrammaton and other divine names in paleo-Hebrew characters, in order that these words, whose sanctity was determined by the writing in this script, might not be erased.

47. S. Talmon, 'Fragments of Scrolls from Masada', *Eretz Israel* 20 (1989), pp. 278-86.

48. See R.S. Hanson, 'Paleo-Hebrew Scripts in the Hasmonean Age', *BASOR* 175 (1964), pp. 26-42.

49. Thus K.A. Mathews: 'The Background of the Paleo-Hebrew Texts at Qumran', in C.L. Meyers and M.O'Connor (eds.), *The Word of the Lord Shall Go Forth: Essays in Honor of David Noel Freedman in Celebration of his Sixtieth Birthday* (Winona Lake, IN: Eisenbrauns, 1983), pp. 549-68.

50. Tov, 'Socio-Religious Background'.

3. *Textual Variety*. The textual variety of the Qumran biblical texts is now an established assumption among scholars.[51] It is probably an equally-accepted assumption of many scholars that these texts derived from different places in ancient Israel, not only from Qumran. Presently scholars are not as naive as the first generation of Qumran scholars who ascribed all the texts found in Qumran to the Qumran community, while some of them even tried to locate in them the characteristic ideas of that community.[52] At the same time, we do not have to go as far as N. Golb, who denies any connection between the scrolls found in the caves and the Qumran community living in Khirbet Qumran very close to Cave 4.[53] I prefer a middle course according to which some of the Qumran texts (probably not more than 25 per cent) were copied by the scribes of the Qumran community, while the remainder were brought to Qumran from outside. I believe that there are criteria in the realm of orthography, morphology and scribal practices for distinguishing between the two groups (see 4. below). As a result, if this opinion is correct, in my view it is justifiable to look for sectarian readings in 1QIsa[a] (although I have not been able to locate them), but it is not justifiable to look for them in any text whose connection with the Qumranites has not been established, such as 4QSam[a], for example.

4. *Classification of the Texts according to Textual Character*. The classification of the Qumran texts remains a difficult assignment. They

51. For recent discussions, see E. Ulrich, 'Pluriformity in the Biblical Text, Text Groups, and Questions of Canon', in Trebolle Barrera and Vegas Montaner (eds.), *The Madrid Qumran Congress*, pp. 23-41; *idem*, 'The Dead Sea Scrolls'.

52. The only clearly recognizable sectarian readings in biblical manuscripts that exclusively reflect the views of one of the religious groups in ancient Israel are of Samaritan background. On the other hand, although many of the Qumran biblical manuscripts were presumably copied by the Qumran scribes (see below), they do not contain readings that reflect the views of the Qumran covenanters (such readings are, however, included in 1QpHab and possibly in other pesharim as well; cf. n. 20 above). According to I.L. Seeligmann, a further exception should be made for Isa. 53.11 in 1QIsa[a] and the LXX, seé 'ΔΕΙΞΑΙ ΑΥΤΩΙ ΦΩΣ', *Tarbiz* 27 (1958), pp. 127-41 (Hebrew with English summary).

53. N. Golb, 'The Problem of Origin and Identification of the Dead Sea Scrolls', *Proc. Am. Phil. Soc.* 124 (1980), pp. 1-24; *idem*, 'Who Hid the Dead Sea Scrolls?' *BA* 48 (1985), pp. 68-82; *idem*, 'Khirbet Qumran and the Manuscripts of the Judaean Wilderness: Observations on the Logic of their Investigation', *JNES* 49 (1990), pp. 103-14.

cannot be classified by cave, since the contents of each individual cave are not homogenous. Nor can they be classified by origin (copied by the Qumranites/brought from outside), since this distinction is not firmly secured. Nor can the texts be classified by date, by palaeographical or codicological criteria, since none of these criteria is firm. Probably the best criterion for classification is according to textual character, even though this criterion is not firm either. But since one of our main interests is to gain insights into the textual nature of the individual texts and the collection as a whole, we nevertheless have to attempt to classify the texts according to this criterion. The first step in this classification is an attempt to determine the principles for describing five textual groups, and to fill in the details for each group. The second step is to see how these groups are distributed in the individual books of the Bible, even though we should not forget that the preservation of the Qumran fragments depends to a large degree on coincidence. But even with these limitations it is relevant to examine, for example, how many texts belonging to the Masoretic family have been preserved in each of the books of the Bible, and whether the various biblical books present a different textual picture.

The following description expands and updates our previous classification of the textual patterns extant in the Qumran scrolls.[54]

The principle behind this classification is the recognition that some texts can be grouped according to common scribal features and others according to the degree of their closeness to the MT, LXX, or the Sam. Pent., without accepting the claim that these three texts are the central pillars (recensions, texts, text-types, etc.) of the biblical text. This classification is valid as long as we are open to the possibility that there are also texts that are not close to any of these three entities (group e. below). I admit that it is rather unusual to classify ancient texts according to the degree of their closeness to later textual witnesses, certainly if these are medieval (MT and Sam. Pent.), but this comparison is merely made for the sake of convenience. The different groups of texts recognized are not all of the same kind, since four groups are identified on the basis of their relation to certain other texts, while the first group

54. Tov, *Textual Criticism*, pp. 114-17; 'Groups of Hebrew Biblical Texts Found at Qumran', in D. Dimant and L.H. Schiffman (eds.), *A Time to Prepare the Way in the Wilderness: Papers on the Qumran Scrolls by Fellows of the Institute for Advanced Studies of the Hebrew University, Jerusalem, 1989–1990* (Studies on the Texts of the Desert of Judah, 16; Leiden: E.J. Brill, 1995), pp. 85-102.

is identified according to its scribal features. This unequal basis for the classification is dictated by the evidence itself and should be kept in mind.

a. *Texts Written in the Qumran Practice*. It has been suggested, especially by the present author, that a large group of Qumran texts stands apart from the other ones because of their common use of a distinctive orthography, morphology, and a set of scribal practices.[55] While in the past my point of departure was that of orthography and morphology, in view of the subjective nature of this criterion, I now start from the scribal features of these texts.[56] It has been recognized that a whole series of scribal features occurs almost exclusively in texts that display a certain system of orthography and morphology. Thus, as recognized in the past on the basis of more partial information, scribal signs such as paragraph indicators, cancellation dots, as well as paleo-Hebrew and Cryptic A letters, occur almost exclusively in texts written in the Qumran scribal practice. This pertains also to the occurrence of guide dots. The fact that virtually all the sectarian texts from Qumran reflect this combined set of features has led to the suggestion that these texts were copied by the group of people who left the texts behind in the Qumran caves. They were possibly written in Qumran itself, although this is not a necessary part of the hypothesis. It is not claimed that these features are characteristic of the Qumran scribal school only. It is only maintained that within the corpus of the texts found at Qumran these features display a peculiar distribution. The criteria for defining the

---

55. E. Tov, 'The Orthography and Language of the Hebrew Scrolls Found at Qumran and the Origin of these Scrolls', *Textus* 13 (1986), pp. 31-57; 'Hebrew Biblical Manuscripts'; *Textual Criticism*, pp. 108-10; 'Further Evidence for the Existence of a Qumran Tribal School', forthcoming. See also J. Lübbe, 'Certain Implications of the Scribal Process of 4QSam^c', *RevQ* 14 (1989–90), pp. 255-65. Cross describes the orthography of these texts as a 'baroque style' and he includes the morphological features under the heading of orthography, F.M. Cross, 'Some Notes on a Generation of Qumran Studies', in Trebolle Barrera and Vegas Montaner (eds.), *The Madrid Qumran Congress*, pp. 1-14; see also my reply, 'Texual Status', in the same volume, pp. 15-21.

56. See 'Scribal Markings in the Texts from the Judean Desert', in D.W. Parry and S.D Ricks (eds.), *Current Research and Technological Developments on the Dead Sea Scrolls—Conference on the Texts from the Judean Desert, Jerusalem, 30 April 1995* (STDJ, 20; Leiden: E.J. Brill, 1996), pp. 41-77.

nature of this group have been refined in recent years. It has, for instance, been recognized that the dichotomy between the texts written in the Qumran scribal practice and those which are not written in this practice pertains to further features, as well, which links many of the texts that are not written in the Qumran scribal practice with rabbinic or Pharisaic circles. Thus texts of the latter group reflect rabbinic rules for copying Scripture more than do texts of the former group.[57] Likewise, *tefillin* belonging to the latter group reflect the rabbinic prescriptions for the contents of the *tefillin*, while the *tefillin* of the former group, written in the Qumran scribal practice, do not.[58] On the basis of these criteria it is now possible to identify a group of biblical texts reflecting the Qumran scribal practice.[59] The great majority of these texts reflect a free approach to the biblical text that manifests itself in adaptations of unusual forms to the context,[60] in frequent errors, in numerous corrections

57. See E. Tov, 'Scribal Practices Reflected in the Documents from the Judean Desert and in the Rabbinic Literature: A Comparative Study', in M.V. Fox *et al.* (eds.), *Texts, Temples and Traditions: A Tribute to Menahem Haran* (Winona Lake, IN: Eisenbrauns, 1996), pp. 383-403.

58. This situation probably implies that these phylacteries were produced by the Qumranites. See E. Tov, '*Tefillin* of Different Origin from Qumran?' in Y. Hoffman and F.H. Polak (eds.), *A Light for Jacob: Studies in the Bible and the Dead Sea Scrolls in Memory of Jacob Shalom Licht* (Jerusalem/Tel Aviv: Mossad Bialik 1997), pp. 44*-54*.

59. While the final list of the texts belonging to this group will be compiled when all the texts are known, sound evidence for the Qumran practice exists with regard to the following texts: 1QDeut[a], 1QIsa[a], 2QExod[a,b], 2QJer, 3QLam, 4QNum[b], 4QDeut[h,j,k,m,t], 4QSam[c], 4QIsa[c], 4QXII[c,e], 4QLam, 4QQoh[a], 11QLev[b]; 4QPhyl A,B,G-I,J-K,L-N,O,P,Q. To this group also belong *all* the sectarian compositions written by the Qumran covenanters (such as 1QH, 1QM, 1QS, and the *pesharim*) and the following biblical paraphrases and collections of Psalms: 4Q158, 4Q364, 4Q365 (all three containing 4QRP), 4QPs[n], 11QPs[a,b]. Although there is no characteristic representative of this group, 1QIsa[a], which contains the longest Qumran text of a biblical book, is often referred to (incorrectly) as if it were the main text written in the Qumran practice.

60. This feature is illustrated in Tov, *Textual Criticism*, pp. 110-11. See further two brief articles by A. Rubinstein illustrating the same point: 'Notes on the Use of the Tenses in the Variant Readings of the Isaiah Scroll', *VT* 3 (1953), pp. 92-95; 'Formal Agreement of Parallel Clauses in the Isaiah Scroll', *VT* 4 (1954), pp. 316-21. In his 1953 article, Rubinstein exemplifies the simplification of the tense system and, in his 1954 article, the adaptation of small grammatical elements in 1QIsa[a] to the parallel stichos.

and sometimes in negligent script. Some of these texts have been copied from proto-Masoretic texts, while others are close to the Sam. Pent., and again others reflect a more complicated textual profile.[61] The documents written in the Qumran practice, often described as typical Qumran texts, comprise some 25 per cent of the Qumran biblical texts. As for the nonbiblical texts, possibly the base text of several pesharim belonged to this group as well.

b. *Proto-Masoretic (or: Proto-Rabbinic) Texts.* Proto-Masoretic (or: Proto-Rabbinic) texts contain the consonantal framework of the MT, one thousand years or more before the time of the Masorah codices, and they do not seem to reflect any special textual characteristics beyond their basic agreement with the MT. The closeness of some of these fragments to the medieval texts is quite remarkable.[62] These texts are usually named proto-Masoretic, but the term 'proto-rabbinic', used by F.M. Cross,[63] probably better describes their nature. These texts comprise some 40 per cent of the Qumran biblical texts, and therefore represent the largest group among the Qumran documents.

c. *Pre-Samaritan (or: Harmonistic) Texts.* The pre-Samaritan Qumran texts (4QpaleoExod[m] 4QExod-Lev[f], and 4QNum[b], and secondarily also 4QDeut[n] and possibly also 4QLev[d])[64] reflect the characteristic features

61. 4QSam[c] is equally close to the MT and the Lucianic text of 2 Sam. 14–15, which in that section probably reflects the Old Greek translation. 4QNum[b], containing a rather lengthy text, is very close to the Sam. Pent., and secondarily also to the LXX. Other texts were copied from sources of a different nature. 4QDeut[k] and 4QXII[c,e] reflect non-aligned texts differing in small details from the other sources, while the textual character of 1QDeut[a], 2QExod[a], 2QNum[b], 2QDeut[c], 3QLam, 4QLam and 4QQoh[a] is not clear.

62. For details, see Tov, 'Groups of Hebrew Biblical Texts'. The proto-Masoretic features are well visible in 4QGen[b], 1QIsa[b], 4QIsa[d], 4QJer[a] and 4QJer[c]. The Qumran proto-Masoretic group ought to be investigated also with regard to possible clusters within this group regarding spelling and content, but because of the paucity of overlapping Qumran texts, this investigation is very limited. A possible clustering of 1QIsa[a,b] and 4QIsa[c,d] (of which 1QIsa[a] and 4QIsa[c] reflect the Qumran orthography), against the medieval text, is visible. Such clusters, if detected, could show how the MT has developed since the Qumran period. It should thus be possible to pinpoint readings in which the medieval text reflects a later development.

63. For the use of the term and the conception behind it, see F.M. Cross, 'Some Notes'.

64. Many of the fragments of the Pentateuch are equally close to the MT and

of the Sam. Pent. with the exception of the latter's ideological readings, but they occasionally deviate from it. It appears that one of the texts of this group formed the basis of the Sam. Pent., and that the Samaritan ideological changes and phonological features were inserted into that text. A characteristic feature of these texts is the preponderance of harmonistic readings, and as a result the group as a whole was named harmonistic by Eshel.[65] F.M. Cross[66] prefers to term this group 'Palestinian', and there is much justification for this characterization, since these texts are not evidenced outside Palestine. The use of this term is, however, problematic, since it may imply that no other texts or groups of texts were extant in Palestine. Of the rewritten Pentateuch compositions, the following reflect a pre-Samaritan biblical text: 4Q158, 4Q364, 4Q365 (all three containing 4QRP). 4QTestim also reflects a similar text. All the pre-Samaritan texts together comprise some five per cent of the Qumran biblical texts, and they are texts of the Pentateuch only. Although this is a small group (for all of the Bible this group would have comprised some 15 per cent), it is very significant for our understanding of the transmission of the Hebrew Bible.

d. *Texts Close to the Presumed Hebrew Source of the LXX.* Although no text was found in Qumran that is identical or almost identical to the presumed Hebrew source of the LXX, a few texts are very close to that translation: 4QJer[b,d] bear a strong resemblance to the LXX in characteristic details, with regard both to the arrangement of the verses and to their shorter text.[67] Similarly close to the LXX, though not to the same extent, are 4QLev[d] (also close to the Sam. Pent.), 4QDeut[q] and secondarily also 4QSam[a] (close to the main tradition and the Lucianic manuscripts of the LXX; see further below, group e.),[68] 4QNum[b], and according to Cross (DJD, 12, 84) also 4QExod[b]. Individual agreements with the LXX are also found in additional texts, in a somewhat large proportion in 4QDeut[c,h,j], but the latter texts actually belong to group e. In Isaiah, MT and LXX are fairly close to each other, so that most of the extant Qumran texts from Cave 4 are equally close to the MT and LXX.

Sam. Pent, because their fragmentary state of preservation does not allow us to identify characteristic features of either MT or the Sam. Pent.

65. Eshel, '4QDeut[n]'.
66. Oral communication.
67. See the discussion in Tov, *Textual Criticism*, pp. 319-27.
68. For an analysis, see Tov, 'The Contribution of the Qumran Scrolls'.

There is insufficient evidence for speculating on the internal relationship between the texts that are close to the LXX. In any event, they should not be considered a textual group. They do not form a closely-knit textual family like the Masoretic family or the pre-Samaritan group, nor have these texts been produced by a scribal school, like the texts written according to the Qumran usage (group a). They represent individual copies that in the putative stemma of the biblical texts happened to be close to the Hebrew text from which the LXX was translated. Since the *Vorlage* of the LXX was a single biblical text, and not a family, recension or revision, the recognition of Hebrew scrolls that were close to the *Vorlage* of the LXX is thus of limited importance to our understanding of the relationship between these texts, but it does have bearing on our understanding of the nature of the LXX and its *Vorlage*. The texts that are close to the LXX comprise some five per cent of the Qumran biblical texts.

e. *Non-Aligned Texts*. Many Qumran texts are not exclusively close to either the MT, LXX or Sam. Pent. and are therefore considered non-aligned. That is, they agree, sometimes significantly, with the MT against the other texts, or they agree with the Sam. Pent. and/or the LXX against the other texts. They furthermore contain readings not known from other texts, so that they are not exclusively close to one of the other texts or groups. Usually the employment of the term *non-aligned* merely implies that the texts under consideration follow an inconsistent pattern of agreements and disagreements with the MT, LXX and Sam. Pent., as in the case of 4Q-Lev[c], 4QDeut[b,c,h,k,m], 6QpapKings, 4QIsa[c], 4Q12[a,c,e], 4QDan[a] and 11QpaleoLev[a]. But the texts that are most manifestly non-aligned, and actually independent, are texts that contain (groups of) readings that diverge significantly from the other texts, such as 4QJosh[a], 4QJudg[a] and 5QDeut. 4QSam[a] holds a special position in this regard, since it is closely related to the *Vorlage* of the LXX, while reflecting independent features as well. A special sub-group of non-aligned texts are scrolls written for a specific purpose, especially 'liturgical' or 'excerpted' texts, such as the aforementioned 4QExod[d], 4QDeut[j,n] and many of the Psalm texts. By extension this also pertains to 4QCant[a,b]. Taken together, all the non-aligned texts comprise some 25 per cent of the Qumran evidence, and this group thus adds an important aspect to our understanding of the nature of the transmission of the biblical text.

Whether we assume that all the aforementioned texts were written at Qumran, or that only some were written there while others were brought from elsewhere, the coexistence of the different categories of texts in the Qumran caves is noteworthy. The fact that all these different texts were found in the same caves probably reflects a certain textual reality in the period between the third century BCE and the first century CE. In our reconstruction of the history of the biblical text in that period this situation is described as textual plurality. At the same time, within that textual plurality the large number of proto-Masoretic texts probably reflects their authoritative status. Since there is no evidence concerning the circumstances of the depositing of the scrolls in the caves or concerning their possibly different status within the Qumran sect, no solid conclusions can be drawn about the approach of the Qumranites towards the biblical text. In any event, they apparently paid no special attention to textual differences such as those described here.

That all these different groups of texts co-existed in Qumran, and in Palestine as a whole shows that no fixed text or textual family had been decided upon as the central text for the country as a whole. However, this conclusion may be slightly misleading, since in certain milieux in Palestine one of the texts or textual families may still have been the only accepted text. This, I believe, is the case for the Masoretic family, which probably was the only acceptable text in temple circles.[69] In a way, this should thus be considered an official text; this assumption would explain the great number of copies of this text found at Qumran. This assumption also explains the aforementioned fact that the Masoretic family was the only text found at Masada, Naḥal Ḥever, and Murabbaʿat. The facts known about Masada also fit into this picture, since the community which lived there would have adhered to the rabbinic text. This also applies to Naḥal Ḥever and Murabbaʿat, reflecting a reality from the time of the Second Jewish Revolt (135 CE).

Within this framework, the presence of the Qumran paleo-Hebrew texts of proto-Masoretic character seems to defy any explanation. After all, against the background of the rabbinic prohibition of the paleo-Hebrew script,[70] it is puzzling to see among the Qumran texts several

---

69. For details, see Tov, *Textual Criticism*, pp. 32-33.

70. See *m. Yadayim* 4.5; *b. Sanh.* 21b; and cf. *b. Meg.* 9a; *t. Sanh.* 5.7; *y. Meg.* 1.71b-c.

manuscripts (probably the majority)[71] of proto-Masoretic character written in that script. The connection between these proto-Masoretic texts
and Pharisaic circles is evident, and some scholars even call the proto-
Masoretic texts 'proto-rabbinic'. When the biblical text is quoted in the
Talmud and midrashim, it is that of the MT, and when the rabbinic circles produced an Aramaic translation, it is again based on a text that is
more or less identical to the MT. It is, therefore, hardly comprehensible
that the same circles that prohibited the use of paleo-Hebrew should
also have produced copies of the proto-Masoretic texts written in paleo-
Hebrew characters. Because of this difficulty, one of the links in our
argumentation must be wrong. Against this background, my aforementioned suggestion should be remembered according to which the
Qumran paleo-Hebrew texts of proto-Masoretic character derived from
Sadducean circles.[72] One of the special characteristics of the paleo-
Hebrew texts is that they display virtually no scribal intervention. The
proto-Masoretic text was presumably kept intact in the temple, and this
description suits the further assumption that the temple also kept the
paleo-Hebrew Masoretic texts alive. The proto-Masoretic texts were
thus embraced, in different scripts, by both the Pharisees and the Sadducees, both of whom were connected with the temple. If this description is correct, texts of proto-Masoretic content were central in Israel,
with the Pharisees in the square script and with the Sadducees in the
paleo-Hebrew script. At the same time, it is not impossible that the
Sadducees embraced proto-Masoretic texts both in the paleo-Hebrew
and the square script.

If the recognition of the aforementioned five groups of texts is correct, by definition some of the textual theories which have been suggested in this century cannot be maintained, especially because of the
fifth group, which is composed of texts not connected with the MT,
LXX, or Sam. Pent. The existence of this group allows for an endless
number of individual texts, thus eliminating the possibility that all the
Qumran texts, and in fact all ancient Hebrew texts, ultimately derived
from a tripartite division of the textual sources. Elsewhere I have tried
to refute that view,[73] claiming that the textual sources of the Bible

71. Thus Ulrich, 'The Palaeo-Hebrew Biblical Manuscripts', p. 128.
72. This conclusion is reached not only by way of elimination, but it is also
based on positive arguments related to the Sadducees; Tov, 'Socio-Religious
Background'.
73. Tov, *Textual Criticism*, pp. 155-60.

cannot be reduced to three traditions and that these textual traditions are not recensions or text-types, but that they are simply 'texts'. It should, however, be conceded that my own view, like all other views, is based on certain suppositions; it is equally subjective, and, like the other views, cannot be proven with absolute proof. The texts themselves should remain our point of departure, but a recent article by Davila on Genesis and Exodus shows how difficult it is to find mutually acceptable criteria.[74] In the wake of others before him, Davila takes as his point of departure that the MT and Sam. Pent. of these books are text-types, rather than texts, and he suggests that they, together with the Qumran texts, belong to the same text-type, and that the LXX reflects a different text-type.[75] Most of the Qumran texts of Genesis and Exodus examined by Davila are indeed close to the MT, but the material is simply too fragmentary to prove that the Qumran texts together with the MT and Sam. Pent. comprise one textual entity and that this entity is a text-type. Had the fragments been more extensive, we would probably have been able to recognize the proximity between some Qumran fragments and the Sam. Pent. For example, one of the rewritten Bible texts, 4QRP[b] (4Q364), reflects significant harmonizing additions in Genesis and Exodus, and if the biblical text upon which this text is based had been found, the statistical picture for these two books would have been different.

In this analysis, I have not referred to the different numbers of copies of the biblical books found in Qumran,[76] nor to the implications of the textual finds from Qumran for our understanding of the development of the biblical text in Palestine in the period covered by the finds from the Judean Desert.[77]

5. *The Textual Evidence for the Different Biblical Books*. Having analyzed the different textual entities recognized among the Qumran

---

74. J.R. Davila, 'Text-Type and Terminology: Genesis and Exodus as Test Cases', *RevQ* 16 (1993), pp. 3-37.

75. In my view, however, the MT and Sam. Pent. of Genesis and Exodus differ sufficiently to be considered different texts, often recensionally different. The LXX reflects yet a third text, again often recensionally different, especially in the genealogies and in Gen. 31. But this evidence does not suffice to prove either my theory or the views of Davila (reiterating those of others before him).

76. Cf. Tov, *Textual Criticism*, p. 104.

77. For which, see Tov, *Textual Criticism*, pp. 117, 187-97.

scrolls, I now turn to the evidence for the individual books, assuming that different textual patterns may emerge for the biblical books, while at the same time I am aware of the dangers inherent in this type of review. The main problem is the vagaries of the textual transmission causing certain texts to be preserved, while others have been destroyed over the centuries. Thus the evidence showing the existence of two different editions of Jeremiah (MT and 4QJer[a,c] on the one hand and 4QJer[b,d] and the LXX on the other) characterizes the textual transmission of that book, while in other books there may likewise have existed different editions, though less clearly defined (Joshua, Samuel, Kings, Proverbs, Daniel, Esther). But how do we know that similar editorial processes did not take place in other books as well, without leaving any trace in the textual witnesses? For example, different recensions may have existed once for Leviticus or Isaiah, even though the present rather homogenous textual traditions of these books give us no indication of such earlier stages.

I turn first to the Pentateuch, in which an approach of less scribal intervention or greater precision was possibly to be expected. However, there is no indication that the textual transmission of the Pentateuch, in fact, differs from that of the other books of the Bible.

In Genesis, there are no major differences between the MT and the Sam. Pent., except for some of the genealogies. The great majority of the texts of Genesis[78] reflect this combined evidence of the MT and the Sam. Pent., although they are somewhat closer to the MT. The deviations of the LXX from this often-common text are not major, but large enough to enable us to recognize that the Qumran texts do not reflect that text. A close relation to the combined text of the MT and the Sam. Pent. is visible in the following texts: 4QGen[c], Gen[e], Gen[f], Gen[g], and Gen[j], while 4QGen-Exod[a] is somewhat closer to the MT and 4QGen[b] is practically identical with that text. The other texts are too fragmentary for analysis. Note that none of the Genesis texts is written in the 'Qumran practice'.

---

78. Beyond the 14 texts of Genesis in the square script, three fragments may reflect additional : 4QGen[h-title], 4QpapGen? (4Q483), and 4Q576. There are also three texts in the paleo-Hebrew script. Two texts also contain Exodus: 4QGen-Exod[a] and 4QpaleoGen-Exod[l].

In Exodus, the 16 texts diverge substantially. Three (four?) texts reflect the Qumran practice: 2QExod^{a,b},[80] 4QExod^j,[81] and possibly 4QExod^b. In this book, the differences between the MT, LXX, and the Sam. Pent. are clear-cut, so that the allegiance of the Qumran fragments can be easily determined if the fragment is large enough. 4Qpaleo-Exod^m is very close to the Sam. Pent., without the latter's sectarian readings, and according to Cross,[82] 4QExod-Lev^f also belongs to this category. The following texts belong to the group of the MT: 1QExod, 4QGen-Exod^a, 4QExod^c, 4QpaleoGen-Exod^l. Statistically independent are: 4QExod^b (close to the LXX according to Cross)[83] and 4QExod-Lev^f. 4QExod^d is independent in terms of content, omitting a large section. The other texts are too fragmentary for analysis.

Several of the 12 manuscripts of Leviticus (four of which are in the paleo-Hebrew script; one also contains Numbers: 4QLev-Num^a) are equally close to the MT and the Sam. Pent. (these two texts do not differ much from each other in Leviticus): 1QpaleoLev^a, 4QLev-Num^a, 4QLev^{b,c,d,e}. Statistically independent is 11QpaleoLev^a. 11QLev^b and 4QLev^g are possibly not biblical compositions.[84] The other texts are too fragmentary for analysis. On the whole, the texts of Leviticus are rather homogeneous, probably due to their contents. None of the manuscripts is written in the 'Qumran practice'.

Two of the seven manuscripts of Numbers (one is in the paleo-Hebrew script) are written in the 'Qumran practice' (2QNum^b, 4QNum^b). It is difficult to define the nature of 4QNum^b, which in its major deviations is close to both the Sam. Pent. and the LXX, and at the same time contains many independent readings. The other texts are too fragmentary for analysis.

Of the 28 manuscripts of Deuteronomy (two of which are written in

---

79. Of the 16 texts, two also contain Genesis (see previous note), and one contains Leviticus: 4QExod-Lev^f. All texts except for 4QpaleoExod^m are written in the square script.

80. 2QExod^b probably contains a rewritten Bible text and not a regular Bible manuscript.

81. The orthography of this small fragment probably reflects the 'Qumran practice', and it also contains the tetragrammaton in paleo-Hebrew characters.

82. DJD, 12, p. 136.

83. DJD, 12, p. 84.

84. 4QLev^g and 11QLev^b have the tetragrammaton in paleo-Hebrew characters, but are too fragmentary for analysis.

the paleo-Hebrew script),[85] the following are equally close to the MT and Sam. Pent.: 1QDeut[b], 4QDeut[d,f,g,i,o,p], 4QpaleoDeut[r]. Seven manuscripts are written in the Qumran practice: 1QDeut[a], 2QDeut[c], 4QDeut[m], 4QDeut[j,k,t] and 5QDeut. The textual nature of several manuscripts cannot be classified easily, since they probably represent excerpted texts, probably for liturgical purposes: 4QDeut[j,k,n,t]. Statistically independent are 4QDeut[b,c,h,m]. 4QDeut[q] is close to the *Vorlage* of the LXX.[86] The other texts are too short for analysis.

One of the two Joshua texts is close to the MT (4QJosh[b]), and one is contents-wise independent (4QJosh[a]). 4QJosh[a] is an unusual biblical text which contains, in addition to an occasional shorter text similar to that of the LXX,[87] the following unusual sequence in frags. 1-2: 8.34-35; X; 5.2-7. Since the pericope which is now known in MT as 8.30-35 and which relates the building of an altar by Joshua on Mt Ebal, occurs in 4QJosh[a] at an earlier stage in the story, that scroll reflects a completely different picture.[88]

85. See F. García Martínez, 'Les manuscrits'; S.A. White, 'Three Deuteronomic Manuscripts from Cave 4, Qumran', *JBL* 112 (1993), pp. 23-42.

86. For an analysis, see Tov, 'The Contribution of the Qumran Scrolls', esp. pp. 29-30. According to White, this text is close to the LXX. See DJD, 14.

87. Frags. 15-16 of this scroll present a recensionally shorter text than the MT, which runs parallel to the shorter text of the LXX, although the two are not identical. Cf. L. Mazor, *The Septuagint Translation of the Book of Joshua: Its Contribution to the Understanding of the Textual Transmission of the Book and its Literary and Ideological Development* (Jerusalem: Hebrew University, 1994 [Hebrew with English summary]), pp. 54-56 and *idem*, 'A Textual and Literary Study of the Fall of Ai in Joshua 8', in S. Japhet (ed.), *The Bible in the Light of its Interpreters: Sarah Kamin Memorial Volume* (Jerusalem: Magnes Press, 1994 [Hebrew]), pp. 73-108.

88. According to that text, immediately after Joshua crossed the Jordan (ch. 4), he built an altar, followed in the scroll by a transitional clause, and the beginning of the account of the circumcision (5.2-7 in the MT). According to this account the altar was thus built at Gilgal, and not on Mt Ebal as in the MT, and in this regard the Joshua scroll resembles the account in Josephus in *Ant.* 5.16-19 according to which Joshua built his altar immediately upon crossing the Jordan. According to Ulrich, '4QJoshua[a]', 96 and A. Rofé, 'The Editing of the Book of Joshua in the Light of 4QJosh[a]', in Brooke with García Martínez (eds.), *New Qumran Texts and Studies*, pp. 73-80, this account presents the more original version of the story. The section describing the implementation of the command of Deut. 27 to erect an altar thus occurs in three different places in the various textual traditions of Joshua: in its present place in MT, in the LXX after Josh. 9.2, and in 4QJosh[a] before the beginning

One of the three texts of Judges is close to the MT (4QJudg[b]), and one is independent in terms of context (4QJudg[a]).[89] The third text is too short for analysis.

Two of the four texts of Samuel are close to the MT (1QSam, 4QSam[b]), one is close to the LXX, 4QSam[a],[90] with features of an independent text, and one is written in the 'Qumran practice' (4QSam[c]).

The two texts of Kings reflect the group of MT, 4QKgs and 6QKgs.

Of the 21 manuscripts the following of Isaiah are close to the MT and secondarily also to the LXX: 4QIsa[a], 4QIsa[e], 4QIsa[f], 4QIsa[g]. This pertains also to the following texts, although they are too short to enable one to pronounce a clear judgment: 4QIsa[h], 4QIsa[i], 4QIsa[j], 4QIsa[k], 4QIsa[l], 4QIsa[m], 4QIsa[n], 4QIsa[o], 4papIsa[p], 4QIsa[q], 4QIsa[r]. Two texts reflect the 'Qumran practice': 1QIsa[a] and 4QIsa[c]. The other texts are too short for analysis.

Two of the six manuscripts of Jeremiah are close to the MT (4QJer[a,c]), one is written in the 'Qumran practice' (2QJer), and two are close to the LXX (4QJer[b,d]). 4QJer[e] is too short for analysis.

Three of the six manuscripts of Ezekiel are close to the MT (4QEzek[a,b], 11QEzek). The other texts are too short for analysis.

Three of the eight manuscripts of the *Minor Prophets* are statistically independent (4QXII[a,c,e]). Two of these are written in the 'Qumran practice' (4QXII[c,e]). The other texts are too short for analysis.

It is difficult to classify the many texts of Psalms because of the uncertainty regarding their nature and the fact that most of the psalters from Cave 4 have not yet been published. What is relatively stable is the recognition that several of the Psalm texts reflect the 'Qumran practice': (1) 11QPs[a], also reflected in 4QPs[e] and 11QPs[b]; (2) 4QPs[f]; (3) 4QPs[n]; (4) 4QPs[q]; (5) 4QPsAp[a]. Also well-established is the recognition that most of the Psalm texts reflect a textual tradition different from the MT and the other textual witnesses. At least eight collections

---

of ch. 5, immediately after the crossing of the Jordan. The evidence of 4QJosh[a] supports the assumption made previously on the basis of the LXX and MT that Josh. 8.30-35 is a separate pericope added to a previous layer of Joshua at different places. For parallel developments, see Tov, 'Some Sequence Differences between the MT and LXX and their Ramifications for the Literary Criticism of the Bible', *JNSL* 13 (1987), pp. 151-60.

89. For an analysis, see Tov, *Textual Criticism*, pp. 344-45.

90. For an analysis and for earlier literature, see Tov, 'The Contribution of the Qumran Scrolls', esp. pp. 30-33.

of Psalms from Caves 4 and 11 contain Psalms in a sequence different from the MT, sometimes with additional psalms being added to the canonical ones: (1) 11QPs^a, also reflected in 4QPs^e and 11QPs^b and probably also in 4QPs^b; (2) 4QPs^a; (3) 4QPs^d; (4) 4QPs^f; (5) 4QPs^k; (6) 4QPs^n; (7) 4QPs^q; (8) 4QPsAp^a. Furthermore, according to Flint,[91] there is no evidence in Qumran of any scroll clearly supporting the Masoretic psalter, which, incidentally, is supported by MasPs^{a,b}. If the view suggested by Sanders, Wilson, and Flint carries the day,[92] it implies that the Psalm fragments from Caves 4 and 11 probably constitute the group of Qumran evidence which diverges most from the MT. However, the arguments adduced in the past in favor of the assumption that 11QPs^a reflects a liturgical collection also hold with regard to the texts from Cave 4,[93] and this view seems preferable to me. The deviations from the MT pertain to both the sequence of the individual Psalms and to the addition and omission of Psalms, including noncanonical Psalms.

Two of the four texts of Job are close to the MT (4QJob^{a,b}), but in this book no other textual traditions are known since the much-deviating LXX text was probably shortened by the translator himself. The other texts are too short for analysis.

Both texts of Proverbs are close to the MT (4QProv^{a,b}).

All four texts of Ruth are equally close to the MT and to the LXX (2QRuth^{a,b}; 4QRuth^{a,b}).

Three of the four texts of Canticles are independent, one statistically (6QCant) and two with respect to content, probably reflecting excerpted texts (4QCant^{a,b}).[94] 4QCant^c is too short for analysis.

One of the two texts of Qoheleth (4QQoh^a),[95] written in the 'Qumran practice', differs relatively frequently from the MT. 4QQoh^b is too short for analysis.[95]

91. Flint, *The Dead Sea Psalms Scrolls*, pp. 157-58.

92. For bibliographical references and an analysis of the data, see Tov, 'Excerpted and Abbreviated Biblical Texts'.

93. 11QPs^a contains prose as well as poetry sections showing the purpose of the collection (focus on David). To one of the Psalms (Ps. 145) the scroll added liturgical antiphonal additions. To these arguments Talmon recently added the fact that 11QPs^a, unlike MasPs^b and other biblical manuscripts, does not present the Psalms in a stichometric arrangement, which was apparently reserved for the biblical texts. See S. Talmon, 'Fragments', pp. 318-27 (324).

94. Tov, 'Three Manuscripts'.

95. See J. Muilenburg, 'A Qoheleth Scroll from Qumran', *BASOR* 135 (1954), pp. 20-28; E. Ulrich, 'Ezra and Qoheleth Manuscripts from Qumran (4QEzra,

Two of the four texts of Lamentations are written in the 'Qumran practice' (3QLam, 4QLam), with a number of deviations from MT in 4QLam. 5QLam[a] is close to MT. The other text is too short for analysis.

One of the eight texts of Daniel is written in the 'Qumran practice' (4QDan[b]), one is independent (4QDan[a]), while two texts are close to the MT (1QDan[a], 6QpapDan). The other texts are too short for analysis.

The one text of Ezra is close to the MT.[96]

The one text of Chronicles is too fragmentary for analysis.

The analysis of the individual books does not leave much room for conclusions on their textual character because of the aforementioned provisos.

6. *Textual Transmission and Literary Criticism.* The relevance of the textual witnesses for certain aspects of the literary analysis has often been discussed, especially in the last two decades.[97] So far, the following Qumran scrolls have been analyzed with regard to their possible contribution to literary criticism: 4QPhyl A,B,J (shorter text in Deut. 5), 4QJudg[a] (shorter text of ch. 6), 4QSam[a] (longer text in 1 Sam. 11), 1QIsa[a] (Isa. 38.21-22), 4QJer[b,d] (shorter text and different arrangement).[98] More recent research has added insights regarding different editorial strands in Joshua (see above with regard to 4QJosh[a]) and the *Song of Hannah* in the MT, LXX, and 4QSam[a].[99] According to some scholars, the different arrangements of the various Psalms scrolls are also relevant to the literary criticism of the Bible, since they display texts differing recensionally from the MT and the other witnesses (above, p. 306). By definition, all of the excerpted and abbreviated texts (above, section 3.a) are secondary, so that their greatly-deviating text does not contribute to the literary analysis of the Bible.

4QQoh[a,b])', in E. Ulrich *et al.* (eds.), *Priests, Prophets, and Scribes: Essays on the Formation and Heritage of Second Temple Judaism in Honour of Joseph Blenkinsopp* (JSOTSup, 149; Sheffield: JSOT Press, 1992), pp. 139-57.

96. See Ulrich, 'Ezra and Qoheleth Manuscripts'.

97. See the discussion in Tov, *Textual Criticism*, pp. 313-50 covering Genesis, Deuteronomy, Joshua, Judges, 1 Samuel, Isaiah, Jeremiah, Ezekiel and Proverbs.

98. For references, see Tov, *Textual Criticism*, pp. 313-50.

99. See E. Tov, 'Different Editions of the Song of Hannah', in M. Cogan *et al.* (eds.), *Tehillah le-Moshe, Biblical and Judaic Studies in Honor of Moshe Greenberg* (Winona Lake, IN: Eisenbrauns, 1997), pp. 149-70.

7. *Scribal Procedures*. The texts from the Judean Desert contribute much to our understanding of many aspects of the textual transmission of the Bible. When dealing with text-critical issues, we need to be constantly aware of the realia of the Qumran manuscripts pertaining to all ingredients of the biblical text, such as: similarity of certain letters, procedures of correcting, size of lines and columns, nature of super-scribed letters and words, sense divisions, scribal marks and proce-dures, special scribal characteristics of certain types of texts (sacred texts, texts written in paleo-Hebrew characters, scribal schools, etc). These and other aspects of the scribal practices reflected in the scrolls from the Judean Desert are described elsewhere.[100]

8. *Correction on the Basis of Other Texts?* It has often been said that some of the Qumran texts were corrected on the basis of proto-Ma-soretic texts or the LXX (5QDeut).[101] Indeed, many of the corrections in the texts which do not belong to the family of the MT (1) correct the base text towards the MT, while others correct away from the MT. The same applies to texts belonging to the Masoretic family (2). If any correcting on the basis of an external source were to have taken place, this could only have been a very inconsistent type of revising, since both in the texts of group (1) and of group (2) most opportunities for correcting were actually overlooked by the presumed revisers. Moreover, in my own analysis of the details corrected in the biblical manuscripts,[102] it was realized that most of the corrections pertain to simple scribal mistakes—mainly different linguistic (morphological, orthographical) forms—and only rarely could the details corrected be taken to refer to different readings transferred from a different source.

---

100. 'Scribal Practices Reflected in the Texts from the Judean Desert', in *The Dead Sea Scrolls after Fifty Years*, pp. 403-29; 'Scribal Markings'; 'Letters of the Cryptic A Script and Paleo-Hebrew Letters Used as Scribal Marks in Some Qumran Scrolls', *DSD* 2 (1995), pp. 330-39.

101. For the latter, see J.T. Milik, *Les 'petites grottes' de Qumran* (DJD, 3; Oxford: Clarendon Press, 1962), pp. 169-71; N. Fernandez Marcos, '5QDt y los tipos textuales bíblicos', in G. Aranda *et al.* (eds.), *Biblia exégesis y cultura* (Coleccíon Teológica, 82; Pamplona 1994), pp. 119-25. The assumption of a cor-rection according to a source closely related to the LXX is based on insufficient evidence. See E. Tov, 'The Textual Base of the Corrections in the Biblical Texts Found in Qumran', in D. Dimant and D. Rappaport (eds.), *The Dead Sea Scrolls: Forty Years of Research* (Leiden: E.J. Brill, 1992), pp. 299-314.

102. Tov, 'The Textual Base', pp. 307-308.

This evidence compels me to posit a correction made on the basis of the different *Vorlagen* from which each individual Qumran text was copied. The fact that those *Vorlagen* were close to the details corrected creates an optical illusion, which has led several scholars to believe that scribes or readers corrected scrolls according to the MT.

THE TEACHER OF RIGHTEOUSNESS, THE HISTORY OF THE QUMRAN COMMUNITY, AND OUR UNDERSTANDING OF THE JESUS MOVEMENT: TEXTS, THEORIES AND TRAJECTORIES

Håkan Ulfgard

1. *Introduction*

The aim of this paper is, first, to give a brief presentation of what we know from the Dead Sea Scrolls about the founding figure of the Qumran community, that is, what we know about the Teacher of Righteousness, as the title מורה (ה)צדק is commonly translated. Secondly, I also want to put him and his community into the larger historical framework of the second century BCE, that crucial formative period for Judaism. Finally, I want to give some indications about what all this might mean for our picture of the relationship between the Teacher's community and that of another great teacher, Jesus of Nazareth. However, I cannot—and I do not want to pretend to—cover all these aspects on the Teacher of Righteousness in an exhaustive way here.[1] I will, instead, limit my investigation to the following points:

1. The following are just a few examples of the scholarly literature on the Teacher of Righteousness and his community: G. Jeremias, *Der Lehrer der Gerechtigkeit* (SUNT, 2; Göttingen: Vandenhoeck & Ruprecht, 1963); P. Wallendorff, *Rättfärdighetens Lärare: En exegetisk undersökning* (Helsingfors, 1964); B.Z. Wacholder, *The Dawn of Qumran: The Sectarian Torah and the Teacher of Righteousness* (Cincinatti: Hebrew Union College Press, 1983); P.R. Callaway, *The History of the Qumran Community: An Investigation* (JSPSup, 3; Sheffield: JSOT Press, 1988); F.M. Schweitzer, 'The Teacher of Righteousness', in Z.J. Kapera (ed.), *Mogilany 1989: Papers on the Dead Sea Scrolls Offered in Memory of Jean Carmignac* (Krakow: Enigma Press, 1991), pp. 53-97. A detailed discussion of certain aspects on the Teacher and his role can also be found in S. Byrskog, *Jesus the Only Teacher: Didactic Authority and Transmission in Ancient Israel, Ancient Judaism and the Matthean Community* (ConBNT, 24; Stockholm: Almqvist & Wiksell, 1994), pp. 115-32, 148-55, 188-93.

For bibliographic surveys, see, e.g. B. Jongeling, *A Classified Bibliography of*

1. In which texts is he mentioned and what do they say about him?

2. In which circumstances, controversies and activities does he appear?

3. How does he fit into the emergence of the Qumran community at a precise moment of history and against the general background of post-exilic Judaism in the Hellenistic period, especially in the wake of the Maccabean revolt?

4. Finally, having studied how the Teacher is depicted in the Dead Sea texts, what might be the consequences for our picture of Jesus and the Jesus movement, when these are seen as later exponents of Judaism in Roman Palestine, but sharing the same focus on a founding figure who was thought to be God's chosen instrument at the End of Days, a religious *virtuoso* around whom the idea of a New Covenant was crystalized?[2]

At first, however, a few words must be said about the term מורה (ה)צדק. Is this a functional description or a personal characterization? Obviously it denotes a certain historical person, set into a certain historical context, but referred to, without proper name, with the formula מורה (ה)צדק.[3] The same kind of expression is also used about his enemies (e.g. מטיף/איש הכזב, 'the Liar'/'the Spouter of Lies'). For some

---

the Finds in the Desert of Judah 1958–1969 (Studies on the Texts of the Desert of Judah, 7; Oxford: Clarendon Press, 1971), pp. 78-93; H. Bardtke, 'Literaturbericht über Qumran. X. Der Lehrer der Gerechtigkeit und die Geschichte der Qumrangemeinde', *TRu* 41 (1976), pp. 97-140; J.A. Fitzmyer, *The Dead Sea Scrolls: Major Publications and Tools for Study* (Atlanta, GA: Scholars Press, rev. edn, 1990); A.S. van der Woude, 'Fünfzehn Jahre Qumranforschung (1974–1988). IV. Ursprung und Geschichte der Qumrangemeinde', *TRu* 57 (1992), pp. 225-53. The bibliography in J. Murphy-O'Connor's article about the Teacher of Righteousness in *ABD*, VI, p. 341, is surprisingly meagre.

2. It would be an interesting task to compare the two figures against the background of what their followers in the Qumran and New Testament texts say about their function and importance, e.g. their roles as teachers, interpreters of Scripture and of Torah, revealers of God's secrets, apocalypticians, messianic figures, fulfillers of Scripture and so on.

3. The expression might have a scriptural background in Hos. 10.12 and Joel 2.23, but cf. also Isa. 30.20-21 and Deut. 33.9-10. In Isa. 9.14 and Hab. 2.18 the opposite formula מורה שקר is found; thus, J.C. Reeves, 'The Meaning of *Moreh Ṣedeq* in the Light of 11QTorah', *RevQ* 13 (1988), pp. 289-90.

reason, the precise identity of these persons is not disclosed.[4] But how to translate the formula? The Hebrew construct phrase (מורה הצדק) could mean two things: either an objective genitive or a personal quali-fication (i.e. either 'he who teaches justice' = 'the Teacher of Righ-teousness', or 'the Just/Righteous Teacher').[5] In the latter, attributive sense, the personal character of the Teacher is stressed,[6] whereas the former translation puts the emphasis on his didactic function.[7] How-ever, there is no need to exclude any of these possibilities. Both nuances should be retained, even if the traditional translation followed here—'the Teacher of Righteousness'—implies an understanding of the term as an objective genitive.[8]

2. *The Teacher of Righteousness in the Texts*

The term מורה (ה)צדק does not appear in very many Qumran texts. More or less explicitly, it occurs in the *Damascus Document* (CD 1.11; 20.32) and in the pesher commentaries on Habakkuk, Micah and Psalms (1QpHab 1.13; 2.2; 5.10; 7.4; 8.3; 9.9; 11.5; 1QpMic 10.6; 4QpPs[a] 3.15 [...ה מורה],[9] 19 [...מור]; 4.27 [...מורה] and 4QpPs[b] 1.4;

---

4.   On the question of anonymity, see Byrskog, *Jesus the Only Teacher*, pp. 148-55. However, his suggestion (pp. 148-49) that the lawgiver (νομοθέτης) mentioned by Josephus, *War* 2.145 (p. 152) could be identified as the Teacher of Righteousness, seems a bit far-fetched.

5.   For earlier discussions, see, e.g. how Jeremias, *Der Lehrer der Gerech-tigkeit*, pp. 308-16, is open to both options (but tends to prefer the former), while Wallendorff, *Rättfärdighetens Lärare*, pp. 27-28 is more certain about the former understanding.

6.   Byrskog, *Jesus the Only Teacher*, pp. 119-22, strongly argues for this trans-lation; see esp. his excursus against the arguments of Jeremias.

7.   Thus J. Blenkinsopp, 'Interpretation and the Tendency to Sectarianism: An Aspect of Second Temple History', in E.P. Sanders *et al.* (eds.), *Aspects of Judaism in the Graeco-Roman World* (Jewish and Christian Self-Definition, 2; Philadelphia: Fortress Press, 1981), p. 23. See further the common English translations listed by Reeves, 'The Meaning of *Moreh Ṣedeq*', pp. 288-89.

8.   Possibly one could speak of a modern tendency among scholars—a sign of the times?—towards stressing the person more than the abstract concept that he represents.

9.   The line number is misprinted to 3.13 in F. García Martínez, *The Dead Sea Scrolls Translated: The Qumran Texts in English* (trans. W.G.E. Watson; Leiden: E.J. Brill, 1994), p. 205.

2.2).[10] This means that the person referred to by this title does not at all play the same prominent role in the Qumran literature, taken as a whole, as does Jesus in early Christian writings. Even if only a small portion of the texts found in Qumran are actually sectarian (Essene) texts—some 40 of them, according to Hartmut Stegemann[11]—and even if we discount the Gospels as being some kind of Jesus-biographies, this fact points to a significant difference in importance between the two 'founding figures' of the ensuing Qumranite and Christian movements.

As to the *Hodayot* Psalms (1QH), whose author often speaks in the first person, it has been suggested that they were composed by the Teacher of Righteousness.[12] I do not, however, want to discuss them at all, since their authorship is very much debated, and—above all—since they do not contribute greatly to the specific questions about the person of the Teacher and about Qumran origins and history. In these texts, the author identifies himself and his situation to a large extent by using and referring to Scripture, which means that it is often difficult to say when the author is speaking about his own personal experience and when he is merely using pre-existing concepts. The reconstruction of Qumranite history from allusions in the *Hodayot* Psalms is even more uncertain. Thus, I find it better not to bring any of these texts into this investigation.[13]

10. Cf. the list in M.A. Knibb, 'The Teacher of Righteousness: A Messianic Title?', in P.R. Davies and R.T. White (eds.), *A Tribute to Geza Vermes: Essays on Jewish and Christian Literature and History* (JSOTSup, 100; Sheffield: JSOT Press, 1990), pp. 51-52. Wallendorff, *Rättfärdighetens Lärare*, p. 29 n. 2, lists 13 examples of the term מורה (ה)צדק, but elsewhere (pp. 75-81) in all 17 cases where the term occurs, more or less complete. Out of these, 15 are considered as referring to the Teacher. Furthermore, there are conjectures like, e.g., 1QpMic 11.4 and 4QpIs^e 1/2.3 in García Martínez, *The Dead Sea Scrolls Translated*.

11. H. Stegemann, *Die Essener, Qumran, Johannes der Täufer und Jesus: Ein Sachbuch* (Freiburg: Herder, 3rd edn, 1994), p. 148.

12. Jeremias, *Der Lehrer der Gerechtigkeit*, pp. 171-77, considers the following *Hodayot* Psalms as composed by the Teacher: 2.1-19, 31-39; 3.1-18; 4.5–5.4; 5.5-19; 5.20–7.5; 7.6-25; 8.4-40. From these *Lehrerlieder*, he argues, it is possible to reach conclusions on the Teacher's self-understanding as teacher and herald of God's secrets, on his religious life, and on his relations with spiritual friends and enemies. Similarly, G. Vermes, *The Dead Sea Scrolls: Qumran in Perspective* (London: SCM Press, 1977), p. 145; cf. also the synthetic picture of the Teacher in the *Hodayot* given by Schweizer, 'The Teacher of Righteousness', pp. 66-73.

13. Murphy-O'Connor, 'Teacher of Righteousness', p. 341, is of the same

a. *The Teacher of Righteousness in the Damascus Document*
One of the most important sources of information concerning the
Teacher of Righteousness is the so-called *Damascus Document* (CD;
also known as 'the Zadokite Document'). Solomon Schechter's edition
of the two medieval manuscripts from the Cairo Genizah[14] has been
complemented by the fragments from Caves 5 and 6,[15] and by the
recent publication of the findings from Cave 4 (4Q266–273).[16] Paleographically, the 4Q fragments have been dated to 75–50 BCE, while
those from 5Q and 6Q are considered to be somewhat younger (first
century CE).[17] Evaluation of all these texts is made difficult, however,
owing to the fragmentary character of the manuscripts from the caves;
also, there is the problem of how to reconstruct the original version of
the text.[18]

As to the basic content and character of the *Damascus Document*,
some leading scholarly opinions are as follows:[19] according to Stegemann, the text presents a historical survey of the conflicts between the

opinion, although he also agrees that the Teacher is the only possible author of the
Lehrerlieder. Cf. Callaway, *The History of the Qumran Community*, pp. 185-90,
and his negative conclusions about the possibility of any historical reconstruction
based on the *Hodayot* Psalms (pp. 196-97), and, before him, S. Holm-Nielsen,
Hodayot: Psalms from Qumran (Acta Theologica Danica, 2; Århus: Univer-
sitetsforlaget, 1960).

14. S. Schechter, *Documents of Jewish Sectaries* I–II (repr. New York: Ktav,
1970 [Cambridge, 1980]).

15. M. Baillet and J.T. Milik (eds.), *Les 'petites grottes' de Qumrân* (DJD, 3;
Oxford: Clarendon Press, 1962).

16. The reconstruction of this text was published by B.Z. Wacholder and M.G.
Abegg, *A Preliminary Edition of the Unpublished Dead Sea Scrolls: Fascicle One*
(Washington: Biblical Archeology Society, 1991), pp. 1-59. Its translation is found
in García Martínez, *The Dead Sea Scrolls Translated*, pp. 37-71, with a brief
description, pp. 492-93. Cf. also the reconstruction in Fitzmyer, *The Dead Sea
Scrolls*, pp. 132-33.

17. Callaway, *The History of the Qumran Community*, pp. 57-58.

18. See the summary of the lively discussion about the composition and character of the CD in Callaway, *The History of the Qumran Community*, pp. 89-133.
Cf. also the bibliography in Fitzmyer, *The Dead Sea Scrolls*, pp. 134-36.

19. A more complete summary of opinions is found in Callaway, *The History of
the Qumran Community*, pp. 91-99, and an exhaustive bibliography in van der
Woude, 'Fünfzehn Jahre Qumranforschung (1974-1988): III. Studien zu früher
veröffentlichten Handschriften', *TRu* 57 (1992), pp. 50-52.

Qumran community and its enemies.[20] In his literary analysis, Jerome Murphy-O'Connor speaks about a pre-Qumranite, Essene missionary and hortatory document, which was later complemented by a Qumranite author.[21] Taking this idea further, Philip R. Davies emphasizes the complex redactional process whereby the pre-Qumranite document was turned into a strongly sectarian text which underlines the central role of the Teacher in his conflict with internal and external enemies.[22]

1. *CD 1.11*. The complete title מורה צדק is found twice in the *Damascus Document*: in 1.11 and 20.32. It occurs first in the context of a survey of the history of the 'Damascus movement' (1.3–2.1). In the translation of Geza Vermes (here and in the following pages, I am mainly using his version), lines 1.10b-13a are as follows:

> And God observed their deeds, that they sought Him with a whole heart, and He raised for them a Teacher of Righteousness to guide them in the way of His heart. And he made known to the latter generations that which God had done to the latter generation, the congregation of traitors, to those who departed from the way.[23]

20. See his dissertation, 'Die Entstehung der Qumrangemeinde' (Rheinische Friedrich-Wilhelms-Universität, Bonn, 1965) (published privately 1971). In his recent popular but detailed study, *Die Essener*, pp. 164-67, the CD is presented mainly as the definitive collection of the post-biblical rules that developed within the Essene movement; thus, it might be regarded as some kind of an early Mishna.

21. J. Murphy-O'Connor, 'An Essene Missionary Document? CD ii,14–vi,1', *RB* 77 (1970), pp. 201-29, and *idem*, 'A Literary Analysis of Damascus Document vi,2–viii,3', *RB* 78 (1971), pp. 212-20.

22. P.R. Davies, *The Damascus Covenant: An Interpretation of the 'Damascus Document'* (Sheffield: JSOT Press, 1982); cf. also his *Behind the Essenes: History and Ideology in the Dead Sea Scrolls* (Brown Judaic Studies, 94; Atlanta, GA: Scholars Press, 1987). A similar opinion is expressed by Schweitzer, 'The Teacher of Righteousness', pp. 84-88.

23. G. Vermes, *The Dead Sea Scrolls in English* (Penguin: Harmondsworth Books, 3rd edn, 1987), p. 83. In the second sentence, Vermes takes the pronoun 'he' as referring to the Teacher, whereas the Hebrew text might as well refer to God, who is the subject of the previous clause; cf. Callaway, *The History of the Qumran Community*, pp. 101-102. García Martínez, *The Dead Sea Scrolls Translated*, p. 33, and E. Lohse, *Die Texte aus Qumran* (Darmstadt: Wissenschaftliche Buchgesellschaft, 3rd edn, 1981), p. 67, take God as the subject in both sentences, while M.A. Knibb, *The Qumran Community* (Cambridge: Cambridge University Press, 1987), p. 22, playing down the problem, is satisfied to see how the Teacher is described as the one who mediates the revelation from God; cf. 1QpHab 7.1-5: the

The Teacher of Righteousness is here characterized as a person who appeared, having been sent by God, in order to give guidance to 'the remnant of Israel' (שארית (ל)ישראל; 1.4-5) at a critical moment in the history of this group. His appearance is put into a larger historical perspective by some chronological data: first there were 390 years ('the age of wrath'; 1.5) from the time of Nebuchadnezzar, that is, the fall of Jerusalem and its temple in 587 BCE. Then the original movement behind the *Damascus Document* was founded ('a plant root...from Israel and Aaron'; 1.7), but its members 'were like blind men groping for the way' for yet another 20 years (1.9-10).

If taken as an actual chronology, this would imply that the early 'Damascus movement' came into being shortly after 200 BCE, and that the Teacher of Righteousness appeared sometime around 177 BCE. In that case, the origin of the movement coincides roughly with the Seleucid political takeover of Palestine after the battle of Baneas, and the emergence of the Teacher could be correlated with the first years of the reign of king Antiochus IV Epiphanes.[24]

However, this is not the only possible way of understanding the chronological information. The figure 390 could represent a theological interpretation of the period from the destruction of the temple, based on Ezek. 4.4-5, where the prophet is commanded to lie on his left side for 390 days—a symbolic carrying of the guilt of Israel, incurred by their 390 years of sin. In other words, the period from the exile onwards has been a time of divinely-sent punishment, and now it is coming to its end. But the text in Ezekiel goes on to speak about another 40 days, during which the guilt of Judah should be carried in a symbolic way

word 'God' in the last sentence is not found in the Hebrew text, but the verb עשה has no explicit subject. Vermes here follows his distinction between the Teacher as the subject in the first part of the last sentence, and God as the subject in the second part. Contrary to this, Stegemann, *Die Entstehung der Qumrangemeinde*, p. 132, and Davies, *The Damascus Covenant*, p. 64, understand God to be the subject in the whole passage.

24. See the discussion in A. Laato, 'The Chronology in the *Damascus Document* of Qumran', *RevQ* 15 (1992), pp. 605-607. Referring to the chronology of the Jewish historian Demetrius (third century BCE), he argues that the chronological system of the CD is 26/27 years too short. Thus, instead of arriving at 197/196 BCE as the date when the movement behind the CD was founded, he suggests that a date around 170 would be more correct. This would infer that the appearance of the Teacher could be dated to about 150, with Jonathan Maccabeus as the 'Wicked Priest' of the pesharim (see further below).

(4.6). This invites speculation about whether another 40 years are expected in the *Damascus Document*, and perhaps there is an allusion to such a period of God's wrath (although directed against Israel, not Judah) in 20.13-16. Here it is predicted that 40 years will elapse after the death of the Teacher until the destruction of those who have turned to 'the Liar'. Evidently, the passage was composed during this period.[25]

It has also been argued that the chronological survey is a redactional addition to the CD, the purpose of which would have been to stress the eschatological and/or messianic significance of the Teacher of Righteousness.[26] However, the intention behind these data might just have been to put the movement behind the *Damascus Document* into the broader framework of postexilic Jewish history, such as it was conceived in the mind of the author. The specific function of the Teacher was to act on God's behalf for the benefit of the 'remnant of Israel'. This is described as a small group within the Jewish people, who realized that they were sinners, and who 'sought him (God) with a whole heart' (כי בלב שלם דרשוהו; 1.10). The Teacher's role was then to guide them in 'accordance with the way of his (God's) heart' (בדרך לבו; 1.11).

Thus, the Teacher of Righteousness is referred to as the historical person to whom the group behind the present versions of the *Damascus Document* owes its existence. But, as the text clearly states, he was not the founder of that larger movement within postexilic Judaism from which this group originated. Before he appeared as their leader, there was a period of 20 years that was later regarded by his followers as a time of 'groping for the way like blind men'.

But the Teacher's group, considered by themselves as belonging to the remnant of Israel, is confronted with enemies, 'the community of traitors' (עדת בוגדים; 1.12). They are those who have departed from the right way, and to them Hos. 4.16 is applied in a long description of their infidelity (1.13-21). In this context a 'Scoffer' (איש הלצון; 1.14) is

25. The figure 390 years approximates the duration of Solomon's temple; thus Knibb, *The Qumran Community*, p. 20. Besides, 390 + 40 = 430 years is the equivalent of the period during which the people of Israel stayed in Egypt (Exod. 12.40). But cf. the sceptical attitude of Vermes, *The Dead Sea Scrolls*, pp. 158-59, pointing out the unreliability of ancient chronological figures, even when it is not a case of interpreted history.

26. Schweitzer, 'The Teacher of Righteousness', p. 54.

mentioned, who appears as a seducer of Israel through his false teaching. Reappearing in 20.15 as 'the Liar' (איש הכזב), this arch-enemy of the Teacher and his community is also mentioned in the Habakkuk commentary under the epithets איש הכזב and מטיף הכזב, 'the Spouter of Lies' (1QpHab 2.1-2; 5.11; 10.9; 11.1[?]).[27]

2. CD 20.32. The role of the Teacher of Righteousness as the one and only authoritative teacher is emphasized also in the second CD passage, where he is explicitly mentioned, 20.32. In this hortatory section, depicting the punishments and rewards of God's judgment, those who are willing to be taught in 'the first commandments' (משפטים הראשונים; 20.31) and who 'have listened to the voice of the Teacher of Righteousness' (וישמעו לקול מורה צדק; 20.32) are promised 'to prevail over all the sons of the earth' (ויתגברו על כל בני תבל; 20.33-34). But already in 20.28 the importance, in view of the impending judgment, of listening to the voice of the Teacher is made clear (however, the reference to his person is here shortened to 'he who teaches', מורה).[28]

Furthermore, the way of referring to 'the voice of the Teacher' in the passages just discussed may be an indication that the author is aware that the Teacher has been dead for a while (cf. 19.35–20.1) and that the people he is writing for have never had the possibility of meeting him and listening to him while he was alive. Now only his 'voice' can be heard—through the community's teaching—and it is to this 'voice' that their allegiance should be directed.

3. CD 20.1 and 14. In two other passages, 20.1 and 14, mention is made of 'the only/unique teacher' (מורה היחיד)/'the teacher of the community' (מורה היחד).[29] The context in cols. 19–20 (Genizah text B) makes a contrast between those who are inside and outside the New Covenant respectively. The 'outsiders' are threatened by God's coming

---

27. See further Wallendorff, *Rättfärdighetens Lärare*, pp. 140-43.

28. Callaway, *The History of the Qumran Community*, p. 114, considers God to be the teacher of 20.28, not noting the parallel way of speaking about 'the teacher' in 20.32.

29. García Martínez, *The Dead Sea Scrolls Translated*, prefers the former reading, while Lohse, *Die Texte aus Qumran*, suggests that the text should be read as מורה היחד. Vermes, *The Dead Sea Scrolls in English*, and J.A. Fitzmyer, *Responses to 101 Questions on the Dead Sea Scrolls* (New York: Paulist Press, 1992), pp. 54, 56, 77, agree with Lohse.

judgment, while salvation is promised for the 'insiders'. However, the threat is not directed against ungodly men in general, but against, in particular, those 'who enter the New Covenant in the land of Damascus, and who again betray it and depart from the fountain of living waters'. These will not 'be reckoned with the Council of the people or inscribed in its Book from the day of the gathering in of the Teacher of the Community (García Martínez: 'the unique teacher') until the coming of the Messiah out of Aaron and Israel' (19.33–20.1).

CD 19–20 is characterized by an acute awareness of the crisis and conflicts experienced by the Teacher's community. Above all, the crisis consists of a schism within the movement called 'the New Covenant'. This would explain the hortatory and threatening language of this text, especially where the Teacher is mentioned. Evidently, some members of the community have rejected the Teacher's authority and will be subjected to God's wrath. But the author is certain that this evil period will be limited: 40 years will pass until the elimination of all the 'men of war' (אנשי המלחמה), that is, those who have defected to 'the Liar' (20.14-15). With this chronological notice, the faithful remnant in the community should be comforted and encouraged to steadfast perseverance.[30] This might conceivably indicate that the Qumranite covenanters understood their situation against the background of the scriptural wilderness traditions. The inspiration behind the statement could come from Deut. 2.7 and 14, where the duration of the wilderness wandering is given as 40/38 years, and where there is a reference to the Lord's oath that none of the 'men of war' (אנשי המלחמה) who went out of Egypt, but who turned their hearts away from him, should enter the Promised Land (cf. Num. 14.29). But, as was noted above in the discussion of CD 1.5-6, there might also be a reference to the symbolical 390+40 days/years in Ezek. 4.4-6.

According to most scholars, there is an allusion to the death of the Teacher of Righteousness in CD 19.35–20.1 and 20.14: 'the day of the gathering in of the Teacher' (מיום האסף מורה/יורה). In the general judgment perspective of cols. 19–20, his death is regarded as an eschatologically significant event, an indication of the coming End.[31] As

---

30. These 40 years are also mentioned in 4QpPs[a] 2.7, an exposition of Ps. 37.10: at the end of the 40 years all the wicked will be wiped out, while 'the Poor' will be saved from the snares of Belial and will inherit the land.

31. But it should be noted that both his death and, before that, his appearance as

Frederick M. Schweitzer has pointed out, CD 19–20 reflects a crisis within an eschatological and messianic movement. In his opinion, the crisis resulted from the death of the Teacher, and led to an increased antagonism between his followers and their opponents. At the same time, this text puts a strong emphasis on fidelity towards the message of the Teacher. Only those who remain attentive to his 'voice' will enjoy salvation (cf. 20.28, 32):

> Here we seem to have a displacement toward 'faith' in the Teacher, an elevation of his word and teaching as the faith to live by, an intensification of sectarian self-identity…which accords salvation to the faithful members alone and resoundingly condemns the rest of Israel and the *goyim.*[32]

According to Davies, this interpretation could be taken even further: While 19.35–20.1 might have been an older formulation from the Teach-er's own lifetime, 20.14 could be regarded as a redactional note that was added after the death of the Teacher. The attack on the defectors in the first text could thus have been directed at those within the 'Damascus movement' who did not accept the Teacher's authority, while the threat in the latter (and later) passage could have been intended for those who, after the death of the Teacher, parted ways with the community that he founded in Qumran as a consequence of the earlier schism within the 'Damascus movement'.[33]

In this connection, it is also worth noting that the messianic character is mainly found in those Qumran texts that can be dated after the death of the Teacher. Thus, in Schweitzer's words, it 'represents various reactions to that trauma and attempts to make eschatological sense of it'.[34] (There are good reasons for seeing a parallel to this phenomenon in the development of Christology within early Christianity).[35]

However, not all scholars agree that there is a reference to the death of the Teacher in CD 19.35–20.1 and 20.14. Against the understanding

---

the leader of the congregation (col. 1), are interpreted as eschatological events, or, rather, they are put into the framework of eschatological calculation.

32. Schweitzer, 'The Teacher of Righteousness', pp. 92-94 (94).

33. Davies, *The Damascus Covenant*, pp. 173-97. This is congruent with his opinion about the Qumranite redaction of the CD; cf. pp. 202-204.

34. Schweitzer, 'The Teacher of Righteousness', p. 92.

35. Schweitzer's exclamation: 'This is to bring us perilously close to the portals of the NT!' ('The Teacher of Righteousness', p. 94) seems unwarranted. Cf. Davies, *The Damascus Covenant*, p. 179.

of practically all translations and commentaries,[36] Ben Zion Wacholder
has remarked that the verb taken as a reference to dying, הֵאָסֵף (niph'al
absolute infinitive), in this context could point to the moment when the
Teacher gathered (to himself; hence the reflective niph'al) his adherents
and founded his community of the New Covenant.[37] Wacholder argues
that this form of the verb nowhere else in the Qumran texts refers to
dying, and that its scriptural references to dying (being gathered to
one's forefathers) nearly always are combined with the preposition אֶל.
Moreover, the death of the Teacher is nowhere else hinted at in the
Qumran texts.[38] Despite these arguments, however, a fundamental objection to Wacholder's idea is that it seems highly unlikely that the the
author of the CD would have emphasized that special day on which the
Teacher started gathering his followers. Both passages use the expression 'from the day when...' (מִיּוֹם), a phrase that rather indicates that
crucial day when the Teacher died, rather than the day when his community was called into existence.

4. *CD 6.2-11*. Another passage with a possible reference to the Teacher
of Righteousness—and a passage that holds some important clues as to
the history of the 'Damascus movement', which means the prehistory
of the Qumran community—is found in CD 6.2-11, which contains a
midrashic exposition of Num. 21.17-18, the song of the well at Be'er
(='well'). The author has just stated how there was a 'time of the deso-
lation of the Land', when it was devastated because its leaders turned
away from God and his commandments (5.20–6.1), but from 6.2 he
recounts how God has acted for the salvation of his chosen ones:

> But God remembered the Covenant with the forefathers, and he raised
> from Aaron men of discernment and from Israel men of wisdom, and He
> caused them to hear. And they dug the Well: *the well which the princes
> dug, which the nobles of the people delved with the stave.*
> The *Well* is the Law, and those who dug it were the converts of Israel
> who went out of the land of Judah to sojourn in the land of Damascus.
> God called them all *princes* because they sought Him, and their renown

36. See, e.g., Knibb, *The Qumran Community*, p. 72, referring to Gen. 25.8, 17
and Num. 27.13.
37. B.Z. Wacholder, 'Does Qumran Record the Death of the *Moreh*? The Meaning of *he'aseph* in *Damascus Covenant* xix, 35, xx, 14', *RevQ* 13 (1988), pp. 323-
30.
38. Wacholder, 'Does Qumran Record the Death?', pp. 324-26.

was disputed by no man. The *Stave* is the Interpreter of the Law of whom Isaiah said, *he makes a tool for His work*; and the *nobles of the people* are those who come to dig the *Well* with the staves with which the *Stave* ordained that they should walk in all the age of wickedness— and without them they shall find nothing—until he comes who shall teach righteousness at the end of days.

This is a most revealing text. 'The well' is equated with the *Torah*, while 'the princes' who have 'dug the well' are identified with a specific group within post-exilic Judaism, 'the converts of Israel'. The expression שבי ישראל has a double meaning: it could refer both to persons who have undergone a mental conversion, but it could as well refer to those that have returned from exile, 'returners' or 'ex-exiles'. These people, who have left 'the land of Judah to sojourn in the land of Damascus', are called 'princes' (שרים) by God, since they have 'sought him' (דרשוהו; cf. 1.10). Yet another figure in the biblical text, 'the stave' (מחוקק), is explained as referring to 'the Interpreter of the Law' (דורש התורה), who will give guidance to the 'nobles of the people' (נדיבי העם), who have come to join 'the converts of Israel' during 'the age of wickedness' (קץ הרשיע). His importance is emphasized by the statement that without his teaching they will obtain nothing,[39] 'until he comes who shall teach righteousness at the end of days' (עד עמד יורה הצדק באחרית הימים).

The question is, who is referred to by the expressions דורש התורה and יורה הצדק in 6.7 and 11? It is clear from the text that these figures are chronologically distinct from each other, and also that דורש התורה clearly refers to someone in the past. Elsewhere in the Qumran texts, the designation appears twice: CD 7.18 and 4QFlor (=4Q174) 1.11. On both occasions it is connected to an eschatological/messianic exposition of Amos 5.26 and linked to the appearance of other eschatological/ messianic figures belonging to the 'end of days'. Could דורש התורה in 6.7 then be another characterization of the Teacher of Righteousness? However, according to CD 1.9-11, the Teacher did not appear until the 'Damascus movement' had been groping for the way for 20 years. Or, if 6.7 speaks about another, and earlier, leader than the Teacher, could this possibly refer to the founder of the 'Damascus movement'? Or to some other past authority?[40]

39. Exactly what is to be obtained (ישיגו) is unclear: Lohse, referring to 1QS 6.14, suggests 'learning'.

40. According to Callaway, *The History of the Qumran Community*, p. 231

But the question is, also, who is meant by יורה הצדק באחרית הימים,
'he who teaches righteousness at the end of days'? Is this the Teacher
of Righteousness, the founder of the Qumran community (not the same
person who founded the 'Damascus movement')? Is he expected to
have a messianic role in the *coming* End? (This is not the case in any
other Qumran texts that are known to us; nor is there any hint of a
resurrected or reincarnated Teacher).[41] Or, in the opinion of the author,
could it be that the 'end of days' has already begun, so that the appearance of the Teacher is just part of God's secret plan for the salvation of
his chosen people?

According to Davies, 6.2-11 speaks about *two distinct persons*, one
of them, 'the Interpreter of the Law', being the founder of the 'Damascus movement'; and the other, 'the Teacher of Righteousness', being
the founder of the Qumran community. In the eyes of his followers, the
appearance of the Teacher meant the beginning of 'the end of days',
while his death (20.14) caused a crisis within the community. This 'cog-
nitive dissonance' was resolved in various ways by his adherents: they
prolonged their eschatological timetable, they expected more action by
God against his enemies, external and internal, and they stressed the
role of the Teacher as a precursor for the coming Messiah(s) of Aaron
and Israel. Thus, Davies thinks that the title 'Teacher of Righteousness'
should be regarded as having messianic implications, and also maintains that the origin of the Qumran community is to be sought not
mainly in a conflict against external factors (enemies, defection from
the true *halakah*), but instead in the 'messianic pretension' of the
Teacher and his sympathizers.[42]

These theories about the two figures in 6.2-11, further developed by
Murphy-O'Connor,[43] have been opposed by Michael A. Knibb: in his

n. 95, there is a general tendency towards identifying the דורש התורה with the
Teacher, but he is personally of the opinion that it is an earlier figure, perhaps Ezra,
that is meant by this term. The next figure mentioned, the יורה הצדק is, in his view,
a designation of the Teacher (pp. 108-11).

41. See, e.g., Fitzmyer, *Responses*, p. 57.

42. Davies, 'The Teacher of Righteousness and the "End of Days"', *RevQ* 13
(1988), pp. 313-17; cf. his earlier *The Damascus Covenant*, pp. 122-25. See also
Schweitzer, 'The Teacher of Righteousness', pp. 176-77, who in his understanding
of the character of the Teacher is strongly influenced by—as he says—Davies's
'iconoclastic' interpretation of CD 6.11.

43. The Teacher would also have appropriated the title נשיא כל עדה, 'Prince of

opinion, it is not clear whether the 'Damascus movement' or the Qumran community ('the teacher-community') is meant in this passage, but he prefers to see a reference to the latter, which means that he is able to regard 'the Interpreter' and 'the Teacher' as one and the same person. This also means that, in his view, the Teacher cannot have been thought of as a messianic figure by his followers.[44] In his recent dissertation, Samuel Byrskog is also of a different opinion, although in another way: like Davies, he realizes that the text speaks about two persons, but these are identified by him as first a historical person (דורש התורה), denoting the Teacher of Righteousness, and then a future priestly messiah, described in terms taken over from the Teacher.[45]

In my opinion, there can be no doubt that 6.2-11 speaks about two distinct persons. But there is nothing convincing in Byrskog's idea that יורה הצדק should refer to a future, priestly messianic figure, who in some ways had been modelled on the Teacher of Righteousness, nor should the expression be understood as a reference to the returning (reincarnated?) Teacher after his death. What is clear from the whole of the CD is that the Teacher's appearance as the leader and founder of the Qumran community is considered as being part of the events of 'the end of days'. This could also be confirmed by the chronological figures in the document, which incorporate his activity in its larger eschatological pattern: 390 years + 20 years + the Teacher's activity + 40 years from his death until the End. If his activity is approximated to 40 years, this would give 490 years, that is, 7×70 years.[46]

The identity of 'the Interpreter of the Law' can only be a matter of speculation, but in my view it could not be the Teacher himself. Possibly, it could be someone like the biblical Ezra figure, the priest, scribe and Torah expert, about whom there really is very little historical knowledge. It could also be the enigmatic Zadok, suggested by Wacholder, as the Teacher of Righteousness, which in that case might give another clue as to the meaning of the appellation 'sons of Zadok' in the Qumran texts (see below). The next character mentioned, however, in 6.11, 'until there arises he who teaches justice at the end of days', I

the whole congregation'; thus J. Murphy-O'Connor, 'The Damascus Document Revisited', *RB* 92 (1985), p. 241.

44. Knibb, 'The Teacher of Righteousness', pp. 56-60.

45. Byrskog, *Jesus the Only Teacher*, p. 125; cf. pp. 127, 129, 192-93.

46. Schweitzer, 'The Teacher of Righteousness', p. 92; Vermes, *The Dead Sea Scrolls*, pp. 147-48.

would like to identify with the historical person of the Teacher of Righteousness. His appearance 'at the End of Days', according to the texts, does not signify a future epoch, but refers to the present experience of the Qumran group itself. His emergence on the scene was but one sign of the approaching judgment, when the true Israel of 'the New Covenant' was called to intensified holy life.

This reconstruction of the Qumranites' view of their prehistory is confirmed by the beginning of the *Damascus Document* (1.5-11), commented upon above. Another hint at the various stages of this process is found in 4.2-4, a text that also helps to clarify the meaning of 6.2-11.[47] In 3.21–4.2 the author quotes from the prophecy of Ezekiel about those who will serve in the temple (Ezek. 44.15). By twisting the biblical text, which in fact only speaks of one kind of priest (והכהנים הלוים בני צדוק), the author arrives at seeing an indication of three separate groups: 'priests', 'levites', and 'sons of Zadok'. 'The priests' are identified as the 'converts/returners of Israel' (שבי ישראל) who have left the land of Judah, 'the levites' are those who have joined themselves to the first group, and 'the sons of Zadok' are the elect of Israel, who have been called by name and who have stood up at the end of days.

The text clearly points to a historical sequence. First, some 'converts/ returners' leave their land, then 'the levites' add to their number, and, finally, at the end of days, they are joined by 'the sons of Zadok'.[48] Then there is the significant similarity between 4.2 and 6.5 in the expression about 'the converts/returners of Israel'. In the context of the passage in 6.5, we have seen how it is stated that God has been faithful to his covenant and raised wise men, who have 'dug the well', that is, who have kept the Law and its commandments (cf. 4.16). But the biblical text interpreted in 6.2-11, namely Num. 21.18, speaks of two groups: 'the princes' and 'the nobles of the people'. The first group, identified as ' the converts/returners of Israel who went out of the land of Judah' are said to have sojourned in 'the land of Damascus'. This could refer to the group that, according to 1.5, emerged 390 years after

---

47. But see also 4QFlor (4Q174) 1.10-17, where a long sequence of scriptural passages are interpreted as applying to the community and its prehistory.

48. But see how the expression שבי ישראל is taken as only referring to spiritual conversion by J.J. Collins, 'Was the Dead Sea Sect an Apocalyptic Movement?', in L.H. Schiffman (ed.), *Archaeology and History in the Dead Sea Scrolls: The New York University Conference in Memory of Yigael Yadin* (JSPSup, 8; JSOT/ASOR Monographs, 2; Sheffield: JSOT Press, 1990), p. 39.

Nebuchadnezzar's capture of Jerusalem. When the second group arrives in order to 'dig the well', that is, study the Torah (6.8-9), this corresponds to the characterization of 'the levites' in 4.3 as people who after some time had passed joined the original group.

Thus, 'the Interpreter of the Law' (דורש התורה) of 6.7 is clearly a person in the past. And when 6.11 goes on to speak about the second important personality in the history of the community, 'he who teaches justice at the end of days' (יורה הצדק באחרית הימים), it would be a mistake to take this as a reference to the future. The members of the Qumran community were convinced that they and their Righteous Teacher/Teacher of Righteousness were living in the final years of the present age. What is said about 'the nobles of the people' in 6.10 (='the levites' of 4.3) should be understood as a retrospective reference, pointing to such people who had 'sought God', but who could not find the true interpretation of the Law until the Teacher of Righteousness appeared (in the final era of the world). After their time, those who were responsible for the existing versions of the CD considered themselves as 'the sons of Zadok' (cf. 1QS 5.2, 9), the third group mentioned in 4.3. Taken together, they formed the congregation of the elect who were able to serve God in the new temple—in its preliminary stage represented by the Qumran community. They all belonged to 'the New Covenant' of 19.33 and 20.12, but the followers of the Teacher could regard themselves as some kind of third-generation covenanters. The person referred to in 6.11 is, therefore, not expected to appear in the future, but he has already come as the Teacher of Righteousness. The whole section of 6.2-11 is a midrashic exposition about the history and prehistory of the Qumran community and its self-understanding.[49]

b. *The Teacher of Righteousness in other Qumran Texts*
Apart from the *Damascus Document*, the Teacher of Righteousness is only mentioned in the pesher literature—often in a fragmentary (*sic*) way. These texts are comparatively late Qumran texts (mainly from Herodian times),[50] whose value as sources for historical knowledge is

49. Note how the idealized depiction of 'the converts/returners of Israel' gives an obvious association to the idealized community of the returning exiles in the books of Ezra and Nehemiah. The 'true Israel' consists of those who have experienced the exile or who can claim such heritage—a central theme in the resultant Scripture and in emerging Judaism.

50. Cf. Callaway, *The History of the Qumran Community*, p. 57.

highly debated.[51] The growth of this particular literary genre reflects the conviction of the community that it is living in the end of days, about which Scripture has spoken. Therefore, the biblical texts can provide detailed information about God's plans for his chosen people and its enemies.[52] In a wealth of sometimes cryptic, sometimes explicit formulations, the authors of the pesharim allude to events and persons from the experience of the community.[53]

The Teacher of Righteousness is, in particular, mentioned often in the commentary on Habakkuk (1QpHab).[54] His role for the community is emphasized by recounting events in which he was involved and by describing important characteristics of his personality. All this serves to highlight his authority and legitimacy as God's instrument.

Like the prophets, he speaks the word of God (2.2-3). Being 'the Priest', he has been given the ability to interpret the words of the prophets of the past (2.8-9; there is no explicit identification of the Teacher with 'the Priest', but this is made clear by the context). This concerns especially the things to come: what will happen to the people and to the land (2.10). God's secrets that were given to the prophets have been revealed to him (7.4-5):

פשרו על מורה הצדק אשר הודיעו אל את כול רזי דברי עבדיו הנבאים.

51. Davies, *Behind the Essenes*, p. 27, is strongly sceptical towards this use of the pesher material: 'The use made of the *pesharim* for historical purposes is nothing less than a shambles'. J. Murphy-O'Connor builds his reconstruction of the history of the 'Damascus movement' and of the Qumran community mainly on the CD; see, e.g., his 'The Essenes and their History', *RB* 81 (1974), pp. 215-44. In his methodological discussion about the use of the pesharim, Callaway, *The History of the Qumran Community*, pp. 140-42, agrees with Stegemann, *Die Entstehung der Qumrangemeinde*, pp. 10-15: it is mainly their polemical statements about the Jewish enemies of the Qumran community that can be utilized.

52. Cf. Stegemann, *Die Essener*, pp. 174-75, in whose opinion the pesher commentaries were composed in the Qumran community in the period between the death of the Teacher and the awaited Day of the Lord, a period understood as analogous with the wilderness wanderings of Israel in Scripture.

53. See the list in Callaway, *The History of the Qumran Community*, p. 135. At the same time, this literature (1QpNah) also contains explicit references to historical persons, Antiochus and Demetrius, two Seleucid kings (although there are many with such names).

54. Cf. Jeremias, *Der Lehrer der Gerechtigkeit*, pp. 140-46; Wallendorff, *Rättfärdighetens Lärare*, pp. 30-51.

Thus, although the prophet Habakkuk had been commanded to write down what would happen to the last generation, he had not been informed about the fulfilment of time (7.1-2).[55] This was disclosed only to the Teacher. The Teacher's importance as the prophetic herald of the secrets of the end of days is also closely related to another feature of his role, namely his soteriological function: it is through their fidelity towards the Teacher and his way of interpreting God's Torah that the pious members of the community will be saved (8.1-3).

Although he is referred to as 'the Priest' in 2.8, the Teacher is never described with a liturgical function in the *Habakkuk Pesher.* Only in 11.2-8, the famous incident when his arch-enemy, 'the Wicked Priest', searched him out at his place of exile on the Day of Atonement, is there any connection with worship. As is shown by several Qumran texts (and as is well known by now), the community followed a solar calendar instead of the 'official' luni-solar one that was in use among the political and religious leaders in Jerusalem.[56] Thus, 'the Wicked Priest' committed a serious offence by appearing in the community on the most sacred day of the year (in the two calendars, the Holy Days would rarely coincide) in order 'to confuse them, and to cause them to stumble on the Day of Fasting, their Sabbath of repose' (11.7-8). But God has given him the punishment that he deserved by delivering him into the hands of his enemies (9.9-12).

In the commentary on Micah (1QpMic 10.6-8), special emphasis is put on the role of the Teacher as the one who gives instruction about the *Torah* to all who join the community, to God's chosen who will thus be saved on the Day of Judgment.[57] This text clearly points to

55. Jeremias, *Der Lehrer der Gerechtigkeit,* p. 142, refers to the similar idea in 1 Pet. 1.10-12.

56. On the important problem of calendars, see, e.g., S. Talmon, 'The Calendar Reckoning of the Sect from the Judean Desert', in C. Rabin and Y. Yadin (eds.), *Aspects of the Dead Sea Scrolls* (Scripta Hierosolymitana, 4; Jerusalem: Magnes Press, 1958), pp. 162-99, but also the general discussions in Stegemann, *Die Essener,* pp. 231-34; J.C. VanderKam, *The Dead Sea Scrolls Today* (Grand Rapids: Eerdmans, 1994), pp. 114-16; and L.H. Schiffman, *Reclaiming the Dead Sea Scrolls: The History of Judaism, the Background of Christianity, the Lost Library of Qumran* (Philadelphia: Jewish Publication Society, 1994), pp. 301-305.

57. There could be a possible reference to the judging function of the Teacher in 11.4, according to the translation of García Martínez. However, the text here seems very conjectural.

the conflict between the Teacher and his enemies, personified in 'the Spouter of Lies' (מטיף הכזב). Possibly (the text is very fragmentary), a quotation from Mic. 1.5 about 'the high places' (for sacrifice) is taken as referring to the cultic establishment in Jerusalem. The attack on the official Jewish leaders continues in fragment 11, an interpretation of Mic. 1.8-9 that accuses the Jerusalemite priests as those who lead the people astray.

The fragmentary *Psalms Pesher* (4QpPs) mentions the Teacher as the founding figure behind the Qumran community in an exposition of Ps. 37.23-24 (4QpPs[a] 3.15-16):

מורה ה[צדק אשר] [ד]בר בו אל לעמוד ו[אשר] הכינו לבנות לו עדת.

In the same context he is identified as 'the Priest'; a qualification taken by many scholars to be important evidence of his liturgically leading and authoritative role for the Qumranites:[58]

פשרו על הכוהן מורה ה[צדק...

However, the main question is whether it is possible to relate the information contained about the Teacher in the pesharim with what is said about him in the CD.[59] If this were the case, the statement in CD 1.11 concerning his fundamental role for the transition from the 'Damascus movement' to the Qumran community could be illuminated by 4QpPs[a] 3.15-16, which speaks about his divine commission to build a congregation for God. However, he is never given the title 'the Priest' in the CD (nor is there any 'Wicked Priest' in this text). Does this mean that it would be rash to identify the historical person of the Teacher with one of the priests who once served in the temple of Jerusalem? Or perhaps one should not expect the CD to give a complete picture of all the functions that were ascribed to the Teacher by his followers after his death.

58. 4QpPs[a] 3.19, together with 4QpPs[b] 1.3; 2.1, are too fragmentary to provide any relevant information about the Teacher, whereas 4QpPs[a] 4.26 might indicate the Teacher's God-given prophetic inspiration.

59. See the caution not to use the pesher-literature in order to explain passages in the CD by Davies, *The Damascus Covenant*, p. 190.

3. The Circumstances, Controversies and Activities
of the Teacher of Righteousness

After this analysis of those Qumran texts in which the Teacher is mentioned, it is time to give a synthesized picture of the circumstances, activities and controversies in which he appears.

From a Nordic perspective, it is fitting to call attention to the fact that one of the pioneering studies on the Teacher of Righteousness was made by a Finnish scholar, Per Wallendorff, whose doctoral dissertation, *Rättfärdighetens Lärare*, subtitled 'En exegetisk undersökning' ('The Teacher of Righteousness: An Exegetical Investigation'), was published in 1964. In his book, Wallendorff concentrated on three possible functions assigned to the Teacher, according to the then-published texts: the Teacher's role as a prophet, his literary activity, and his eschatological and messianic roles in the Qumran community. His conclusion was that while the two latter functions are not stressed in the texts, it is mainly the prophetic and historical functions of the Teacher that occupy the foreground.[60]

In brief, Wallendorff underlines how the Teacher is consistently depicted in a situation of conflict. Having founded and led a community, in which he was the primary authority, he is a figure to believe in, though in a limited, legalistic way. He appears as a divinely-inspired expert in the *Torah* and its interpretation and application, but also as the charismatic interpreter of the prophetic texts—and, even more, as a prophet himself. Thus, his supporters can claim that divine judgment will come upon those who do not recognize his authority, and biographical incidents from his career are remembered as signs of his exceptional qualities as a divinely-chosen instrument at the End of Days.[61]

Subsequent research, with more material available, has proven Wallendorff right in many respects, but has also added some specific aspects

---

60. See, e.g., Wallendorff's analysis of 1QpHab 7.4 in *Rättfärdighetens Lärare*, pp. 39-40. In his view, the Teacher occupies a middle position between the era of the prophets and the coming judgment. Thus, in relation to the prophet Habakkuk the Teacher represented the 'end of days', and in relation to the Qumran community he represented the revelation of God's secrets. However, according to Wallendorff, he does not belong to the actual final events in a direct way.

61. Wallendorff, *Rättfärdighetens Lärare*, pp. 80, 134.

on the Teacher's activities.[62] For instance, his involvement in the formulation of sectarian *Torah* and *halakah* has been much discussed: Yigael Yadin,[63] and after him (among others) Wacholder,[64] Michael O. Wise,[65] and Schweitzer,[66] have suggested that the Teacher was the author of the *Temple Scroll* (11QT). Similarly, Murphy-O'Connor has argued that the Teacher was involved in the formulation of the *Community Rule* (1QS).[67] And recently, one of the most hidden, but long-awaited Qumran scrolls, the so-called 'halakic letter' (4QMMT), has been presented by its editors, Elisha Qimron and John Strugnell, as a letter from the Teacher of Righteousness (or, possibly, his adherents) to the establishment party in Jerusalem.[68] Other scholars have stressed the function of the Teacher as, in some sense, an *apocalyptician*, one through whom God's hidden meaning in Scripture is revealed. Joseph Fitzmyer and Joseph Blenkinsopp, respectively, have pointed to the Teacher's importance for the shaping of the pesher genre,[69] and to his role as an apocalyptic scribe like the *maskilim* of the book of Daniel or in the calmer style of Jesus ben Sira, the ultimate fusion of prophecy and scribal activity.[70] Following this lead, John J. Collins has shown how the Teacher's inspired exegesis comes close to the mode of revelation in the apocalyptic literature.[71]

As is shown by the *Damascus Document* and the pesher literature, the Teacher continued to play a role for his sympathizers even after he died. In fact, his decisive role grew after his death, as his followers

62. See, e.g., the synthetic picture given by Schweitzer, 'The Teacher of Righteousness'.

63. Y. Yadin, *The Temple Scroll: The Hidden Law of the Dead Sea Sect* (London: Weidenfeld & Nicolson, 1985), pp. 87, 195-96, 226-28.

64. Wacholder, *The Dawn of Qumran*, pp. 202-12.

65. M.O. Wise, *A Critical Study of the Temple Scroll From Qumran Cave 11* (Chicago: Oriental Institute of the University of Chicago, 1990), cf. e.g. p. 184.

66. Schweitzer, 'The Teacher of Righteousness', pp. 55-57, 95; he also regards part of the *Rule of the Community* (1QS 8.1-16a and 9.3–10.8) as his work (p. 59).

67. J. Murphy-O'Connor, 'La genèse littéraire de la *Règle de la Communauté*', *RB* 76 (1969), p. 531.

68. E. Qimron and J. Strugnell (eds.), *Qumran Cave 4. V. Miqṣat Ma'aśe ha-Torah* (DJD, 10; Oxford: Clarendon Press, 1994), pp. 119-21.

69. Fitzmyer, *Responses*, pp. 33-34.

70. Blenkinsopp, 'Interpretation', p. 23.

71. J.J. Collins, *The Apocalyptic Imagination: An Introduction to the Jewish Matrix of Christianity* (New York: Crossroad, 1987), pp. 120-21.

accorded him more and more characteristic traits that emphasized his importance as an authoritative, divinely-inspired teacher and interpreter of Scripture in an eschatological context. It was *his halakah* that was to be followed by God's chosen people in the New Covenant, just as it was *he* who was able to disclose God's hidden secrets in the words of the prophets, showing how these could be applied to the community of the elect at the End of Days.[72]

Thus, as a result of the Teacher's activities, and as a consequence of the loyalty to his teachings as they were preserved within the congregation, the Qumran movement developed into an ever more closely knit and institutionalized community, as is shown by the many detailed sectarian rules. These should be seen as related to the rabbinical *halakah* that was later codified in the Mishna, although the special structure of authority in the Qumranite movement excludes the typical rabbinic halakic discussions.[73]

Thus, the person of the Teacher of Righteousness came to be formative for the Qumran community. However, since he was not the original founder of that larger Jewish movement that came into existence as a reaction to the political, social and cultural conditions in the Hellenistic age, and especially during the second century BCE, he as an individual does not constitute the focus of all contemporary texts found in Qumran, nor is he the crucial figure in God's secret plans for the salvation of

---

72. Thus, correctly, Byrskog, *Jesus the Only Teacher*, p. 193.

73. Cf. the synthetic characterization of the Teacher by S. Talmon, 'The Internal Diversification of Judaism in the Early Second Temple Period', in S. Talmon (ed.), *Jewish Civilization in the Hellenistic-Roman Period* (JSPSup, 10; Sheffield: JSOT Press, 1991), p. 41: 'The Teacher apparently did not innovate any religious concepts and maxims, but rather was an inspired interpreter of the traditional lore. He was instrumental in forging the group's anarchistic utopian messianism into the basis of a new social and religious structure. During his term of office and through him, the amorphous cluster of men who had reckoned the dawn of the 'World to Come' by millenarian speculations developed their own religious and societal structures. The erstwhile anarchistic dissenters' community hardened into an institutionalized socioreligious establishment which was soon to surpass in social rigidity and legalistic exactitude the old order from which they had seceded.

This transformation generated at Qumran a gradual increase in specific covenant precepts which culminated in their codification. Before long, the particular tenets of the Covenanters solidified into what may be termed a written appendix to the traditional law ... With all due caution and reservations, this particular body of laws may be viewed as a sectarian parallel to the rabbinic law codified in the Mishnah.'

the chosen people. Accordingly, he does not assume all the religious functions that Jesus does, later on, in a new situation, when political conditions, messianic expectations and scriptural interpretation have developed even further. Therefore, he does not have the pivotal role for the developing self-understanding of his supporters as Jesus has, according to the canonized early Christian literature. After all, what the Teacher does is to point to God and the *Torah*, rather than to himself. What Jesus is claimed to have done in the Gospels, especially in the more reflective Johannine Gospel, is to point to God *through* himself. Within this current of early Christian thought, Jesus is regarded as the personified *Torah*, God's Wisdom, and as conveyor of Holy Spirit—but what the real Jesus would have thought about this remains obscure and a matter of faith.

Another aspect of the Teacher's activities—also with certain similarities to the figure of Jesus—is shown by his conflicts. They concern mainly the Jerusalemite establishment, but also, according to the texts, those who had joined 'the New Covenant' for a while but who for unknown reasons had defected. The latter group of opponents of the Teacher and his community can be traced in cols. 19–20 of the *Damascus Document*. Evidently, the appearance of the Teacher caused a split within the 'Damascus Movement', the parent group of the Qumranites. For some members of this 'Damascus Movement', the Teacher would always remain the one and only authoritative leader, while those who did not agree with this opinion withdrew from the congregation and were condemned as defectors.[74] The former group of enemies, the Jerusalemite establishment, is especially prominent in the pesher literature, that is, in texts later than the *Damascus Document*. The Teacher, who now appears as 'the Priest', is opposed by those from 'Ephraim and Manasseh' (4QpPs[a] 2.17-18). Not explained here, these cryptic designations appear elsewhere in the pesher literature (4QpNah 2.2; 3.9), in a way that suggests that they may have been identified with Pharisees and (possibly) Sadducees.[75]

---

74. Maybe these will later become known as 'the Pharisees' (פרושים)? Or is this to put too much meaning into the use of a common word? In 4QMMT (4Q397 frag. 7+8.7), the verb פרש, 'to separate (oneself)' is used by the author(s) to indicate how the group has separated from 'the rest of the people'.

75. 'Ephraim' in 4QpNah 2.2 is characterized as 'those who seek smooth things (חלקות)'. Earlier in the same text (4QpNah 1.6-7) the same characterization is used in a context usually understood as referring to how Alexander Jannæus once had

Foremost among the opponents of the Teacher and of his Qumranite version of God's Torah, 'the Wicked Priest' is especially prominent in the *Habakkuk Pesher*, as we have seen above. In the *Psalms Pesher* (4QpPs[a] 4.8-9), it appears that 'the Wicked Priest' tried to seek out the Teacher and kill him 'because of the law that he had sent him'. If this 'law' should refer to the so-called 'halakic letter' (4QMMT), and if it were possible to identify this 'Wicked Priest', then the identity of the Teacher would be much less of a problem. Suggestions are not lacking, but it will then also be necessary to look closely at the various theories concerning the history and prehistory of the Qumran community.

4. *The Teacher of Righteousness as a Historical Person and against the Background of the History of the Qumran Community*

We have seen how, according to the *Damascus Document*, the Teacher of Righteousness played a decisive role during part of the history of the 'New Covenant'/'Damascus movement', not as its founder, but as one who, after a period of uncertainty, appeared as a strong, God-sent and charismatic leader. However, it is also clear that his appearance caused a schism within the 'Damascus movement'. From the pesher literature, where he is identified as 'the Priest', it is evident that some of the most influential of his enemies were located in the Jerusalemite priesthood. All this points to a complicated history, full of questions concerning both the Teacher as a historical person and the history/prehistory of the 'Damascus'/Qumranite movement. Consequently, this is a very active research front where many more or less probable hypotheses have been put forth, although over the years some main theories have crystallized.

a. *The Teacher of Righteousness as a Historical Person: Some Attempts at Identification*

It has sometimes been suggested that the title, 'Teacher of Righteousness', may not have been the title of only one person, but that it might have been used to denote many historical figures.[76] However, it is very

---

800 Pharisaic opponents crucified (cf. Josephus, *War* 1.4, 6 and *Ant.* 13.14, 2); on this, see, e.g., Knibb, *The Qumran Community*, pp. 212, 215. But while the reference to the Pharisees is thus rather clear, it is difficult to find arguments for an allusion to the Sadducees in the text.

76. In the opinion of I. Rabinowitz, 'The Guides of Righteousness', *VT* 8 (1958), pp. 391-404, the Teacher of Righteousness of the texts can be identified

difficult to ignore the fact that the Qumran texts actually indicate a certain individual, fitted into a certain historical context, as its authoritative founding figure, leader and teacher. But already on paleographical grounds, such sensational and populistic ideas as the notion that the Teacher should be identified with John the Baptist,[77] Jesus,[78] or James the Just, the Lord's brother,[79] can be dismissed. The Teacher appears in texts that can be dated well before the appearance of these figures.[80]

Among the historical persons of the pre- or early Maccabean period with whom the Teacher is identified, one of the earliest is Zadok, who flourished about 200 BCE (a pupil of Antigonos from Socho, known from *m. Avot* 1.3, and whose opponent, according to this theory, could have been the High Priest Simon the Just/Simon II, who is praised in Sir. 50).[81] Other suggestions include Onias III, the deposed High Priest, who had to flee from Jerusalem in 175 BCE and was killed five years later, the early Pharisees Yose ben Yoezer or Eleazar, the critic of John Hyrcanus, Judas the Essene, a prophet known to have been active

with several past, present and future figures: Nehemiah, Mattathias (the father of the Maccabean brothers)/Judas Maccabeus and the Messiah. Similarly, M. Smith, 'The Dead Sea Sect in Relation to Ancient Judaism', *NTS* 7 (1961), pp. 347-60, has proposed that this designation, like 'the Wicked Priest', could refer to several persons. Cf. A.S. van der Woude, 'Wicked Priest or Wicked Priests? Reflections on the Identification of the Wicked Priest in the Habakkuk Commentary', *JJS* 33 (1982), pp. 349-59, and *idem*, 'The Dead Sea Scrolls: Some Issues', *SEÅ* 57 (1992), pp. 99-100. See below on the so-called 'Groningen-hypothesis'.

77. B. Thiering, *Jesus and the Riddle of the Dead Sea Scrolls: Unlocking the Secrets of his Life Story* (San Francisco: Harper, 1992); see also her earlier *Redating the Teacher of Righteousness* (Sydney: Theological Explorations, 1979).

78. Thus according to the former professor of English at the University of Gothenburg, A. Ellegård, *Myten om Jesus: Den tidigaste kristendomen i nytt ljus* (Stockholm: Bonnier, 1992).

79. R. Eisenman, *James the Just in the Habakkuk Pesher* (Leiden: E.J. Brill, 1986); cf. R. Eisenman and M.O. Wise, *The Dead Sea Scrolls Uncovered: The First Complete Translation and Interpretation of 50 Key Documents Withheld for Over 35 Years* (Shaftsbury: Element Book, 1992).

80. Thus, emphatically, e.g. van der Woude, 'Fünfzehn Jahre Qumranforschung, IV', p. 233, and García Martínez, *The Dead Sea Scrolls Translated*, 'Introduction', pp. xlvii-viii.

81. Wacholder, *The Dawn of Qumran*, pp. 141-48, 182-84, based on *Aboth de-Rabbi Nathan* (A) 5 and (B) 10.

towards the end of the second century BCE, or even Jesus ben Sira.[82] Later identifications are Eleazar the Pharisee, a well-known critic of John Hyrcanus, or the Essene prophet Judas, both of whom were living towards the end of the second century BCE.[83]

But the mainstream opinion on the Teacher places him somewhere in the middle of the second century BCE, in a situation of conflict on many levels among the Jews of that period. There was the violent struggle against the Syrians for national independence, and there was also the tension within Judaism itself between conservatives and hellenizing modernists. The latter struggle was an old one, dating far back into the postexilic period. It is this tension between various groups that sets the stage for the many varieties of Judaism from the Maccabean period onwards—and, if Morton Smith is right in his provocative *Palestinian Parties and Politics that Shaped the Old Testament*,[84] Scripture itself reflects this struggle for dominion among those who in the postexilic era claimed an Israelite heritage. One of the focal points of this tension was the struggle for control over the temple and its cult, the foremost symbols of the Jewish nation.

After Judas Maccabeus had restored Jewish control over the temple in 162 BCE and following his death in 160, his brother Jonathan managed to consolidate the Maccabean/Hasmonean rule and the relative independence of the Jewish nation. But from 159 until 152, the period between the death of Alcimus, the last High Priest of the ancient Zadokite family (1 Macc. 9.56), and the appointment of Jonathan as High Priest by the Seleucid throne pretender Alexander Balas (1 Macc. 10.15-21), it seems that there was an *interregnum* on the highest office of the temple. According to 1 Maccabees, no High Priest seems to have

82. See the summary of opinions in, e.g., Bardtke, 'Literaturbericht über Qumran', p. 139 and Callaway, *The History of the Qumran Community*, p. 211 n. 4.

83. Thus according to, among others, J. Carmignac, 'Qui était le Docteur de Justice?', *RevQ* 10 (1980), pp. 235-246. Cf. the list in Vermes, *The Dead Sea Scrolls*, p. 160, or in the 'new' Schürer, G. Vermes, F. Millar and M. Goodman (eds.), *The History of the Jewish People in the Age of Jesus Christ (175 BC–AD 135)*, III.1 (Edinburgh: T. & T. Clark, 1986), p. 436 n. 7. See also the excursus in Byrskog, *Jesus the Only Teacher*, pp. 153-55.

84. (New York: Columbia University Press, 1971; second, corrected edition London: SCM Press, 1987).

been officially appointed after Alcimus's death, and Josephus, following 1 Maccabees as his source, speaks explicitly of a period of seven years, during which there was no High Priest in Jerusalem.[85]

The fact that there was no official appointment of a successor to Alcimus until 152 BCE does not, however, mean that nobody fulfilled the duties of the High Priest during this period. Especially the sacrifices on the Day of Atonement required that someone fulfil his role. Thus, many scholars today identify the Teacher of Righteousness with an anonymous priest, who was closely connected with (maybe a member of) the previous Zadokite High Priestly family, and who filled the office of High Priest between Alcimus and Jonathan.[86] Whether this was during the whole seven-year period, or for a shorter time, is not clear.[87]

85. Information in Josephus on this point is contradictory and confusing. In *Ant.* 20.237 it is stated that there was no High Priest in Jerusalem for seven years, thus in congruence with the chronology of 1 Macc. (the main source of Josephus's narrative). But according to other notices in *Ant.*, the High Priestly office was given to Judas, the brother of Jonathan, after the death of Alcimus (12.414), and was held by him for three years (12.439; cf. 12.419), and from 13.46 we learn that Jonathan became High Priest four years after the death of Judas, which occurred in 160 BCE. But in the narrative of 1 Macc. nothing is said about Judas as High Priest before Jonathan. Would not that have been mentioned in a pro-Maccabean writing? And according to 1 Macc. 9.3, 18, Judas dies in the year 152 (= 160 BCE), i.e. while Alcimus is still alive. Does Josephus want to put Judas on par with his brothers, who—all of them—after him obtained the prestigious office as High Priests? Or, when he says that it was the *people* who made Judas High Priest, does this imply that this was no formal appointment, in which the supreme political power confirmed the legitimacy and authority of the leading temple official?

86. See, among others, Murphy-O'Connor, 'Teacher of Righteousness'; *idem*, 'The Essenes and their History'; O. Betz and R. Riesner, *Jesus, Qumran and the Vatican: Clarifications* (London: SCM Press, 1994), pp. 47-48, Stegemann, *Die Essener*, p. 205; VanderKam, *The Dead Sea Scrolls Today*, pp. 103-104. The detailed historical reconstruction by H. Burgmann, *Vorgeschichte und Frühgeschichte der essenischen Gemeinden von Qumrân und Damaskus* (ANTJ, 7; Frankfurt am Main: Peter Lang, 1987), pp. 189-228, assumes the same general idea (but is often too speculative; cf. the criticism in van der Woude, 'Fünfzehn Jahre Qumranforschung, IV', pp. 244-47).—Another variant of this theory is given by J.H. Ulrichsen, 'Menighetsforståelsen i Qumrantekstene', *NTT* 83 (1982), p. 156: the Teacher would, as the second highest official in the temple hierarchy (סגן הכוהנים), have been the acting High Priest after Alcimus's death, but he had to wait in vain for the official recognization from the ruling Seleucids. Finally, in 152 BCE, Jonathan's intrigues between the Seleucid throne pretenders put him out of office.

87. According to Stegemann, *Die Essener*, p. 205, there might have been several

Support from the Qumran texts for this identification of the Teacher of Righteousness rests mainly on information about his opponents from the pesher literature. From the *Habakkuk Pesher*, it is clear that the hated 'Wicked Priest', who had persecuted the Teacher on the Day of Atonement (1QpHab 11; cf. above), had been punished both by his enemies and by God, and that he and his successors, 'the last priests of Jerusalem' had also lost to the pagans what they had amassed unjustly (1QpHab 9; cf. 4QpPs[a] 4.9).[88] Among the illegitimate Hasmonean High Priests, the most likely candidate—whose life story best fits the details of the pesharim—would then be Jonathan, who after having usurped political power in 160 and religious power in 152, eventually was killed in 143 after having been taken captive by the Syrian general Tryphon (1 Macc. 13.12-23).

Hence, from 152 onwards, the supreme Jewish office remained in the hands of the non-Zadokite Hasmonean rulers, thus marking a breach in both political leadership and in traditional Jewish worship. From now on, the same dynasty controlled the highest political and religious institutions. Even though the Hasmoneans were Jewish nationalists, ideologically they did not belong to the conservative traditionalists. Having taken control of the highest office through Jonathan's intrigues with the Syrians, they did not restore it to its rightful possessors, but inaugurated a new, illegitimate High Priestly family (cf. 1 Macc. 14.41). The pro-Maccabean ideology of 1 and 2 Maccabees cannot obscure the fact that their ascent to power meant another complicating factor in the tension between different groups within postexilic Judaism. Although depicted as pious defenders of the Jewish traditions in the books of Maccabees, these usurpers were highly hellenized, and—still worse—true worship in the Temple was now made impossible, not by pagans, but by power-hungry Jews!

b. *The Teacher of Righteousness against the Background of the History of the Qumran Community*
The question about the identity of the Teacher of Righteousness is closely connected with the question about the place of the Qumran covenanters within postexilic Judaism—sociologically, ideologically,

persons who substituted for the High Priest during the years 159–152. As the last of these, the Qumran Teacher of Righteousness would then have been deposed by Jonathan.

88. Cf. Vermes *et al.*, *The History of the Jewish People*, p. 434.

chronologically. How do he and his community fit into the larger perspective of postexilic Judaism in the Hellenistic period, especially in the aftermath of the Maccabean revolt? When and where does the history of the 'Damascus movement', 'the New Covenant' and the Qumran community begin? Some time in the pre-Maccabean period, around 200 BCE, or even before that? In early Maccabean times (from about 175 and some decades after)? Or during the Hasmonean era, some time between about 150 until 90?

Some scholars are inclined to emphasize the roots of the Qumran community in pre-Maccabean times, sometimes far back in the postexilic period. Thus, Murphy-O'Connor has argued that the Qumran movement emerged from the larger Essene movement, which in its turn had its origins among Jewish exiles in Babylon. Hence, the original, pre-Qumranite version of the *Damascus Document* expressed Essene ideology. The 'Damascus movement' would then have consisted of Essenes who had returned to Palestine in connection with the Maccabean uprising, and 'Damascus' in, for example, CD 19.34 should then be understood as a cover name for Babylon. Being disappointed with the Maccabeans, and following the appearance of the Teacher of Righteousness, however, the 'Damascus movement' was split up. The Teacher and his sympathizers withdrew to form the Qumran community.[89] Cf. the analysis of CD 4.2-4 and 6.2-11 above; these passages indicate the successive stages of the community behind the resultant 'Damascus Document'.

But the question is whether the roots of the Essene/Qumranite movement should be sought for as early as this, and outside Palestine as well. Josephus, for example, mentions the Essenes for the first time in connection with the rule of Jonathan, that is, some time between 160 and 143 BCE (*Ant.* 13.171). Another theory, advocated by (among others) Hartmut Stegemann, rejects the idea that the background of the Essenes is to be looked for in Babylonia and in groups of Jews who had returned

---

89. Murphy-O'Connor, 'The Damascus Document Revisited'. See also the summary of his theory in Callaway, *The History of the Qumran Community*, p. 214 n. 56. His opinion is to a great extent shared by P.R. Davies; see his article, 'The Prehistory of the Qumran Community', in D. Dimant and U. Rappaport (eds.), *The Dead Sea Scrolls: Forty Years of Research* (Studies on the Text of the Desert of Judah, 10; Leiden: E.J. Brill, 1992), pp. 116-25, but cf. also his *The Damascus Covenant*.

from the Babylonian exile.[90] Instead, a more plausible background could be found in Jewish revivalist groups within Palestine itself during the chaotic first years of the Maccabean revolt.[91] The *hasidim*, pious Jews known from 1 Macc. 2.42, could have been one exponent of this traditionalist form of Palestinian Judaism, resulting from the strong tendency towards hellenization from about 200 BCE (the time of the Syrian take-over).[92]

In Stegemann's detailed historical reconstruction,[93] the anonymous Zadokite ex-High Priest deposed by Jonathan in 152 is identical with the Teacher of Righteousness. He and his followers flee to Syria, where they find refuge 'in the land of Damascus' among a group called 'the New Covenant' (cf. CD 6.5; 7.18-20). From here, he tries to exert his influence on the Jerusalem establishment (Jonathan and other pro-Maccabean leaders) through the now famous 'halakic letter' (4QMMT). However, this is a failure, which results in an attempt from the Jerusalemites to murder the Teacher (4QpPsᵃ 4.7-9). Even worse, the Teacher causes a schism within the 'Damascus movement'. Some remain loyal to the Teacher, while three other groups emerge: some 'New Covenanters' remain unmoved by the Teacher and his ambitions for authority; these will come to be known as Essenes. Some separatists defect; these are later called 'Pharisees', that is, 'those who separate themselves'. Yet others try to compromise with the new Hasmonean temple leadership; from them the Sadducees of the New Testament period will emerge.

This is roughly where to put the Teacher and the beginnings of the Qumran settlement, according to (among others) Stegemann's view.

90. But he agrees that the Essene movement absorbed many concepts commonly held by Jews returning from exile; thus, e.g. (and it could be of some significance in contrast to the idea of a pandemic *Babylonian* influence on post-exilic Judaism) the solar-based calendar could have been introduced by Jews returning from Egypt after 538 BCE; cf. Stegemann, *Die Essener*, pp. 234, 280. This example might be of great significance for the understanding of the prehistory of the Qumranites, but I have no possibility of going further into the topic here.

91. See Stegemann, *Die Essener*, pp. 198-213, for a general sketch of Essene history.

92. Note how these *hasidim* seek refuge to the east of Jordan, i.e., outside Palestine proper. Cf. also 1 Macc. 7.13-18: the High Priest Alcimus orders the execution of 60 *hasidim*, who have arrived to negotiate about how to conduct worship in the temple of Jerusalem.

93. Stegemann, *Die Essener*, pp. 205-212.

The decisive point that marked the end of the Teacher's influence on political and religious affairs would then be the proclamation of Simon Maccabee as Jonathan's successor as High Priest in 142 BCE.[94] From now on, the Essenes remained neutral regarding political leadership, but instead they turned to polemicize against the Pharisees, whose influence in Jewish society was growing. The conflict was mainly a religious one, focused on halakic matters, in which Pharisaic opinions had become more and more widespread, while the conflict with the emerging Sadducee 'party' had different, political, reasons.[95]

To continue this overall picture of Qumranite history presented by Stegemann, political ambitions were replaced by increased eschatological expectation. The Teacher cancelled his political claims and waited for the End, when the Davidic Messiah would appear—there was no need to expect a priestly Messiah as long as the Teacher was alive, himself being the true Priest. However, after his death, about 110 BCE, there emerged the belief in two Messiahs, the priestly from Aaron and the royal from Israel.[96] At the same time there was an *Eschatologieverzögerung*. Studying Scripture to find the reason why the End had not come, 40 years were added to the eschatological time-table (CD 20.13-17; cf. Deut. 2.7, 14), that is, until about 70 BCE.[97] Then, when no End, but only Roman power was in sight (Pompey's entry of Jerusalem and the Holy of Holies in 63), the prophecy in Hab. 2.3 was taken as a comfort in prolonged waiting: God's secrets are greater than man can comprehend (cf. 1QpHab 7.7-16).[98] The delay would mean that the sins of mankind could grow even greater, that is, the coming judgment would be even more certain! A rereading of the book of Daniel, finally, gave a new date for the End, according to Stegemann: it would come another 140 years after the first 40-year delay; that is, by

94. Stegemann, *Die Essener*, pp. 213-14. Cf. John C. Trever, *The Dead Sea Scrolls: A Personal Account* (Upland, CA: Upland Commercial Printers, 1988), p. 162, who claims that it was the ascent to power of Simon that made the conservative circles around the Teacher withdraw into the wilderness and found the Qumran settlement.

95. Stegemann, *Die Essener*, p. 216.

96. Stegemann, *Die Essener*, pp. 219-20.

97. Stegemann, *Die Essener*, p. 220, cf. p. 174.

98. The crisis for eschatological speculation is thus reflected in the Habakkuk pesher, dated to about 50 BCE. The same applies to the commentaries on Nahum and Hosea, also dated to the period after 70 BCE; Stegemann, *Die Essener*, pp. 180-85.

our reckoning, in 70 CE—and so it did, in a way! Thus, resulting from this Essene rereckoning, neither John the Baptist nor Jesus could be regarded by the Essenes as true messianic figures. They showed up at the wrong time![99]

Beside this elaborate hypothesis, there is the so-called 'Groningen' hypothesis associated with Florentino García Martínez and Adam van der Woude.[100] The prehistory of the 'Damascus movement' is here not taken as far back in time as by Murphy-O'Connor, nor in such detail as by Stegemann. Its background is seen in the apocalyptic brand of Judaism that emerged in the third century BCE in Palestine. According to this theory, the appearance of the Teacher of Righteousness towards the middle of the second century BCE, during the reigns of Jonathan and Simon as High Priests, caused a split within the movement.[101] As a result, he and his followers withdrew and formed the Qumran community. The 'Wicked Priest' who persecuted the Teacher, according to the *Habakkuk Pesher*, is not Jonathan, but his nephew, John Hyrcanus. Otherwise, it is characteristic for this theory that the term 'Wicked Priest' could indicate several Hasmonean High Priests from Judas until Alexander Jannæus.

But even if 'the Wicked Priest' could be identified with such late Hasmonean rulers as Alexander Jannæus (103–76) or Aristobulus II (67–63), it is difficult to see that this would greatly affect the date of the founding of the Qumran community.[102] There is a general scholarly consensus, supported by archaeological investigations, to put the early stages of the congregation's settlement at Qumran to the last decades of

99. Stegemann, *Die Essener*, p. 221.

100. See, e.g., García Martínez, 'Qumran Origins and Early History: A Groningen Hypothesis', *FolOr* 25 (1988), pp. 113-36; García Martínez and van der Woude, 'A "Groningen" Hypothesis of Qumran Origins and Early History', *RevQ* 14 (1990), pp. 521-41. A short summary by van der Woude is found in his 'The Dead Sea Scrolls', pp. 95-98, and by García Martínez in his *The Dead Sea Scrolls Translated*, 'Introduction', pp. lv-lvi; cf. also Knibb, 'The Teacher of Righteousness', pp. 61-62.

101. In this theory, the *Temple Scroll* (11QT) would have been dated to the period before this schism within the Essene movement, while 4QMMT would have been composed immediately after it.

102. For such identifications, see, respectively, J.P.M. van der Ploeg, *The Excavations at Qumran* (London: Longmans, 1958), and A. Dupont-Sommer, *The Jewish Sect of Qumran and the Essenes* (London: Vallentine, Mitchell & Co., 1955).

the second century BCE.[103] But what must be discussed further is the question about the Judaism of the Qumran community in relation to the other Jewish 'parties' that emerged during the Hasmonean period. The commonly-held opinion that the Qumran covenanters were some kind of Essenes is no longer unproblematic.

Thus, another theory on Qumranite origins is presented in the energetic claims of Lawrence H. Schiffman: that the character and early history of the Qumran community as part of an Essene form of Judaism need to be reassessed.[104] According to him, there are significant examples of how the *halakah* in the Qumran texts, especially in 4QMMT, are comparable to opinions ascribed to the Sadducees in later rabbinic literature.[105] However, the 'Sadducees' (or rather 'Zadokites') of the Qumran community are not to be identified with the Sadducees of Josephus or the New Testament. It is, thus, necessary to distinguish between two groups of Sadducees.[106] Similarly, he points out that the MMT contains criticism of opinions later ascribed to the Pharisees. His conclusion is, therefore, that either the Qumran community was dominated by Sadducees (=adherents to the traditional Zadokite High Priestly family) instead of Essenes, or that it is necessary to rewrite the theories about the early history of the Essenes. Furthermore, 4QMMT is an important proof that there was an halakic discussion going on already

103. Some of the 'wilder' hypotheses about the history of the Qumran community are described in Callaway, *The History of the Qumran Community*, p. 13.

104. See Schiffman, *Reclaiming the Dead Sea Scrolls*, pp. 65-112; the main points of his hypotheses are also stated in L.H. Schiffman, 'The Sadducean Origins of the Dead Sea Scroll Sect', in H. Shanks (ed.), *Understanding the Dead Sea Scrolls: A Reader from the Biblical Archaeology Review* (New York: Random House, 1992), pp. 36-49.

105. Some examples of Sadducean *halakah* in 4QMMT are the questions about purity concerning the red heifer, and the issue about whether liquid poured from a clean vessel to an unclean vessel can convey uncleanness 'in the wrong direction', i.e., to the first vessel; cf. E. Qimron, 'Miqṣat Maʿaśe Hatorah', *ABD*, IV, p. 844.

106. Opposition to the ideas of Schiffman concerns mainly his terminology for characterizing the Qumran community. It is clear that the Sadducees of Josephus and of the New Testament cannot be of the same ideological kind as the Qumranites. But it is confusing to apply the same (or similar) epithet(s) to different groups. It would be better to speak about the Qumranites only as 'Zadokites'—or else he runs the risk of evoking the kind of confusion produced by Eisenman in his way of talking about 'Herodian' and 'Messianic' Sadducees in *The Dead Sea Scrolls Uncovered*. See further the criticism in VanderKam, *The Dead Sea Scrolls Today*, pp. 93-95.

in Maccabean times (in Schiffman's view, the MMT was written even before the appearance of the Teacher of Righteousness), which could indicate that the halakic discussions in the rabbinic writings do not necessarily have to refer to the situation after 70 CE.[107]

5. *Consequences for the Picture of Jesus and the Early Jesus Movement in Palestine*

Finally, then, from a New Testament perspective: what does all this mean for our understanding of Jesus and of the Jesus movement— another Jewish messianic and eschatologically-oriented 'New Covenant' movement?

Reflecting on this question, it is necessary to begin with certain fundamental and well-known facts: it seems, from the texts, that the Teacher and his community separated themselves from, and were gradually marginalized from, contemporary forms of mainstream Judaism. In their self-understanding, fidelity towards the Teacher and his *halakah* became a decisive criterion. His followers inherited his eschatological way of interpreting Scripture in an actualizing way, applying its prophecies to themselves and their contemporary situation, based on the conviction that they were God's chosen true remnant of Israel, the New Covenant at the End of Days. Within this ideological framework, several messianic ideas and concepts were created—many of which are found in the New Testament where they are applied to Jesus and the Church. At the same time, an awareness of their special cultic qualities and heritage created and enhanced ideas of a transcending, within the context of liturgy, of the spatial and temporal framework shaped by traditional beliefs and eschatological speculations.

In comparing Jesus and his Jewish reform movement with the Teacher of Righteousness and his community, I think we must be aware of the obvious similarities between these two exponents of Jewish ideology in a situation of internal and external crisis. However, it would not be correct to put the emphasis on a comparison of the two founding figures, or to regard the Jesus movement as a simple copy of the preexisting Qumran community.[108] But there are many good reasons to

107. In contrast to Schiffman, Qimron, 'Miqsat Ma'aśe Hatorah', p. 844, is of the opinion that 4QMMT was written by the Teacher himself, about 150 BCE, shortly after the conflict hinted at in the text.

108. Cf. VanderKam, *The Dead Sea Scrolls Today*, pp. 160-61, for criticism of,

study the ideological and sociological preconditions from which these two figures came to have such fundamental importance for their adherents. In both cases, the voice of God was thought to be heard by people who considered themselves to be living at the End of Days.[109] Both were charismatic leaders, religious *virtuosi*, who were convinced that they were acting as God's instruments in the coming of the *eschaton*. For both, it was important to gather a community of the New Covenant in the Last Days. Both movements carry messianic ideas and eschatological convictions, into which the founding figures were fitted.

They differed widely in *halakah*, but both came into conflict with the authorities over halakic issues. But while Jesus was executed as a criminal, nothing is known about the fate of the Teacher. However, both continued to play a decisive role for their sympathizers after they died. Their particular actualizing interpretation of Scripture and their self-understanding as being God's chosen instruments governed their ideas about correct *halakah*, which was regarded as normative, but developed in the spirit of the respective masters by their communities after them.

But while there are no signs of the Qumranites borrowing from the Jesus movement, I think there are good reasons for believing that there was an exchange in the opposite direction. In the early history of the Palestinian Jesus movement, we can see how the legacy of Jesus, and his originally-Galilean protest movement, was taken over and adapted into various levels of the contemporary Palestinian society. Some of it was moulded into a more Jerusalemite, temple-oriented ideological framework. Some of it found expression in diaspora-based, temple-critical groups. While it seems to have attracted some Pharisees, according to certain information, it is also depicted as having its worst enemies among the Pharisees elsewhere in the early Christian documents.

Thus, I will conclude by putting the question forward of whether we should not be more open to the possibility of seeing how the legacy of Jesus was fused into the ideological framework of, among others, ex-Qumranites, who changed loyalties from obeying the voice of the

among others, the ideas of Dupont-Sommer on how the New Testament depiction of Jesus could have been influenced by conceptions about the Teacher.

109.   See further the article by Stegemann, 'The "Teacher of Righteousness" and Jesus: Two Types of Religious Leadership in Judaism at the Turn of the Era', in S. Talmon (ed.), *Jewish Civilization in the Hellenistic-Roman Period* (JSPSup, 10; Sheffield: JSOT Press, 1991), pp. 196-213.

Teacher to listening to the word of God through his Son and Servant, Jesus the Messiah. (This does not, I should like to emphasize, mean that one has to subscribe to the fanciful ideas of Robert Eisenman about the true nature of early Palestinian Christianity).[110] After all, is it not the case that much of the early Christian propaganda emphasizes how Jesus is the fulfilment of all messianic and eschatological expectation that was the legacy of Scripture? Such a fusion of pious *Torah*-centered Judaism with Jesus-focused messianic belief would explain the emergence and growth of the conservative Jewish Christianity, witnessed by early Christian documents in the decades before and after the great turmoil in Palestine around the revolt in 66–73 CE. It would also provide a *Sitz im Leben* for the apocalyptic currents within early Christianity. I, for my part, am increasingly convinced that the dominating ideological presuppositions behind the book of Revelation, to take but one example, originate in a Judaism with strong ties to concepts and beliefs found especially in the Qumran texts. Perhaps we should be more open to the fact that there was also considerable variation within early Christianity in Palestine, and not just, as is commonly accepted, within the Judaism from which it originated.

110. Cf. Eisenman, *James the Just*, but see also Eisenman and Wise, *The Dead Sea Scrolls Uncovered.*

HISTORIOGRAPHY OF QUMRAN:
THE SONS OF ZADOK AND THEIR ENEMIES

Ben Zion Wacholder

1. *Introduction*

The history of a schismatic movement may be told from the viewpoint of (1) its own adherents, (2) its opponents, or (3) an external perspective. This paper collects evidence from the Cairo Genizah and Qumran's caves to view the history of the sect and its adversaries. Often sectarian, as well as orthodox, movements present a rewriting, or new vision, of the past illuminated by contemporary ideas. This is especially true of Second Temple Judaism, in which various sects sought advantage by reinterpreting Scripture and history. Manuscript evidence of the Yaḥad divides sectarian history into three periods: origins—the sect and its adversaries emerge from biblical lore; contemporary—the sectarian perspective of Second Temple Jewish and foreign dignitaries; and eschatological—the prophecies of Ezekiel serve as a springboard to advance the sect into the eschaton. The sect's chronographers delineated these three epochs by superimposing biblical events and eras upon the Jubilean timeline.

From the perspective of the Yaḥad's historians the fracture of the Solomonic state pictured the conflict between the 'proto–Pharisees', represented by the northern kingdom of Ephraim, and 'true Israel', portrayed by the southern kingdom of Judah. 4Q169 (*Pesher Nahum*) and 4Q398 (MMTᵉ) confirm the *Damascus Document*'s assignment of apostate headship to Jeroboam, the progenitor of Pharisaism. Echoing these earlier polemicists, the medieval Karaite writer al-Qirqisani depicts Jeroboam as true Israel's nemesis. From this genesis, 4Q247 (Apocalypse of Weeks) specifies the period from Jeroboam's rise to Jerusalem's fall as lasting for 430 years. 4Q385–90 (*Second Ezekiel*) translates the prophet's vision of the dry bones into postexilic history.

The scraps from Qumran's Cave 4 continually extend the list of identifiable historic figures from the Hellenistic period. John Allegro's 1965 publication of *Pesher Nahum* mentions the historical figures of Antiochus IV and Demetrius III.[1] Since then the rogues' gallery of the Qumranites has been expanded to include Jewish apostates as well as foreign persecutors, 4Q477 (*Decrees of Sect*).[2] These villainous characters, as this paper argues, have as their seminal head Jeroboam. The almanacs of 4Q322–24 (4QMish C^{a-e}) chronicle the events surrounding Pompey's conquest of Judea in 63 BCE. Hasmonean rulers, as well as Roman legates, are named in these diaries. Sectarian propagandists had also mastered covert polemical tactics. Into the popularly circulating Ben Sira the Yaḥad's editorialists inserted a sectarian discourse within the wisdom poem of ch. 51. Dating presumably from the post-70 CE era, this song, an imitation of Psalm 136, proclaims the Zadokite clan as that chosen by God for the office of the high priesthood.

In their polemics the sect also used Ezekiel. Interpreting Ezekiel 37–39, the sectarian *Second Ezekiel* stretches postexilic history to the horizon of the eschaton, at which time a blasphemer would arise. The sectarian prophet also recalls the ancient Jewish enemy, Haman, and his ancestors, the Amalekites, forecasting their absolute destruction. Civil war may be the appropriate term for this tumultuous epoch in which the sect battles its timeless opponents.

2. *Origins of Jewish Sects: Pharisees versus True Israel*

The sectarian writers sought legitimation through historical grounding. But their lot was a protracted struggle; the ancestry of their opponents had roots as old as their own. The historiography of the sect was bound up in that of their opponents. A clear view of the ascension of their adversaries opens the scene of sectarian origins.

---

1.   J.M. Allegro and A.A. Andersen, *4Q158-4Q186* (DJD, 5; Oxford: Clarendon Press, 1968–77), p. 39. F. García Martínez and J. Trebolle Barrera, *The People of the Dead Sea Scrolls* (Leiden: E.J. Brill, 1968), p. 80, say Antiochus V, not Antiochus Epiphanes.

2.   For other references to historical figures, see M. Broshi and A. Yardeni, 'On Netinim and False Prophets', *Tarbiz* 62 (1992), pp. 45–54.

3. *History of the Sect's Opponents:*
Jeroboam, the Pharisaic Progenitor

The *Damascus Document* (CD) opens the pages of sectarian historiography with a single theme: to tell the history of Israel by noting its epochs.[3] Modern scholarship misinterprets the main thrust of the non-legal sections of the *Damascus Document* by branding them Admonitions.[4] Losing the historical perspective advanced by the sectarian writer, scholarship prefers to reconstruct its own understanding of history instead. According to the author of CD, the most important event on Israel's timeline was the building of the Solomonic temple when God came to dwell in the midst of Israel. What then, CD speculates, could have caused God to hide his face from his people, destroy Jerusalem along with its temple, and exile the survivors to Babylon? CD seconds the biblical chroniclers who assign to Jeroboam the authorship of the adulterous practices that led to the fall of the northern kingdom. The sect is the true Israel of old living in David's Judah, whereas their Pharisaic and Sadducean opponents are the northern kingdom's Ephraim and Manasseh. Why then did God hand Judah over to the Babylonians? Because, as the sect saw it, the Rehoboamite kingdom adopted the practices of Jeroboam and his progeny. God, however, did not destroy all of Judah but preserved a faithful remnant in the midst of apostasy. Among the Israelite captives taken to Babylonia, a pietistic minority congregated in the land of Damascus, bonded by a new covenant under the appellation of the Sons of Zadok.

The initial lines of CD describe God's confrontation with Israel over their continued apostasy.

CD 1.1-4a: The LORD's Dispute

1 ועתה שמעו כל יודעי צדק ובינו במעשי
2 אל כי ריב לו עם כל בשר ומשפט יעשה בכל מנאציו
3 כי במועלם אשר עזבוהו הסתיר פניו מישראל וממקדשו
4 ויתנם לחרב ובזכרו ברית ראשנים השאיר שאירית
5 לישראל ולא נתנם לכלה ובקץ חרו שנים שלוש מאות
6 ותשעים לתיתו אותם ביד נבוכדנאצר מלך בבל
7 פקדם ויצמח מישראל ומאהרן שורש מטעת

---

3. 4Q266 (*Damascus Document*ª) adds eight lines prior to the first line of the Geniza text.

4. P.R. Davies, *The Damascus Covenant* (Sheffield: JSOT Press, 1983), p. 48.

1. Now hear me all you who know righteousness and understand the acts of

2. God. For he (God) has a dispute with all flesh; and he will execute judgment against all those who have angered him.

3. Because of their profanation by which they have profaned him, he hid his face from Israel and his temple.

4. And he put them to the sword. However, when he remembered the covenant of the very first, he saved a remnant

5. for Israel and did not deliver them up to destruction. And at the period of wrath, three hundred and

6. ninety years after having delivered them up into the hands of Nebuchadnezzar the king of Babylon,

7. he visited them and caused to sprout from Israel and from Aaron a shoot of the planting.

Two questions must be asked. When did this confrontation, ריב לו, begin? And how long did it continue? Qumran scholars take it for granted that this expression refers to the Babylonian exile, an epoch which at most relates to the sect's prehistory, but more typically predates the birth of the sect. Generally speaking, reconstructions of Qumran's history may be classified into one of three theories. Vermes is the standard-bearer for the Hellenistic theory, which begins the history of the sect with the rift between the Hasideans and Jonathan the Maccabee. Vermes understands the period of wrath in CD 1.5 as included within the 390 years, beginning with Nebuchadnezzar's destruction of Jerusalem. García Martínez's 'Groningen' hypothesis locates the roots of the community within the Palestinian apocalyptic tradition. He interprets Josephus's account of the beginning of the sect, 'since the most ancient times', to indicate its origin in postexilic Judaism prior to the advent of Hellenism. Murphy-O'Connor places the sect's origins earlier and locates its foundation within the diaspora community in Babylon. All three theories similarly address the pre-history Qumran as postexilic, but extend it no further. What these historical reconstructions ignore is the plain meaning of CD that the dispute and the period of wrath refer to the apostasy which began with Jeroboam and continued to the exile.

a. *Jeroboam, the Progenitor of Apostasy*
That the era of the wrath begins with Jeroboam is attested in other passages from CD.

CD 1.11-15: The Jeroboamite Generation

11 ויקם להם מורה צדק להדריכם בדרך לבו ויודע
12 לדורות אחרונים את אשר עשה בדור אחרון בעדת בוגדים
13 הם סרי דרך היא העת אשר היה כתוב עליה כפרה סוריה
14 כן סרר ישראל בעמוד איש הלצון אשר הטיף לישראל
15 מימי כזב ויתעם בתוהו לא דרך

11. (God) raised up for them a teacher of righteousness to lead them in the way of his heart. And he made known

12. to later generations what he had done to the last generation a congregation of traitors.

13. They are the turners from the way. That was the time about which was written: 'like a wandering heifer

14. so did Israel stray'—when the man of scoffing arose who spouted water of deceit to Israel and led them astray in a wilderness without a way.

Beginning with the last word of CD 1.11, ויודע, the text reviews the Jeroboamite rebellion and its consequences. Note especially the following: what had been related in general, is now amplified, and what had been first narrated, is now attributed to the Moreh Zedek. ויודע may be taken to refer to God, but it is more reasonable to attribute 'he made known' to the Teacher since the previous clause relates to the Teacher's instruction of Israel. God sends a message through his prophet the Moreh Zedek. Exegesis of CD 1.12 makes this point: 'And he [the Moreh] made known to later generations what he [God] had done to the last generation'. This clause makes best sense supposing that the 'last generation, the congregation of traitors', is an epithet for the Jeroboamites. They were the traitors, the heretics who led Israel astray.

The editor of CD quotes (line 13) Hos. 4.16, 'like a rebellious cow so Israel has rebelled', in its context referring to the apostasy of the northern kingdom. Line 14 introduces a 'man of scoffing' as the one who led Israel astray. The identity of this scoffer has been the subject of many studies, but none has identified him correctly.[5] All propositions assume a figure of the second temple, but the context leads elsewhere. Jeroboam is the referent, the model chosen by the sectarian writers in their diatribes with the Pharisees.

---

5. Refer to E. Schürer, *The History of the Jewish People in the Age of Jesus Christ* (3 vols.; ed. G. Vermes, F. Millar and M. Goodman; Edinburgh: T. & T. Clark, 1973-87), II, pp. 585-88, for a summary of the literature.

CD 7.10-12a describes apostate Ephraim's departure from faithful Judah.

10 עליהם בבוא הדבר אשר כתוב בדברי ישעיה בן אמוץ הנביא
11 אשר אמר יבוא עליד ועל עמך ועל בית אביך ימים אשר <לא>
12 באו מיום סור אפרים מעל יהודה

> 10. When there shall come to pass the word which is written in the words of Isaiah, son of Amoz, the prophet
> 11. who said: 'There shall come upon you and upon your people and upon your father's house days which have (not)
> 12. come since the day when Ephraim departed from Judah'.

Quoting Isa. 7.17, the writer states directly that the Jeroboamite rebellion, which ruptured the Davidic empire, kindled the divine wrath. Eventually this wrath would culminate in Nebuchadnezzar wielding the sanctioned sword. In many Qumranic texts, moreover, Judah and Ephraim stand for the sectaries and the Pharisees. For example, *Pesher Nahum* warns against the false Talmud of the Pharisees.

4QpNah (4Q169) 2.7, 8: The False Talmud

7 מרוב זנוני זונה טובת חן בעלת כשפים הממכרת גוים בזנותה
ומשפחות ב[כש]פיה
8 פשר[ו ע]ל מתעי אפרים אשר בתלמוד שקרם ולשון כזביהם
ושפת מרמה יתעו רבים

> 7. And all for the countless harlotries of the harlot, graceful and of deadly charms, who betrays nations with her harlotries, and peoples with her charms.
> 8. Its interpretation concerns those who lead Ephraim astray, who by their false Talmud, their lying tongue, and lip of deceit will lead many astray.

The pesherite exegesis of Nahum gives a sectarian sense to Nah. 3.4 in which the prophet charges the prostitute Assyrian with not only defiling weaker nations but also leading them away. As read by the Qumranic exegete, this verse manifestly applies to the Ephraimites who lead the people astray with their 'false Talmud'. Many translations mislead by rendering תלמוד as 'teaching'. The use of successive epithets 'false Talmud', 'lying tongue', and 'lip of deceit' emphasizes the oral aspects of Talmud. The designation of the oral teachers of the Talmud as the misleaders of Ephraim links the Ephraimites with the Pharisaic oral teachers.

A final implicit reference to Jeroboam occurs in CD 1.21: עם ויסיסו
לריב, 'and they rejoiced for the dispute of the people'. In fact לריב עם
seems to be a pun on Jeroboam's name; c.f. Jerubbaal in Judg. 6.32,
'Therefore on that day he was called Jerubbaal, that is to say, "Let Baal
contend against him"'. In CD, the allusion is to the dispute, ריב, and its
origin, 'let God contend against Jeroboam'.

Other sectarian texts support the claims of CD. 4Q398 (MMTᵉ), part
of a letter that articulates differences of opinion within the sect itself,
makes explicit what CD implies: Jeroboam's apostasy induced the fall
of Jerusalem during the reign of Zedekiah.

4Q398 Fl: Jeroboam's Apostasy Caused Jerusalem's Fall

2 [ ]בֿן[ ] בֿ[ ] בֿ[ ]בֿימי שלומוה בן דויֿד ואֿף הקללותֿ/
3 [ש]/ בא [ן] בוֿ מיֿ[מי †יֿ]רֿבעֿםֿ בן נבט וער כֿלֹוֹתֿ‡† ירושלם וצדקיה מלך יֿ[הודה]/
4 [ש]/יֿבֿ[יֿ]אֿם בֿ]בלה [

† מֿימי versus Qimron in DJD, 10 בֿימי.

‡† Qimron reads גֿלות.

2. (The blessings which came upon Israel) in the days of Solomon the
son of David and also the curses

3. which came upon him (Israel) since the days of Jeroboam son of
Nebat right up to the capture of Jerusalem and Zedekiah king of Judah.

4. He (the king of Babylon) brought them (Israel) to Ba[bylon.

Contrary to Qimron's reconstruction of בֿימי, which understands the
period from Jeroboam to Zedekiah, reading מֿימי implies that Jeroboam
was responsible for Jerusalem's collapse under Zedekiah. Strugnell
wondered whether this column really belonged in a text that is not concerned with history.[6] But the alleged rise of proto-Pharisaism in the
aftermath of Solomon's death coheres well with the polemics of MMT
against its Pharisaic opponents.

The final evidence that equates the foundation of Pharisaism with
the Jeroboamite rebellion comes from a source outside of Qumran: the
tenth-century Karaite, al-Qirqisani. Writing in 1894, Abraham Harkavy
mentioned that the Karaite encyclopedist had access to sectarian writings from the Second Temple period in addition to rabbinic sources.[7]

6. J. Strugnell, 'MMT: Second Thoughts', in E. Ulrich and J. VanderKam
(eds.), *The Community of the Renewed Covenant* (Notre Dame: University of Notre
Dame Press, 1994), p. 69.

7. W. Bacher, 'Qirqisani, the Karaite, and his Work on Jewish Sects', *JQR* 7

From both perspectives Qirqisani presents the rise of rabbinism, giving first the claims of the sectaries, followed by the rabbinic position found in the Mishnah and Talmud. That Jeroboam was the first Pharisee is a belief, says Qirqisani, of the sectarians. One argument in this proof concerns Jeroboam's calendric manipulations (1 Kgs 12.33), which CD adopts, charging the adversaries with altering seasons and festivals (CD 3.14). Qirqisani goes on to cite *M. Aboth* and the talmudic sources which locate the roots of rabbinism during the rise of the Great Assembly, the time of Ezra and Nehemiah.[8] A close reading of the Qumranic sources verifies Qirqisani's claims, although he wrote a millennium after the sectarian compositions.

b. *The Epoch of God's Wrath*
The phrase 'at the end of the wrath' (CD 1.5) is not the inaugural event of the 390-year abandonment, but the apex of an ever-increasing apostasy that finally brought down the temple. CD interprets Ezekiel to set the period of wrath on the biblical time table.

וְיָדְעוּ הַגּוֹיִם כִּי בַעֲוֺנָם גָּלוּ בֵית־יִשְׂרָאֵל עַל אֲשֶׁר מָעֲלוּ־בִי וָאַסְתִּר
פָּנַי מֵהֶם וָאֶתְּנֵם וָאֶתְּנֵם בְּיַד צָרֵיהֶם וַיִּפְּלוּ בַחֶרֶב כֻּלָּם
Ezek. 39.23

> And the nations shall know that the house of Israel went into captivity for their iniquity, because they profaned me. I hid my face from them and I handed them to their oppressors so that they all fell by the sword.

Distinguished by Ezekiel and mirrored by the Zadokite Fragments, Israel's transgressions caused God to hide his face from his disobedient people. As a result of Israel's recreance, God turned them over to their enemies. The question needs to be asked: how long was God lenient with Israel prior to destroying them? Rabinowitz argued some years ago that the period of 390 years referred to the time prior to Nebuchadnezzar.[9] This view has often been criticized and rightly so,[10] but Rabinowitz was not entirely wrong. In CD 1.1-7a, the author draws on

(1895), p. 691. al-Qirqisani, a follower of Anan, the founder of Karaism, composed a history of Jewish sectarianism in 937 CE.

8.   L. Nemoy, 'al-Qirqisani's account of the Jewish Sects and Christianity', *HUCA* 7 (1930), p. 325.

9.   I. Rabinowitz, 'A Reconsideration of "Damascus" and "390 Years" in the "Damascus" ("Zadokite") Fragments', *JBL* 73 (1954), pp. 11–35.

10.   H. Ringgren, *The Faith of Qumran: Theology of the Dead Sea Scrolls* (trans. E.T. Sander; New York: Crossroad, expanded edn, 1995), p. 37.

Ezek. 4.5, 6, which describes the prophet's atonement for the sins of the past; he lies 390 days on his left side for the years of Israel's transgression and 40 additional days on his right side for the sins of Judah. CD applies the Ezekielian figure bidirectionally. Not only had 430 (390 + 40) years elapsed from the Jeroboamite schism to the destruction, but an allusion to chrono-messianic methodology asserts that the period from the *hurban* to the rise of the Moreh Zedek would likewise elapse 390 years.[11] Continuing this line of exegesis, CD notes that of Ezekiel's 40 years for Judah's rebellion, 20 years of blind groping had elapsed, with an additional 20 years expected to fulfill the prophetic 430 years.

That the time from the Jeroboamite schism to the captivity of Israel lasted 430 years is attested in the Apocalypse of Weeks (4Q247).

4Q247 F1: 430 Years until the Exile

1 קץ ח[קוֹק]

2 ויבו]א השבוע החמ[ש]ישי

3]ארבע מאות שלו[שים שנה

4 צד]קיֹה מלך יהודה [

5 ו]בני לוי ועם האר[ץ

6 [מל]ך[כתיים]

1. era en]graved
2. and the fif[th] week [of years of the (?) Jubilee ca]me
3. four hundred thir[ty years
4. Zede]kiah king of Judah
5. and] the sons of Levi and the people of the lan[d
6. the ki[ng] of the Kittim

Whereas line 1 makes it apparent that 4Q247 relates to a chronological schema, line 2 specifies the method of measurement as Jubilean. Although the number of the Jubilee in which this fifth week of years occurs is missing, the data available is important. Milik reconstructs,[12] שנים שמונים ו[ארבע מאות שלו]מה, suggesting that line 3 refers to the date of the building of the Solomonic sanctuary as referenced in 1 Kgs 6.1, 'In the four hundred and eightieth year after the people of Israel came out of the land of Egypt'. In contrast to Milik, it is more plausible to reconstruct שלו[שים שנה, 'thir[ty years', for a sum of 430 years, as

11. This numeral is an attested chrono-messianic number, typified by the period of the Israelites stay in Egypt (Exod. 12.40, 44).

12. J.T. Milik (ed.), *The Books of Enoch, Aramaic Fragments of Qumran Cave 4* (Oxford: Clarendon Press, 1976), p. 256.

the context demonstrates that this time-period of 430 years dates the destruction of the First Temple. Line 4 mentions Zedekiah, Judah's last king; and line 5 refers to the captivity of the Levites and the people of the land who, according to Jer. 52.15 and 2 Kgs 25.11, were taken captive to Babylon by Nebuchadnezzar, the king of the Kittim (line 6).

The author of 4Q247 employs two kinds of chronography—the Jubilean era of creation and the epoch of the Egyptian sojourn (430 years) as a metaphor for a time of suffering. According to *Jubilees*, the exodus occurred 2410 years after creation, followed by Israel's entry into the promised land 40 years later. As to the actual chronology of 4Q247, 430 years represents the length of time that began either with the building of the Solomonic temple or with the schism that occurred 40 years later. From one or the other, the chronicler employed 1 Kgs 6.1 as the point of departure for dating the *hurban* of Solomon's temple.[13]

4. *History of the Sect: Zadok and his Progeny in Scripture and Qumran*

Parallel to the rise of the apostates, the sectarian beginnings may concomitantly be traced to the monarchic schism. Initially, under the rubric 'true Israel', the sect remained faithful as the progeny of Rehoboam fell to the seduction of the Jeroboamite apostasy. A concordance of Qumranic manuscripts lists the name Zadok often. Many entries refer to the priest who served under David and Solomon and whose line continued as chief priests during the Davidic monarchy. A branch of this Zadokite clan also served as high priests during the postexilic period, being replaced only during the stormy days after the rebellion against the Seleucid rulers in 152 BCE. It is not the purpose here to deal with the complex history of the Zadokite clan; only to stress the peculiar sense that the sobriquet בני־צדוק, the sons or progeny of Zadok, assumes in Ezekiel and in the manuscripts from Qumran and the Genizah. In contrast to the biblical references of Zadok and his descendants, the mention of Zadok, and especially the Sons of Zadok, in Ezekielian, Qumranic, or Genizah texts always alludes to a line apart from progeny of Aaron. Throughout this literature, there exists a continuity of both terminology and concept that downplays the Aaronites when compared to the Zadokites. For example, Ezekiel 40–48 distinguishes the faithful Sons of Zadok from the other sacerdotal clans which had gone astray.

---

13. That the temple's construction did not begin until the fourth year of Solomon's reign is not addressed in these general calculations.

As a reward for their fidelity, the Zadokite clan, and it alone, would serve in the eschatological sanctuary and have the authority to teach and adjudicate Torah.

Students of Ezekiel will, of course, debate the question whether this was what the prophet had intended. Abraham Geiger, Julius Well-hausen, and many scholars after them have interpreted Ezekiel's words as referring to the political role of the Zadokites and their Sadducean party. Needless to say, the authors of the non-biblical texts of Qumran and the Genizah understood Ezekiel 40–48 differently from nineteenth-century biblical scholarship. Claiming Ezekiel's promises as their own, the members of the Yaḥad emerged from the *hurban* of Jerusalem in 586 BCE.

The *Damascus Document* picks up the trail of the Sons of Zadok where Ezekiel left off. The sect, as well as Israel, endured the exile, although Damascus was the place of their resettlement, not Babylon. After its three prefatory discourses, CD 3.12 turns to the history of faithful Israel, that is, the sect. What follows describes God's preser-vation of an exilic remnant in the land of Damascus. CD 4.2 calls the chosen priests who had gone out from the land of Judah 'the captives of Israel' (שבי ישראל).[14] This phrase has been variously interpreted as 'the penitents of Israel', 'the returnees of Israel', or 'the captives of Israel', but only the latter fits the exilic context of CD 6.5, 'The captives of Israel who went out from the land of Judah and settled in the land of Damascus'. Murphy-O'Connor has already noted that CD dates the origin of the sect in exilic times. As proposed here, the solidification of the sect in Damascus dates contemporaneously with the exile (c. 586–570 BCE). CD fixes the rise of the Teacher of Righteousness by Neb-uchadnezzar's capture of Jerusalem because it was then, in the sect's chronography, that the Yaḥad covenanted in Damascus under the epi-thet 'the Sons of Zadok'.

These captives, who became the architects of the sect, chose to dif-ferentiate among themselves according to a priestly model. As many scholars have noted, CD 4.4-6 knows of a list of priests whose names are inscribed along with their accolades.[15] Although CD's copy of the

14. S. Iwry, 'Was there a Migration to Damascus? The Problem of שבי ישראל', *EI* 9 (1969), pp. 80-88 (83). The phrase should be translated 'captives of Israel', not 'converts of Israel'. Contrast García Martínez, *People of the Dead Sea Scrolls*, p. 81.

15. Davies, *Damascus Covenant*, p. 97.

roster is lost, most, if not all, Qumranic allusions to this term refer to the Sons of Zadok through 1 Chron. 24.7-18, the recorded list of David's 24 priestly administrators. Chronicles and Ezra-Nehemiah list many of these clans as having played a prominent role during the post-exilic period. That the sect indeed regarded the 24 priestly courses as specially favored comes from an unexpected source. Qumran's calendars, known as the Mishmerot Ha-kohanim, use the priestly clans, for example, the sons of Gamul, the sons of Delaiah, and so on, as the 52 week names within the schematic solar year of 364 days.[16]

The six manuscripts of *Second Ezekiel* (4Q385–90) have peculiarities not, or only rarely, found in other texts; they reveal the post-exilic epochs of Israel beginning with the return of the faithful from exile in Damascus. Expositing Ezekiel's vision of the dry bones (Ezek. 37), *Second Ezekiel* reflects what may be called the sect's futurist historiography.[17]

The 11 lines of 4Q390F1 compensate for CD's silence on the 390-year interval between Nebuchadnezzar's conquest and the coming of the Moreh Zedek with a pesher-type exegesis of the prophecy of Ezekiel regarding the dead bones' revival. This text presents the earliest returnees, who went back to Jerusalem to rebuild the temple under Zerubbabel, as beneficiaries of God's forgiveness. The editor of *Second Ezekiel* associated Zerubbabel and his followers with the sect, the Sons of Zadok.

4Q390 F1: The Rebuilders of the Temple

1 ‏[ ]‏[·]ממן‏ [שוב]‏ [··]ד בני אהר̇ו̇]ון‏ [שבעים שנה] ומשלו בהק
2 /ומשלו בני אהרון̇ בה ולא יתהלכו [בדר]כ̇י אשר אנ̇וכי מצו̇ה א̇שר/
3 /תעיד בהם ויעשו ג̇ם̇ הם את הרע̇ בעיני ככל אשר עשה ישראל/
4 /בימי ממלכתו הרישונים מלבד העולים רישונה מארץ שבים לבנות/
5 /את המקדש ואדברה בהמה ואשלחה אליהם מצוה ויבינו בכול אשר/
6 /עזבו הם ואבותיהם ומתום הדור ההו̇א ביובל השביעי/
7 /לחרבן הארץ ישכחו חוק ומועד ושב̇ת וברית ויפרו הכול ויעשו/
8 /הרע בעיני והסתר̇תי פני מהמה ונתתים ביד איביהם והסגרת̇י̇ם]/
9 /להרב

16. Interestingly, the earliest sources for the reckoning of the 364-day year, *1 En.* 72–82 and *Jub.* 6 make no allusion to the chronicler's onomasticon.

17. Interspersed within the Ezekielian prophecies are excerpts from works relating to the formation of the monarchy, the reign of Solomon, and, most of all, Jeremiah's role in the migration to Egypt.

1. sons of Aaron [ruled over] them 70 years
2. And the sons of Aaron will rule over it. But they will not walk [in my ways] that I command you (Ezekiel) that
3. you will forewarn them. And they also will do what is evil in my eyes as they had done
4. in the early days of his (Jeroboam's) kingdom, except for those who had returned first from the land of their captivity to build
5. the sanctuary. And I will speak to them and I will send them commandments and they will understand all that
6. they and their ancestors had forsaken. And from the end of that generation in the seventh jubilee
7. after the destruction of the land (586 BCE) they will forget statute, season/festival, sabbath, and covenant; and they will abrogate everything. And they will do what is
8. evil in my eyes, and I will hide my face from them, and I will give them over to their enemies, and I will hand them over
9. to the sword.

The readable words of line 1 corresponding to the length of the exile make the sons of Aaron morally responsible for the fall of Jerusalem. The present Aaronite priesthood, concurrent with the rule of Joshua ben Jehozadak and Zerubbabel ben Shealtiel, is castigated as being as sinful as their forebearers. Exempted from this pattern of unbelief are 'those (lines 4-6a) who had returned first from the land of their captivity to build the sanctuary'. This attempt to rebuild Jerusalem's sanctuary by the new covenanteers failed (lines 6b-7). Israel again forgets statute, festival, sabbath, and covenant, abrogating everything. God responds as before, hiding his face from them and handing them over to their enemies, to the sword (lines 7-9).

The wording of this text is clear, but its sense is obscure. Who were these repentant builders of the post-exilic sanctuary? Three possible solutions are available: (1) the exilees who returned under Cyrus's decree; (2) the second wave of immigrants under Ezra; and (3) the Sons of Zadok, who returned from Damascus under their new covenant. Following Ezekiel, the sectarian historiographers assumed that the Sons of Zadok would be the chief priests in the sanctuary. The text then asserts that the covenanters were ready, indeed had started, to rebuild Jerusalem and its temple, but were frustrated by their enemies. This list of transgressions, forgetting statute, festival, sabbath, and covenant, is an often-repeated charge against the sect's Pharisaic enemies.[18]

18. For example *Jub.* 1.5.

Recognition of Zadokite primacy extends beyond Qumran's caves. The Cairo Genizah collection contains at least two fragments recognizing the preeminence of this priestly family. One fragment demonstrates the authorization by which the Sons of Zadok served in the Temple.

Genizah Text: Only the Sons of Zadok Serve in the Temple[19]

1 כהן
2 בכול ע[ת יורוני<ו> מבני
3 עדת בני צדוק
4 על חוק טמא וט[ה]הור
5 משפטיי <י> ישטפ <ישפטו>
6 להבדיל] קדושו וחול
7 [ש]ם יסובו דוכני
8 [וב]שיר יהללו או[נ]תך
9 יי עז לעמו יתן

1. Priest
2. [at all ti]mes some of the Sons of [Zadok] would instruct me (us)
3. congregation of the Sons of Zadok
4. regarding the rule of purity and impurity
5. the law(s) of the LORD they will adjudicate
6. [they will separate what is] holy to him from [what is] ordinary
7. [the]re they will encircle the platforms of (the altar)
8. [with] song they will chant the Hallel to y[ou]
9. The LORD will give strength to his people (Ps. 29.11a)

The size of this narrow strip of Genizah parchment is disproportionate to its importance. The initial three lines confirm that the sobriquet, 'Sons of Zadok' was the genuine name of the sect; they call themselves 'the congregation of the Sons of Zadok'. As in name, so in function: it is the Sons of Zadok who distinguish between the sacred and the profane. Their responsibilities extend from the altar to the court. The authority of adjudication given to Levi in Deut. 33.8-11 is here, as in Ezek. 44.23, 24, assigned to the priests of Zadokite lineage. Line 7, 'they will encircle the platforms', gives the Zadokites the liturgical

19. Refer to I. Levi, 'Document relatif à la "Communauté des fils de Sadoc"', *REJ* 65 (1913), pp. 24-31; J.A. Fitzmyer, 'Prolegomenon', to S. Schechter, *Documents of Jewish Sectaries* (New York: Ktav, repr., 1970), p. 14; and S. Talmon, 'The "Manual of Benedictions" of the Sect of the Judaean Desert', *RevQ* 2 (1960), pp. 475-500.

monopoly of granting priestly benedictions as well as leading the recitation of the Hallel (line 8), 'The LORD will give strength to his people'; [the LORD will bless his people with peace], reproducing the concluding line of Psalm 29 seems to have been the finale of this liturgical piece as well.

The date of composition is not known, but it appears to have been a medieval copy. This does not preclude the possibility that its composition may go back to the pre-*hurban* (70 CE) era. If these liturgical lines predate the Roman destruction of Qumran in 68 BCE,[20] this text regards the title, 'the Sons of Zadok', as paramount. This composition's retrieval from the Geniza could indicate that it emanated from a sectarian group allied to that of Qumran but flourishing in a different geographical location. If composed after Qumran's destruction, its importance increases, as it would then verify the Sons of Zadok's existence during the post-*hurban* era.

A second mention of the Sons of Zadok in the Geniza collection illustrates that propaganda was not beyond the capabilities of the sect in their conflict with the Pharisees. For example, the sectarian editors covertly modified the popular work of the sage Ben Sira. In one of the five Ben Sira Hebrew manuscripts recovered from the Cairo Genizah, 16 additional lines have been inserted between two autobiographical hymns to wisdom, Ben Sira 51.1-12 and 13-28. No other extant version of Ben Sira, Hebrew, Greek, or Syriac, parallels the radical alterations of the Genizah's Manuscript B. Scholars have long recognized 51.12a-p as an insertion, but have failed to associate this ghostwriting with a Qumran-like sectarianism.

Ben Sira 51.12a-p: Sectarian Propaganda[21]

כי לעולם חסדו	a) הודו לייי כי טוב
כי לעולם חסדו	b) הודו לאל התשבחות
כי לעולם חסדו	c) הודו לשומר ישראל
כי לעולם חסדו	d) הודו ליוצר הכל
כי לעולם חסדו	e) הודו לגואל ישראל
כי לעולם חסדו	f) הודו למקבץ נדחי ישראל
כי לעולם חסדו	g) הודו לבונה עירו ומקדשו

20. The putative supposition that the Romans wiped out the Zadokite sect is a modern thought. No ancient army, not even that of Vespasian and Titus, could do that.

21. M. Segal, *The Book of Ben Sira* (Jerusalem: Mosad Bialik, 1959).

h) הודו למצמיח קרן לבית דוד	כי לעולם חסדו
i) הודו לבוחר בבני צדוק לכהן	כי לעולם חסדו
j) הודו למגן אברהם	כי לעולם חסדו
k) הודו לצור יצחק	כי לעולם חסדו
l) הודו לאביר יעקב	כי לעולם חסדו
m) הודו לבוחר בציון	כי לעולם חסדו
n) הודו למלך מלכי מלכים	כי לעולם חסדו
o) וירם קרן לעמו	תהלה לכל חסידיו
p) לבני ישראל עם קרבו	הללויה

a) Glorify the LORD, for he is good, for his favor endures to eternity.

b) Glorify the LORD, the God of praises, for his favor endures to eternity.

c) Glorify the LORD, the guardian of Israel, for his favor endures to eternity.

d) Glorify the LORD, the creator of everything, for his favor endures to eternity.

e) Glorify the LORD, the redeemer of Israel, for his favor endures to eternity.

f) Glorify the LORD, who gathers the scattered of Israel, for his favor endures to eternity.

g) Glorify the LORD, who builds his city and temple, for his favor endures to eternity.

h) Glorify the LORD, who grows the horn of the house of David, for his favor endures to eternity.

i) Glorify the LORD, the chooser of the Sons of Zadok for the priesthood, for his favor endures to eternity.

j) Glorify the LORD, the shield of Abraham, for his favor endures to eternity.

k) Glorify the LORD, the rock of Isaac, for his favor endures to eternity.

l) Glorify the LORD, the strength of Jacob, for his favor endures to eternity.

m) Glorify the LORD, the chooser of Zion, for his favor endures to eternity.

n) Glorify the LORD, the king of kings, for his favor endures to eternity.

o) He raises the horn of his people, a tehillah for all his pious ones.

p) For Israel the people close to him, Hallelujah.

Of these parenthetic 16 lines, 14 (a-n) begin with הודו, 'Glorify the LORD', and end with the formula, כי לעולם חסדו, 'For his favor endures to eternity'. The insertion's first line (a) duplicates Ps. 136.1, while the last two lines (o and p) reproduce Ps. 148.14. The presence of line (i) identifies the quill's owner as a scribe belonging to a Qumran-like sect, הודו לבוחר בבני צדוק לכהן 'Glorify the LORD, the chooser of the Sons of Zadok for the priesthood'. With this line, the sectarian poet disqualifies any non-Zadokite from sacerdotal office. Only those priests associated with the Mishmarot clans have authority to serve in the innermost sancta of the temple.

As Ben Sira manuscript B derives from the Genizah, the date of the original composition of 51.12a-p cannot be determined. Di Lella nevertheless dates the psalm before 152 BCE, apparently taking it as an anti-Hasmonean composition.[22] Such a chronological assessment is inadmissible because it could be argued with equal plausibility that the pro-Zadokite author of the psalm feared to circulate his composition independently after 152 BCE. To avoid censure, he incorporated his doctrine into the widely-copied work of Ben Sira. It is also conceivable that the inserted psalm was authored after the destruction of Qumran in 68 CE. When placed alongside the discovery of the *Damascus Document*, the *Testament of Levi*, and other writings from Qumran and the Genizah, Ben Sira Manuscript B evidences a continuous scribal tradition extending from Qumran to the eleventh century.

The rabbis of the Mishnah were of two opinions with regard to Ben Sira. Some, like Rabbi Akiba, quoted in *M. Sanh.* 10.1, condemned his work. In spite of this hostility, Ben Sira continued to circulate among the Amoraim, attesting that this work attracted a following that the Sages could not entirely resist. Rabbi Akiba's opposition to Ben Sira may not have stemmed from the work as such, but to a contaminated Ben Sira containing pro-Zadokite passages such as Manuscript B from the Genizah. This is not the only classic Jewish text that the sectarians corrupted. Even the Torah did not escape insertions, for example 4Q364–67 (Reworked Pentateuch) or the Psalms of David 11QPs[a] 21, 22.[23] These pseudonymous contaminations demonstrate the existence of a *Kulturkampf* during the period of the second temple and, thereafter, between the Pharisees and the Zadokites, in which no falsification was barred.

5. *Contemporary History*

The doctoring of Ben Sira to make its author proclaim the sect's teaching is the only example in Qumran's library of a historical figure being

22. A.A. Di Lella, 'Wisdom of Ben-Sira,' *ABD*, VI, p. 938.
23. E.g. note E. Tov, 'Biblical Texts as Reworked in Some Qumran Manuscripts with Special Attention to 4QRP and 4QParaGen-Exod', in E. Ulrich and J. VanderKam (eds.), *The Community of the Renewed Covenant*, pp. 111-34.

treated positively. As minor players at a turbulent time, the sect had to confront enemies from within and without. Often sectarian historiographers chastized their opponents viciously. In other settings, only brief historical comments accompany the entry of a historical figure. Texts such as 4Q248 (*Acts of a Greek King*) tantalize with historical inference but are too brief to establish the context conclusively.

Sectarian polemics were not always subtle. 4Q477, the so-called *Decrees of the Sect*, sets a precedent, cursing by name those whose wrath had been vented upon the Qumranites. Only four names survive from what must have been a long list of authorities who opposed or even persecuted the Yaḥad.

4Q477 F1i: Persecution of the Sect

‏[ ]וגם אנשי היֿחֿד[ ]	1
לעמוד עֿ[ל נפשמה ולהוכיח אֿתֿ/	2
[ ]ֿמֿחני הרבים על/	3
[מֿעֿלֿוֿ	4

1. And also the people of the Yaḥad
2. to stand up (to be ready to sacrifice) their lives, and to reproach
3. the camp of the many upon
4. (and) they profaned

According to line 2, several members of the community may have become martyrs for the cause. The phrase 'to stand up for their lives' as used in the book of Est. 8.11 means 'to defend their lives'. The chastisements were issued by the camp of the multitude because their enemies had desecrated the holy things of God (lines 3 and 4).

Column 2 lists the condemned together with the charges against them.

4Q477 f1ii: Condemnation of the Wicked

			‏לֿ]לֿ 1
‏[מחני	‏אשֿ[ר היה מרעֿ]		‏[אֿשֿרֿ]/ 2
	‏וֿ[אֿת יוחנן בן מֿתֿ [תיה הוכיחו		‏[הרבים]/ 3
‏[עמו ואֿ [ת רוֿ]ֿעֿ העין עמו וגם רוח פֿאֿרֿה עמוֿ[ו]		‏[הואה קצר אפים]	‏/ 4
‏[הֿ הואה [ו] הֿם לשֿחֿ[ת -]- ואת חנניה נתוס הוכיחו אשר הואֿה]			5
‏[לֿ]לֿ[הֿ]סֿיר את רוח היחֿ[ד וֿ]גם לערב אֿ[ת ישר[אל]			6
‏]-/ ואת טוביה? בן יוֿ[סֿ]ֿף הוֿלֿ[י]ֿלֿֿו אֿשר רוע הֿ[עֿין] עמו וגם אשר איננו חֿ[-]			7
‏[ורו וגם אוהב את שיֿר בשֿרֿו]			8
‏[-- ואת חנניה בן שמ]ֿעֿון הוכיחו			9
‏וגֿ[ם אוהב את טֿ]מֿא			10

2. is one who does evil [. . . the camp of

3. the many; [and] Johanan the son of Mat[tathias they chastized.

4. He was short tempered and had [an ev]il eye and a greedy spirit.

5. He [and] they will go to the pi[t.] They chastized Hananiah Notos who

6. to [cor]rupt the spirit of the Yaḥ[ad and] also to intermingle (corrupt sexually) [Isra]el

7. They chastized [Tobias the son of Jo]seph who has an evil [eye] and also he does not

8. and he loves his kin (incestuous relations)

9. and [they chastized] Hananiah son of Sim[on

10. [and al]so he loves the de[filed person

Four names survive: John the son of Mattathias, Hananiah Notos, the son of Joseph, and Hananiah the son of Simon. These were not ordinary people, but the politically and economically powerful. The charges brought to bear against them were equally weighty, including corrupting the spirit of the Yahad and inducing sexual transgressions. Accusations also include being short-tempered, evil-eyed, having a greedy spirit and sexual transgressions. Such indictments could only refer to the leaders of the opposition, rather than to ordinary members of the Yaḥad who had fallen away.[24]

Can any of these four figures be identified, even if only conjecturally? John the son of Mattathias could refer to the elder brother of Judas Maccabaeus, John Gaddes, slain by marauding Arabs in c. 160 BCE (1 Macc. 9.36). The son of Joseph may be Hyrcanus, the great-grandson of Tobias, some of whose gold was stored in the temple (2 Macc. 3.11).[25] Two of the figures are named Hananiah; one Hananiah Notos, the other Hananiah son of Simon. As to Hananiah Notos, the absence of a patronymic possibly shows a blemish on his pedigree. In fact 'notos' (νόθος) designates something counterfeit or a child born outside of wedlock. Josephus (*Ant.* 5.233) calls Abimelek the son of Gideon 'a notos'. Herod's children alleged that their brother Archelaeus was unqualified to succeed his father because he was the son of a concubine (*War* 1.52). It is possible that the replacement of the patronymic by 'notos' in regard to this Hananiah indicates his illegitimate status.

It is conceivable that Hananiah Notos is the infamous Menelaus who succeeded Jason to the high priesthood, 171 BCE. 2 Maccabees 4.2

24. E. Eshel, '4Q477: The Rebukes by the Overseer', *JJS* 45 (1994), p. 121, sees those being chastized as common members of the community.

25. Compare 2 Macc. 3.11 with Schürer, *History of the Jewish People*, I, p. 150.

describes Menelaus as having 'the hot temper of a cruel tyrant and the rage of a savage wild beast'. According to Josephus, Menelaus was the brother of Jason (*Ant.* 7.239), but 2 Macc. 4.23 designates him as the brother of Simon, the manager (προστάτης) of the temple. The ancient sources claim that Menelaus instigated Antiochus Epiphanes to introduce Hellenism into Jerusalem. It is conceivable that some, including the author of 4Q477, thought that only a notos could have acted so despicably.

The second-censured Hananiah, Hananiah ben Simon,[26] could be Simon the Just's son, Onias II, who flourished during the second half of the third century BCE or the son of Simon II, Onias III, a contemporary of Seleucus IV and Antiochus IV. Whatever the identifications, the importance of this text is its unique condemnation of the sect's opponents by name.

Historical figures also emerge from the five calendar manuscripts of Mishmarot C (4Q322–24). Compared with the doubtful identifications above, the names in these lists are recognizable figures who played a leading role in Hasmonean history. The entry of these names into sectarian calendars or almanacs reflects the group's interest in the affairs of Jerusalem. Unfortunately the dates cannot be accurately reconstructed.

4Q322 F1: Gabinius?

3 בעשרים ו[שבעה בחודש]הששי
4 [הושיב גֹ]בניויס
5 כתי[אים וגֹם]
6 א[ג]ֹורי הנפשו]ֹת
7 [אסירים]

---

26. 4Q339 (list of false prophets) names a certain Simon as 1 of 8 false prophets. E. Qimron, 'Note: On the List of False Prophets from Qumran', *Tarbiz* 63 (1992), pp. 273-75, conjectures that the full name was Johanan ben Simon, John Hyrcanus I. However, this Simon may be the patronymic of the Hananiah ben Simon rebuked in this text.

Interestingly, 4Q340 (list of Nethinim) names 5 or 6 Nethinim, servants in the sanctuary. According to the editors, these were listed on account of their inferior pedigree, i.e., not to intermarry with them.

Broshi and Yardeni say that כונו is not attested in rabbinic literature, but see Jastrow, *ad loc.* As to the sense of כונו, it is probably an Aramaic rendition of Num. 1.17 נקבו בשמות. If this is so, the list is not pejorative, as claimed by Broshi and Yardeni. Certainly Num. 1.17 is intended to be positive. Thus, the list of Nethinim may record those who became members of the sect.

3. On the twenty-seventh of the sixth month

4. G[abinius] returned

5. Kitt]im and also

6. cu]rsed souls

7. prisoners

4Q322 F2: *Shelamzion*

† ה[רמ]ה בערמן ל[ת]ת לו יקר ל[1

זה] אר]בעה לשבט 2

ה[שהוא עֹשרים בחודֹשֹ] 3

[•ֹ•יֹסֹוד באה שלֹמֹציון] 4

להקביל אֹתֹן פנֹי 5 [

ב]ב[הרקנוס מֹ•ֹ] 6

להֹקֹבֹיֹל] 7 [

† Eisenman and Wise read בערבים 'among the Arabs'.[27]

1. to pay tribute to him by deceit

2. on the fourth of Shebat this

3. that is the twentieth of the month

4. foundation, Shelamzion came

5. to welcome

6. Hyrcanus

7. to welcome

4Q323 F3: *Aristobulus*

•ֹ•אנֹשֹ]יֹ[5

וֹנגד אר[ֹ•ֹ]יֹסטבולוס? 6

5. men

6. and against Ar[istobulus

4Q324a F2: *Aemilius*

/עשרים[ ] 1

ושמונֹ]הֹ ואחד בוא ביאת פתחיה בעשרים 2 [

שהוא/ בֹוא ביאת יחזקאל יום שלישי ביֹ[חזקֹאֹל 3 [

אמליוס/ שלושים ואחד בחודש הששי שיום]הֹרֹגֹ 4 [

השביעֹי/ יום רביעי ביחזקאל זה אחד בחודֹ]שֹ 5 [

גמול/ בארבעה בוא ביאת יכין באחד עשד בוא בֹ]יֹ[אֹת] 6 [

הֹוֹא/ בשמונה עשד בוא ביאת דליהו יום ששי בדליהו שֹ]הֹוֹא 7 [

אמליוס/ עשדים ואדבעה בחודש שביעי שיום] הֹרֹגֹ 8 [

27. R. Eisenman and M. Wise, *The Dead Sea Scrolls Uncovered* (New York: Element Books, 1992), p. 125.

1.]The twenty-
2. first of it, the entrance of Pethahiah. On the twenty-eigh[th
3. of it, the entrance of Jehezkel. The third day of Je]hezkel that is
4. the thirty-first in the sixth month, that day]Aemilius killed.
5. The fourth day of Jehezkel that is the first of the] seventh [mon]th.
6. On the fourth of it, the entrance of Jachin. On the eleventh of it, the]
   [ent]rance of Gamul.
7. On the eighteenth of it, the entrance of Delaiah. The sixth day of
   Delaiah that] is
8. the twenty-fourth in the seventh month, that day] Aemilius killed.[28]

Composite of 4Q324b

Fragment 1	Fragment 2
	1
	2
אנ ש] משמר	̊ם[ ]̊ה ̊ם[3
[א]ת הזיי̊י̊	4 ה]כוהן א̊ש̊ר כו̊ל
שלמצי̊ו̊ן]	[ ]א̊ל̊] יוחנן להבי 5

1.
2.
3. the members of the priestly course
4. the] priest who all...
5. Johanan brought to [...] Shalomzion

4Q324b f2: Johanan

4 ה]כוהן א̊ש̊ר כו̊ל
5 [יוחנן להבי א̊ל̊]

4. High] Priest who all
5. Johanan to bring

These calendars have three remarkable characteristics: (1) for the first
time Jewish and Gentile historical events are dated; (2) historical figures are catalogued according to sectarian chronography; and (3) the
sect's schematic solar calendar is synchronized with the standard luni-

---

28. The reconstruction of this text is indebted to the unpublished dissertation by
George Snyder, Jr, *Mishmarot Calendars From Qumran Cave 4: Convergence and
Divergence* (Cincinnati: Hebrew Union College—Jewish Institute of Religion,
1997), pp. 252-53.

solar calendation. These almanacs reference foreign invaders, univer-
sally called the Kittim, but also well-known personalities like Aemilius
Scaurus and Aulus Gabinius, legates in Pompey's army that conquered
the near east in 64–63 BCE. Hasmonean princes, such as John Hyrcanus
I or Hyrcanus II and the pro-Pharisaic queen Shelamzion (Salome 76–
67 BCE), stand out within the usual redundant calendric format.
Mishmarot calendars reckon according to the sectarian year of 364
days. Uniquely, here, the fragment 4Q322 frag. 2 synchronizes the
sectarian and Judaic systems referring to the month of Shebat, but the
nature of the equivalence is lost.

4Q248 (*Acts of a Greek King*) describes a tyrant who captures Jerusalem, taking its children captive to Egypt, but Egypt was not home to
this conqueror, as he also oppresses that land.

4Q248 Fl: Acts of a Greek King

2 [	[וֹ מִצְרִים וֹצִיון]
3 [	[בֹכן יאכלו] [ם הגוֹי]ם
4	[ויתן ב]נֹֹ'הם ובנותי[ה]ם במצור ב]ירושלים?
5	[וה]עֹביר **** רוח[ו ב]חֹצרותיהם ו]
6	[ו]בֹא למצרים ומכר את עפרה ואת] אבניה
7	אֹל עיר המקדש ותפשה עם כ]ל קודשיה
8	והפֹך בארצות גוים ושב למצרי]ם
9	[ו]בֹבציר עם הק]יץ שודד נפל
10	כל אלה ישוֹבוֹ בנֹי] ישראל?

2. Egypt and Zion and
3. the nations thus they will consume
4. and he will besiege their sons and daughters in [Jerusalem
5. and Yahweh would cause his spirit to move over their courtyards
6. and he came to Egypt and sold her soil and [stones
7. and he would come to the city of the temple and seize her together
with a[ll her holy things
8. and he turned to the lands of the nations and returned to Egypt
9. and during the fig harvest together with the summer fruit the ravager
has fallen (Jer. 48.32)
10. after] all these (events) the children of Israel will return.

The editors entitled this remnant, *Acts of a Greek King*, although neither king nor Greek is specifically mentioned. The besieging ruler is not
named but several candidates come to mind: Ptolemy I Soter, Antiochus IV, and Pompey. Does 4Q248 supply enough evidence to determine if its description fits what is known of these figures? The remains

of line 2 mention Zion and Egypt. Line 3 further develops the context by speaking of Gentiles who consumed, in all probability, Jerusalem. A hostile entry into Jerusalem (line 4) results in the city's offspring being taken away into captivity. The spirit introduced in line 5 may refer to the Antiochene attempt to abolish the Jewish way of life. The conqueror enters Egypt, despoiling her land (line 6). Next (lines 7 and 8), he launches a second expedition against what only could be Jerusalem, from which he seizes her sacred objects. Replaying the above sequence, the ravager again turns south to Egypt. Paraphrasing Jer. 48.32 line 9 refers to the invading army's despoiling the land. Finally a consolation (line 10) promises that God's people, Israel, would avenge the intrusions of this despot.

Ptolemy I Soter, as Josephus narrates, conquered Jerusalem following his victory over Demetrius at Gaza in 312 BCE. His triumphant return to Alexandria does not correspond with the text of 4Q247, which describes a subsequent appropriation of Egyptian lands. Pompey's candidacy, although including Jerusalem's capture, fails to address the manuscript's Egyptian expedition, since, with his victory, Pompey turned north, not south. The allusions in this fragmentary text best fit Antiochus Epiphanes because 4Q247 depicts two conquests of Egypt as some sources relate of Antiochus IV.[29]

6. *Futuristic Historiography*

The several texts of *Second Ezekiel* afford glimpses of the actors, events, and places projected onto the time frame of sectarian historiography. These manuscripts move sectarian historiography from the recent past, described above, to the apocalyptic future. Commandeering the pen of Ezekiel, the Yaḥad prophecies the demise of wicked Haman as one of the sons of Belial. A blasphemer assisted by his cohorts, the sons of the Mastemahs, is shown to arise, performing abominations against Israel. The geographic span over which these actors move extends from the River Chebar to Egypt's Memphis, with Jerusalem and Zion sandwiched between. Civil war looms ever more imminent on the horizon as the eschatological epoch of ten Jubilees nears conclusion.[30]

---

29. Dan. 11.28-30; 1 Macc. 1.16; 2 Macc. 4.5; and Josephus, *Ant.* 7.242-43.

30. R.T. Beckwith, 'The Significance of the Calendar for Interpreting Essene Chronology and Eschatology', *RevQ* 10 (1980), pp. 166-202.

Placing these events within sectarian historiography is complicated by generic vocabulary. For example, the terms גוים and כתיאים, representing pagan nations that have occupied Israel, may refer to Babylonians, Persians, Macedonians, Seleucids, or Romans, but why not also Ezekiel's Gog and Magog? The people and places mentioned on the fragments of 4Q385–90 (*Second Ezekiel*) correspond to any of three backgrounds, two historical and one futuristic. First, Alexander's conquest of the Ancient Near East heralded the change from Persian to Macedonian rule, an occidental despot disposed an oriental potentate. The Diadochian civil wars played out upon Palestine's plains and hills ravaged the land for twenty years. Could Alexander have been the Ezekielian blasphemer, גדפן, and the diadochoi the sons of the Mastemahs? Secondly, after one hundred years of Ptolemaic peace the balance of power shifted north with the rise of the Seleucid, Antiochus the Great. But it would have been his son, Antiochus IV, whom Qumran's historiographers would have portrayed as the evil enemy. Antiochus Epiphanes invaded Egypt and seized control of Jerusalem; these are events to which these fragments could allude. Finally, the historiographer's deliberate ambiguity casts an apocalyptic screen over the material. Applying the eschatology of the prophet Ezekiel, the revival of the dry bones sets loose the coming of the hordes of Gog and Magog. Perhaps the blasphemer represents their leader, who was reminiscent of John's beast from the sea, and who 'was given a mouth uttering haughty and blasphemous words' (Rev. 13.5).

One might object presaging through Ezekiel the story of Haman and his ten sons. If so, the concomitant widening of the horizon to include Egypt would accentuate this doubt. But surely this archetypal enemy in an apocalyptic setting could hold sway throughout the regions from which Israel's persecutors had risen. In concord with Deut. 25.17-19, the Amalakites, here represented by Haman, were ordained to be obliterated. *Second Ezekiel* 4Q386 frag. 1 makes this point at some length.

4Q386 F1ii Second Ezekiel: Defiled Haman

1 [ ]־ו[ידעו כי אני יהוה]] Vacat [[ויאמר אלי התבונן/
2 בן אדם באדמת ישראל ואמר ראיתי יהוה והנה חרבה/
3 ומתי תקבצם ויאמר יהוה בן בליעל יחשב לענות את עמי/
4 ולא אניח לו ומשרו לא יהיה והמן הטמא זרע לא ישאר/
5 ומנצפה לא יהיה תירוש ותזיז לא יעשה דבש [ ] ואת/
6 הרשע אהרג במף ואת בני אוציא ממף ועל ש[א]רם אהפך/

1. And they will know that I am the LORD [their God]. And he said to me (Ezekiel), Look closely,
2. son of man, in the land of Israel. And I said, I have seen O LORD and behold (the city is) destroyed.
3. And when will you gather them in? And the LORD said, the son of Belial will plot to oppress my people,
4. but I shall not let him. And there will not be any of his relations, and the defiled Haman[31] will not leave any seed.
5. And from the caper bush there will be no wine, neither will the bee produce honey.
6. And I will slay the wicked in Memphis and I will bring out my children from Memphis and I will turn to their remnant.

Lines 1 and 2 insure the Ezekielian association, placing in the prophet's mouth the question, 'when will the bones be regathered?'. The story relates to Haman and his offspring, whose deserved deaths are attributed to God's intervention on behalf of the Jews. Critical to understanding this fragment is the translation of והמן in line 4. Eisenman and Wise, as well as García Martínez, render 'multitude', which makes little sense in the context, since the subject is the 'son of Belial'.[32] The rendition as 'Haman' also fits well with the qualifier 'defiled'. The metaphor from nature (line 5) emphasizes that this oppressor of Israel would be the last; he would not have any successors. Having shown the divine salvation of the Persian Jews, line 6 takes up the fate of the Jews in Egypt, Memphis in particular. Here again, the wicked will be judged and the faithful redeemed. This הרשע is not further identified, but judging from the extant context, the persecutor of the Egyptian Jews bore some resemblance to Haman. The bones, awaiting revival, stretch from Egypt to Persia.

From the following two fragments and 4Q390 frag. 1 discussed above, three chronographic references fix events within an epoch of judgment and redemption.

31. The fact that no manuscripts of Esther have been identified among the Dead Sea manuscripts does not invalidate this rendition, as this may be a coincidence.
32. Eisenman and Wise, *The Dead Sea Scrolls Uncovered*, p. 63; and F. García Martínez, *The Dead Sea Scrolls Translated: The Qumran Texts in English* (trans. W.G.E. Watson; Leiden: E.J. Brill, 1994), p. 287.

4Q390 frag. 2.1 Second Ezekiel[e]: Seventy Years of Contention

כמו הו כי לא[אֵת מקדש הקו[דש   ] בֵית [   ] 1
[הֹו   כול] אלה יבואו עליהם [   ] נעשֹׁה וֹכן /2
/ממשלת בליעֹל בהם להסגירם לחרב שבועֹ שנ[ים ב]יֹובל ההוא יהיו 3
/מפרים את כול חקותי ואת כל מצותי אשר אצוה ל[הם בי]דֹ עבדי הנביאים 4
/וֹ[ח]ֹל[וֹ] להריב אלה באלה שנים שבעים מיום הפר הברית אשר יפרו ונתתים 5
/[ביד מל]אֹכי המשטמות ומשלו בהם ולא ידעו ולא יבינו 6
/כי קצפתי עליהם במועלם 6

1. [and my] house, [my altar and] my ho[ly] temple which like it had never

2. been and thus [all] these things will happen to them [ ] and there will come

3. the dominion of Belial upon them to deliver them up to the sword for a week of yea[rs In] that jubilee

4. they will abrogate all my statutes and all my commandments which I will command t[hem by the ha]nd of my servants the prophets

5. and they will begin to contend with one another for seventy years from the day of the rejection of the covenant that they will abrogate. And I shall hand them over

6. [to the hands of the mes]sengers of the Mastemahs. And they will rule over them. And they will not know and will not understand that I have been angered by them on account of their profanation.

Belial's reign spans a definite period of time, of which the Haman text (4Q386 frag. 1.2) describes the end. Previously, his full force had weighed heavily. Israel's unfaithfulness precipitates the unleashing of God's wrath, which takes the form of foreign dominion. In the model of CD 1, Israel stretches God's mercy to its breaking point, causing him to turn his back upon his people, abandoning them for seventy years. Without achieving the desired result, disobedient Israel is turned over to the sword of Belial and the messengers of the Mastemahs for a week of years. In a historic context, these messengers may have been Alexander's *somatophylakes*, his inner circle who superintended the rending of the Macedonian empire. In a futuristic sense, there may be a parallel with the angelic locusts that John saw released upon the world led by their king ʼΑβαδδών (Rev. 9.11).

4Q387 F3ii Second Ezekiel: The Rise of the Blasphemer

/בֹם וֹתחֹזקֹוֹ לעבדני בכל לבבכם[   ] 1
/ובכֹ.ל נפשכם לא אבקֹ[ש]]בֹם בצר להם ולֹא אדרש להם 2
/בעבור מעלֹםֹ א[שֹׁרֹ מעֹלוֹ [בי] עֹדֹי שלמות עשרה 3
/יבלי שנים וֹתֹתֹוֹ[ל]כתם בֹשֹׁ[גען]ובעורון ותמהֹן 4

5 /הלבב ובתֹם הדור הֹהוא א[וציא] אֹת הממלכה מיד המחזיקים/

6 /אֹתֹה ֹוֹ[ה]קֹימוֹתֹ[י] עֹליה אחרֹים מעם אחר ומשל/

7 /[האחֹ]רֹון וֹבֹ[כֹ]וֹ[ל] [האֹ]רֹץ וממלכֹת ישראל תֹאבד בימים/

8 /ההמה הֹ] ואז יקום [הֹוֹא גדפן ועשה תעבות וקרעתי/

9 /[אֹת] ממלכֹ[ה הרשעה הֹ]הֹיא למכל[י]ם <למלכֹ[י]ם> ופני מסתרים מישראל

10 †[?ל] והממלכה תשוב ל[גוים רבים ובֹנֹי ישראל זעקים/

11 [עֹלֹי בבכי על כבר בארצות שבֹי[ם [ואין מושֹיֹ[ע להם/

12] יען ביֹען חוקותי מאסו ותורותי געלה נפשם

† Reconstructed from 4Q389 frag. 2.2-4.

1. You will be strong to serve me with all your heart
2. and with al]l your soul. But I will not seek them anymore in their trouble and I will not respond to them
3. on account of their unfaithfulness that they had profaned me until the completion of ten
4. Jubilees. And they will walk in madness and with blindness and with numbness of
5. heart (Deut. 28.28). And at the completion of that generation I will remove the kingdom from those who are holding
6. it. Then I will establish over it others from another nation and the last one who will rule over (them and over)
7. all the land. And the kingdom of Israel will be destroyed in those days.
8. Then he will arise, the *Gadfan* (blasphemer) and he will perpetrate abominations and I will rend
9. tha[t wicked]kingdom unto (other) kings while my face is hidden from Israel.
10. And the kingdom will return to] many nations and the children will cry [unto me with tears on (the river) Chebar in the lands of their captiv]ity, [but there is no one to sav]e them
12. [for surely they despised my statutes and my Torah their soul rejected.

Brief as it is, this fragment portrays an apocalyptic event. Citing time and place, the writer couches judgments within language common to the chronography of Ezekiel and *Jubilees*. Deuteronomic nomenclature demonstrates that Israel's destruction would be the result of violating law and commandment. Even the designation גדפן resounds out of the sectarian prophet's mouth, 'Thus says the Lord GOD: In this again your fathers blasphemed me, by dealing treacherously with me' (Ezek. 20.27). *Second Ezekiel*'s chronology extends to the rise of the apocalyptic blasphemer, apparently a chrono-messianic date 490 years after the fall of Jerusalem.

7. *Conclusion*

A new hypothesis as to the origins of the Yaḥad emerges from this study. Three views on the history of the sect currently dominate: (1) Vermes—the sect derived from the Hasidim of the Antiochene crisis; (2) García Martínez—the pre-Hellenistic Jewish apocalyptic movement gave birth to the Essenes of the classical sources from which the Qumranites split; and (3) Murphy-O'Connor—the sect originated in the diaspora of Babylon, migrating to Palestine in the second century.

Both the so-called Vermes and García Martínez theories unacceptably presuppose a sect at Qumran whose total existence spans less than two centuries. The literature found in Qumran's caves, with its various intellectual trends, requires a period of maturation longer than these theories allow. If read correctly, the recently-published texts included in this study indicate an established community that dueled with the founders of the Maccabean dynasty. The Babylonian hypothesis contributed by Murphy-O'Connor does not have the temporal defect of the others, so that some of its views can be incorporated into this study's proposal. Its weakness lies in its methodology of literary criticism in which texts are selected or rejected depending on their questionable support of the hypothesis.

The virtue of this study is a fresh look at Qumran's history through many of the Cave 4 manuscripts recently made available. What emerges from this paper is historiography, not the history of the above opinions. Ignored in these proposals is the sect's own historical vision. Granted, the testimony from the caves includes mistakes and outright lies, but it also contains some elements which may be accurate. It is the task of the reader to sift the evidence to distinguish fact from fancy.

Sectarian historiography saw the split of the monarchy as its genesis. The sect identified with Judah as true Israel, whereas Jeroboam's northern kingdom represented the apostate Pharisees and Sadducees. 430 years later, only the sectarian contingent would rise with their faith intact from Jerusalem's ruins. The first reference to the community comes from the prophet Ezekiel who convokes the Sons of Zadok as the faithful remnant of Israel. Citing Ezekiel, the *Damascus Document* reiterates this view, interpreting the Sons of Zadok as the captives who sojourned in the land of Damascus under a new covenant. The charismatic Righteous Teacher appeared 390 years later at the dawn of a new age. He was to be followed in 40 years by the anointed of Aaron and Israel who would usher in the eschatological expectation.

The group received a fully developed ideology in two works, *1 Enoch* and *Jubilees*. The ideology stood on three points: (1) a new covenant and a newly-revealed Torah; (2) a new calendar that could not be subjected to partisan manipulations; and (3) a stand on new rules of purity that differentiated it from the defilement of the masses.

Some of the claims presented by the sect's scribes may be historical. Certainly the charge that Jeroboam was the founder of Pharisaism is absurd. But the founding of the Sons of Zadok by exiles in Damascus during the first half of the sixth century BCE may contain a grain of truth. Ezekiel's architectural plans of the sanctuary are eschatological, but the Sons of Zadok to whom he ascribes the ecclesiastical leadership must have existed already in his day as reported in 1 Chronicles 24 and Ezra–Nehemiah.

Much of the history of the sect still remains obscure. The texts published in recent years have added new material much of which remains undigested. It is important that the students of these manuscripts do not become captives of unproven hypotheses.

Schematic Chronology of Sectarian History

Counting from the Jubilean date of the exodus, the following chronological table emerges:

2410—Exodus from Egypt (*Jub*. 50.4).
2450—Entry into Canaan (*Jub*. 50.4).
2451—Crossing of the Jordan (4Q379 frag. 12 [Pseudo-Joshua]).
2890—Beginning of the building of the sanctuary (1 Kgs 6.1) 480 years after the Exodus.
2930—Death of Solomon and Rise of Jeroboam (1 Kgs 11.42-43).
3360—Destruction of the Temple 430 years after Jeroboam (4Q247 frag. 1.3-6).

Additional dates with imprecise chronology yet to be incorporated into sectarian historiography:

1. An event occurring in fifth week of years in an unspecified Jubilee prior to the *hurban* of 586 BCE (4Q247 frag. 1.2).
2. 70 years of Aaron's rule and the rebuilding of the sanctuary (4Q390 frag. 1).
3. End of the seventh Jubilee (7 x 49 =) 343 + 3360 (destruction of the Temple) = 3703 (4Q390 frag. 2).
4. A week of years for Belial's reign (4Q390 frag. 2.1).

5. 70 years of civil war (4Q390 frag. 2.1).
6. A supposed date for King Jonathan is not included in this paper, as the paleography is inconclusive.[33]

33. E. and H. Eshel, 'A Scroll from Qumran which Includes Part of Psalm 154 and a Prayer for King Jonathan and his Kingdom', *Tarbiz* 60 (1991), p. 295-324.

I wish to thank my students George Snyder, Jr and David Maas for their editorial assistance.

21	274	1.2	133, 145	86.11	93
22.6	81	2.7	122, 268	88.3	241
24	376	2.12	241	89.26-27	268
24.7-18	358	5.11	241	89.27-28	122
		7.1	247	89.28	123
2 Chronicles		7.7	241	89.40	244
1	274	7.8-9	19	93.5	244
1.1-4	274	7.11	244	94.15	244
5	273	8	128, 271	94.19	241
5.11-14	273	8.5	271	96.1-13	268, 272
7	273	16.5-11	121	96.6	244
7.3-6	273	17-118	238	97.10	241
7.6	273	18	273	97.11	244
29–32	267	18.1	247	98.1	241
		22.2	247	102.26	241
Ezra		22.17	183	102.27	248
1.3	269	22.32	241	103.11	241
9.8	74	25.21	241	105.1-15	268, 272
9.13-15	74	29	361	105.5-6	273
		29.11	360	105.27	247
Nehemiah		31.20	241	106	272
1.1–7.3	185	32.11	244	106.1	272
		35.18	241	106.47-48	268
Esther		35.20	247	106.47	272
8.11	364	35.23	241	109.3	247
		36.4	247	114.2	244
Job		36.10	120	119	286
1.14	242	36.11	244	119.7	241
4.8	242	37	127	119.105	244
4.12-20	137	37.11	126	119.147-48	133
4.17-19	271	40.17	241	119.163	248
5.1	137	44.27	241	119.168	241
5.8	137	48.12	241	119.49	238, 243
6.10	137	51.20	241	119.55	133
7.17	271	52.6	247	119.62	133
15.2-16	137	55.24	241	119.68	241
15.14	271	64.11	244	119.85	241
15.16	271	65.4	247	119.93	241
21	271	69.29	146	119.97	241
21.14-16	271	73.1	244	122.7	248
22	271, 272	73.23-28	121	125.4	238, 244
22.17-18	271	77.13	145	129.3	242
28	136	78.54	244	132.11	268
28.20-1	137	78.69	244	132.18	243
		79.9	241	135.12	286
Psalms		80.8	241	135.18	248
1–2	23	82.1-2	19	136	348
1	23	84.6	241	136.1	362

Ps. Philo		*T. Abr.*		*T. Levi*	
16.5	123	12	123	4.2	122, 123

Pss. Sol.		*T. Jud.*			
11.3-8	149	24.1-3	123		

QUMRAN

1QH		9.32	173, 177	4.27-28	140
1	163	12	177	4.31	124
1.7-8	163	12.6-7	44	4.32-33	123, 124
1.8-9	163, 178	12.11-13	177	6.15	116, 126, 127
1.9-10	163	12.12	173		
1.9	164	12.13	166	6.17-18	120
1.15	163, 164, 167	12.22-23	166	7.27	132
		12.23	166	7.29-30	123
1.22	172	13.13	172	8.4-26	127
1.27-31	165, 167	14.11-12	169	8.5-6	132
1.27-30	167	14.11	163	8.6	116, 126
1.27-29	165	14.13	173, 177	8.8	120
1.27-28	163, 164	14.15	91	8.10	116, 120
1.30-31	167	14.17	173	8.11	132
1.31-32	167	14.31	178	8.20	116
1.31	165, 166	15	177-79	8.31	120
1.32	167	15.13	173, 178	9.23	132
1.33	167	15.14-16	177	9.35-36	122
2.1-19	313	15.17	177	9.35	123
2.31-39	313	15.21-22	177, 178	10.27-28	116
3.1-18	313	15.21.2	178	10.30	120
3.20-23	171	15.23	91	11.9	123, 124
3.21-22	172	16.11-12	173	11.10-11	121
3.21	90, 171, 172	16.11	173	11.10	132
3.22	172	16.12	173, 177	11.11-12	122
4	178	16.13	91	11.11	123
4.5–5.4	313	17.21	91	11.12	120
4.5-6	174	17.26	173	11.21	145
4.19	174			12	134
4.24	174	*1QHa*		12.7-8	135
4.25	90, 174	1.4	120	12.13	132
4.29-33	174	1.11	132	12.15	116, 127
4.31	174	1.21	132	12.20	132
5.5-19	313	1.23-24	140, 146	13.5-6	173
5.20–7.5	313	2.13	132, 140	13.6	140
7.6-25	313	2.18	120	14.10-11	120
7.6-7	177	3.22	120	15.7	120
8.4-40	313	3.28-29	129	18.10	120
8.6	173	3.29-36	148	18.12	120
9.15-16	175	4.19	120	18.13	120

73	43, 45, 46, 59	18.18	48-50, 56, 57	2.126	52, 57, 59
				2.127	52, 57
75-78	41	18.19	50, 56-58	2.128	52, 54, 57, 59
75-76	44	18.20	50, 56-59, 62		
75	43, 46, 59			2.129	52, 56, 57, 59, 61
77	44	18.21	50, 56-59		
78	44	18.22	50, 56, 58	2.130	52, 57, 59
80	42, 44, 60	20.237	337	2.131	52, 56, 57, 59
81-82	44, 60				
81	43	*Apion*		2.132-33	52
83-84	44, 60	1.1-56	62	2.132	52, 57, 59
85-88	44, 60			2.133	52, 57, 59
89	41, 44, 52, 59, 60	*Life*		2.134	52, 56, 57
		10–11	46, 47, 56, 60	2.135-42	53
90	44	12	49, 56, 57, 59, 62	2.135	53, 57, 61
				2.136	53, 57, 59, 61, 64
Josephus					
Ant.				2.137-42	43, 53, 54, 57, 59, 61
3.172	48	*War*			
5.16-19	304	1.4	334	2.137	51, 56
5.233	365	1.6	334	2.138	53
7.239	366	1.52	365	2.139	53, 57, 61
7.242-43	370	1.78-79	46	2.141	53, 57, 61
12.414	337	1.78	47, 57, 58	2.142	53, 57, 61, 145
12.419	337	3.11	46, 47, 56, 60		
12.439	337			2.143-51	54
13.2	334	2.113	46, 47, 57, 58	2.143	54, 57, 61
13.14	334			2.144	54, 57, 61
13.46	337	2.119-61	46-49, 55, 56, 60, 61	2.145	54, 57, 61
13.171-73	46, 48, 56			2.146	54, 57, 94
13.171	339	2.119-24	51	2.147	54, 57, 59, 61, 64
13.298	46	2.119	51, 57, 58, 61		
13.311-13	46, 47, 57, 58	2.120-21	51	2.148-49	54, 57, 59, 61, 64
13.311	47, 57	2.120	51, 56, 57, 59, 61	2.148	52, 53
15.371-73	46			2.150	54, 57
15.371	49, 53, 56, 57, 59, 62	2.122	51, 52, 56, 57, 59, 61, 94	2.151-58	55
				2.151	54, 57, 61
				2.152-60	55
15.373-79	47, 57, 58			2.152-53	48, 55, 61
15.374-79	46	2.123	51-53, 56, 57, 59, 61, 64, 94	2.154	55, 56
17.346-48	46, 47, 57, 58			2.155-58	55, 56
		2.124	49, 51, 56, 58, 61	2.155	55, 56
18.11-25	48			2.159	47, 55-58
18.11	46, 49, 56, 57, 59, 62	2.125-34	52	2.160-161	51, 56
18.18-22	46, 49, 50	2.125	48, 52, 56, 57, 61, 253	2.160	55-57, 61, 64

INDEX OF AUTHORS